California
Preschool Program
Guidelines

Publishing Information

California Preschool Program Guidelines was prepared under the direction of the Early Education and Support Division, California Department of Education. This publication was edited by Faye Ong and John McLean, working in cooperation with Laura Bridges, Child Development Consultant. It was designed and prepared for printing by the staff of CDE Press, with the cover and interior design created and prepared by Karen Phillips. It was published by the Department of Education, 1430 N Street, Sacramento, California 95814. It was distributed under the provisions of the Library Distribution Act and *Government Code* Section 11096.

Ordering Information

Copies of this publication are available for purchase from the California Department of Education. For prices and ordering information, please visit the Department Web site at http://www.cde.ca.gov/re/pn/rc/ or call the CDE Press sales office at 1-800-995-4099.

Notice

The guidance in *California Preschool Program Guidelines* is not binding on local educational agencies or other entities. Except for the statutes, regulations, and court decisions that are referenced herein, the document is exemplary, and compliance with it is not mandatory. (See *Education Code* Section 33308.5.)

Contents

A Message from the State Superintendent of Public Instruction

I am pleased to present the *California Preschool Program Guidelines*, a critical publication providing administrators, teachers, and college instructors with guidance on the essential elements of high-quality preschool programs. A better preschool program will ensure success in our efforts to close the school-readiness gap. This publication complements and builds upon policies adopted by the State Board of Education and recent publications by the California Department of Education, Early Education and Support Division. The guidelines in this publication present a broad picture of high-quality preschool programming, based on the most recent research available, that optimize our ability to meet the needs of children in California's diverse preschool settings and communities.

The Preschool Program Guidelines draw both upon current research and the collective professional wisdom of California's numerous early childhood educators who have contributed to the creation of the California Early Learning and Development System. This publication features three main sections: Part One: Setting the Stage for Program Quality; Part Two: Supporting Young Children's Learning and Development; and Part Three: Program Guidelines. This publication is best used in conjunction with other California Department of Education publications in the California Early Learning and Development System. Of particular note is a chapter on research-based program approaches and practices that best support the learning and development of young dual language learners. Considerations for inclusion of children with disabilities or other special needs are integrated throughout the publication, and a chapter on using technology and interactive media in preschool settings is included. To highlight key points from the *California Preschool Program Guidelines*, a companion DVD set is available to deepen professional knowledge and understanding.

The guidelines and examples in this publication offer to preschool professionals a comprehensive view of policies and practices that establish a solid foundation on which to build high-quality preschool programs for California's future. The *California Preschool Program Guidelines* speaks to new early childhood administrators and teachers as well as experienced ones. The publication recognizes the best practices already in place in many preschool programs while providing new insights and strategies to optimize the enduring positive impacts of high-quality preschool learning experiences that help ensure the well-being and successful development of our state's young children.

Tom Torlakson

TOM TORLAKSON
State Superintendent of Public Instruction

Acknowledgments

The development of the *California Preschool Program Guidelines* involved many people. The following groups contributed: project leaders; principal writers; advisers on English-language development; universal design advisers; consultants and reviewers; project staff and advisers from the WestEd Center for Child and Family Studies; staff from the California Department of Education; and early childhood education stakeholder organizations.

Project Leaders

The following staff members are gratefully acknowledged for their contributions: **Elita Amini Virmani**, **Peter L. Mangione**, and **Katie Monahan**, WestEd.

Principal Writers

Special thanks are extended to the principal writers for their expertise and contributions:

Introduction

Elita Amini Virmani, WestEd

Peter L. Mangione, WestEd

Chapter 1: Current Issues in Early Childhood Education

Elita Amini Virmani, WestEd

Peter L. Mangione, WestEd

Chapter 2: The Preschool Child

Elita Amini Virmani, WestEd

Peter L. Mangione, WestEd

Chapter 3: The Role of the Preschool Teacher

Elita Amini Virmani, WestEd

Peter L. Mangione, WestEd

Chapter 4: The Role of the Administrator

Janet Thompson, University of California, Davis

Chapter 5: Use of the California Preschool Curriculum Framework

Peter L. Mangione, WestEd

Chapter 6: Support for Young Dual Language Learners

Linda Espinosa, Center for Early Care and Education Research—Dual Language Learners, Frank Porter Graham Child Development Institute, University of North Carolina, Chapel Hill

Chapter 7: Using Technology and Interactive Media with Preschool-Age Children

Osnat Zur, WestEd

Chapter 8: Guidelines for Operating Preschool Programs

Elita Amini Virmani, WestEd

Linda Brault, WestEd

Laura Bridges, Early Education and Support Division, CDE

Linda Espinosa, Co-Principal Investigator, Center for Early Care and Education Research—Dual Language Learners, Frank Porter Graham Child Development Institute, University of North Carolina, Chapel Hill

Cecelia Fisher-Dahms, Early Education and Support Division, CDE

Peter L. Mangione, WestEd

Desiree Soto, Early Education and Support Division, CDE

Adviser on English-Language Development

Particular thanks are extended to the following adviser in appreciation of her extensive involvement in the project:

Linda Espinosa, Co-Principal Investigator, Center for Early Care and Education Research—Dual Language Learners, Frank Porter Graham Child Development Institute, University of North Carolina, Chapel Hill

Universal Design Adviser

The following universal design expert is gratefully acknowledged for her contributions:

Linda Brault, WestEd

Additional Consultants and Reviewers

Particular thanks are extended to the following consultants in appreciation of their involvement in the project:

Advisory Group: California's Best Practices for Young Dual Language Learners

Linda Espinosa, Co-Principal Investigator, Center for Early Care and Education Research—Dual Language Learners, Frank Porter Graham Child Development Institute, University of North Carolina, Chapel Hill

Oscar Barbarin, Tulane University

Luz Marina Cardona, Cabrillo Community College

Deborah Chen, California State University, Northridge

Barbara Conboy, University of Redlands

Claude Goldenberg, Stanford University

Vera Gutiérrez-Clellen, San Diego State University

Linda Halgunseth, University of Connecticut

Gisela Jia, Lehman College

Karen Nemeth, Language Castle LLC

Catherine Sandhofer, University of California, Los Angeles

Yuuko Uchikoshi, University of California, Davis

Marlene Zepeda, California State University, Los Angeles

WestEd Center for Child and Family Studies—Project Staff and Advisers:

Linda Brault

Melinda Brookshire

Jenae Leahy

Gina Morimoto

Caroline Pietrangelo Owens

Teresa Ragsdale

Amy Schustz-Alvarez

Laurel Stever

Ann-Marie Wiese

California Department of Education*

Thanks are extended to the following staff members: **Richard Zeiger**, Chief Deputy Superintendent; **Lupita Cortez Alcalá**, Deputy Superintendent of Instruction and Learning Support Branch; **Debra McMannis**, Director, Early Education and Support Division; **Cecelia Fisher-Dahms**, Administrator, Quality Improvement Office; **Desiree Soto**, Administrator, Northern Field Services; **Laura Bridges**, Child Development Consultant, for ongoing revisions and recommendations. During the development process, many CDE staff members were involved at various levels. Additional thanks are extended to **Deborah Sigman**, Deputy Superintendent, District, School, and Innovation Support Branch; **Gavin Payne**, former Chief Deputy Superintendent, and the following Early Education and Support Division staff members: **Gail Brodie**, **Sy Dang Nguyen**, and **Charles Vail** and the following Special Education Division staff member: **Meredith Cathcart**.

Early Childhood Education Stakeholder Organizations

Representatives from many statewide organizations provided perspectives affecting various aspects of the program guidelines.

Action Alliance for Children

Alliance for a Better Community

Asian Pacific Islander Community Action Network (APIsCAN)

Association of California School Administrators

Baccalaureate Pathways in Early Childhood & Education (BPECE)

Black Child Development Institute (BCDI), Sacramento Affiliate

California Alliance of African American Educators (CAAAE)

California Association for Bilingual Education (CABE)

California Association for the Education of Young Children (CAEYC)

---

*The names and affiliations of all individuals were current at the time of the development of this publication.

California Association for Family Child Care (CAFCC)

California Association of Latino Superintendents and Administrators (CALSA)

California Child Care Coordinators Association (CCCCA)

California Child Care Resource and Referral Network (CCCRRN)

California Child Development Administrators Association (CCDAA)

California Child Development Corps

California Commission on Teacher Credentialing (CCTC)

California Community College Early Childhood Educators (CCCECE)

California Community Colleges Chancellor's Office (CCCCO)

California County Superintendents Educational Services Association (CCSESA)

California Early Childhood Mentor Program

California Early Reading First Network

California Federation of Teachers (CFT)

California Head Start Association (CHSA)

California Kindergarten Association (CKA)

California Preschool Instructional Network (CPIN)

California School Boards Association

California State PTA

California State University Office of the Chancellor

California Teachers Association

Californians Together

Campaign for Quality Early Education (CQEE)

Center for the Study of Child Care Employment (CSCCE) at UC Berkeley

Child Development Policy Institute (CDPI)

Child Development Training Consortium (CDTC)

Children Now

The Children's Collabrium

Coalition of Family Literacy in California

Council for Exceptional Children/ California Division for Early Childhood (Cal-DEC)

Council of CSU Campus Child Care (CCSUCC)

Curriculum Alignment Project (CAP)

Curriculum and Instruction Steering Committee (CISC)

David and Lucile Packard Foundation— Children, Families, and Communities Program

Desired Results *access* Project

Early Edge California

Early Learning Advisory Council

Faculty Initiative Project

Federal/State/Tribes Collaboration Workgroup

Fight Crime: Invest in Kids California

First 5 Association of California

First 5 California (California Children & Families Commission)

Head Start State-Based Training and Technical Assistance Office for California

Infant Development Association of California (IDA)

Learning Disabilities Association of California

Los Angeles Universal Preschool (LAUP)

Mexican American Legal Defense and Educational Fund (MALDEF)

Migrant Education Even Start (MEES)

Migrant Head Start

National Council of La Raza (NCLR)

Professional Association for Childhood Education (PACE)

Special Education Administrators of County Offices (SEACO) Committee

Special Education Local Plan Area Administrators of California (SELPA)

TeenNOW California

The Tribal Child Care Association of California

University of California, Child Care Directors

University of California, Office of the President (UCOP)

Voices for African American Students, Inc. (VAAS)

Zero to Three

Photographs

Many photographers contributed to a large pool of photographs taken over the years and collected by WestEd. Special thanks are extended to WestEd and the photographers. The following child care agencies deserve thanks for allowing photographs to be taken of staff members, children, and families:

Child Development Center, American River College, Los Rios Community College District, Sacramento

El Jardín de los Niños at University Preparation School at California State University Channel Islands, Camarillo

Friends of Saint Francis Childcare Center, San Francisco

Lincoln Street State Preschool, Tehama County Department of Education, Red Bluff

Thermalito Learning Center Preschool, Oroville

West Grand Head Start, Oakland

Introduction

California Preschool Program Guidelines provides the detailed guidance needed by **administrators**[1] and **teachers** to offer high-quality preschool programs that prepare children to arrive in kindergarten with the foundational skills necessary for school success. The purpose of this publication is to present an overview of key issues to be considered in planning and implementing a high-quality preschool program.

The primary audience for this publication is early childhood education (ECE) professionals who are responsible for preschool program planning. When the document is used in combination with other resources (detailed below) offered by the California Department of Education (CDE), it can also be helpful and informative to a broader audience of policymakers, school administrators, teaching staff, parents, and others who are committed to high-quality preschool education for all of California's children.

Need for the Guidance

This publication responds to the need for a common understanding about what constitutes high-quality programming across a broad spectrum of curriculum and practice for preschools. It also takes into account what high-quality preschool programming means in the context of California's move toward higher expectations for all students at the elementary and secondary school levels. It complements and builds upon policies adopted by the State Board of Education and documents published by the CDE.

The guidelines in Part Three present a broad picture of high-quality programming that should be used to meet the needs of children in California's diverse preschool settings and communities. Although the guidelines are not mandatory,

they represent the best practices based on current scientific evidence in early childhood education and are strongly recommended by the CDE for all preschool programs.

This publication recognizes that one of the great attractions for professionals in early childhood education is the potential to make a significant and lasting impact on the lives of young children and their families. Rather than attempt to prescribe exactly what should be happening in a program at any given time or specifically what should be taught and what methods should be used, it proposes principles and related practices for developing preschool programs that support the diverse learning needs of young children in California.

Organization of the Content

This publication is divided into three main parts:

- **Part One—Setting the Stage for Program Quality**

- **Part Two—Supporting Young Children's Learning and Development**

- **Part Three—Program Guidelines**

Part One, Setting the Stage for Program Quality, consists of chapters 1–4. Chapter 1 presents key background information and the many resources available to preschool administrators and early childhood educators in California, highlighting resources developed by the CDE that are cited in this publication. It presents the background and context of early childhood education, especially recent developments in the field in California. Chapter 2 focuses on the major advances that occur during the preschool years in the areas of physical, cognitive, language, and social–emotional development. The chapter uses the five essential domains of school readiness and the *California Preschool Learning Foundations* to organize what is known about children's

---

1. Terms in boldface are defined in the glossary.

learning and development. Chapter 3 discusses the role of the preschool teacher in supporting children's high-quality early learning experiences. Chapter 4 focuses on the role of the preschool program administrator in designing and implementing a high-quality preschool program.

Part Two, Supporting Young Children's Learning and Development, consists of three chapters about best practices in preschool settings. Chapter 5 provides readers with an overview of the *California Preschool Curriculum Framework*, highlighting aspects of curriculum planning that are most relevant for program directors or administrators. Chapter 6 addresses program practices and approaches that support the learning and development of young dual language learners. Chapter 7 has suggestions on how to integrate the use of technology into preschool programs to support children's learning and development.

Part Three, Program Guidelines, consists of a single chapter (8) covering guidelines for operating preschool programs. Considerations regarding practices that best support young dual language learners,[2] as well as children with disabilities or other special needs, are attended to throughout the following 10 guidelines:

(1) Aspiring to Be a High-Quality Program

(2) Addressing Culture, Diversity, and Equity

(3) Supporting Relationships, Interactions, and Guidance

(4) Engaging Families and Communities

(5) Including Children with Disabilities or Other Special Needs

(6) Promoting Health, Safety, and Nutrition

(7) Assessing Children's Development and Learning

(8) Planning the Learning Environment and Curriculum

(9) Supporting Professionalism and Continuous Learning

(10) Administering Programs and Supervising Staff

Appendixes A through K offer a variety of resources for program implementation and improvement.

The guidelines and examples in this publication offer clear directions on the best practices for preschool professionals. This material draws on current research and on the collective professional experience of California's numerous early childhood educators who have contributed to the creation of the California Early Learning and Development System. The guidelines represent a solid foundation on which to build high-quality preschool programs for California's future.

Related Publications

This publication is a resource to be used in conjunction with other publications developed by the CDE to support early childhood education professionals. Over the past 10 years, the CDE's Early Education and Support Division (formerly called the Child Development Division) developed the California Early Learning and Development System. The system provides early childhood education professionals with an integrated set of programs, publications, and initiatives based on state-of-the art science of early learning and development and best practices in education: "Each component area in the system provides resources that focus on a different aspect of supporting preschool teachers and links to the resources provided in every other component of the system" (CDE 2010b, 30). The following section provides an overview of the components of the California Early Learning and Development System, highlighting those resources in the system that support preschool programming. The section also introduces readers to resources related to the California Early Learning and Development System and designed to be used in conjunction with the *California Preschool Program Guidelines*.

---

2. *Dual language learners* are young children learning two or more languages at the same time, as well as those learning a second language while continuing to develop their first (or home) language.

1. California Learning and Development Foundations

At the center of the California Early Learning Development System are the California preschool and infant/toddler learning and development foundations. The preschool foundations describe competencies—knowledge and skills that all children typically learn between the ages of three and five with appropriate support. Three volumes of the *California Preschool Learning Foundations* (CDE 2008, 2010c, and 2012c) have been developed that, taken together, cover nine developmental domains. Volume 1 includes foundations in the domains of Social–Emotional Development, Language and Literacy, English-Language Development, and Mathematics. Volume 2 covers the domains of Visual and Performing Arts, Physical Development, and Health. Finally, volume 3 focuses on the domains of History–Social Science and Science. Together, the foundations present a comprehensive view of what preschool children learn through child-initiated play and teacher-guided experiences within the context of emotionally supportive environments that are well supplied with engaging and appropriately challenging learning materials. The foundations describe major areas of learning in which intentional teaching can support young children's progress in preschool (adapted from CDE 2010b, 30).

2. California Curriculum Frameworks

California's curriculum frameworks offer guidance on how teachers and programs can support the learning and development that are described in the foundations, through environments, routines, and interactions, and teaching strategies that are developmentally appropriate as well as individually and culturally meaningful and connected. In the field of early education, the CDE created the *California Infant/Toddler Curriculum Framework* (CDE 2012b) and the three-volume *California Preschool Curriculum Framework* (2010b, 2011, and 2013a). The preschool curriculum framework consists of

resources in the early learning system that pertain to planning for children's learning. Each volume of the curriculum framework addresses domains in the corresponding volume of foundations. Volume 1 has chapters on each of the domains addressed in the *California Preschool Learning Foundations, Volume 1*: social–emotional development, language and literacy, English-language development, and mathematics. The curriculum framework presents an integrated approach to the planning of environments, interactions, and strategies to support young children's learning in those domains. (CDE 2010b, 31)

Volume 2 has chapters on each of the domains addressed in the *California Preschool Learning Foundations:* Visual and Performing Arts, Physical Development, and Health. Finally, volume 3 focuses on planning children's learning in the domains of History–Social Science and Science.

3. Program Guidelines and Other Resources

The California Early Learning and Development System also includes the *California Preschool Program Guidelines*, as well as *Guidelines for Early Learning in Child Care Home Settings* (CDE 2010a); *Preschool English Learners: Principles and Practices to Promote Language, Literacy, and Learning* (PEL Resource Guide) (CDE 2009b); *Inclusion Works!* (CDE 2009a); *California Striving Readers Comprehensive Literacy Plan: A Guidance Document* (CDE 2013c); and *The Alignment of the California Preschool Learning Foundations with Key Early Education Resources* (CDE 2012a). These publications provide recommendations for program elements that lead to the creation of high-quality preschool programs.

Guidelines for Early Learning in Child Care Home Settings. An adaptation of the original *Prekindergarten Learning and Development Guidelines*, the CDE publication *Guidelines for Early Learning in Child Care Home Settings* (CDE 2010a) was designed to help home-based child care providers offer high-quality early care and learning experiences to the children and families they serve. The publication covers

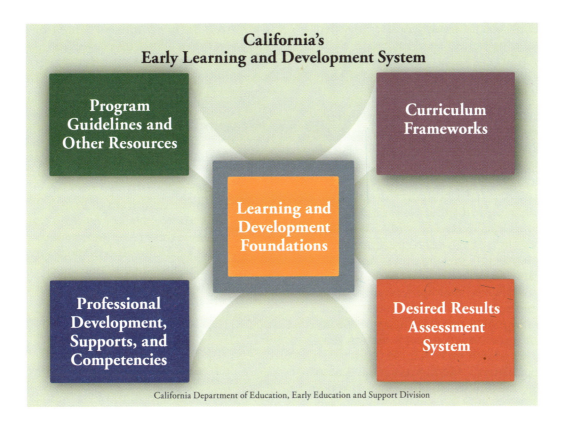

California's Early Learning and Development System

Program Guidelines and Other Resources

Curriculum Frameworks

Learning and Development Foundations

Professional Development, Supports, and Competencies

Desired Results Assessment System

California Department of Education, Early Education and Support Division

topics such as the roles and relationships involved in home-based child care; how to create safe, inclusive environments that foster early learning and development; ideas for implementing appropriate curriculum; professional development for home-based providers; and things to consider when infants and toddlers receive care in mixed-age group settings.

Preschool English Learners: Principles and Practices to Promote Language, Literacy, and Learning. The publication *Preschool English Learners: Principles and Practices to Promote Language, Literacy, and Learning* (PEL Resource Guide) provides guidance on how to support preschool children who are learning English as a second language. This resource guide highlights the role of families in language and literacy development as well as the importance of connecting preschool and the home language. It is organized around 10 principles and accompanying practices. For example, Principle 2 states, "Children benefit when their teachers understand cultural differences in language use and incorporate them into the daily routine." It goes on

to state, "Culturally responsive teaching practices in the preschool classroom create a positive learning environment. They incorporate the linguistic and cultural resources that children bring with them and thereby promote their learning and overall growth."

The PEL Resource Guide works in tandem with the preschool learning foundations. It provides expanded information about the domain of English-language development. It also provides details on strategies to support children's ongoing learning and use of their home language as well as their English-language development. Teachers can draw on these strategies as they engage in curriculum planning (CDE 2010b, 35).

Inclusion Works! This publication (CDE 2009a) is designed to provide information and proven strategies that promote belonging and inclusion for all children. Building on research and the experience of years of effective implementation, this handbook contains stories and examples, as well as background information and resources that support strategies for successful inclusion. Suggestions for ways to adapt the environment are provided, along with examples of inclusive strategies. A glossary and appendixes make this handbook a practical tool for care providers.

The Alignment of the California Preschool Learning Foundations with Key Early Education Resources: California Infant/Toddler Learning and Development Foundations, California Content Standards, the Common Core State Standards, and Head Start Child Development and Early Learning Framework. This online publication presents the developmental continuum of learning for children from birth through kindergarten (an abbreviated version is included as an appendix in the *California Preschool Learning Foundations, Volume 3* [CDE 2012c]). It shows the connections that the nine domains of the *California Preschool Learning Foundations* have with the content of these other important resources. This alignment demonstrates that early learning is a significant part of the educational system and that the knowledge and skills of young children are foundational to all future learning. Of particular note is the alignment of the preschool learning foundations with the California content standards and the California Common Core State Standards for kindergarten. The vertical alignment between the areas of learning and development at the preschool and kindergarten levels supports children's transition from preschool to early elementary school and provides for continuity in the building of children's knowledge and skills across those settings.

4. Professional Development, Supports, and Competencies

Professional development is provided through the state's extensive higher education system, the California Preschool Instructional Network, the Faculty Initiative Project, and other CDE activities. The California Early Childhood Educator (ECE) Competencies were developed to describe educators' knowledge and skills and to inform professional development learning outcomes (see appendixes A and B for a comprehensive list).

California Early Childhood Educator Competencies. The California Early Childhood Educator Competencies serve several interrelated purposes. First, the competencies provide coherent structure and content to foster the professional development of California's early childhood workforce. Second, they inform the course of study that early childhood educators follow as they pursue study in institutions of higher education. Third, they provide guidance in the definition of ECE credentials and certifications. And fourth, they give comprehensive descriptions of the knowledge, skills, and dispositions that early childhood educators need to support young children's learning and development across program types. The competencies were developed for early childhood educators and for people who are responsible for ECE professional development—such as higher-education faculty, training organizations and consultants, and human resources departments of large agencies that provide early care and education services.

5. Desired Results Assessment System

The Desired Results assessment system is designed to document the progress made by children and families in achieving desired results and provides information to help practitioners improve their child care and development services. Desired Results for Children and Families are the outcomes (or results) that California wants for all children and families. Please see chapter 1 for more detail on the Desired Results for Children and Families.

Complementary Resources

California Content Standards and Common Core State Standards. The California academic content standards and the Common Core State Standards (CCSS) fit within a broad approach to K–12 standards. The standards are considered educational goals at each grade level. The curriculum and instruction at a given grade support students' learning of the knowledge and skills established for that grade level. The content standards were formally adopted by California's State Board of Education. Standards for kindergarten cover English Language Arts, Mathematics, English-Language Development, Health Education, History/Social Science, Physical Education, Science, and Visual and Performing Arts. The CCSS provide standards for every grade level, from kindergarten through twelfth grade, for English Language Arts and Literacy in History/Social Studies, Science, and Technical Subjects; and for Mathematics. California stands among numerous states that have adopted the CCSS (CDE 2012a, 9–10).

Head Start Child Development and Early Learning Framework. The *Head Start Child Development and Early Learning Framework* (U.S. Department of Health and Human Services 2010) outlines the developmental building blocks essential for children's school and long-term success. This framework is intended for early care professionals who work with children three to five years old, covering all aspects of child development and learning. Head Start programs use the framework to establish school-readiness goals and to guide teachers in curriculum, assessment, and program planning. The *Head Start Child Development and Early Learning Framework* takes a broad approach to early development and learning. It is organized into 11 domains: Physical Development and Health, Social and Emotional Development, Approaches to Learning, Logic and Reasoning, Language Development, English-Language Development, Literacy Knowledge and Skills, Mathematics Knowledge and Skills, Science Knowledge and Skills, Creative Arts Expression, and Social Studies Knowledge and Skills. These domains stem from the history of Head Start research and practice. There is considerable overlap between this framework and the content standard domains typically used for the kindergarten level, but the framework also has some distinct ways of identifying young children's developing knowledge and skills. The framework covers areas generally addressed by a comprehensive preschool curriculum (CDE 2012a, 9–10).

California Striving Readers Comprehensive Literacy Plan. The *California Striving Readers Comprehensive Literacy (SRCL) Plan* is a comprehensive literacy development and education program to advance literacy skills for students from birth to grade twelve. The goal of the SRCL Plan is to provide every child with the instruction and support to achieve advanced literacy skills that traverse academic disciplines and translate into meaningful personal, social, civic, and economic outcomes. The plan extends California's literacy focus and addresses the state's current urgent literacy needs, which have been identified through a review of state assessment data collected over the past 15 years (CDE 2009c and DataQuest 2014). For school-age children, California's plan places a particular focus on underachieving students: English learners, African American and Hispanic students, students with disabilities, and those who are socioeconomically disadvantaged (CDE 2013b).

References

California Department of Education. 2006. *Infant/Toddler Learning & Development Program Guidelines.* Sacramento: California Department of Education.

———. 2008. *California Preschool Learning Foundations, Volume 1.* Sacramento: California Department of Education.

———. 2009a. *Inclusion Works! Creating Child Care Programs That Promote Belonging for Children with Special Needs.* Sacramento: California Department of Education.

———. 2009b. *Preschool English Learners: Principles and Practices to Promote Language, Literacy, and Learning* (PEL Resource Guide). 2nd ed. Sacramento: California Department of Education.

———. 2009c. Standardized Testing and Reporting (STAR). Sacramento: California Department of Education. http://www.starstamplequestions.org (accessed June 26, 2014).

———. 2010a. *Guidelines for Early Learning in Child Care Home Settings.* Sacramento: California Department of Education.

———. 2010b. *California Preschool Curriculum Framework, Volume 1.* Sacramento: California Department of Education.

———. 2010c. *California Preschool Learning Foundations, Volume 2.* Sacramento: California Department of Education.

———. 2011. *California Preschool Curriculum Framework, Volume 2.* Sacramento: California Department of Education.

———. 2012a. *The Alignment of the California Preschool Learning Foundations with Key Early Education Resources: California Infant/Toddler Learning and Development Foundations, California Content Standards, the Common Core State Standards, and Head Start Child Development and Early Learning Framework.* Sacramento: California Department of Education. http://www.cde.ca.gov/sp/cd/re/documents/psalignment.pdf (accessed June 12, 2015).

———. 2012b. *California Infant/Toddler Curriculum Framework.* Sacramento: California Department of Education.

———. 2012c. *California Preschool Learning Foundations, Volume 3.* Sacramento: California Department of Education.

———. 2013a. *California Preschool Curriculum Framework, Volume 3.* Sacramento: California Department of Education.

———. 2013b. *California Standardized Testing and Reporting (STAR).* Sacramento: California Department of Education.

———. 2013c. *California Striving Readers Comprehensive Literacy Plan: A Guidance Document.* Sacramento: California Department of Education. http://www.cde.ca.gov/pd/ca/rl/documents/srclplan.pdf (accessed June 12, 2015).

California Department of Education and First 5 California. 2012. *California Early Childhood Educator Competencies.* Sacramento: California Department of Education and First 5 California.

California MAP to Inclusion & Belonging: Making Access Possible. http://www.cainclusion.org/camap/ (accessed June 12, 2015).

DataQuest. 2014. Sacramento: California Department of Education. http://data1.cde.ca.gov/dataquest/ (accessed June 12, 2015).

National Governors Association Center for Best Practices and Council of Chief State School Officers. 2013. *Common Core State Standards.* Washington, DC: National Governors Association Center for Best Practices; Council of Chief State School Officers.

U.S. Department of Health and Human Services. 2010. *The Head Start Child Development and Early Learning Framework: Promoting Positive Outcomes in Early Childhood Programs Serving Children 3–5 Years Old.* Arlington, VA: U.S. Department of Health and Human Services Administration for Children and Families Office of Head Start.

Part One:
Setting the Stage for
Program Quality

Chapter 1
Current Issues in Early Childhood Education

This chapter consists of two major sections. The first elaborates on issues that are central to early childhood and preschool education throughout the United States. The second focuses specifically on recent developments in early childhood and preschool education in California.

General Issues

The general issues in this section cover the benefits of high-quality **preschool programs**, societal benefits of investing in early childhood education (ECE) programs, research on brain development and its implications for supporting young children's learning and development, and key features of preschool that have been shown to be important to young children's school readiness and long-term achievement.

Evidence from Research

The preschool years are critically important for children's later development, subsequent performance in school, and later success in life. High-quality preschool programs make significant contributions to gains in children's academic, language, and social skills. This premise has been substantiated over the past 25 years by a wide body of research:

- Children who attend high-quality child care and education programs show significant cognitive gains during early childhood and perform better academically compared with children in low-quality programs (Mashburn et al. 2008; Gormley et al. 2011; Curby et al. 2009). In particular, cognitive and language gains are most evident when teachers engage in high-quality instructional practices, including responsive and stimulat-

ing interactions around learning. Research suggests that the benefits of high-quality early childhood programs extend into the early school years (Belsky et al. 2007; Peisner-Feinberg et al. 2001).

- Children who experience high-quality preschool programs, as indicated by high-quality teacher–child interactions and a positive emotional climate, demonstrate greater social competence and display fewer behavior problems (Howes et al. 2008; Mashburn et al. 2008; Peisner-Feinberg et al. 2001).

- Although studies find that all young children potentially benefit from high-quality preschool programs, benefits tend to be the most pronounced for children from economically disadvantaged backgrounds.

Longitudinal studies of high-quality early childhood programs reveal that the positive effects may persist well into adolescence and adulthood. A 36-year follow-up study of the Perry Preschool Program in Ypsilanti, Michigan, showed that children from low-income families who attended preschool as four-year-olds were more likely to graduate from high school, hold a job, have higher earnings, and have committed fewer crimes than those adults who had not attended preschool as four-year-olds. Remarkably, it is estimated that this preschool program yielded more than $9 in benefits for every $1 invested (Heckman 2009).

Most studies of ECE program features and children's outcomes have either not included dual language learners or administered cognitive and social–emotional assessments exclusively in English. Consequently, a comparable research base that can offer guidance on how to design early childhood programs that provide effective and high-quality education for young dual language learners is only beginning to emerge. Some of the elements of early care and education settings that have been shown to be salient for dual language learners are (1) attendance/participation rates, (2) language of instruction, (3) global quality of the ECE environment (including the positive emotional climate of the setting), (4) specific instructional and assessment practices, (5) teacher/provider qualifications and language abilities, and (6) home–school collaboration practices (Espinosa 2013).

Research on the elements of quality in inclusive preschool classrooms that predict positive outcomes for children with disabilities or other special needs is limited. Even so, there is emerging evidence to suggest that individualization, as a measure of high-quality inclusive practice, is positively associated with children's developmental outcomes in the areas of cognition, communication, and motor skills (Odom, Buysse, and Soukakou 2011).

How is quality in preschool measured?

Preschool quality is typically measured according to two dimensions—structural quality (teacher education, class size, length of day, teacher–child ratio) and process quality (teacher–child interactions, appropriate learning activities and materials, and effective instructional practice). The structural quality of the early childhood program plays an important role in influencing process features of the program environment. For instance, low adult–child ratios likely make it more possible for teachers to engage in the responsive interactions known to contribute to positive child outcomes.

Research findings from a large study of approximately 700 randomly selected, state-funded preschool prekindergarten classrooms (Howes et al. 2008) revealed the following findings about preschoolers who had experienced high-quality instructional practices and high-quality teacher–child relationships:

- greater proficiency in language and literacy skills

- higher ratings on social competence

- fewer reported behavior problems

Additionally, the National Institute of Child Health and Human Development (NICHD) Study of Early Care and Youth Development (Vandell et al. 2010), one of the most exhaustive recent national studies of early childhood care and education (between birth and four and a half years of age), found that

- quality of child care is important, whether at a child care center, family child care home, or other early childhood setting;

- high-quality care was predictive of higher academic achievement at age fifteen with more positive effects associated with higher levels of child care quality;

- high-quality care predicted less externalizing behavior, as indicated by self-reports of the children during adolescence;

- the number of hours in nonrelative care mattered. More hours in care predicted greater risk taking and impulsivity at age fifteen. However, those children who attended programs of higher quality had fewer behavior problems than those who attended low-quality programs.

The Need for High-Quality Preschool Programs

Despite growing evidence of the importance and long-term benefits of early childhood education, a number of studies have shown that the quality of typical child care programs in the United States is, at best, mediocre (Helburn 1995). A recent report, *Prepared to Learn: The Nature and Quality of Early Care and Education for Preschool-Age Children in California*, suggests that "center-based ECE programs fall short on key quality benchmarks, particularly those related to early learning environments that foster school readiness and later school success" (Karoly et al. 2008).

Further, although preschool program quality is a necessary condition for promoting positive outcomes for all young children, the field's understanding of the essential elements of preschool program quality continues to evolve.

As *preschool program quality* has been defined in the research literature to date, it is a necessary but not sufficient condition for supporting the learning needs of dual language learners (Castro, Espinosa, and Paez 2011) and children with disabilities or other special needs (Soukakou 2012).

For example, Castro, Espinosa and Paez (2011, 268) have made a strong case for the following expanded definition of *high-quality ECE* for dual language learners:

> Providing high-quality early education experiences to young dual language learners will require a revision of the indicators of quality being used. Regarding structural quality, adult–child ratios may need to be smaller to allow educators time to conduct small-group and one-on-one activities with dual language learners. Also, to implement classroom activities in the children's primary language, to conduct valid and reliable assessments in children's primary language and English, and to plan activities that are responsive to young dual language learners' individual developmental and learning needs, programs will need to increase the number of bilingual and qualified staff, as well as offer ongoing professional development.

Early Childhood Program Effectiveness

1. Effective services build supportive relationships and stimulating environments.

2. Effective interventions address specific developmental challenges.

3. Effectiveness factors distinguish programs that work from those that don't.

4. Effective early childhood programs generate benefits to society that far exceed program costs.

Source: Center on the Developing Child at Harvard University, n.d.

There is also a growing realization that the definition of *high-quality early care and education* needs to include serving children with identified disabilities, learning or behavioral difficulties, or other special needs (Odom, Buysse, and Soukakou 2011). The Division for Early Childhood and the National Association for the Education of Young Children (2009) joint position statement on inclusion highlights the concern that high-quality inclusion extends beyond the way in which program quality is typically conceptualized. Thus, high-quality inclusive practice should be an integral part of high-quality care.

Early Childhood Investments and Societal Impacts

Current statistics on early child care and education suggest that approximately 7.5 million children, or 68 percent of children under the age of five in the United States, experience some type of routine nonparental child care. Approximately 48 percent of these young children spend some time in organized care settings (National Association of Child Care Resource and Referral Agency [NACCRRA] 2010). Because of the large numbers of children in the United States experiencing nonparental child care, researchers parents, and policymakers have sought to understand the effects of early child care experiences on children's long-term developmental outcomes (Belsky et al. 2007; NICHD Early Child Care Research Network 2003; Greenspan 2003).

Studies conducted over the past 30 years indicate that early childhood investments can yield substantial benefits for young children when programs intentionally support young children's development and early learning. Cost–benefit analyses conducted by Heckman (2006) suggest that investing in the preschool years yields the highest rates of return on investment as compared to any other period of human development.

Recent Research on Brain Development

Research on brain development in the early years further substantiates society's need to ensure that children's early experiences are of high quality. Recent research on brain development suggests that while all children come to the world with their own biological and genetic makeup, early experiences also contribute to shaping their developing brain and who they are. In particular, the quality of care that a child receives both in early childhood settings and at home plays an important role in influencing how specific genes are expressed in behavior. It follows that what is expressed in children's behavior can neither be determined by "nature" (genes, biology) nor "nurture" (parenting influences, child care experiences, neighborhood quality) alone, but a complex interaction between the two (Thompson and Virmani 2012).

Babies are born ready to learn. In a review of research on early brain development, Conboy states, "By the time an infant is born, his or her brain possesses most of the neurons it will ever have and major sensory pathways have already become organized to process visual and auditory information and are thus ready to learn from the external environment. Yet the brain is far from fully formed at birth" (State Advisory Council on Early Learning and Care 2013, Paper 1: Neuroscience Research). Although a vast majority of neurons are established by the time one is born, connections between neurons, or synapses, are a result of one's experiences. Connections made are solidified and made more efficient by repeated use. Although the brain continues to be shaped

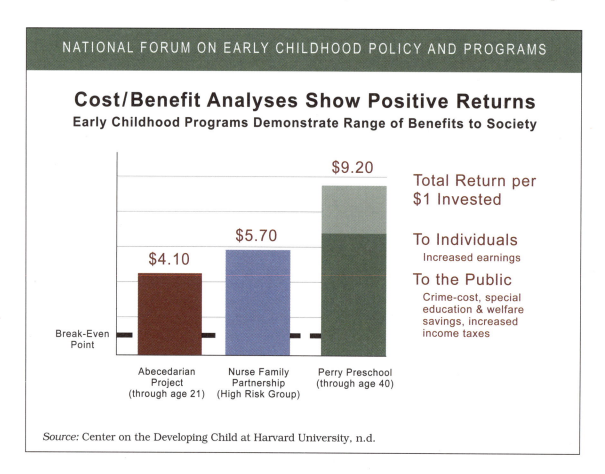

NATIONAL FORUM ON EARLY CHILDHOOD POLICY AND PROGRAMS

Cost/Benefit Analyses Show Positive Returns
Early Childhood Programs Demonstrate Range of Benefits to Society

$9.20

$5.70

$4.10

Break-Even Point

Abecedarian Project (through age 21)

Nurse Family Partnership (High Risk Group)

Perry Preschool (through age 40)

Total Return per $1 Invested

To Individuals
Increased earnings

To the Public
Crime-cost, special education & welfare savings, increased income taxes

Source: Center on the Developing Child at Harvard University, n.d.

The Science of Early Childhood Development

Research by the Center on the Developing Child at Harvard University suggests that:

1. **Brains are built over time, from the bottom up.** Sensory pathways, like those for vision and hearing, are the first to develop, followed by early language skills, and then higher cognitive functions.

2. **The interactive influences of genes and experiences shape the developing brain.** The "serve and return" relationships between children and their parents and other caregivers in the family and community play a central role in one's early experiences.

3. **The brain's capacity for change decreases with age.** The brain is most flexible or plastic early in life to accommodate a wide range of environments and interactions, but as the maturing brain becomes more specialized to assume more complex functions, it is less capable of reorganizing and adapting to new or unexpected challenges.

4. **Cognitive, emotional, and social capacities are inextricably intertwined throughout life.** The emotional and physical health, social skills, and cognitive–linguistic capacities that emerge in the early years are all important prerequisites for success in school and later in the workplace and community.

5. **Toxic stress damages the developing brain architecture, which can lead to lifelong problems in learning, behavior, and physical and mental health**. Scientists now know that chronic, unrelenting stress in early childhood, caused by extreme poverty, reported abuse, or severe maternal depression, for example, can be toxic to the developing brain.

Source: Center on the Developing Child at Harvard University, n.d.

by experiences throughout a life span, it is the experiences children have in the early years that help to lay the foundation for later learning and development (CDE 2012c). Remarkably, an estimated 85 percent of children's core brain structures are developed by the age of four (Child and Family Policy Center and Voices for America's Children 2005).

How are the brain and its related functions studied?

Various brain imaging techniques have been used successfully to increase understanding of how the brain works. Positron-emission tomography scans and functional magnetic resonance imaging have been used to map brain activity, and event-related potentials are often used to study changes in the brain's electrical activity as related to a specific event or stimulus (Nelson and McCleery 2008). The above-mentioned techniques are some of the most widely used by researchers to investigate, for instance, the negative impacts of stress on the developing brain and the positive impacts of early language experiences on the developing brain.

Marian Diamond (Diamond and Hopson 1998) and a research team at the University of California, Berkeley, have found that enriched environments can influence

NIEER Preschool Policy Brief

Connecting Neurons, Concepts, and People: Brain Development and Its Implications

Policy Recommendations

- Government and business should support prenatal and well-child health care, good nutrition, efforts to eliminate children's exposures to harmful pollutants and toxins, and high-quality preschool programs in striving to support healthy early brain development.

- Early prevention is better and less expensive than later remediation. Health care services, early intervention programs, and preschools should ensure that they provide early hearing, vision, language, cognitive, and behavioral screenings, and link children to necessary services.

- Sensitive interactions with adults do more to promote brain development than any toy, CD, or DVD. Preschools should deliver services that enable adults to have rich interactions with children.

- Preschools should embrace educational approaches that encourage child-oriented discovery over adult-directed instruction.

- Since social–emotional development and cognitive development are intertwined, preschool programs should recognize and focus on both.

- Exposure to chronic early stress is harmful. Mental health experts can help preschool staff work with children who have behavioral problems and learn to identify and refer children and families to other services as needed.

Source: Thompson, n.d.

brain growth significantly. According to Diamond, an enriched environment

- includes a steady source of positive emotional support;

- provides a nutritious diet with enough protein, vitamins, minerals, and calories;

- stimulates all the senses (but not necessarily all at once);

- has an atmosphere free of undue pressure and stress but suffused with a degree of pleasurable intensity;

- presents a series of novel challenges that are neither too easy nor too difficult for children at their stages of development;

- allows social interaction for a significant percentage of activities;

- promotes development of a broad range of mental, physical, aesthetic, social, and emotional skills and interests;

- gives children an opportunity to choose many of their efforts and to modify them;

- allows children to be active participants rather than passive observers.

When the impact of enriched environments on dual language learner popula-

The Bilingual Brain: What Is Known from Neuroscience

Although bilingual learners share many characteristics of language development with monolingual learners of each of the same languages, differences across groups have been noted for various aspects of how the brain processes language. For example, there is evidence that both languages are activated for the same concept, such that a speaker needs to select from a wider range of words to retrieve the correct word, using cognitive (executive) control mechanisms to a greater extent than in monolingual word retrieval (for more information, see Paper 2, Development Across Domains). There is limited evidence regarding how the bilingual lexicon is organized in children, but evidence from studies reviewed in this paper has suggested a greater use of attentional control processes than during monolingual processing. This difference is noted as early as seven months of age, even before vocabulary is developed, and is therefore probably induced by the need for bilingual children to pay attention to different cues across languages. Thus, differences in the brain areas used for dual versus monolingual language processing should not be interpreted as delays or deficits; instead, they should be viewed, as adaptations to the need for using additional cognitive resources. In fact, many of the differences in cognitive control functions across bilingual and monolingual individuals may be construed as bilingual advantages. Such advantages might be made accessible to all children through various degrees of bilingual programming (p. 34). . . .

The research [from cognitive neuroscience] . . . suggests that, because experience shapes children's learning mechanisms, models of learning need to consider that bilingual children may learn differently from monolingual children. For example, monolingual models do not account for the fact that the dual language learner needs to discover different sound systems, stress patterns in words, and grammatical rules. Although there is no evidence that dual language learners become confused by learning different sets of language rules, practitioners should recognize that language systems interact during processing. While these differences may affect performance on tests, they do not necessarily indicate a delay or deficit. (p. 35)

Source: State Advisory Council on Early Learning and Care 2013, Paper 1 (Neuroscience Research), 34–35.

tions is considered, it is important to take into account specific adaptations and strategies, which are presented in chapter 6, in addition to those listed above.

Conversely, a stressful environment and a lack of developmentally appropriate experiences and learning opportunities can impair healthy brain development.

One of the primary ways to buffer stressful experiences for young children in early childhood settings is to ensure that teachers develop stable, predictable, and secure relationships with children in their care. To engage in cognitively complex tasks, young children first need to feel safe and emotionally secure.

Highlighting the Impact of Language Experiences on the Brain

1. Language experience affects the organization of the neural systems involved in learning, storing, processing, and producing language (i.e., evidence for structural and functional differences between the brains of monolingual and dual language learners).

2. Dual language learning and use involves different cognitive processes than do single language learning and use.

3. The effects of language learning experiences on the brain facilitate and constrain further learning.

School Readiness

As the NAEYC's position statement on school readiness suggests, school readiness involves more than children being prepared for school; it involves ensuring that families, schools, and communities are ready to support children's success in school. Past conceptualizations of school readiness that focused primarily on children's specific skills in areas such as literacy and mathematics have recently been broadened to include areas such as social and emotional development and executive functioning. The prevailing view today envisions children's school readiness as the development of skills and competencies during early childhood that contribute to children's success in school later in life. Readiness now reflects a range of dimensions, such as a child's physical well-being and motor development, social and emotional development, communication and language use, cognition and general knowledge, and approaches to learning (NAEYC 2009; National Educational Goals Panel 1995, 1998; CDE 1997).

In California, school-readiness programs funded by First 5 use the First 5 California-adapted National Education Goals Panel[1] definition of school readiness:

1. National Education Goals Panel, "Getting a Good Start in School" (Washington, DC: National Education Goals Panel, 1997).

1. **Children's readiness for school**

   • Promoting physical well-being and motor development

   • Promoting positive social and emotional development

   • Developing approaches to learning

   • Fostering language development

   • Instilling cognitive development and general knowledge

2. **Schools' readiness for children**

   • Creating a smooth transition between home and school

   • Ensuring continuity between early care and education programs and elementary grades

   • Focusing on helping children learn through a student-centered environment

   • Being committed to the success of every child

   • Using strategies that have been shown to raise achievement for each student

   • Being willing to alter practices and programs if they do not benefit children

   • Making sure that students have access to services and support in the community

3. **Family and community support and services that contribute to children's readiness for school success**

   • Providing access to high-quality and developmentally appropriate early care and education experiences

   • Providing parents with access to training and support that allows parents to be their child's first teacher and promotes healthy, functioning families

   • Providing access to prenatal care for mothers and nutrition, physical activity, and health care to children need so they arrive at school with healthy bodies and minds to maintain mental alertness

Many recent efforts at the national, state, and local levels have focused on putting the necessary supports in place to ensure that families, schools, and communities are prepared to support children during early childhood to succeed in school.

The California Context

Demographics

Compared with most other states, California has an extraordinarily diverse population of young children, particularly those under the age of five. Of California's 3.2 million children under the age of five, approximately 53 percent are Latino, 28 percent are white, 10 percent are Asian, and 6 percent are African American (Children Now, n.d.).

Dual Language Learners

Young children with home languages other than English make up the fastest-growing segment of the population nationwide, with California being at the forefront of this trend (State Advisory Council on Early Learning and Care 2013, Paper 3, Program Elements and Teaching Practices). The California Department of Education (CDE) reports that 25 percent of children in public schools serving preschool through twelfth grade are English learners (ELs).[2]

The diversity of families across the nation reflects an increase in young dual language learners (State Advisory Council on Early Learning and Care 2013, Paper 4, Family Engagement).

---

2. As stated on page 91 of Paper 3, Program Elements and Teaching Practices (State Advisory Council on Early Learning and Care 2013), "The term *English learner* is commonly used in K–12 schools to identify children who speak a language other than English at home and are not yet proficient in English. Preschoolers with a home language other than English are often a distinct group, however, since they are still developing the basics of oral language in their home language even as they begin to learn English. Therefore, many preschool programs choose to use the term *dual language learners* to describe children who are learning English while also developing proficiency in their native language (Severns 2012)" (State Advisory Council on Early Learning and Care 2013, Paper 3, Program Elements and Teaching Practices).

> ### What Is School Readiness?
>
> School readiness involves more than just children. School readiness, in the broadest sense, is about children, families, early environments, schools, and communities. Children are not innately "ready" or "not ready" for school. Their skills and development are strongly influenced by their families and through their interactions with other people and environments before coming to school (Maxwell and Clifford 2004, 42).
>
> *Source:* National Association for the Education of Young Children (NAEYC) 2009.

Growth in dual language learners has occurred predominantly among younger children (National Center for Children in Poverty 2010) and is reflected in early childhood education (ECE) programs, such as Head Start, in which 30 percent of the children served nationwide are dual language learners (Office of Head Start 2011). Despite immense growth in their numbers, children who are dual language learners are disproportionately from low-income households (Fortuny, Hernandez, and Chaudry 2010), and dual language learners who have been educated in American schools since preschool are consistently outperformed by their peers on achievement tests, and the gap widens at higher grades (Batalova, Fix, and Murray 2007; Cannon and Karoly 2007; Espinosa 2007; Hammer et al. 2009; Lee and Burkham 2002; Páez, Tabors, and Lopez 2007).

Socioeconomic Status

California's young children live in families of varying levels of socioeconomic status. In 2010, it was estimated that approximately 45 percent of California's young children live in low-income families (below 200 percent of the federal poverty level) and that 22 percent live in poverty (National Center for Children in Poverty 2010). According to the National Center for Children in Poverty, young children of immigrant parents are more likely to live in a low-income household as compared with children of native-born parents. Moreover, 60 percent of young children of immigrant parents live in low-income families. Young Latino, African American,

Native American, and Asian children in California are more likely to live in low-income families compared with white children. In California, 50 percent of four-year-olds are children of immigrant parents, and 20 percent of these children live in linguistically isolated households (Cannon, Jacknowitz, and Karoly 2012).

Children with Disabilities or Other Special Needs

It is estimated that between 5 and 14 percent of the population under age five has a special health care need (U.S. Department of Health and Human Services 2007, 57) as defined by having or being at risk for "chronic physical, developmental, behavioral, or emotional conditions that have lasted or are expected to last at least 12 months." There are approximately 45,000 children with identified disabilities in the CDE preschool system (see appendix C, California Children Enrolled in Special Education). This number does not include children at risk of disability or developmental challenges. Three-, four-, and five-year-old children with identified disabilities have individualized education programs (IEPs). These IEPs must reflect the CDE's preschool learning foundations. Under the Individuals with Disabilities Act (2004), all children must have access to the general preschool curriculum, and their progress measured accordingly (CDE 2010a, 5).

Readiness Gap

California's young children vary substantially in their progress toward becoming ready for school. Likewise, schools and communities vary in their readiness to support children toward this aim. "Achievement data for students in kindergarten through grade twelve confirm a persistent gap between white students and African American students, Hispanic students, socioeconomically disadvantaged students, English learners and students with disabilities" (CDE 2013a). Further, information in the 2011–12 California Report Card confirms that

> Latino and African American students, economically disadvantaged students and other vulnerable young, such as those in foster care, are much more likely to lag behind their peers in school. These students often lack sufficient support from an early age. By third grade, Latino and African American students are half as likely as Asian and white students to score proficient or advanced on the English Language Arts portion of the California Standardized Testing and Report (STAR) test (Children Now n.d., 32).

Although the readiness gap in California persists, as a part of the American Recovery and Reinvestment Act of 2009, the Race to the Top–Early Learning Challenge (RTT-ELC) program is designed to close the achievement gap for children with high needs. As one of nine states to win the competitive RTT-ELC federal grant in 2011, California has received funding to work toward narrowing the readiness gap and improving the early learning and development of young children by

1. increasing the number and percentage of low-income and disadvantaged children in each age group of infants, toddlers, and preschoolers who are enrolled in high-quality early learning programs;

2. designing and implementing an integrated system of high-quality early learning programs and services;

3. ensuring that the use of assessments conforms to the recommendations of the National Research Council's reports on early childhood.

Desired Results for Children and Families

The Early Education and Support Division of the CDE has established the Desired Results assessment system (http://www.desiredresults.us [accessed June 27, 2014]) to improve program quality in early care and education programs across the state. The system includes the Desired Results Developmental Profile (DRDP), which is an observational assessment instrument of children's progress in development and learning; the Environment Rating Scale, which assesses global program quality according to a program's arrangement of space, materials and activities, interactions, daily schedule, and support given to families and staff; and the Desired Results Parent Survey.

Profile of Preschool Children in California

- Number of preschool-age children in California ages three, four, and five years old in 2011: 1,546,310 (Annie E. Casey Foundation 2011)

- Total number of children from birth through age five estimated to be served in state and federal programs (FY 2011–2012):*
  State-funded: 436,936
  Early Head Start (birth to three years old): 16,480
  Head Start (three to five years old): 95,479

- Ethnic breakdown of children from birth to five years old (estimated for 2011 [Children Now, n.d.])

Hispanic	53%
White	28%
Asian/Pacific Islander	10%
African American	6%

- Number of English learner students in kindergarten (FY 2011–12): 186,717[†]

- Number of children aged three, four, and five years old (FY: 2011–2012) with Disabilities or Other Special Needs within California State Funded Preschool Programs: 73,720[†]

---

* Based on California Department of Education, Child Development Division, Child Care Annual Aggregate Report (CD-800). Number of Children Served by Program Type During Fiscal Year (2009–2010) (CDE 2010c) and Early Head Start and Head Start information from the Administration for Children and Families, U.S., Department of Health and Human Services, Head Start Bureau, 2011–2012, http://www.caheadstart.org/facts (accessed June 27, 2014).

[†] The source of these figures may be found at the Ed-Data Web site (https://www.ed-data.k12.ca.us [accessed June 27, 2014]). The number of children with disabilities or other special needs can be found in appendix C (California Children Enrolled in Special Education).

Note: Demographics that refer to the number of dual language learners in California's preschool programs are not included because it is common for programs not to track the specific enrollment of dual language learner students (NIEER 2011).

Background of Desired Results for Children and Families

The CDE's Desired Results (DR) system is designed to improve the quality of programs and services provided to all children, birth through twelve years of age, who are enrolled in early care and education programs and before- and after-school programs, and their families (see appendix D). Desired Results are defined as conditions of well-being for children and families. Each Desired Result defines an overall outcome. The DR system was developed based on six Desired Results—four for children and two for their families.

The Desired Results for Children and Families are as follows:

DR1. Children are personally and socially competent

DR2. Children are effective learners

DR3. Children show physical and motor competence

DR4. Children are safe and healthy

DR5. Families support their child's learning and development

DR6. Families achieve their goals

The DR system implemented by the CDE is a comprehensive approach that

Figure 1.2. **Standardized Testing and Reporting (STAR) English-Language Arts (ELA)**

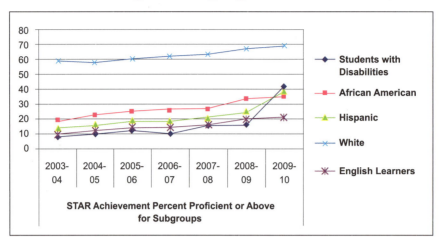

STAR Achievement Percent Proficient or Above for Subgroups

Legend:
- Students with Disabilities
- African American
- Hispanic
- White
- English Learners

Percentage of Students Identified as Proficient or Above, by Subgroups, 2004–2010

Source: 2004-2010 STAR Test Results.

facilitates the achievement of the Desired Results identified for children and families. California is one of the very few states in the nation that has developed its own system for measuring child progress toward desired outcomes. The system is aligned with both the state's learning and development foundations for early care and education programs and the content standards for kindergarten.

To assess dual language learners' English-language development in preschool, the DRDP has four measures in the domain of English–language development (ELD)—comprehension of English, self-expression in English, understanding and response to English literacy activities, and symbol, letter, and print knowledge in English. Furthermore, in the DRDP training documents (CDE 2010d, viii), the instructions state:

- Children who are dual language learners may demonstrate mastery of developmental levels in their home language, in English, or in both.

- The teacher who completes the assessment for a child who is a dual language learner should speak the

child's home language. If not, the teacher must receive assistance from another adult, such as an assistant teacher, director, or parent, who does speak the child's home language. It is important that the program plans for time during the day when the child and adult have time to interact if the adult is not the child's parent or the assistant teacher in the child's classroom.

- Overall, the development of language and literacy skills in a child's first language is important for the development of skills in a second language, and therefore should be considered as the foundational step toward learning English.

This guidance to teachers is intended to ensure that the assessors of dual language learners have the capacity to judge the child's abilities in any language, not just English. Especially for children who are in the early stages of English acquisition, it is crucial that someone who is proficient in the children's home language determines their understanding of mathematical concepts, their social skills, and their progress in the other developmental domains (more information on this system appears in appendix D).

Overview of Preschool Learning Foundations

The California preschool learning foundations (CDE 2008, 2010c, 2012a) outline key knowledge and skills that most children can achieve when provided with the kinds of interactions, instruction, and environments that research has shown to promote early learning and development. The foundations provide early childhood educators, parents, and the public with a clear understanding of the wide range of knowledge and skills that preschool children typically attain when given the benefits of a high-quality preschool program (http://www.cde.ca.gov/sp/cd/re/psfoundations.asp [accessed June 27, 2014]).

The foundations were developed using an inclusive and deliberative input process, including statewide stakeholder meetings, public input sessions held throughout the state, public hearings, and public comment. The materials were developed with the principles of universal design, so as to be inclusive of children with disabilities and other special needs. Input from the reviews was considered and incorporated as appropriate.

The California preschool learning foundations are divided among three volumes. Volume 1 focuses on the domains of social–emotional development, language and literacy, English-language development, and mathematics. Volume 2 focuses on the domains of visual and performing arts, physical development, and health. Volume 3 focuses on the domains of history–social science and science.

> The English-language development (ELD) foundations are specifically designed for children entering preschool with a home language other than English. Unlike the other foundations, in which the foundations are linked to age, the English-language development foundations are defined by three levels of development—Beginning, Middle, and Later. Depending on their prior experience with using their home language and English to communi-

cate with others, preschool dual language learners will go through these levels at different paces. Once children reach the Later level, they will still need support to continue acquiring English and to applying their developing linguistic abilities in every domain. (CDE 2008, xiii)

Closing Thoughts

The benefits of high-quality preschool are powerful and far-reaching. Research on the impact of quality includes significant economic benefits. Investments in early education have been shown to lead to students' success in school and long-term positive financial returns. In addition, research on early brain development illuminates the crucial importance of early experience. This research makes clear that, in order for young children's brains to develop and function well, children need sensitive interactions with adults and protection from toxic stress.

Recent research findings also indicate that early bilingual experience, if properly supported, enhances children's early development and learning. Moreover, the benefits of early intervention are particularly strong for children from low-income backgrounds and children with disabilities or other special needs. Yet knowledge alone has not remedied the readiness gap that persists in California. As the number of young dual language learners, children in low-income families, and children who live in stressful environments continues to increase, so does the readiness gap for these groups of children.

This publication, along with other resources in an aligned, research-based system of support, has been developed by the CDE to offer guidance on how to enhance the quality of preschool programs in California. Research and practice on how to foster early learning and development have increased understanding of the value of early education. There is now an opportunity to invest in high-quality early education and take necessary steps to ensure that all of California's young children develop well and become ready for success in early elementary school and beyond.

References

Annie E. Casey Foundation, Kids Count Data Center. 2011. *Population Estimates for California (2011)*. http://datacenter.kidscount.org (accessed June 27, 2014).

Belsky, J., D. L. Vandell, M. Burchinal, K.A. Clarke-Stewart, K. McCartney, and M. T. Owen. 2007. "Are There Long-Term Effects of Early Child Care?" *Child Development* 78 (2): 681–701.

California Department of Education (CDE). 1997. *Continuity for Young Children: Positive Transitions to Elementary School*. Sacramento: California Department of Education.

———. 2008. *California Preschool Learning Foundations, Volume 1*. Sacramento: California Department of Education.

———. 2010a. *California Preschool Curriculum Framework, Volume 1*. Sacramento: California Department of Education.

———. 2010b. *California Preschool Learning Foundations, Volume 2*. Sacramento: California Department of Education.

———. 2010c. *Child Care Annual Aggregate Report (CD-800): Number of Children Served by Program Type During Fiscal Year (2009-2010)*. http://www.cde.ca.gov/sp/cd/re/acf800.asp (accessed June 27, 2013).

———. 2010d. *Desired Results Developmental Profile: Preschool*. DRDP-PS. Sacramento: California Department of Education.

———. 2012a. *California Preschool Learning Foundations, Volume. 3*. Sacramento: California Department of Education.

———. 2012b. *Desired Results Developmental Profile: School Readiness*. Sacramento: California Department of Education.

———. 2012c. *Infant/Toddler Caregiving: A Guide to Cognitive Development and Learning*. 2nd ed. Sacramento: California Department of Education.

———. 2013a. *California Striving Readers Comprehensive Literacy (SRCL) Plan*. Sacramento: California Department of Education.

Cannon, J., A. Jacknowitz, and L. Karoly. 2012. *Preschool and School Readiness: Experiences of Children with Non-English-Speaking Parents*. San Francisco: Public Policy Institute of California.

Castro, D., L. Espinosa, and M. Paez. 2011. "Defining and Measuring Quality Early Childhood Practices that Promote Dual Language Learners' Development and Learning." In *Quality Measurement in Early Childhood Settings*. Edited by M. Zaslow, I. Martinez-Beck, K. Tout, and T. Halle. Baltimore: Paul H. Brookes Publishing.

Center on the Developing Child at Harvard University. n.d. *InBrief Series: Early Childhood Program Effectiveness*. Cambridge, MA: Harvard University. http://developingchild.harvard.edu/index.php/resources/briefs/inbrief_series/inbrief_program_effectiveness/ (accessed June 25, 2013).

Child and Family Policy Center and Voices for America's Children. 2005. *Early Learning Left Out: Closing the Investment Gap for America's Youngest Children*. 2nd ed. Des Moines, IA: Child and Family Policy Center.

Children Now. n.d. *California Report Card, 2011–12: Setting the Agenda for Children*. Oakland, CA: Children Now.

———. 2011. *Policy Priorities Early Learning & Development*. Oakland, CA: Children Now. www.childrennow.org/ (accessed June 27, 2013).

Curby, T. W., J. LoCasale-Crouch, T. R. Konold, R. C. Pianta, C. Howes, M. Burchinal, D. Bryant, R. Clifford, D. Early, and O. Barbarin. 2009. "The Relations of Observed Pre-K Classrooms Quality Profiles to Children's Academic Achievement and Social Competence." *Early Education and Development* 20: 346–72.

Diamond, M., and J. Hopson. 1998. *Magic Trees of the Mind: How to Nurture Your Child's Intelligence, Creativity, and Healthy Emotions from Birth Through Adolescence*. New York: Dutton.

Division for Early Childhood and National Association for the Education of Young Children. 2009. *Early Childhood Inclusion: Joint Position Statement of the Division for Early Childhood (DEC) and the National Association for the Education of Young Children (NAEYC)*. Chapel

Hill: The University of North Carolina, Franklin Porter Graham Child Development Institute.

Early Head Start and Head Start information from the Administration for Children and Families, U.S., Department of Health and Human Services, Head Start Bureau, 2011-2012. n.d. http://www.caheadstart.org/facts.html (accessed July 3, 2014).

Ed-Data. Fiscal, Demographic, and Performance Data on California's K–12 Schools. https:/www.ed-data.k12.ca.us (accessed June 27, 2014).

Espinosa, L. 2013. *Early Education for Dual Language Learners: Policies and Practices That Promote School Readiness and Early School Success.* Washington, DC: Migration Policy Institute.

Gormley, W. T., Jr., D. A. Phillips, K. Newmark, and K. Perper. 2011. "Social-Emotional Effects of Early Childhood Education Programs in Tulsa." *Child Development* 82:2095–2109.

Greenspan, S. I. 2003. "Child Care Research: A Clinical Perspective." *Child Development* 74:1064–68.

Heckman, J. J. 2006. "Skill Formation and the Economics of Investing in Disadvantaged Children." *Science* 312:1099–1902.

———. 2009. "The Economics of Inequality: The Value of Early Childhood Education." *American Educator* Spring: 31–47.

Helburn, S.W., ed. 1995. *Cost, Quality, and Child Outcomes in Child Care Centers.* Technical report. Denver: Department of Economics, Center for Research in Economics and Social Policy, University of Colorado at Denver.

Howes, C., M. Burchinal, R. Pianta, D. Bryant, D. Early, R. Clifford, and O. Barbarin. 2008. "Ready to Learn? Children's Pre-Academic Achievement in Pre-Kindergarten Programs." *Early Childhood Research Quarterly* 23 (1): 27–50.

Karoly, L. A., B. Ghosh-Dastidar, G. L. Zellman, M. Perlman, and L. Fernyhough. 2008. *Prepared to Learn: The Nature and Quality of Early Care and Education for Preschool-Age Children in California.* Santa Monica, CA: Rand Corporation. http://www.rand.org/pubs/technical_reports/TR539 (accessed March 24, 2013).

Mashburn, A. J., C. Howes, M. Burchinal, R. Pianta, D. Bryant, D. Early, R. Clifford, and O. Barbarin. 2008. "Measures of Pre-K Quality and Children's Development of Academic, Language and Social Skills." *Child Development* 79 (3): 732–49.

National Association for the Education of Young Children (NAEYC). 2009. *Developmentally Appropriate Practice in Early Childhood Programs Serving Children from Birth through Age 8: Position Statement.* Washington, DC: National Association for the Education of Young Children.

National Association of Child Care Resource and Referral Agency (NACCRRA). 2010. http://www.naccrra.org (accessed July 3, 2014).

National Center for Children in Poverty. 2010. *English Language Proficiency, Family Economic Security, and Child Development.* http://www.nccp.org/publications/pub_948.html (accessed June 15, 2015).

National Education Goals Panel. 1995. *The National Education Goals Report: Building a Nation of Learners, 1995.* Washington, DC: U.S. Government Printing Office, Superintendent of Documents.

———. 1997. *The National Education Goals Report: Getting a Good Start in School, 1997.* Washington, DC: U.S. Government Printing Office, Superintendent of Documents.

———. 1998. *The National Education Goals Report: Building a Nation of Learners, 1998.* Washington, DC: U.S. Government Printing Office, Superintendent of Documents.

National Institute for Early Education Research (NIEER). 2011. *Are Hispanic Children Losing Out in Preschool?* http://preschoolmatters.org/2011/05/ (accessed April 7, 2014).

National Institute of Child Health and Human Development (NICHD), Early Child Care Research Network. 2003."Child

Care and Mother-Child Interaction from 36 Months through First Grade." *Infant Behavior and Development* 26: 345–70.

National Research Council and Institute of Medicine. 2000. *From Neurons to Neighborhoods: The Science of Early Childhood Development*, edited by J. P. Shonkoff and D. A. Phillips. Committee on Integrating the Science of Early Childhood Development and Board on Children, Youth, and Families, Commission on Behavioral and Social Sciences and Education. Washington, DC: National Academies Press.

Nelson, C. A., and J. P. McCleery. 2008. "The Use of Event-Related Potentials in the Study of Typical and Atypical Development." *Journal of the American Academy of Child and Adolescent Psychiatry* 47 (11): 1252–61.

Odom, S. L., V. Buysse, and E. Soukakou. 2011. "Inclusion for Young Children with Disabilities: A Quarter Century of Research Perspectives." *Journal of Early Intervention* 33 (4): 344–56.

Peisner-Feinberg, E.S., M. R. Burchinal, R. M. Clifford, M. L. Culkin, C. Howes, S. L. Kagan, and N. Yazejian. 2001. "The Relation of Preschool Child-Care Quality to Children's Cognitive and Social Developmental Trajectories through Second Grade." *Child Development* 72 (5): 1534–53.

Soukakou, E. P. 2012. "Measuring Quality in Inclusive Preschool Classrooms: Development and Validation of the Inclusive Classroom Profile (ICP)." *Early Childhood Research Quarterly* 27 (3): 478–88.

State Advisory Council on Early Learning and Care. 2013. *California's Best Practices for Young Dual Language Learners: Research Overview Papers*. Sacramento: California Department of Education. http://www.cde.ca.gov/sp/cd/ce/documents/dllresearchpapers.pdf (accessed April 3, 2014).

Thompson, R. A. n.d. "Connecting Neurons, Concepts, and People: Brain Development and Its Implications." *National Institute for Early Education Research Preschool Policy Facts*.

Thompson, R. A., and E. A. Virmani. 2012. "Socioemotional Development." In *Encyclopedia of Human Behavior*, edited by V. S. Ramachandran. 2nd ed. Oxford, UK: Elsevier.

U. S. Department of Health and Human Services, Health Resources and Services Administration, Maternal and Child Health Bureau. 2007. *The National Survey of Children with Special Health Care Needs Chartbook 2005–2006*. Rockville, MD: U. S. Department of Health and Human Services.

Vandell, D. L., J. Belsky, M. Burchinal, L. Steinberg, N. Vandergrift, and NICHD Early Child Care Research Network. 2010. "Do Effects of Early Child Care Extend to Age 15 Years? Results from the NICHD Study of Early Child Care and Youth Development." *Child Development* 81 (3): 737–75.

Chapter 2
The Preschool Child

The preschool years are a time of major physical, cognitive, language, and social–emotional growth. Recent research indicates that brain development in the early years is foundational to all later development. Brain development in the preschool years builds on the dramatic changes in brain structure and functioning that occur during the first three years of life. In the preschool years, the brain changes most significantly in the area of the **prefrontal cortex** (see figure 2.1). In particular, growth in the prefrontal cortex is related to the development of **executive function skills**, which lay the foundation for children's emerging abilities to inhibit impulses (**inhibitory control**), hold and use information (**working memory**), and adjust to changing demands of the classroom environment (**cognitive flexibility**) (Diamond et al. 2007).

The executive function skills of inhibitory control, working memory, and cognitive flexibility appear to be particularly important to school readiness because they affect children's capacity to engage in learning activities, to persist when doing challenging tasks, and to regulate their behavior when frustrations arise in daily interactions with peers (Vitiello et al. 2011). As social relationships influence brain development, children's daily experiences with family members, teachers, and peers play a central role in the development of social–emotional and cognitive skills that are needed to thrive in school and life.

Figure 2.1. **Brain Areas and Functions**

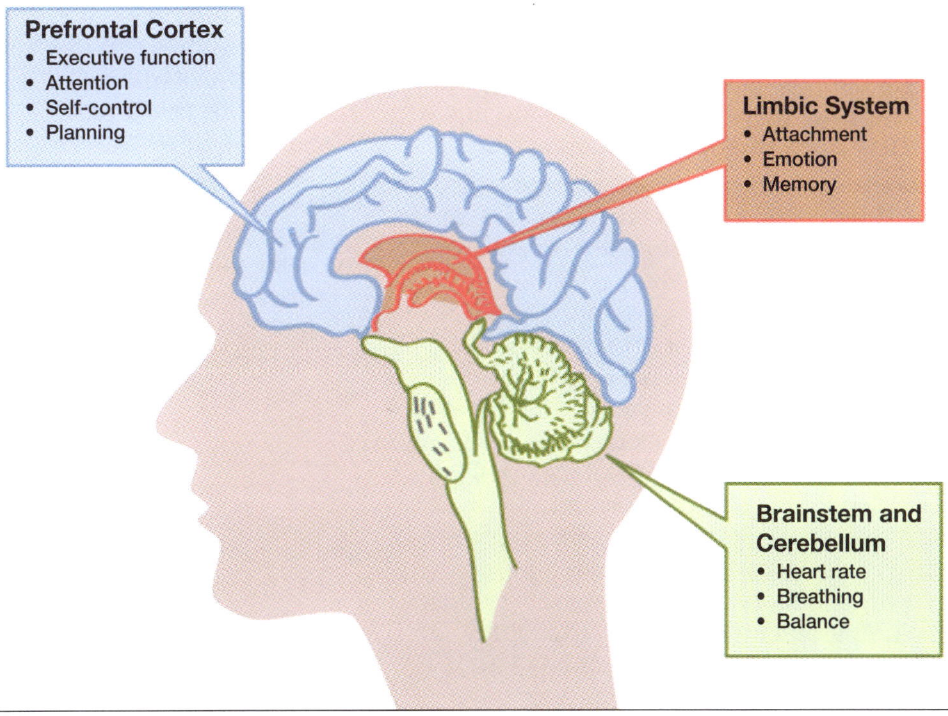

Prefrontal Cortex
- Executive function
- Attention
- Self-control
- Planning

Limbic System
- Attachment
- Emotion
- Memory

Brainstem and Cerebellum
- Heart rate
- Breathing
- Balance

Young children's growing social–emotional, cognitive, and language skills are inextricably linked, with development in one domain affecting development in the other domains. For instance, in the context of social interactions with adults and peers, children develop language that enables them to communicate their needs, desires, and ideas. For children whose **home language** is English, expanded language learning opportunities in both the preschool and home settings strengthens their language development. Additional considerations come into play for children who are dual language learners. When supported to communicate and use language in a preschool environment, children begin to use their growing language skills to interact and build positive relationships with peers and adults. For example, during play with peers, one child asks another, "Why are you crying?" The question demonstrates both the child's growing social–emotional skills as well as a developing ability to communicate effectively with others. Moreover, experiences with language contribute to the growth of children's social–cognitive skills, including executive function capacities. It is noteworthy that research has found that young dual language learners have an advantage over monolingual children in several areas of cognitive and social development (see State Advisory Council on Early Learning and Care 2013, Paper 2, Development Across Domains).

For young dual language learners, there is scientific consensus that children have the capacity to learn two languages from birth and that this early dual language exposure does not confuse children or delay development in either language. In fact, dual language learning provides children with many cognitive benefits across multiple domains (e.g., executive function and executive control skills, measures of creativity, mental flexibility, interpersonal skills, and long-term memory). The cognitive and social advantages of bilingualism appear strongest when children are proficient in both languages. No discernible benefits to dual language learning have been found when children's experience with one of the languages is limited (see State Advisory Council on Early Learning and Care 2013, Paper 2, Development Across Domains). Because dual language learners are developing language proficiency in two languages simultaneously during the preschool years, both languages need to be supported and fostered for all children, including those with special needs.

As young children engage with adults and peers, they learn through play and exploration. Rich learning environments with a variety of activities enhance young children's learning and development. In an environment in which children have the opportunity to make observations, ask questions, plan investigations, gather and interpret information, and communicate findings and ideas (CDE 2012b, 53), they explore concepts in domains such as science, math, and history–social science. Dance, music, and drama not only introduce children to the arts, they provide opportunities for children to learn to regulate their behavior and take the perspective of another person.

Children's physical development is a critical aspect of children's overall development, allowing them to engage with others, to explore, to learn, and to play (CDE 2010b, 37). Preschool-age children develop and refine fundamental movement skills, including gross and fine motor manipulative skills, that enable them to move confidently through space; manage finer, more complex tasks; and take care of personal needs, such as going to the toilet and getting dressed. Together, children's physical, cognitive, language,

and social–emotional capacities enable them to observe, investigate, and engage with the physical and social environment in new ways. To ensure that children with disabilities, or other special needs, have opportunities to use their capacities to their fullest and benefit from what high-quality preschool programs offer, programs and teachers make appropriate adaptations of the environment, curriculum, and instructional strategies.

Culture, age, and individual differences, as well as socioeconomic status and availability of learning opportunities, affect the learning and development of preschool-age children. Typically developing children of the same age vary widely in their mastery of various social, cognitive, and physical skills; nevertheless, progressions of skill development are common to all children. The young three-year-old is markedly different from the five-year-old across all developmental domains. Most three-year-olds are more interested in unstructured play, for example, than in organized games with rules, whereas five-year-olds show an emerging interest in the challenge of more structured games that involve strategies and rules. Another way three-year-olds differ from five-year-olds

is that they are typically not yet developmentally ready to engage in activities that build skills in phonological awareness, such as blending and segmenting compound words. In contrast, five-year-olds often find such activities engaging and are ready to make progress with building phonological awareness. Research-based information on the learning and development that occurs during the preschool years in each domain can deepen families' and parents' understanding of who the preschool child is and how best to nurture and support the preschool child.

The Five Essential Domains of School Readiness

Over the past several years, federal, state, and local organizations have used the five essential domains of learning and development to organize school-readiness goals and assess children's learning and development (National Education Goals Panel [NEGP] 1995). The five essential domains of school readiness, as identified by the NEGP are

(1) Social and Emotional Development;

(2) Language and Literacy Development;

(3) Cognition and General Knowledge;

(4) Physical Well-Being and Motor Development;

(5) Approaches Toward Learning.

In addition to the work of the NEGP, two national initiatives—the Common Core State Standards (K–12; does not include pre-K) and the Head Start Child Development and Early Learning Framework (Head Start Learning Framework)—have contributed to early childhood educators' understanding of children's learning and development in the early years. Collectively, the NEGP, Common Core State Standards, and Head Start Learning Framework have helped to define the knowledge and skills that children acquire during the first years of life that are essential for later success in school.

Mirroring the national initiative, California has created early learning and development foundations to describe knowledge and skills that align with the California kindergarten content standards, the Com-

mon Core State Standards, the Head Start Learning Framework, and the NEGP (see *The Alignment of the California Preschool Learning Foundations with Key Early Education Resources* [CDE 2012a]). The development of content standards for K–12 education established the context for the development of the early learning foundations. Specifically, over the past 15 years, the California Department of Education (CDE) has collaborated with academic content experts, K–12 educators, and other stakeholders to define what children are expected to learn in California public schools from kindergarten through twelfth grade. From this collaborative effort, content standards for grades K–12 emerged. In 2006, experts were convened to write foundations that describe the learning and development of children during the years from birth to age three. The publication *California Infant/Toddler Learning & Development Foundations* (CDE 2009) emerged from this work. After creating the infant/toddler learning and development foundations, the CDE organized researchers, early childhood educators, and other stakeholders to conceptualize and delineate preschool learning foundations. As a result of this effort, the three-volume set of the *California Preschool Learning Foundations* was published.

The California preschool learning foundations describe knowledge and skills that most children, with appropriate support, can be expected to demonstrate as they complete their first and second years of preschool. Foundations in eight of the nine domains focus on learning and development at around 48 months of age and at around 60 months of age. Unlike the other foundations, in which the foundations are linked to age, the English-language development foundations are defined by three levels of development—beginning, middle, and later. Depending on their prior experience with using their home language and English to communi-cate with others, dual language learners will go through these levels at different paces. The following nine domains make up the preschool learning foundations:

- Social–Emotional Development
- Language and Literacy
- English-Language Development
- Mathematics
- Visual and Performing Arts
- Physical Development
- Health
- History–Social Science
- Science

Table 2.1. Alignment of the Five Essential Domains of School Readiness with Nine California Preschool Learning Foundations	
Five Essential Domains of School Readiness	**California Preschool Learning Foundations**
1. Social–Emotional Development	• Social–Emotional Development
2. Language and Literacy Development	• Language and Literacy • English-Language Development[1]
3. Cognition and General Knowledge	• Mathematics • Science • History–Social Science • Visual and Performing Arts
4. Physical Well-Being and Motor Development	• Physical Development • Health
5. Approaches Toward Learning	• Social–Emotional Development • Science

Taken together, the preschool learning foundations provide administrators with a profile of the preschool child across all domains of development as he or she progresses developmentally. The foundations offer preschool teachers and administrators a comprehensive look at the developing child and what the child learns during the preschool years.

Both the federal Head Start programs and the U.S. Department of Education underscore the importance of early learning and development through the five essential domains of school readiness. The alignment between the five essential domains of school readiness and the nine California preschool learning foundations is shown in the table above.

As table 2.1 indicates, some domains of the California preschool learning foundations completely overlap with an essential domain of school readiness. In other cases, a domain of the preschool learning foundations covers an aspect of one of

1. Although English-language development cuts across all domains of learning and development, it is most closely associated with the Language and Literacy domain.

the five essential domains. Starting with Social–Emotional Development, the next section of this chapter delineates how the content of the *California Preschool Learning Foundations* addresses each of the five essential domains of school readiness.

Social–Emotional Development

Social–emotional development is foundational to children's learning in all other domains. Through children's experiences in close relationships with parents and teachers, children develop and learn the social–emotional skills necessary to act and interact with self-confidence, regulate their behavior, and be successful in the early school years and beyond. With the guidance of responsive and caring adults, "young children develop an understanding of other people's feelings and needs, are encouraged to feel empathy and caring, learn to manage their own behavior as responsible group members, and acquire a variety of other capabilities that will be directly related to their success in managing the classroom environment of kindergarten or the primary grades" (CDE 2008, 4).

Social–Emotional Foundations

The California preschool learning foundations[2] are organized according to the following strands of children's social–emotional development: Self, Social Interactions, and Relationships. In the strand of Self, between the ages of 48 and 60 months, preschoolers grow in five areas (substrands): their capacity for *self-awareness, self-regulation, social and emotional understanding, empathy and caring, and initiative in learning.* In the area of self-regulation, for instance, at around 60 months of age, preschool children more consistently regulate their attention, thoughts, feelings and impulses, yet they still rely on adults to help guide pro-social interactions with peers. For example, with a teacher's prompt, a preschooler remembers to use words to convey strong feelings (e.g., "It makes me mad when you push!").

In the strand of Social Interactions, the substrands focus on children's *interactions with familiar adults, interactions with peers, skills in group participation,* and *cooperation and responsibility.* For instance, at around 60 months of age, in the area of group participation, children participate positively and cooperatively as group members, sometimes sharing spontaneously and thinking of turn-taking without adult prompting.

In the Relationships strand, the substrands include children's *attachment relationships to parents,* and their *close relationships with teachers and caregivers.* By the end of the preschool years, at around 60 months, the *friendships* substrand describes children' friendships as becoming more reciprocal, exclusive, and enduring. In the area of friendships at the end of the preschool years, children's skills include engaging in recurrent, familiar, and cooperative role-play activities with one or more favorite friends.

Language and Literacy

Similar to their functioning in all other domains, children's functioning in the Language and Literacy domain depends on their learning and development in other domains (CDE 2008, 47). An understanding of the influence of learning and development in one domain on functioning in other domains is particularly important in supporting dual language learners.

Over the past two decades, the number of young children in California who have a home language other than English has increased dramatically (CDE 2006a, b). The California preschool learning foundations in English-language development provide an overview of how dual language learners make progress in learning English. These foundations specifically focus on children's progress with learning English, while the language and literacy foundations help classroom teachers understand children's progress in the Language and Literacy domain whether the child is monolingual English or a dual language learner.

---

2. The preschool learning foundations are organized by domains. Each domain is divided into strands that define its scope. Each strand is further divided into substrands. Each substrand section includes a brief overview of the substrand.

In the case of dual language learners, knowledge and skills in the Language and Literacy domain may be demonstrated in the home language or in English or in both languages. Taken together, the language and literacy foundations and English-language development foundations address the needs of all learners, regardless of their home language.

Language and Literacy Foundations

The Language and Literacy domain of the preschool learning foundations consists of three broad categories (or strands): Listening and Speaking, Reading, and Writing.

The Listening and Speaking strand focuses on preschool children's increasing competence in the substrands of *language use and conventions, vocabulary,* and *grammar.* While preschool children's language and literacy development tends to follow a general developmental progression, their early experiences with language and communication often vary. By 60 months of age, those with appropriate support tend to speak clearly enough to be understood by both familiar and unfamiliar adults and children. For example, in order to understand a 60-month-old child, most listeners do not to ask the child to say something a second time.

In the Reading strand, children grow in substrand areas that include understanding of *concepts about print, phonological awareness, alphabetics and word/print recognition, comprehension and analysis of age-appropriate text,* and *literacy interest and response.* Phonological awareness, or "an individual's sensitivity to the sound (or phonological structure) of spoken language," has been identified as a particularly important skill that children start to acquire in preschool. It contributes to learning to read in elementary school. By the end of preschool, at about 60 months of age, children develop age-appropriate phonological awareness. For instance, while playing in the dramatic play area, a child may respond "hairbrush" when

asked, "What word do you get when you put 'hair' and 'brush' together?" Even though phonological awareness is defined as an oral language skill, it is also important for children who are deaf or hard of hearing (CDE 2012b, 64).

In the Writing strand, preschoolers demonstrate increasing emergent writing skills in substrand areas, such as writing letter-like shapes to represent words or ideas and writing their first name neatly and correctly, although they may make a few mistakes, such as omitting some letters.

English-Language Development Foundations

The foundations describe preschool English learners' developmental progressions in four general strands: Listening, Speaking, Reading, and Writing. These foundations illustrate a progression for children who enter preschool knowing very little, if any, English. As children make progress in learning English, they are developing the underlying linguistic knowledge needed to learn from a curriculum that is taught in English (CDE 2008, 108). The structure of the English-language development foundations is defined by a continuum of levels: beginning, middle, and later. At the beginning level, young dual language learners communicate in their home language and nonverbally. They may understand a few English words. At the middle level, young dual language learners continue to rely heavily on their home language to understand communication and express themselves. In addition, they start to express themselves in English using telegraphic and formulaic speech and may mix their home language and English. At the later level, dual language learners understand and use English, but they continue to need support to build their knowledge and skills in English and occasionally may mix their home language and English.

The Listening strand addresses various aspects of children's *attending to English language.* Listening to English and understanding it depend on children's receptive comprehension in their home language. In other words, children apply listening strategies in their home language to strategies for learning English (Bialystok

2001). In particular, this strand addresses listening with understanding to beginning words, requests and directions, and basic and advanced concepts.

The Speaking strand addresses three substrand areas: the use of nonverbal and verbal strategies to *communicate with others, including communication of needs, vocabulary production, conversation, utterance length and complexity, grammar, and inquiry; understanding and using social conventions in English*; and *using language to create oral narratives about personal experiences.*

In the Reading strand, the foundations cover the substrands of *appreciation and enjoyment of reading and literature*, which children gain through participating in read-aloud activities and demonstrating interest in books and reading; and an *increasing understanding of book reading*, which children learn through making personal connections to the story and focusing on story structure. The Reading strand also addresses the substrands of the *demonstration of an understanding of print conventions*, which children manifest through book handling; the *demonstration of awareness that print carries meaning*, which involves the *recognition of environmental print; demonstrating*

progress in knowledge of the alphabet in English, which focuses on showing letter awareness and letter recognition; and *demonstrating phonological awareness*, which children acquire through rhyming, recognizing onset (initial sound), and sound differences in the home language and English.

Finally, the Writing strand consists of the substrand areas of the *use of writing to communicate ideas, the use of writing as communication, writing to represent words or ideas, and writing one's name.*

Cognition and General Knowledge

Areas in which preschool-age children expand their cognitive skills and general knowledge of the world are mathematics, history–social science, science, and visual and performing arts. The preschool learning foundations address the various domains of cognitive development across volumes 1, 2, and 3 (CDE 2008, 2010, 2012b).

Mathematics Foundations

During the preschool years, children are motivated to use informal math in sophisticated ways in their everyday environments. They continue to develop their understanding of Number Sense, Algebra and Functions (or Classification and Patterning), Measurement, Geometry, and Mathematical Reasoning.

In the Number Sense strand, between 48 and 60 months of age, preschoolers expand their *understanding of numbers and quantities in their everyday environments*, and *understanding of number relationships and operations in their everyday environments.* For instance, in the area of numbers and quantities, preschoolers can recite numbers in order to 20 with increasing accuracy. At around 60 months of age, one child may skip a few numbers when reciting 1–20 (e.g., "One, two, three, four, five . . . nine, ten, eleven, twelve, thirteen, fifteen, seventeen, eighteen, twenty," whereas another child the same age might chant one through twenty without skipping any numbers.

In the Algebra and Functions (Classification and Patterning) strand, children between 48 and 60 months of age

"Preschool children experience the world and build knowledge in an integrated manner, during simple moments of play and interaction with objects and other people. They constantly gather information and strive to make sense of it. Their minds take in words, numbers, feelings, and the actions and reactions of people, creatures, and objects and integrate new information into an increasingly complex system of knowledge. Effective curriculum for young children engages their active minds and nurtures their enthusiastic search for meaning and understanding."

—CDE 2010a, 13–14.

increase their understanding of sorting and classifying objects in their everyday environment and their *understanding of simple, repeating patterns.* For instance, at around 60 months of age, children begin to extend and create simple repeating patterns such as by clapping, "clap, clap, hop, hop" in rhythm to a song.

In the Measurement strand, children at 60 months of age expand their understanding of comparing, ordering, and measuring objects, for instance, by ordering four or more objects by size. In the Geometry strand, children at around 60 months *identify and use a variety of shapes in their everyday environment,* and *understand the positions of objects in space.* For instance, in the substrand of understanding positions in space, a child follows along with the directions, "Simon Says, put your hands in front of your legs."

In the Mathematical Reasoning strand, children continue to develop their use of mathematical thinking to solve problems that arise in their everyday environment. They identify and apply a variety of mathematical strategies to solve problems, such as predicting the number of small balls in a closed box and then communicating to a peer, "Let's count."

Science Foundations

Preschool-age children are naturally curious. They explore and experiment with things in their environment in inventive ways. By offering a planned, play-based, supportive environment, teachers give children ample opportunities to observe and investigate objects and events in their daily environment (CDE 2012b, 49). The *California Preschool Learning Foundations, Volume 3,* organizes Science into four strands. The first strand, Scientific Inquiry, addresses language and skills that are fundamental to the process of doing science. The other three strands focus on age-appropriate ideas and concepts in the areas of Physical Sciences, Life Sciences, and Earth Sciences that children develop during the preschool years through everyday interactions and activities.

During the preschool years, children develop skills of Scientific Inquiry through *observation and investigation* and *documentation and communication* (substrands). In the observation and investigation substrand, at around 60 months of age children can compare and contrast objects and events and describe similarities and differences in increasing detail. A child distinguishes objects that can roll down a ramp (e.g., balls, marbles, wheeled toys, cans) from objects that cannot roll down (a shovel, block, book). Pointing to the objects that can roll down the ramp, the child may communicate, "These are round and have wheels."

In the Physical Sciences strand, the substrands address children's ability to *understand the properties and characteristics of nonliving objects and materials* and of *changes in nonliving objects and materials*. For instance, at around 60 months of age, children demonstrate knowledge of the difference between animate and inanimate objects, recognizing that living things undergo biological processes such as growth, illness, healing, and dying. The child may communicate, "This roly-poly is alive. It looks like a little ball when I hold it in my hand, but when I put it on the ground, it starts moving."

In the Life Sciences strand, the substrands cover how children *identify properties and characteristics of living things* and *changes in living things*. For example, children identify characteristics of an increasing variety of plants and demonstrate an increased ability to categorize them. They may sort fruit such as mangoes, avocados, apples, grapes, peaches, and apricots based on whether one seed or many seeds are inside. One child may point to an avocado and apricot and say in her home language, "Look! They both have one big seed."

In the Earth Sciences strand, the substrands involve children's *understanding of properties and characteristics of earth materials and objects* and *changes in the earth*. Between the ages of 48 and 60 months, children demonstrate increased ability to investigate and compare characteristics of earth materials such as sand, rocks, soil, water, and air. A child may investigate surfaces of different rocks and sort the rocks based on how shiny they are and then communicate, "Here are very shiny rocks, and here are not-so-shiny rocks."

History–Social Science

Between the ages of 48 and 60 months, children grow in their understanding of the social world in which they live. In the Self and Society strand, children demonstrate developmental progress in the substrand areas of *culture and diversity*, *relationships*, and *social roles and occupations*. For instance, in the area of culture and diversity, preschoolers at around 48 months of age start to develop a sense of self that incorporates the culture, ethnic, and racial identities of their families. Children also display curiosity about diversity in human characteristics, but tend to prefer those of their own group. They demonstrate a sense of their cultural, ethnic, and racial identities in their everyday interactions with their peers. For example, while patting play dough, a child may tell a friend, "My *abuela* makes tortillas." Children share their understanding of how their families do things and how this might be different from or similar to what other families do.

Children learn about the strand of Becoming a Preschool Community Member (Civics). As they learn, they are *developing skills for democratic participation, responsible conduct, demonstrating fairness and respect for other people*, and *conflict resolution* (substrands). In the area of conflict negotiation, children at around 60 months of age are more capable of negotiating, compromising, and finding cooperative means of resolving conflict with peers or adults. For example, when two children want to use the same tricycle, one child might suggest that they take turns.

During the preschool years, children's Sense of Time becomes more sophisticated. This strand consists of *understanding of past events, anticipating and planning future events, understanding of their own personal history*, and *understanding of historical changes in people and the world*. For instance, in the area of personal history, at around 60 months of age children compare their current abilities with their skills when they were younger, sharing autobiographical stories about recent experiences. Along these lines, a child may share with other children that he was once little and that soon they will be big like him.

In addition, preschool children develop a Sense of Place (Geography and Ecology). The Sense of Place strand pertains to *navigating familiar locations, demonstrating an interest in caring for the natural world,* and *demonstrating understanding of the physical world through drawings and maps.* For instance, at around 60 months of age, children show an interest in a wide range of natural phenomena and increasing concern about caring for the natural world. A child may tell a teacher, "Mommy does not like plastic bags because they are bad for the environment."

Young children also develop an understanding of Marketplace (Economics), demonstrating understanding of some complex economic concepts at around 60 months, such as the concept that more money is needed for things of relatively great value. For example, one preschool child may tell a friend that her family needs a new car, but they need lots of money first.

Visual and Performing Arts Foundations

Visual and Performing Arts foundations reflect the many ways in which young children experience the joys of learning, creativity, self expression, and playful exploration. The arts provide varied and meaningful opportunities for all children, including children with disabilities or other special needs, to engage in integrated learning experiences that contribute to their development in all domains. During the preschool period, the arts are more about the *process* (in the sense of participation, engagement, and involvement) than about the *product*, or the end result, of artistic activity.

The Visual and Performing Arts domain in the preschool learning foundations comprises four strands: Visual Art, Music, Drama, and Dance. Within the strands of Visual Art, Music, and Drama, young children's developmental progress is similarly organized across three substrand areas, children: *notice, respond, and engage; develop skills*; and *create, invent, and express themselves.* In contrast, the Drama strand consists of two substrands: *notice, respond, and engage* and *develop skills to create, invent, and express through drama.*

In the Visual Art strand, at around 60 months age, children demonstrate noticing, responding, and engaging by communicating about elements appearing in art and describing how objects are positioned in the artwork. A child who is visually impaired may describe art in sensory terms that relate to his experience—for example, "This ____ feels smooth."

In the Music strand, at around 48 months of age, children display developing skills in music by exploring vocally and singing repetitive patterns and parts of songs alone or with others. For example, early in the preschool years, a child may sing "De Colores" while holding hands with other children and swaying from side to side.

Within the Dance strand, at around 48 months of age children invent dance movements, for example, by striking a pose and then jumping while dancing. At around 60 months of age, children communicate and express feelings through dance (for example, a girl circles slowly with a stealthy movement, indicating she is a cat trying to catch a mouse).

In the Drama strand, children develop substrand skills to *create, invent, and express through drama*— for instance, at around 60 months children demonstrate extended role-play skills with increasing imagination and creativity. A group of older preschoolers might create an extended sequence of a dialogue when improvising with peers in a role. One child may act as a tiger expressing, "Let's hide the woodcutter's ax!" Another child may act as a parrot saying, "He can buy another one." Tiger: "I'm a tiger, I can eat him up!" Parrot: "That's not nice. Let's jump down from a tree and scare him away." Tiger: "Okay."

Physical Well-Being and Motor Development

During the preschool years, children's physical activity and health are central to their overall development. Preschool programs that provide opportunities for young children to be physically active offer them the opportunity to develop a foundation for physical development and well-being that can last a lifetime (CDE 2010, 37). Volume 2 of *the California Preschool Learning Foundations* states, "In partnership with parents preschool programs can have an important impact on the health knowledge, skills, attitudes, and practices of the children and families they serve" (page 70). That volume addresses important aspects of children's physical development and health.

Physical Development Foundations

As with all domains of learning and development, there is great variability in physical development among children of the same age. Even so, research on this domain has identified developmental progressions in the skill development of children from ages 48 months to 60 months. Development depends on appropriate support from adults. Because of the central importance of physical activity and development for preschool children's overall growth, effective preschool programs provide regular and frequent periods of active play across all areas of the curriculum.

The Physical Development foundations are organized according to three broad strands: Fundamental Movement Skills, Perceptual–Motor Skills and Movement Concepts, and Active Physical Play. Children demonstrate improvements in Fundamental Movement Skills during the preschool years by making developmental progress in the following substrand areas: *greater balance and enhanced locomotor skills, more fine-tuned gross motor manipulative skills, and fine motor manipulative skills*. For instance, at around 60 months of age, preschool children demonstrate increasing ability and body coordination in a variety of locomotor skills such as galloping, sliding, hopping, and leaping. During play with peers, a preschooler may leap over a "river" represented by two ropes by starting with a run, taking off with one foot, and landing on the other foot.

In the Perceptual–Motor Skills and Movement Concepts strand, preschoolers exhibit increasing knowledge and skills in the substrand areas of *body awareness, spatial awareness*, and *directional awareness*. In the area of body awareness, at around 60 months of age children demonstrate knowledge of an increasing number of body parts. For example, while drawing, a child may name and add body parts to his drawing.

The third strand of the Physical Development foundations, Active Physical Play, is an essential part of early learning and development and has been linked to enhanced social competence and cognitive performance (Lobo and Winsler 2006; Coe et al. 2006; also see CDE 2010b, p. 39 for more references). The Active Physical Play strand includes the substrands of *active participation, cardiovascular endurance*, and *increased muscular strength, endurance, and flexibility*. In the area of active participation, at around 60 months of age, a preschooler is likely to initiate increasingly complex physical movements for a sustained period of time, riding a tricycle for an extended period of time alone or in a made-up game with another child who is also riding a tricycle.

Health Foundations

The Health foundations consist of three broad strands: Health Habits, Safety, and Nutrition.

By developing health habits, preschool children begin to contribute to their own sense of well-being, although they may have trouble understanding that their actions can contribute to their health. The Health Habits strand consists of the substrands of *basic hygiene, oral health, knowledge of wellness*, and sun safety. In the area of basic hygiene, at around 60 months of age, children demonstrate more knowledge of the steps in the handwashing routine than at around 48 months of age. For example, during toileting, a child may show a friend how to wash hands properly while singing the handwashing song and then may communicate, "Oops! I forgot to dry my hands."

Safety is another important aspect of well-being and health that children learn about in preschool. With adult support and supervision, preschoolers can follow basic safety rules, such as injury prevention (1.0). For instance, at around 60 months of age children demonstrate increased ability to follow transportation and pedestrian safety rules, with adult support and supervision. Following the model of an accompanying adult, a child stops at the curb, looks both ways, and keeps looking for cars while crossing, staying within the lines of the crosswalk.

During the preschool years, children's understanding of Nutrition grows in the substrands of *nutrition knowledge, nutrition choices*, and *self-regulation of eating*. In the area of self-regulation of eating, at around 60 months of age children indicate increased awareness of their own hunger and fullness. For example, at snack time, a child may communicate, "I'm not hungry anymore, so I'm going to go play."

Approaches Toward Learning

Research indicates that children who approach learning in more positive, effective ways tend to be more likely to succeed in preschool and elementary school in the areas of early math and literacy, as well as demonstrate more positive interactions with their peers (Fantuzzo, Perry, and McDermott 2004; McWayne, Fantuzzo, and McDermott 2004). Young children's curiosity and initiative are funda-

mental to their ability to take advantage of learning opportunities presented to them in the classroom (Thompson 2002). When preschool-age children ask "why" questions, they demonstrate their initiative in learning and their curiosity about how the world works.

Some foundations within the Social–Emotional and Science domains of the preschool learning foundations address approaches to learning as identified by the NEGP.

In the Social–Emotional Development domain, under Self, section 5.0 describes how initiative in learning changes through the preschool years. At around 48 months of age, children enjoy learning and are confident in their ability to make new discoveries, although they may not persist at solving difficult problems. By around 60 months of age, children take greater initiative in making new discoveries, identifying new solutions, and persisting in figuring things out. They are self-confident learners who become actively involved in formal and informal learning opportunities by asking questions, proposing new ways of doing things, and offering their ideas and theories. For instance, at 60 months of age a preschooler demonstrates initiative in learning and curiosity about the way things work by asking "why" questions fairly often. For instance, a preschooler may ask, "Why is the worm doing that?" (CDE 2008, 10).

The strand Scientific Inquiry, in the Science foundations, addresses preschool children's curiosity, a fundamental component of approaches to learning. For example, in the substrand of *observation and investigation*, between around 48 months and 60 months of age, children demonstrate curiosity and an increased ability to raise questions about objects and events in their environment. Along these lines, while on the playground, a child at about 60 months of age may look up and ask the teacher, "How come I can see the moon in the daytime?" Ample opportunities to make discoveries, identify solutions, and try to figure things out develop children's initiative in learning and helps them to become self-confident learners (CDE 2012b, 49).

The Role of Play in Children's Learning and Development

Preschool programs use numerous strategies to support children's play, such as planning the learning environment, providing engaging and appropriately challenging materials, and being responsive to children's interest in engaging in play. Through observations of children's play, teachers can deepen their appreciation of the value of play in early learning. For example, imaginary play is an important means of exploring ideas and social behavior and roles among preschool-age children. While older infants and toddlers engage in solitary imaginary play, such as feeding a stuffed animal or making a roaring sound while pushing a toy truck across the carpet, preschoolers engage with one or more peers in the more complex and elaborate form of imaginary play called "sociodramatic" play. In this type of play, children cooperate with one another to create a story and "script," assume various roles, figure out appropriate "costumes" and "props," and negotiate new ideas for play, such as, "I want to be a wolf, not a dog!"

Because imaginary play holds such rich potential for promoting children's cognitive, linguistic, social, and physical development, high-quality preschool programs recognize play as a key element of the curriculum. Children's spontaneous play is a window into their ideas and feelings about the world. As such, it is a rich source of ideas for curriculum planning (Lockett 2004). For example, if a teacher observes a group of children repeatedly engaging in imaginary play about illness or hospitalization, she or he might decide to convert the playhouse area into a veterinary clinic for a week or two. The teacher might also read children stories involving doctors, hospitals, getting sick, and getting well. The teacher's observations of children's resulting conversations and activities would suggest ways to deepen or extend the curriculum further. In thinking of ways to extend the curriculum, it will be important that teachers ensure that the materials used and themes built upon are culturally familiar to the children and value children's cultural heritage. Refer to chapter 3 (The Role of the Preschool Teacher) and chapter 5 (Use of the California Preschool Curriculum Framework) for a more in-depth discussion of how teachers can use their observations to build on children's play experiences.

While involved in play, children are challenged to meet the language, problem-solving, and social competencies of their peers. When play is interesting and important to children, they are eager to learn the new vocabulary, new physical skills, and new social behaviors that will allow them to stay engaged in play (Jones and Reynolds 2011). Many three-year-olds, for example, have not yet mastered socially appropriate ways to enter other children's play. Coaching by a sensitive, observant teacher on appropriate language for asking to join play can help a child overcome this hurdle, thereby opening a new area for learning.

When teachers regularly observe and document brief, subtle moments of chil-

Play and Discovery as a Way to Facilitate Young Children's Learning

Alison Gopnik, professor of psychology at the University of California, Berkeley, studies how young children come to know about the world around them. Her research suggests that preschoolers, like scientists, test hypotheses against available information and make inferences about the way things work based on conducting informal experiments and observing those around them. Gopnik suggests that young children learn best when they can explore, inquire, play, and discover the world around them with the support of expert adults who help to guide children's learning.

dren's learning through play, those records can help parents and others understand how useful and important play is in helping children to learn and grow. For example, a teacher might report a child's language and social development to the parent of a three-year-old: "I watched Sarah standing outside the playhouse area today. Instead of just watching the other children or wandering through their play without getting involved as she often does, she brought the children a book to read to the 'baby' in the family. They asked her if she wanted to be the big sister, and she said yes and joined right in. I have been thinking about ways to help her learn how to use her language to get involved in play with other children, but she figured out her own, creative way to join them."

Closing Thoughts

During the preschool years, children grow markedly in their knowledge and skills in all areas of development. The dramatic increase in their emotional, social, cognitive, and language knowledge and skills occurs hand in hand with development of key areas of the brain, particularly the prefrontal cortex and its connections with the limbic system. Preschool-age children are naturally curious and driven to learn about the way the world works and often develop and test hypotheses through observation and experimentation. Their learning and development in all domains progresses well when they are provided with appropriately challenging opportunities for play and exploration, with the support of skilled teachers who scaffold learning experiences.

Excerpts from an Interview with Alison Gopnik

How might your research influence the work of preschool teachers?

"Preschoolers are extremely well designed for learning. They are naturally curious. We now have evidence that actually confirms what I think a lot of preschool teachers already know intuitively—that children learn through exploring and playing."

Could you elaborate on what your research shows about the value of play?

"One of the things we've learned is that when children engage in pretend play, have imaginary friends, or explore alternative worlds, they are learning what people are like, how people think, and the kinds of things people can do. This helps children learn to understand themselves and other people. We also have evidence that this kind of understanding leads to social adjustment in school and social competence in life."

Source: NAEYC 2009.

The five essential domains of school readiness and the content of the preschool learning foundations provide a comprehensive overview of children's learning and development during the preschool years. In particular, the preschool learning foundations identify for preschool administrators and teachers what children come to know and are able to do as they make progress in learning and development and move toward entry into early elementary school.

References

Bialystok, E. 2001. *Bilingualism in Development: Language, Literacy, and Cognition.* Cambridge, UK: Cambridge University Press.

California Department of Education (CDE). 2006a. *Statewide English Learners by Language and Grade, 2005–6.* Sacramento: California Department of Education. http://dq.cde.ca.gov/dataquest/ (accessed June 30, 2014).

———. 2006b. *Statewide Enrollment by Ethnicity, 2005-6.* Sacramento: California Department of Education. http://dq.cde.ca.gov/dataquest/ (accessed June 30, 2014).

———. 2008. *California Preschool Learning Foundations, Volume 1.* Sacramento: California Department of Education.

———. 2009. *California Infant/Toddler Learning & Development Foundations.* Sacramento: California Department of Education.

———. 2010a. *California Preschool Curriculum Framework, Volume 1.* Sacramento: California Department of Education.

———. 2010b. *California Preschool Learning Foundations, Volume 2.* Sacramento: California Department of Education.

———. 2012a. *The Alignment of the California Preschool Learning Foundations with Key Early Education Resources: California Infant/Toddler Learning and Development Foundations, California Content Standards, the Common Core State Standards, and Head Start Child Development and Early Learning Framework.* Sacramento: California Department of Education. http://www.cde.ca.gov/sp/cd/re/documents/psalignment.pdf (accessed June 30, 2014).

———. 2012b. *California Preschool Learning Foundations, Volume 3.* Sacramento: California Department of Education.

Coe, D. P., J. M. Pivarnik, C. J. Womack, M. J. Reeves, and R. M. Malina. 2006. "Effect of Physical Education and Activity Levels on Academic Achievement in Children." *Medicine and Science in Sports and Exercise* 38 (8): 1515–19.

Diamond, A., W. S. Barnett, J. Thomas, and S. Munro. 2007. "Preschool Program Improves Cognitive Control." *Science* 318 (5855): 1387–88.

Fantuzzo, J., M. A. Perry, and P. McDermott. 2004. "Preschool Approaches to Learning and Their Relationship to Other Relevant Classroom Competencies for Low-Income Children." *School Psychology Quarterly* 19 (3): 212–30.

Jones, E., and G. Reynolds. 2011. *The Play's the Thing: Teachers' Roles in Children's Play.* New York: Teachers College Press, Columbia University.

Lobo, Y. B., and A. Winsler. 2006. "The Effects of a Creative Dance and Movement Program on the Social Competence of Head Start Preschoolers." *Social Development* 15 (3): 501–19.

Lockett, A. 2004. *The Continuous Curriculum: Planning for Spontaneous Play.* Kirklees School Effectiveness Service. UK: Kirklees Children & Young People Service Learning.

McWayne, C. M., J. W. Fantuzzo, and P. A. McDermott. 2004. "Preschool Competency in Context: An Investigation of the Unique Contribution of Child Competencies to Early Academic Success." *Developmental Psychology* 40 (4): 633–45.

National Association for the Education of Young Children (NAEYC). 2009. "News from the Field: A Conversation with Dr. Alison Gopnik." *Teaching Young Children* 3 (2): 26–27.

National Education Goals Panel (NEGP). 1995. *Reconsidering Children's Early Development and Learning: Toward Common Views and Vocabulary.* Washington, DC: NEGP.

State Advisory Council on Early Learning and Care. 2013. *California's Best Practices for Young Dual Language Learners: Research Overview Papers.* Sacramento: California Department of Education. http://www.cde.ca.gov/sp/cd/ce/documents/dllresearchpapers.pdf (accessed April 3, 2014).

Thompson, R. A. 2002. "The Roots of School Readiness in Social and Emotional Development." *The Kaufmann Early Education Exchange* 1:8–29.

Vitiello, V. E., D. B. Greenfield, P. Munis, and G. J'Lene. 2011. "Cognitive Flexibility, Approaches to Learning, and Academic School Readiness in Head Start Preschool Children." *Early Education and Development* 22 (3): 388–410.

Further Reading

Young Dual Language Learners

Downer, J. T., M. L. López, K. J. Grimm, A. Hamagami, R. C. Pianta, and C. Howes. 2012. "Observations of Teacher–Child Interactions in Classrooms Serving Latinos and Dual Language Learners: Applicability of Classroom Assessment Scoring System in Diverse Settings." *Early Childhood Research Quarterly* 27:21–32.

Garcia, E., and E. Frede. 2010. *Enhancing Policy and Practice for Young Dual Language Learners: What Is the Research Base?* New Brunswick, NJ: National Institute for Early Education Research (NIEER).

Gonzalez, J. E., and B. M. Uhing. 2008. "Home Literacy Environments and Young Hispanic Children's English and Spanish Oral Language: A Community Analysis." *Journal of Early Intervention* 30 (2): 116–39.

Gormley, W. T. 2008. "The Effects of Oklahoma's Pre-K Program on Hispanic Children." *Social Science Quarterly* 89 (4): 916–36.

Oades-Sese, G. V., G. B. Esquivel, P. K. Kaliski, and L. Maniatis. 2011. "A Longitudinal Study of the Social and Academic Competence of Economically Disadvantaged Bilingual Preschool Children." *Developmental Psychology* 47 (3): 747–64.

Rumberger, R. W., and L. Tran. 2006. *Preschool Participation and the Cognitive and Social Development of Language-Minority Students.* CSE Technical Report 674, UC LMRI Technical Report 1–118. Santa Barbara, CA: University of California.

Soltero-Gonzalez, L. 2009. "Preschool Latino Immigrant Children: Using the Home Language as a Resource for Literacy Learning." *Theory Into Practice* 48:283–89.

High-Quality Early Education And Related Outcomes

Belsky, J., D. L. Vandell, M. Burchinal, K. A. Clarke-Stewart, K. McCartney, and M. T. Owen. 2007. "Are There Long-Term Effects of Early Child Care?" *Child Development* 78 (2): 681–701.

Burchinal, M. R., C. Howes, R. Pianta, D. Bryant, D. Early, R. Clifford, and O. Barbarin. 2008. "Predicting Child Outcomes at the End of Kindergarten from the Quality of Pre-Kindergarten Teacher–Child Interactions and Instruction." *Applied Developmental Science* 12 (3): 140–53.

Burchinal, M, R., J. E. Roberts, R. Riggins, Jr., S. A. Zeisel, E. Neebe, and D. Bryant. 2000. "Relating Quality of Center-Based Child Care to Early Cognitive and Language Development Longitudinally." *Child Development* 71 (2): 339–57.

Committee on Early Childhood, Adoption, and Dependent Care. 2005. "Quality Early Education and Child Care from Birth to Kindergarten." *Pediatrics* 115 (187): 187–91.

Curby, T. W., J. LoCasale-Crouch, R. R. Konold, R. C. Pianta, C. Howes, M. Burchinal, D. Bryant, R. Clifford, D. Early, and O. Barbarin. 2009. "The Relations of Observed Pre-K Classroom Quality Profiles to Children's Achievement and Social Competence." *Early Education and Development* 20 (2): 346–72.

Espinosa, L. M. 2002. "High Quality Preschool: Why We Need It and What It Looks Like." *Preschool Policy Matters, NIEER* 1:1–11.

Goldenberg, C., K. Nemeth, J. Hicks, M. Zepeda, and L. M. Cardona. 20012. "Program Elements and Teaching Practices for Young Dual Language Learners." In *California's Best Practices for Young Dual Language Learners: Research Overview Papers*, edited by the State Advisory Council on Early Learning and Care. Sacramento: California Department of Education.

Gormley, W. T., Jr., T. Gayer, D. Phillips, and B. Dawson. 2005. "The Effects of

Universal Pre-K on Cognitive Development." *Developmental Psychology* 41 (6): 872–84.

Gormley, W. T., Jr., D. A. Phillips, K. Newmark, and K. Perper. 2011. "Social Emotional Effects of Early Childhood Education Programs in Tulsa." *Child Development* 82 (6): 2095–109.

Melhuish, E. C. 2011. "Preschool Matters." *Science* 333:299–300.

National Scientific Council on the Developing Child, Science Briefs. 2007. "How Early Child Care Affects Later Development." http://www.developingchild.net (accessed October 1, 2014).

National Institute of Child Health and Human Development (NICHD) Early Child Care Research Network. 2001. "Child Care and Children's Peer Interaction at 24 and 36 Months: The NICHD Study of Early Child Care." *Child Development* 72 (5): 1478–1500.

———. 2002. "Child-Care Structure→ Process→Outcome: Direct and Indirect Effects of Child-Care Quality on Young Children's Development." *Psychological Science* 13 (3).

National Institute of Child Health and Human Development (NICHD) Early Child Care Research Network, and G. J. Duncan. 2003. "Modeling the Impacts of Child Care Quality on Children's Preschool Cognitive Development." *Child Development* 74 (5): 1454–75.

Preschool California. n.d. *Closing the Achievement Gap for Dual Language Learners: How Early Learning Programs Can Support English Language Development.* Oakland, CA: Preschool California.

Vandell, D. L., J. Belsky, M. Burchinal, N. Vandergrift, and L. Steinberg. 2010. "Do Effects of Early Child Care Extend to Age 15 Years?" Results from the NICHD Study of Early Child Care and Youth Development. *Child Development* 81 (3): 737–75.

INCLUDING CHILDREN WITH DISABILITIES OR OTHER SPECIAL NEEDS

Cavallaro, C. C., M. Ballard-Rosa, and E. W. Lynch. 1998. "A Preliminary Study of Inclusive Special Education Services for Infants, Toddlers, and Preschool-Age Children in California." *Topics in Early Childhood Special Education* 18 (3): 169–82.

SCHOOL READINESS

Barton, P. E. 2002. *Raising Achievement and Reducing Gaps: Reporting Progress Toward Goals for Academic Achievement in Mathematics.* A Report to the National Education Goals Panel. Lessons from the States. Washington, DC: National Education Goals Panel.

Bodrova, E., D. Leong, and R. Shore. 2004. "Child Outcome Standards in Pre-K Programs: What Are Standards; What Is Needed to Make Them Work?" *Preschool Policy Matters, NIEER* 5:1–11.

Gormley, W. T., D. Phillips, and T. Gayer. 2008. "Preschool Programs Can Boost School Readiness." *Science* 320 (27): 1723–24.

Magnuson, K. A., M. K. Meyers, C. J. Ruhm, and J. Waldfogel. 2004. "Inequality in Preschool Education and School Readiness." *American Educational Research Journal* 41 (1): 115–57.

Magnuson, K. A., C. Ruhm, and J. Waldfogel. 2007. "The Persistence of Preschool Effects: Do Subsequent Classroom Experiences Matter?" *Early Childhood Research Quarterly* 22: 18–38.

BRAIN DEVELOPMENT

Bremner, D. J. 2002. "Neuroimaging Studies in Post-traumatic Stress Disorder." *Current Psychiatry Reports* 4:254–63.

Center on the Developing Child at Harvard University. 2007. *In Brief: The Science of Early Childhood Development.* http://www.developingchild.harvard.edu (accessed July 3, 2014).

Frey, N., and D. Fisher. 2010. "Reading and the Brain: What Early Childhood Educators Need to Know." *Early Childhood Education Journal* 38:103–10.

Georgieff, M. K. 2001. "Nutrition and the Developing Brain: Nutrient Priorities and Measurement." *The American Journal of Clinical Nutrition* 85: 614S–20S.

Gilkerson, L. 2001. "Integrating and Understanding of Brain Development into Early Childhood Education." *Infant Mental Health Journal* 22:174–87.

Gunner, M. 1998. "Quality of Care and the Buffering of Stress Physiology: Its Potential Role in Protecting the Developing Human Brain." *Newsletter of the Infant Mental Health Promotion Project* 21.

Hines, P., M. McCartney, J. Mervis, and B. Wible. 2011. "Laying the Foundation for Lifetime Learning." *Science* 333:951.

King, R. M. 2008. *Enriching the Lives of Children: Creating Meaningful and Novel Stimulus Experiences to Promote Cognitive, Moral and Emotional Development.* Newcastle upon Tyne: Cambridge Scholars Publishing.

Marshall, J. 2011. "Infant Neurosensory Development: Considerations for Infant Child Care." *Early Childhood Education Journal* 39:175–81.

Nakahata, A. K. 2005. "Understanding Brain Development." *CACSAP Newsletter* 34 (4).

National Scientific Council Center on the Developing Child at Harvard University. 2005. *Excessive Stress Disrupts the Architecture of the Developing Brain.* Working Paper 3. Cambridge, MA: National Scientific Council on the Developing Child, Harvard University.

———. 2007. *The Science of Early Childhood Development: Closing the Gap Between What We Know and What We Do.* Cambridge, MA: National Scientific Council on the Developing Child. Harvard University.

Nelson, C. A., and J. P. McClerry. 2008. "Use of Event-Related Potentials in the Typical and Atypical Development." *Journal of American Academic Child Adolescent Psychiatry* 47:11.

Rosales, F. J., S. J. Reznick, and S. H. Zeisel. 2009. "Understanding the Role of Nutrition in the Brain & Behavioral Development of Toddlers and Preschool Children: Identifying and Overcoming Methodological Barriers." *National Institutes of Health* 12 (5): 190–202.

Rushton, S. 2011. "Neuroscience, Early Childhood Education and Play: We Are Doing It Right!" *Early Childhood Education Journal* 39:89–94.

Rushton, S., J. Eitelgeorge, and R. Zickafoose. 2003. "Reading and Connecting Brian Cambourne's Conditions of Learning Theory to Brain/Mind Principles: Implications for Early Childhood Educators." *Early Childhood Education Journal* 31 (1): 11–21.

Rushton, S., A. Juola-Rushton, and E. Larkin. 2010. "Neuroscience, Play and Early Childhood Education: Connections, Implications and Assessment." *Early Childhood Education Journal* 37:351–61.

Rushton, S., and E. Larkin. 2001. "Shaping the Learning Environment: Connecting Developmentally Appropriate Practices to Brain Research." *Early Childhood Education Journal* 29 (1): 25–33.

The Science of Early Childhood Development. The InBrief series of presentations at the National Symposium on Early Childhood Science and Policy. www.developingchild.harvard.edu (accessed July 3, 2014).

Shonkoff, J. P. 2011. "Protecting Brains, Not Simply Stimulating Minds." *Science* 333:983.

Thompson, R. A. 2001. "Development in the First Years of Life." *The Future of Children* 11 (1): 20–33.

———. 2008. "Connecting Neurons, Concepts, and People: Brain Development and its Implications." *Preschool Policy Brief, NIEER* 17.

Zambo, D. 2008. "Childcare Workers' Knowledge About the Brain and Developmentally Appropriate Practice." *Early Childhood Education Journal* 35:571–77.

Zero to Three. 2008. "Frequently Asked Questions: Brain Development." *Zero to Three* 28 (5): 44–45.

CALIFORNIA CONTEXT

Administration for Children and Families, U.S. Department of Health and Human Services, Head Start Bureau, 2010-2011. www.caheadstart.org/facts.html (accessed July 3, 2014).

The Annie E. Casey Foundation, Data Center Kids Count. http://www.datacenter.kidscount.org/data#CA/2/0 (accessed August 26, 2014).

California Department of Education (CDE), Child Development Division, Child Care Annual Aggregate Report (CD-800) Number of Children Served By Program Type During State Fiscal Year 2009–10. Sacramento: CDE. http://www.cde.ca.gov/sp/cd/re/acf800sfy200910.asp (accessed June 12, 2015).

Children Now. 2009. http://datacenter.kidscount.org/data/bystate/Rankings.aspx. (accessed June 25, 2013).

———. 2010. *California Report Card 2010: Setting the Agenda for Children.* Oakland, CA: Children Now.

———. 2011a. *California Report Card 2011–12: Setting the Agenda for Children.* Oakland, CA: Children Now.

———. 2011b. Policy Priorities Early Learning & Development. www.childrennow.org/ (accessed June 25, 2013).

"Early Childhood Program Effectiveness." n.d. The InBrief series of summaries of the scientific presentations at the National Symposium on Early Childhood Science and Policy. http://developingchild.harvard.edu (accessed June 16, 2015).

Heckman, J. J. 2006. "Skill Formation and the Economics of Investing in Disadvantaged Children." *Science* 312: 1900.

Love, J. M., S. Atkins-Burnett, C. Vogel, N. Aikens, Yange Xue, Maricar Mabutas, B. Lepidus Carlson, E. Sama Martin, N. Paxton, M. Caspe, S. Sprachmen, and K. Sonnenfeld. 2009. *Los Angeles Universal Preschool Programs, Children Served, and Children's Progress in the Preschool Year: Final Report of the First 5 LA Universal Preschool Child Outcomes Study.* Princeton, NJ: Mathematica Policy Research, Inc.

Lynch, R. G. 2005. "Early Childhood Investment Yields Big Payoff." WestEd *Policy Perspectives.* San Francisco, WestEd.

Preschool California. http://www.preschoolcalifornia.org/resources/resource-files/dll-policy-brief.pdf (accessed June 24, 2013).

DEMOGRAPHICS

Shin, H. B., and R. A. Kominski. 2010. "Language Use in the United States: 2007." *American Community Survey Reports.* Washington, DC: U.S. Census Bureau.

United States Census Bureau. 2011. *Who's Minding the Kids? Child Care Arrangements: Spring 2010.* Washington, DC: United States Census Bureau. http://www.census.gov/hhes/childcare/data/sipp/2010/tables.html (accessed July 10, 2014).

Chapter 3
The Role of the Preschool Teacher

Preschool teachers[1] play a central role in ensuring the preschool program is of high quality. They bring a wide range of skills and qualities to the job of guiding young children's learning and development. Teachers promote school-readiness skills by striking a skillful balance of engaging in sensitive and warm interactions with children and actively **scaffolding** children's developing skills, providing them with frequent and relevant feedback (Howes et al. 2008). Effective teachers engage collaboratively with one another, drawing upon their collective experience with the children in their care to paint a more complete picture of who each child is. Preschool teachers who work with dual language learners also need to engage in sensitive and warm interactions with them while promoting school-readiness skills. In addition, teachers need to understand the process of second language acquisition during the preschool years and how to intentionally support home language development while promoting English-language development (ELD). Teachers who take the time to learn about the children's home background, culture, and language are able to connect learning activities to the child's world and create a meaningful context for learning. Knowledge about the child's stage of English-language development is crucial for setting realistic language goals.

As stated in the *California Early Childhood Educator Competencies*,

an effective early childhood educator must be knowledgeable about child development, skillful at observing and assessing learning, and intentional in planning experiences to support children's exploration, play, and learning. . . . Intentional early childhood educators are mindful about the daily schedule, the materials available to children, adaptations that individual children may need, indoor and outdoor play environments, and the engagement of families in supporting children's learning." (California Department of Education and First 5 California 2012, 3)

The major responsibilities of preschool teachers are to

- build and maintain positive relationships with children;
- build and maintain positive relationships with families;
- create an environment for social and emotional learning;
- be responsive to children's cultural and linguistic experiences;
- understand children's needs and capabilities;
- plan the learning environment and curriculum in the domains of school readiness;
- balance child-initiated and teacher-initiated activities;
- assess how well the program meets children's needs.

Build and Maintain Positive Relationships with Children

Teachers build meaningful relationships with children during day-to-day interactions with them. Since relationships are central to young children's learning and development, effective preschool teachers engage in consistent efforts to develop positive and nurturing relationships with each child they serve. Preschool teachers understand the importance of consistency, continuity, and responsiveness in

---

1. A *teacher* is defined as an adult with education and care responsibilities in an early childhood setting. Teachers include adults who interact directly with young children in preschool programs.

supporting children's healthy social and emotional development (adapted from California Department of Education and First 5 California 2012, 121). In cases in which children display challenging behaviors, teachers can focus even more directly on cultivating a relationship with the children during less stressful times (when children behave appropriately) and rely on additional support through ongoing mentoring and coaching (e.g., reflective supervision, early childhood mental health consultation) to put in place effective strategies to establish and sustain positive relationships with young children. When teachers engage in positive, nurturing relationships with young children, children feel safe and confident to engage deeply in exploration and learning. For those children who come to the classroom displaying challenging behaviors, nurturing, stable, and positive relationships with teachers often help to provide them with the emotional support needed to develop future positive relationships with teachers and peers (Buyse et al. 2008). Additionally, when a child with a disability is enrolled, it is crucial that the teacher develop a relationship with the child and see the child as "a member of the class" in order to promote authentic belonging.

It is especially important for teachers to foster close, positive relationships with children who are dual language learners. There is some evidence that when teachers and children do not speak the same language, children are perceived to be less socially competent, and children receive fewer language learning opportunities (Chang et al. 2007). When a teacher does not speak the language of a child in the classroom, it is often possible to recruit family members, community volunteers, or other support staff members who are fluent in the child's home language to provide read-alouds, enriched conversations, or targeted literacy activities. Thus, even though a teacher may not understand the language a child is using, she or he must still engage the child in frequent responsive, nurturing interactions on a daily basis.

Build and Maintain Positive Relationships with Families

Honest, caring, understanding, and respectful exchanges with family members lead to their sharing important information with teachers that help to inform how to care and support each child's learning and development. Taking the time to find out from family members about their child's unique characteristics and needs plays an important role in providing teachers with the information needed to set up appropriate learning environments for individual children. Establishing positive relationships with families helps to bridge children's experiences between preschool and home, and it fosters children's sense of belonging in the early education setting.

Teachers view families as children's first teachers and seek their assessments of a child's needs, interests, and abilities. Different families and communities have different views and expectations of three- through five-year-olds. The effective preschool teacher recognizes, understands, and respects the values of children's families and communities and attempts to make the preschool environment as congruent with those values as possible. In high-quality preschool programs, the teacher speaks frequently with family members and, whenever appropriate, strengthens the links between the home and program. Frequent communication between preschool program staff and family members is important, especially in the case of children with disabilities or other special needs. Through collaboration with families, preschool teachers can gain insight into ways in which they can be important contributors to the child's learning and development. To support children's learning across home and school contexts, the program can encourage family participation in activities at the early care and education program.

Create an Environment for Social and Emotional Learning

Teachers in a high-quality preschool program ensure that all the children feel safe and nurtured. They know how to create a classroom climate of cooperation, mutual respect, and tolerance and support children in developing skills needed to solve problems and resolve conflicts with peers.

> "Family engagement with schools has been linked to important outcomes for children of all families, including families with children who are dual language learners . . . Numerous positive developmental child outcomes have been associated with family engagement, including early literacy skills, cognitive and language development skills . . . socio–emotional skills . . . and academic achievement."
>
> *Source:* State Advisory Council on Early Learning and Care 2013, Paper 4, Family Engagement, 121.

Social and emotional learning is central to young children's development in the preschool years and works hand in hand with cognitive and academic learning. To learn well, they need to feel safe, to feel comfortable with their preschool teacher, and to be supported in their play with other children. All these factors interact with each other and either promote or detract from children's learning and well-being.

The Teaching Pyramid Framework for Supporting Social Competence

Fox and colleagues (2003) describe a pyramid framework for supporting social competence and preventing young children's challenging behavior (see http://www.CAinclusion.org/teachingpyramid [accessed July 7, 2014]). The pyramid includes four levels of practice to address the needs of all children: (1) building nurturing and responsive relationships with children, families, and colleagues; (2) implementing high-quality supportive environments; (3) using social and emotional supports and teaching strategies; and (4) planning intensive individualized interventions. The focus of the pyramid model is on promotion and prevention, with the top level—individualized interventions—used only when necessary. The premise is that when the bottom-three levels are in place, only a small number of children will require more intensive support.

Source: Center on the Social and Emotional Foundations for Early Learning.

Be Responsive to Children's Linguistic and Cultural Experiences

Creating an environment that reflects the cultural and linguistic diversity of the children and families served in the preschool program is essential to providing a safe and welcoming place for children to thrive. When preschool teachers draw upon children's experiences at home and integrate those familiar experiences into the classroom, children and families will feel seen and heard and develop a strong sense of belonging. Including teachers who share a common language with the children is essential to creating an environment that supports continued development of the home language and progress toward English-language development.

Ideally, all the children's home languages and cultural backgrounds will be represented in the program staffing. When this is not possible, there are many instructional strategies that support home language development while also promoting ELD and incorporate the cultural knowledge and strengths of the family. These strategies are described in more detail in chapter 6 (Support for Young Dual Language Learners).

Include Children with a Wide Range of Abilities and Approaches to Learning

Effective preschool teachers do not expect all children to be ready for a learning activity according to the same developmental timetable. Teachers actively encourage acceptance of children with disabilities or other special needs by promoting positive social interactions among all children through the adaptation of the environment, curriculum, and instructional practices. They follow guidance from families and service providers to support the learning of all children and respond sensitively to children's cues and unique preferences (for example, those of a child with sensory processing needs). In cases in which a child has a special need or disability, teachers use *people-first* language, referring to a child first, rather than the disability or special need. Teachers adapt the environment to include children with disabilities or other special needs in all learning activities, as well as support the development of friendships with other children in the group.

Teachers respect each child's need to move away from an activity, approach it in a new way, or be encouraged to persist. Sometimes a preschool child who has been doing well in a particular activity for two or three days will lose focus, wander aimlessly, and want to sit or play alone.

At the same time, other children in the group may persist in the activity because they find it stimulating and satisfying. Essential to accommodating a wide range of abilities and approaches to learning is the teacher's recognition that the goal is not just to get the children to do what the teacher wants them to do. More important is understanding what children can do and need to do at any particular time and making adaptations as necessary to support children's individual learning needs. In the case of a child with an individualized education program (IEP), adaptations and accommodations should be made in collaboration with the child's IEP team and be consistent with the Americans with Disabilities Act recommendations for reasonable accommodations.

Role of the Preschool Teacher as a Part of the IEP Team

The role of the preschool teacher as a part of the IEP team is to:

- provide information regarding the child's current level of performance in the preschool education environment;

- provide information on the preschool foundations, curriculum, and expectations;

- participate in discussions about how best to teach the student;

- assist in determining:

  - appropriate positive behavioral interventions and strategies;

  - special education services, activities, and supports needed by the student;

  - support needed for preschool personnel.

Dual Language Learners with Disabilities or Other Special Needs

Research indicates that many families of preschoolers with special needs value home language maintenance and bilingualism for their children. Given the significance of the culture of a family, parent–child interactions, a child's sense of identity and belonging, and the parents' sense of competence and confidence, families should be encouraged to maintain the home language with their children. . . . [I]t is most noteworthy that emerging research suggests that children with a wide range of abilities and language difficulties can learn more than one language. This is a significant message to share with practitioners and families of young dual language learners with special needs.

Source: State Advisory Council on Early Learning and Care 2013, Paper 6, Early Intervention and Special Needs, 225–26.

Understand Children's Needs and Capabilities

Based on their understanding of child development, preschool teachers engage in a process of assessing children's learning and development and work closely with children's families and colleagues to articulate goals for children's learning and development in all domains. Through the process of observing, documenting, and reflecting on children's learning and development, teachers can plan and structure all aspects of the environment, curriculum, and instructional strategies to support these learning goals. Whether children are learning about conservation of volume during free play at the water table or are increasing phonological awareness through teacher-guided rhyming and word-play activities, the effective teacher is aware of children's progress toward learning goals—for individual children and for the group as a whole. Continuing observation of children's learning helps the teacher make needed changes in the environment and curriculum.

The effective preschool teacher understands how young children think, feel, and reason. Teachers work together to provide learning experiences that involve experimentation, inquiry, play, and exploration to guide children's learning. They support children's development as independent thinkers by asking open-ended questions and helping children extend their thinking with thoughtful follow-up comments or questions. Teachers have realistic expectations of what young children can do and offer them activities that are interesting and stimulating and promote growth.

> "As teachers, we ask ourselves every day, every hour—What questions should we be answering, and what questions should we not answer?"
>
> *Source:* Journal entry of Bryn Potter, early childhood educator at Cow Hollow School in San Francisco, 2013.

Plan the Learning Environment and Curriculum in the Domains of School Readiness

Because preschool children are naturally curious and learn best in meaningful contexts, teachers responsible for planning the learning environment and curriculum will best support children's learning and development when they use a variety of strategies to support children's learning—such as focusing on interactions, scaffolding learning experiences, engaging in explicit instruction, changing the environment and materials, and making adaptations to the learning environment. As discussed in Guideline 8, "Planning the Learning Environment and Curriculum," in chapter 8, teachers can set up play-based interest areas to support children's learning across a variety of domains, capitalizing on children's natural curiosity.

In planning and implementing the learning environment and curriculum, effective preschool teachers simultaneously attend to all five domains of children's school readiness: (1) Social and Emotional Development (2) Language and Literacy Development, (3) Cognition and General Knowledge, (4) Physical Well-Being and Motor Development, and (5) Approaches Toward Learning. Please refer to chapter 2 for a more detailed discussion of how to effectively use the *California Preschool Learning Foundations* to facilitate understanding of growth across these developmental areas.

Teachers make use of daily routines as an important context for learning, integrating engaging learning opportunities into the everyday routines of arrivals, departures, mealtimes, naptimes, handwashing, setup, and cleanup, both indoors and outdoors. Children enthusiastically practice and apply emerging skills when they are helpers who ring the bell to signal it is time to come inside; when they count how many are ready for lunch; when they move a card with a child's photo and name from the "home" column to the "preschool" column of a chart near the room entry; when they put their name on a waiting list to paint at the easel; or when they help set the table for a meal, making sure that each place has a plate, utensils, and a cup. Such routines offer opportunities for children to build language skills, to learn the rituals of sharing time with others, and to relate one action in a sequence to another" (adapted from CDE 2010, 18).

The skilled teacher is a thoughtful observer of young children and makes use of her observations, in collaboration with colleagues, *to implement a curriculum planning process* that builds upon the interests children are actively pursuing (see chapter 5 for further guidance on a curriculum planning process). The effective preschool teacher observes, listens, documents, and reflects on learning. Documentation serves many purposes. A primary purpose is to share it with the children so they can reflect on their past engagement in learning and revisit those experiences in multifaceted ways.

In collaboration with children's families and in conversation with colleagues and specialized professionals (when appropriate), teachers also reflect on documentation to assess what children know and use this information to inform how to set up the learning environment and plan instructional activities and interactions with children in their classroom. Based on teachers' assessments of individual children's learning, the teachers might add materials to play-based interest areas, decide to read books with small or large groups, adapt activities to meet the diverse learning needs of children in the classroom, and think of a particular topic area that children would be interested in investigating. Guided by the California preschool learning foundations, teachers use their understanding of children's learning and development as a way to ensure they adequately support children's development across all domains. With clear ideas or objectives in mind, teachers plan curriculum that includes strategies to enhance the learning of all children in a group, as well as strategies to support the learning of individual children (adapted from CDE 2010a, 21). Please refer to chapter 5 for a closer look at the curriculum planning process.

Balance Child-Initiated and Teacher-Initiated Activities

The preschool curriculum should offer a carefully considered balance between child-initiated and teacher-initiated learning activities. When preschool teachers collaboratively plan and implement learning activities for young children, one of the most fundamental questions should always be, *How much of my direct involvement, guidance, or explicit instruction is needed to make this activity the most beneficial for children's learning?* The nature of the activity; the personality, skills, and interests of the child involved; or even the time of day can influence this decision.

For many open-ended activities involving materials that are easy to manipulate—for example, sand or water play—only minimal teacher intervention or guidance may be necessary to achieve the teacher's goals. As learning activities become more complex or abstract, the teacher's skilled guidance or explicit instruction may help a child build understanding or skill in a particular area. For example, an older four-year-old who has shown no interest in early literacy skills may benefit from an engaging teacher-initiated and teacher-guided activity focusing on alphabet letters in children's

names. If a teacher notices that few girls are working in the block or puzzle areas, she or he might augment the materials in those centers or structure a small-group activity to attract more girls to these important learning activities.

Whether an activity is principally child-initiated and child-directed, teacher-initiated and teacher-guided, or somewhere in between, the effectiveness of teachers' interventions may vary. Effective intervention requires knowledge of the individual child and the child's learning needs, knowledge of the parents' educational goals for their children, and appropriate instructional goals for both individual children and the group.

Throughout an activity, flexibility is key to the teacher's effectiveness in meeting goals. An activity may start out to be child-initiated, but if children have difficulty in focusing, they may need additional teacher guidance. Similarly, a teacher-guided activity may not meet the teacher's original goals, but it may change and improve as a result of children's interaction with it. A variety of strategies that teachers can use to facilitate children's learning and development (e.g., scaffolding, explicit instruction, modeling, demonstration, and environmental adaptations) are discussed in chapter 8, Guideline 8, "Planning the Learning Environment and Curriculum."

Questions for Reflection

1. How did the writing experiences engage children in the family dinner activities in ways that the reading activities could not?

2. What do you think Mrs. Nguyen did when a child refused to write the names of family members on name tags, saying, "I can't write." What would you do?

3. How can you help parents understand the early phases of children's writing?

4. Would you feel a need to write the correct and recognizable words (e.g., *salads, desserts*) on the food table signs that children prepared? Why or why not?

5. How might these meaningful experiences with writing affect children's motivation to write?

6. Do you think that preschool children should have only meaningful writing experiences, such as the ones they used for the preschool family dinner event, or should children be asked to practice writing letters and their names simply for practice? Why?

7. If you have ever seen children practice writing on their own—a teacher had not asked them to—what environmental materials, structure, or previous experiences might have influenced and supported their decision to practice some aspect of writing?

Source: CDE 2010, 167.

Assess How Well the Program Meets Children's Needs

Effective preschool teachers are continually aware of the effects of the program structure, the learning environment, activities, and the routines on the children. Teachers are also attentive to the influence of their behavior and other adults' behavior on the children. The program environment should be stimulating without being overwhelming and offer learning activities that are challenging without being frustrating. While helping children choose and stay engaged with activities, the effective teacher is a close observer of which activities are especially engaging or of the ways in which a particular activity may be frustrating for children. In addition, the effective teacher is familiar with a wide range of assessment procedures that help in understanding the progress and development of individual children and the group throughout the year.

Becoming a Reflective Teacher
"A reflective teacher . . .

- examines his or her own reactions to children or their actions to understand their source

- is curious about children's play and watches it closely

- documents details of children's conversations and activities

- takes time to study notes and photos to puzzle out what is significant

- eagerly shares stories about children's learning with families and co-workers

- asks co-workers and children's families for their insights

- reads professional literature to learn more

- shows children photos and stories of themselves to hear their views

- changes the environment and materials to encourage new play and learning possibilities"

Source: Carter et al. 2010.

Thinking Lens

1. **Know yourself**
   - What captures my attention as the children engage, explore, and talk with each other and with me?
   - What delights me as I watch and listen?
   - How might my background and values influence how I respond to the children?
   - What adult perspectives (e.g, standards, health and safety, time, goals) are on my mind?

2. **Find the details that touch your heart and mind**
   - What do I notice in the children's faces and actions?
   - Where do I see examples of children's strengths and abilities?
   - What are the children learning from this experience?

3. **Seek the child's perspective**
   - What is the child drawn to and excited about?
   - What might the child be trying to accomplish?
   - Why might the child be talking to and playing with others this way?
   - What ideas might the child be exploring?

4. **Examine the physical and social–emotional environment**
   - How do schedules, routines, the physical space, and materials support or limit the children's play?
   - What changes or additions to the space or materials would help to strengthen children's relationships?
   - How do schedules and routines influence this experience?

5. **Explore multiple points of view**
   - How might the child's culture and family background be influencing this situation?
   - What questions could I ask to get the perspective of the child's family?
   - Who else or what other perspectives should I consider?
   - What child development or early learning theories apply to this experience?
   - How does this child's play (or other activity) demonstrate desired early learning outcomes or standards?

6. **Consider opportunities and possibilities for next steps**
   - What values, philosophy and desired outcomes do I want to influence my response?
   - What new or existing relationships could be strengthened?
   - Which learning goals could be addressed?
   - What other materials and activities could be offered to build on this experience?
   - What new vocabulary can teachers introduce?

Source: Adapted from Carter and Curtis 2009, 359.

Closing Thoughts

Preschool teachers play a vital role in providing high-quality learning opportunities and environments for young children. At the heart of the role is building and maintaining positive relationships with children and families and creating environments for social and emotional development. An essential part of supporting social and emotional development is being responsive to children's cultural and linguistic experiences and understanding individual children's needs and capabilities. To help prepare children for kindergarten entry, effective preschool teachers plan and implement the environment and curriculum to support learning in all five domains of school readiness in an integrated way. They balance teacher-initiated activities with child-initiated play and learning. Then they assess how well the program addresses children's interests and needs and help children make progress toward school readiness. Reflective, intentional teaching based on knowledge of child development; sensitive observation; and documentation of learning can have a positive impact on children's well-being and success in the preschool years and beyond.

References

Buyse, E., K. Verschueren, S. Doumen, J. Van Damme, and F. Maes. 2008. "Classroom Problem Behavior and Teacher–Child Relationships in Kindergarten: The Moderating Role of Classroom Climate." *Journal of School Psychology* 46 (4): 367–91.

California Department of Education (CDE). 2010. *California Preschool Curriculum Framework, Volume 1*. Sacramento: California Department of Education.

California Department of Education and First 5 California. 2012. *California Early Childhood Educator Competencies*. Sacramento: California Department of Education.

Carter, M., W. Cividanes, D. Curtis, and D. Lebo. 2010. "Becoming a Reflective Teacher." *Teaching Young Children* 3 (4): 18–20. http://www.naeyc.org/files/tyc/file/TYC_V3N4_Reflectiveteacherexpanded.pdf (accessed July 7, 2014).

Carter, M., and D. Curtis. 2009. *The Visionary Director: A Handbook for Dreaming, Organizing, and Improvising in Your Center*. St. Paul, MN: Redleaf Press. http://www.naeyc.org/files/tyc/file/TYC_V3N4_Reflectiveteacherexpanded.pdf (accessed July 7, 2014).

Chang, F., G. Crawford, D. Early, D. Bryant, C. Howes, M. Burchinal, O. Barbarin, R. Clifford, and R. Pianta. 2007. "Spanish-Speaking Children's Social and Language Development in Pre-Kindergarten Classrooms." *Early Education and Development* 18 (2): 243–69.

Fox, L., G. Dunlap, M. L. Hemmeter, G. E. Joseph, and P. S. Strain. 2003. "The Teaching Pyramid: A Model for Supporting Social Competence and Preventing Challenging Behavior in Young Children." *Young Children* 58 (4): 48–52.

Howes, C., M. Burchinal, R. Pianta, D. Bryant, D. Early, R. Clifford, and O. Barbarin. 2008. "Ready to Learn? Children's Pre-Academic Achievement in Pre-Kindergarten Programs." *Early Childhood Research Quarterly* 23 (1): 27–50.

State Advisory Council on Early Learning and Care. 2013. *California's Best Practices for Young Dual Language Learners: Research Overview Papers*. Sacramento: California Department of Education. http://www.cde.ca.gov/sp/cd/ce/documents/dllresearchpapers.pdf (accessed April 3, 2014).

Further Reading

Dual Language Learners

Conboy, B. T. 2013. "Neuroscience Research: How Experience with One or Multiple Languages Affects the Developing Brain." In *California's Best Practices for Young Dual Language Learners: Research Overview Papers*, edited by the State Advisory Council on Early Learning and Care. Sacramento: California Department of Education.

Petitto, L. A., M. Katerelos, B. G. Levy, K. Gauna, K. Tétreault, and V. Ferraro. 2001. "Bilingual Signed and Spoken Language Acquisition from Birth: Implications for the Mechanisms Underlying Early Bilingual Language Acquisition." *Journal of Child Language* 28 (2): 453–96.

Sandhofer, C., and Y. Uchikoshi-Tonkovich. 2013. "Relationship Between Dual Language Development and Development of Cognition, Mathematics, Social-Emotional Development, and Related Domains." In *California's Best Practices for Young Dual Language Learners: Research Overview Papers*, edited by the State Advisory Council on Early Learning and Care. Sacramento: California Department of Education.

DUAL LANGUAGE LEARNERS AND SPECIAL NEEDS

Bedore, L. M., and E. D. Pena. 2008. "Assessment of Bilingual Children for Identification of Language Impairment: Current Findings and Implications for Practice." *International Journal of Bilingual Education and Bilingualism* 11 (1): 1–29.

EXECUTIVE FUNCTION AND SCHOOL READINESS

Barnett, W. S., K. Jung, D. J. Yarosz, J. Thomas, A. Hornbeck, R. Stechuk, and S. Burns. 2008. "Educational Effects of the Tools of the Mind Curriculum: A Randomized Trial." *Early Childhood Research Quarterly* 23 (3): 299–313.

Bierman, K. L., R. L. Nix, M. T. Greenberg, C. Blair, and C. E. Domitrovich. 2008. "Executive Functions and School Readiness Intervention: Impact, Moderation, and Mediation in the Head Start REDI Program." *Development and Psychopathology* 20:821–43.

McClelland, M. M., C. McDonald Connor, A. M. Jewkes, C. E. Cameron, C. L. Farris, and F. J. Morrison. 2007. "Links Between Behavioral Regulation and Preschoolers' Literacy, Vocabulary, and Math Skills." *Developmental Psychology* 43 (4): 947–59.

National Scientific Council on the Developing Child: Science Briefs. 2008. *Focus and Planning Skills Can Be Improved Before a Child Enters School.* Cambridge, MA: National Scientific Council on the Developing Child, Harvard, University.

LANGUAGE AND LITERACY

National Institute for Literacy. 2008a. *Developing Early Literacy, Report of the Early Literacy Panel: A Scientific Synthesis of Early Literacy Development and Implications for Intervention.* Jessup, MD: National Institute for Literacy/RAND.

———. 2008b. *Executive Summary: Developing Early Literacy: Report of the National Early Literacy Panel.* Jessup, MD: National Institute for Literacy/RAND.

MATHEMATICS

Clements, D. H. 2001. "Mathematics in the Preschool." *Teaching Children Mathematics* 7 (5): 270–75.

Molfese, V. J., E. Todd Brown, J. L. Adelson, J. Beswick, J. Jacobi-Vessels, L. Thomas, M. Ferguson, and B. Culver. 2012. "Examining Associations between Classroom Environment and Processes and Early Mathematics Performance from Pre-Kindergarten to Kindergarten." *Gifted Children* 5 (2) Article 2.

SOCIAL AND EMOTIONAL DEVELOPMENT

CLASS: Building Connections, Enhancing Learning. "Summary of CLASS Research." Reference list of papers/abstracts. Charlottesville, VA: Teachstone. http://www.teachstone.com/resources/research-dna (accessed July 7, 2014).

Greater Good: The Science of a Meaningful Life. n.d. The Greater Good Science Center, University of California, Berkeley. http://greatergood.berkeley.edu (accessed 6/24/13).

Pitel, J., and E. Provance. 2006. *Social and Emotional Well-Being: The Foundation for School Readiness.* Sacramento: WestEd, Center for Prevention and Early Intervention.

Thompson, R. A., and H. A. Raikes. 2007. *The Social and Emotional Foundations of School Readiness.* Baltimore, MD: Paul H. Brookes Publishing Co.

Webster-Stratton, C., and M. J. Reid. 2004. "Strengthening Social and Emotional Competence in Young Children-The Foundation for Early School Readiness and Success: Incredible Years Classroom Social Skills and Problem-Solving Curriculum." *Infants and Young Children* 17 (2): 96–113.

SCIENTIFIC THINKING

Gopnik, A. 2012. "Scientific Thinking in Young Children: Theoretical Advances, Empirical Research, and Policy Implications." *Science* 337:1623.

Chapter 4
The Role of the Administrator

Effective administrative practices are essential for ensuring high-quality outcomes for young children and their families. Research has documented strong relationships between observed program quality and directors' beliefs, leadership, and management practices (Rohacek, Adams, and Kisker 2010). When directors are well prepared for their positions and their program decisions are guided by well-informed beliefs, their programs' classrooms demonstrate higher observed quality. Key practices of effective administration include communication of high expectations, respect, and support for staff; integration of new learning to inform decision making; an emphasis on sound financial management; prioritization of staff wages, benefits, and professional development; and the establishment of program practices that exceed minimum licensing requirements (McCormick Center for Early Childhood Leadership 2011).

The role of the program administrator is complex and requires specialized training and expertise in addition to a solid grounding in child development knowledge and best practices in early childhood education. An early childhood "administrator" may hold a wide variety of titles and positions: sole center director in a small, single-site program; site supervisor within a large, multiple-site program; or a program coordinator for a network of centers. Regardless of the particular size or characteristics of a program, the same issues and concerns must be addressed at all levels.

Administrative responsibilities may be divided into two general categories: leadership and management. It is critical to a successfully managed child development program that the administrator be able to perform the following functions:

- Manage budgets, including an internal system of oversight to ensure appropriate expenditures.
- Maintain accurate attendance and fiscal reports.[1]
- Document compliance with health and safety licensing regulations (http://ccld. ca.gov/PG555.htm [accessed July 8, 2014]).
- Abide by applicable contract funding terms and conditions, laws, and regulations.[2]
- Record program inventory and follow a bid process for acquisition of new equipment.
- Enroll children by applying appropriate priority and eligibility requirements.
- Maintain family files with accurate documentation.
- Develop and implement a system to ensure the administration of management responsibilities is effectively maintained over time.
- Conduct evaluations and provide ongoing observation and feedback.
- Communicate policies, schedules, and decisions to the program's staff and families.

---

1. Refer to the Early Education and Support Attendance & Fiscal Reporting & Reimbursement Procedures for information about attendance, fiscal reporting, and reimbursement procedures for CDE contractors. This document, also known as the Greenbook, is updated by the Fiscal and Administrative Services Division of the California Department of Education (http://www.cde.ca.gov/fg/aa/cd/ [accessed July 8, 2014]).

2. Each California Department of Education (CDE), Early Education and Support Division (EESD) contractor must adhere to the funding terms and conditions of its contract in addition to all other applicable laws and regulations (http://www.cde.ca.gov/fg/aa/cd/ftc2010.asp). Title 5 regulations define the requirements for program operations in order to obtain child care services funds made available by the California Department of Education (http://www.cde.ca.gov/sp/cd/lr [accessed July 8, 2014]).

Each of these tasks generally falls within the administrator's scope of work; together they represent the management category of responsibility. Although crucial to a program's day-to-day functioning and overall effectiveness, competent management alone is not enough to ensure high-quality outcomes for young children and their families.

Leadership is also essential. It is widely acknowledged that any successful organization's administrator must be, above all else, a leader (Bloom 2003). Although the context of early childhood program leadership is different from that of corporate leadership, many core principles and practices are shared. The effective leader in each setting articulates the organization's mission (i.e., its purpose for existing) as well as its vision (i.e., what it will achieve if successful in accomplishing its goals). The leader sets the tone, or organizational climate, of the program for all the participants. In an early childhood setting, this climate begins with the leader's own attitudes, values, and competence and translates into the recruitment and selection of well-qualified teaching staff, the provision of sufficient resources and guidance to enable them to teach effectively, and the collaborative support they need to design and implement a program that exemplifies best practices in all areas. An effective leader demonstrates cultural competence, the willingness and ability to partner with children's families and communities, and strong support for dual language learners and children with special needs. All of these aspects of the role are discussed in detail later in this chapter (also refer to chapter 8, Guideline 10).

Professionals with many different backgrounds and personal styles can be effective program leaders. They can demonstrate their commitment to their teaching staff in a variety of ways, while affirming the diverse strengths each person brings to their shared work. "Leaders are those who provoke or nudge or elevate others into thinking, feeling, or behaving in ways they would not otherwise have demonstrated" (Espinosa 1997). A leader's

positive regard, expressed consistently through words and actions, establishes and maintains a warm and trusting organizational climate for all staff members. A skilled program leader employs strategies that motivate everyone to contribute to achieving the program's goals. For many experienced directors, this entails visiting the program's classrooms regularly and incorporating experiences and impressions gathered there into reflective conversations with the teaching team. Engaging with the staff in assessment and planning conversations based on shared experiences builds and supports a collaborative community.

Within the broad range of individual styles, several specific traits and dispositions are shared by many effective leaders. These include a passion for their work and a focus on goals, willingness to take risks and consider different perspectives, unwavering commitment to their core values, and the capacity to understand and manage their own emotions and to support others in managing theirs (Bloom 2003). Professionals who commit themselves to leadership in the field of early childhood education often exhibit these qualities.

Reflective Curriculum Planning

One formative way in which the administrative leader shapes an early childhood program is by establishing the curriculum approach[3] it will adopt. This approach will align with the *California Preschool Learning Foundations*, and the program's curriculum planning and teaching strategies will be guided by the accompanying preschool curriculum framework. Both resources address all early childhood developmental domains and curriculum content areas. They can be used by program administrators and teachers as a guide for building a curriculum tailored to an individual program's context and needs. Alternatively, they can steer program leaders to select an established curriculum judged to be a good fit for the program's children, families, teachers, and community.

The selection of a curriculum approach is one of the most significant decisions a

3. *Curriculum approach* can be defined as "a conceptual framework and organizational structure for decision making about educational priorities, administrative policies, instructional methods, and evaluation criteria" (Goffin 2000, 1).

"Family engagement with schools has been linked to important outcomes for children of all families, including families with children who are dual language learners . . . Numerous positive developmental child outcomes have been associated with family engagement, including early literacy skills, cognitive and language development skills . . . socio-emotional skills . . . and academic achievement."

Source: State Advisory Council on Early Learning and Care 2013, Paper 4, Family Engagement, 121.

program administrator will make. It will be informed by the program's mission and vision and should reflect the developmentally appropriate philosophy and practices outlined by the CDE's Early Education and Support Division's guidance in the preschool learning foundations and the preschool curriculum frameworks. Active play and exploration, guided by children's interests and choices within a thoughtfully planned environment and with the skilled, responsive support of teachers,

will be valued as a primary avenue for young children's learning. These key elements of best practice can be found within a variety of curriculum approaches grounded in current understanding of early developmental processes. They can and must be individualized to reflect the cultural context, values, personal strengths, and learning needs of the children the program serves.

The choice between selecting a packaged curriculum and designing a program-specific curriculum will depend on several factors. These include the level of experience and demonstrated skill of the teaching staff in environment and curriculum design, the staff's ability to access and adapt a wide variety of teaching resources as needed, and the amount of time available for the teaching staff, often with the guidance of an administrator or instructional coach, to devote to curriculum planning and preparation.

A well-designed curriculum provides a general structure for organizing daily routines and activities, as well as guidelines for equipping a classroom's various learning centers, while allowing for flexibility. It suggests academic content and learning objectives for teacher-led and child-led portions of each preschool session. A high-quality product provides multiple options that teachers can use or modify based on their assessment of children's

learning needs, as well as the teachers' skills and preferences. Many teachers, especially those who are beginning to build their skills, will find that this level of detailed guidance enhances their own professional growth. The program administrator will assess whether this will be an appropriate route to take and provide teachers with additional professional development in implementing the lesson plans, activity instructions, materials templates, and book suggestions.

Developing a curriculum based on the administrator's and teachers' shared philosophy and knowledge base and tailored to the children and community can also be a rewarding choice. Success will depend, in large part, on the expertise of the administrator and teachers, their willingness to experiment while still maintaining high standards, and the opportunities they have to plan, prepare, observe, and evaluate as a team. Allotting ample time for staff members to engage in each of these steps is essential to developing a high-quality curriculum. A program that is rich in all of these areas can excel in designing an approach that is tailored to those it serves. Innovation in early childhood education results from the creative efforts of leaders willing and able to experiment with novel ways to engage young children in the learning process.

As children from diverse cultural, ethnic, and linguistic backgrounds are a significant proportion of all children served in California's early childhood education (ECE) programs, administrators will need to adopt policies and choose or develop program approaches for preschool dual language learners, including curriculum and instructional practices that are culturally and linguistically appropriate (see chapter 6; and State Advisory Council on Early Learning and Care 2013, Paper 3, Program Elements and Teaching Practices). In general, high-quality ECE practices benefit young dual language learners, but may not be sufficient for achieving learning outcomes comparable to those of other children. Specific instructional adaptations are critical aspects of a quality environment for young dual language learners. Methods of supporting home language development and classroom enhancements are described in chapter 6 (Support for Young Dual Language Learners) and Paper 3, Program Elements and Teaching Practices (State Advisory Council on Early Learning and Care 2013). Administrators will need to facilitate the development of policies for supporting dual language learners, adopt a program approach that supports those language policies, monitor the language of instruction, and continually evaluate the progress of all children in their programs, including dual language learners (see chapter 6). The English-language development foundations provide a description of the typical developmental progression of preschool dual language learners and should be used in combination with the other preschool foundations and the Desired Results Developmental Profile to document children's progress and thus inform curriculum planning (see State Advisory Council on Early Learning and Care 2013, Paper 5, Assessment).

As described in chapter 6 and in Paper 3, Program Elements and Teaching Practices (State Advisory Council on Early Learning and Care 2013), two basic program approaches are appropriate for preschool dual language learners in different local contexts: (1) English-language development with home language support, and (2) balanced English and home language development. These program ap-

proaches vary in their goals, use of home language, and certain features of instruction. It is important for administrators to work with both program staff and local communities, including family members, in selecting the specific program approach that is most appropriate for children and families. This decision will be based on many factors (e.g., program resources and capacity, local values and priorities, and characteristics of the children enrolled); however, all preschools that serve dual language learners will need to intentionally promote English-language development while building on the home language knowledge and skills of young dual language learners and promote bilingual development as possible.

When a curriculum approach is selected and designed, children with disabilities or other special needs should be considered. These children often require some type of accommodation or adaptation due to differences in learning, mobility, or behavior. In order to modify or adapt the curriculum, it is crucial that the underlying goals, objectives, and concepts for the activities are thoroughly understood. The administrator plays a key role in clearly articulating the various goals and concepts and is often relied upon to support modifications for children with disabilities or other special needs. More information on typical modifications can be found in chapter 8 (Guideline 5) and in *Inclusion Works!* (CDE 2009). The Americans with Disabilities Act (ADA) and accompanying state laws (such as the Unruh Civil Rights Act in California) provide protection for people with disabilities.[4] This law protects children in child care settings as well as employees. More information is available in appendix E (State and Federal Laws Regarding People with Disabilities).

Many children with special needs are not diagnosed until they enroll in early childhood settings. At that point, teachers may notice delays or differences in development from that of the children's peers. Administrators should be familiar

---

4. Turning children away from a child care program solely because they have a disability or other special need is a violation of the ADA and accompanying state laws, such as the Unruh Civil Rights Act in California.

with steps for screening and referral in the community. Some children may qualify for services through the Individuals with Disabilities Education Act (IDEA), the federal legislation for early intervention and special education services (see appendix E for more information). Generally, a child who is receiving special education services will have an individualized education program (IEP). As stated in chapter 1, these IEPs must reflect the CDE's preschool learning foundations. Under IDEA 2004, all children must have access to the general preschool curriculum and have their progress measured accordingly (CDE 2010, 5).

Regardless of the specific curriculum approach and overall program approach chosen, it is the administrator's responsibility to ensure that the philosophy, including the core principles and strategies outlined in the preschool foundations and frameworks and other documents in the California Early Learning and Development System, is clearly articulated to staff members. The program's curriculum approach may be introduced during an initial orientation period, but also addressed on an ongoing basis through group collaboration, individual observation and coaching, and times set aside for professional development, discussion, and reflection. A large portion of an effective program leader's time and energy will be devoted to working with staff members in the context of their teaching while providing constructive feedback and engaging in collaborative instructional improvement.

Setting the Conditions for Work

Many factors influence how staff members perceive their working conditions. Although some perceptions are based on prior experiences and personal preferences, staff members' positive or negative ratings of an organization's overall climate are usually widely shared. Collective perceptions are based on the following elements: the work environment's attractiveness and adequacy of physical facilities and supplies; quality of supervisory support; clear communication of expectations and policies; opportunities for professional growth, challenge, and advancement; fairness of the reward system; degree of professional autonomy and par-

ticipatory decision making; effectiveness of organizational functioning; openness to new ideas; and a spirit of collegiality among staff members (Bloom 2010).

All of these program elements are strongly influenced by the program director's leadership. An administrator may have to work with a less-than-ideal physical setting, limited funds for equipment and materials, and some policies that were set by the organization sponsoring the program. Even within these constraints, much can be done to create a positive, effective workplace environment that leads to greater job satisfaction for staff.

The first step is to create a culture of open sharing of information about everything that affects people's workplace lives. Being transparent and specific with staff members about budgets, accountability requirements, personnel policies, and broader organizational structures and priorities builds trust and collaboration between the administrator and teaching staff. Additionally, the administrator's willingness to answer questions from staff and engage in ongoing discussion reinforces a sense of teamwork. Even when some substantive changes cannot be made, open team discussions with a supportive administrator help staff members work together within organizational realities and move on to collaboration on important program areas where decision making and management can be shared. Although some aspects of a program cannot be changed, those that can be changed may be strengthened.

Participative management is now widely practiced in both corporate and nonprofit settings. This democratic leadership model recognizes that job satisfaction increases when employees have a voice in making decisions that affect their lives. It increases their perception that they are respected and treated fairly, and consequently it strengthens their commitment to the organization. When teachers have a meaningful role, for example, in solving a staff scheduling problem, planning a school community event, addressing adult needs in the physical environment, or choosing new equipment and materials, they more fully understand and have

a greater commitment to implementing the decisions that are made (Bloom 2011). Being recognized for regularly making positive contributions to improve a program's functioning reinforces early childhood educators' perceptions of themselves as professionals.[5]

A critical area in need of improvement is the compensation of early childhood educators. Compensation for those providing education for young children is much lower than compensation for almost every other profession requiring postsecondary training, including teaching in the K–12 educational system. Salaries of early childhood teachers with a college degree are about two-thirds of what other women college graduates earn (Brandon, Stutman, and Maroto 2009). Only 25 percent of prekindergarten teachers nationally receive health benefits (Herzenberg, Price, and Bradley 2005). Teacher aides and other early childhood workers earn far less—$9.73 per hour on average (United States Bureau of Labor Statistics 2008). The combination of low pay and often-challenging working conditions can compromise the quality of early child-

hood educators' work with children (Gilliam 2008). These factors also contribute to high rates of staff turnover in many programs, even though it is well established that the youngest children need the most consistency in adult caregiving. To address this situation, attention must be paid to the entire employee compensation package, beginning with establishing a formal salary scale with increases based on education, performance, and additional professional activities. Health and retirement benefits should be included in an agency's fair and reasonable compensation package for its teaching staff.

Although program administrators often lack the fiscal authority to increase all wages and benefits in their programs, they can be strong voices for better support of early childhood education and systemic change. They can work within their sponsoring organizations to place high priority on improving staff compensation as well as funding for credit-bearing course work and other specialized professional development and training. As visible leaders in the field, they can also educate policymakers at all levels about the inadequacies and potential harmful effects of the current system for families with young children, for the early childhood workforce, and for a society looking to prepare its youngest members for future productivity.

---

5. Additional information about examining, assessing, and improving the working environments of early childhood educators can be found in the SEQUAL tool developed by the Center for the Study of Child Care Employment (Whitebook and Ryan 2012).

Creating a Collaborative Work Environment and Learning Community

High-quality early childhood education always stems from collaboration. Collaboration with sponsoring organizations is essential for obtaining the space and resources necessary to build a program's infrastructure and to ensure ongoing support. Collaboration with members of the particular community whose children and families are served is essential for creating a program that reflects the community's culture and values. Collaboration with each family is essential for designing a program that meets their child's learning needs and supports their own parenting efforts, while bridging learning environments at home and in the classroom. All of these collaborations will involve the ongoing attention of the program administrator.

Collaboration *with a program's community and a sponsoring agency* most often includes an administrator's active engagement with a board of directors, or at least a community advisory board or committee. A board can provide a major source of support, as well as expertise, to a program administrator. A board usually includes members of the community served, representatives of the sponsoring agency, children's adult family members, and others with specific areas of expertise related to the program's needs or context, such as a pediatric health care provider or social worker (Sciarra and Dorsey 2009). In oral and written communications with a board, the administrator functions as the official "face" of the program. Effectiveness in this role requires regular reports and discussions that document both responsible management practices and competent program leadership. In this sense, the administrator is accountable to the board. Equally important is the board's potential as a resource for the administrator. Along with reports and business-oriented decisions, an effective director brings to the board or, at times, to its committees, broader or deeper topics for focused discussion. These sometimes relate to ways to enlist the community's support for aspects of the program's mission or questions about how to better achieve specific desired outcomes for children and families. This kind of active collaboration between administrator and board can strengthen a program considerably.

Ongoing collaboration *between program staff and families* is crucial to ensure high-quality outcomes for children and their family caregivers. A program's leader and teaching staff will need to be thoroughly familiar with the community contexts and cultural frameworks of the families they serve. Ideally, this will begin with including qualified members of the community on the teaching team. It can continue through staff efforts to invite children's adult family members to work with the staff in building a strong school community that values cultural and linguistic diversity. Adult family members should be invited to share thoughts, informally or in group gatherings, about their goals for their children.

It is especially important for families that do not speak English in the home to have opportunities to express their language preferences for their children. Conversations with families with dual language learners about how the program supports both English-language development and home language development will facilitate collaboration to create rich language learning at preschool and at home. All families can be encouraged to bring or suggest culturally authentic items and activities from their own lives to enrich the preschool's physical environment and the curriculum. Family members can assist or take leadership in planning events that will promote a sense of belonging for everyone, including book readings and other literacy activities in the home language. Most importantly, all adults in the program can be engaged together in a reciprocal learning model, one in which both adult family members and teachers are viewed as givers and receivers of important information in ways that are respectful, honorable, and instructive (Paratore 2005). A program leader who takes the time to build strong relationships with families will set the tone for mutual engagement throughout the year.

Collaboration *within the program's teaching staff* is essential for ensuring high-quality outcomes for children and families and for ensuring job success and satisfaction for the teachers themselves. Like the children in a high-quality early education program, the adults also see themselves as learners. Professional development often will consist of gatherings intended for collaboration in which teaching teams share ideas, use their observational data to inform curriculum planning, seek and receive support in addressing challenging situations, and exchange other information helpful for everyone to know. Additional blocks of time are scheduled for periodic reassessment of the program's indoor and outdoor classroom environments and materials so that all staff members who use the spaces have opportunities to contribute to design and purchasing decisions.

Effective collaboration requires careful planning by the program administrator. Full-scale staff meetings may be difficult to build into the schedule on a weekly basis, but regular meetings, held as often as possible, are crucial to maintaining and improving program quality. During these gatherings, a program administrator can set the tone for collaborative inquiry and problem solving and reinforce a message of inclusive teamwork across job classifications. Staff members can assume varying roles in any group setting; however, in a culture of consistent collegial support and collaboration, most will become confident enough, in time, to actively participate. It is the program administrator's responsibility to adapt communication strategies to meet the diverse language and literacy abilities of staff members. Many excellent books and online resources are available to guide leaders in facilitating collaborative learning communities (see appendixes A and B).

Integrating Reflective Practice, Reflective Supervision, and Mentorship

An administrator who structures the early childhood program as a learning community for the adults as well as the children views staff supervision through the lens of a mentor and coach. The goal is to encourage reflective practice—approaching the educational setting with the intention to observe mindfully, respond thoughtfully, and take time

afterward to share reflections, thereby deepening one's own understanding and improving one's own work. Reflective supervision is a way of guiding teachers to draw lessons from their own experiences that will influence their next steps (Heffron and Murch 2010).

When the administrator is also the person evaluating or rating the teacher's performance, it can be challenging to act in the role of mentor or coach. Through reflective practice, teachers may feel vulnerable as they examine their own actions, impacts, and experiences. The ability to reflect may be impeded by fear or concern over what the supervisor wants to hear. It is important to have an open discussion with teaching staff regarding the desire to separate the evaluative observations and meetings from observations for reflective practice and coaching sessions. Some administrators have made the purpose clear by having the meeting in a different setting, or even wearing a hat to indicate that they are in a coaching role. It is helpful if the administrator also has an opportunity to reflect in order to maintain the neutral stance needed. In some cases, a teacher will indicate that he or she cannot separate the evaluation from the person. In those cases, an administrator may partner with a mental health consultant for reflective practice meetings.

Use of the techniques of reflective supervision with a teacher requires the administrator to spend time observing the teacher during periods of active engagement with children. This builds familiarity with the teacher's context and enables the administrator to tailor questions and responses to the challenges observed as well as to focus on the strengths displayed. The process of reflecting together about the work afterward provides individualized coaching and feedback that are valuable to teachers at each stage of their professional development. With time and familiarity, it may not always be necessary to precede reflective supervision meetings with an observation. At times, reflective supervision may take place during group meetings where teaching team members take turns providing and receiving reflective support. The kinds of concerns and perspectives raised will vary depending on each teacher's level of experience, but the model of providing a regular setting for reflection remains valuable.

Mentoring is a related means of supporting professional growth. In a mentoring relationship, a more experienced teacher or administrator serves as a learning partner in the work setting as a newer teacher strives to grow in expertise. The mentoring partnership can be formal or informal and can involve modeling, observation, and coaching as the mentee learns new skills. This kind of context-based professional coaching has been shown to lead to more concrete changes in early education practices than have other, more common approaches to professional development such as workshops or tutorials (Pianta et al. 2008). Collaboration itself can serve as a valuable mentoring tool. Research indicates that early childhood teachers who work in teams and have regular opportunities to make decisions about practice, together with more experienced team members, demonstrate enhanced performance (Leana, Appelbaum, and Shevchuk 2009).

A formal framework for individual mentoring may be found in the California Commission on Teacher Credentialing's Professional Growth Plan, a part of its Child Development Permit Matrix system. During the process of developing a Professional Growth Plan, a teacher meets with an experienced early childhood educator who serves as an ongoing adviser. Together, they discuss professional goals, challenges, and possible ways of overcoming barriers to further education or training. They outline a plan and meet periodically to discuss progress and next steps. Planning a path toward professional advancement with the assistance of a mentor increases the likelihood of successful progress toward goals. A teacher's supervising administrator can facilitate participation in this program by making initial arrangements with registered Professional Growth Advisers in the program's region and even by scheduling times for initial meetings—an important step for those teaching staff members who are new to the field.

Professional development techniques tailored to individuals are especially important in a culturally and linguistically diverse workplace. An administrator may

not share the home culture and language of all teaching staff members. In a diverse context, it is especially important to recognize and respect the varied perspectives teachers bring from their own backgrounds. Although the early childhood program must be built around shared goals for child and family outcomes, each person will contribute differently.

> ## View Teachers as Competent Thinkers and Learners
>
> "How you see teachers and the scope of their work is critical to your success in helping them develop. If you view your staff as people with problems, only noticing their lack of skills and knowledge to manage behavior or plan lessons for learning, you will most likely approach your coaching with quick fixes, one-size-fits-all techniques, and impatience rather than engage with them in the dynamics of the teaching and learning process. Most current approaches to professional development reinforce remediation, emphasizing techniques rather than reflective practice. In contrast, if you acknowledge the complexities of working with children and regard your teachers as competent human beings with rich life experiences, important perspectives, and the potential to rise to their best selves, you will invest the time, resources, and enthusiasm to engage with them in their work."
>
> *Source:* Carter and Curtis 2010, 131.

When hiring teaching staff, the program administrator must have in place a supervision plan that will support the staff members' professional growth and the development of competencies important for successful job performance. If a teaching staff member and program administrator or supervising teacher do not share enough language in common to form an effective mentoring partnership, the administrator may contract with an outside instructional coach or master teacher who can provide these services in the teacher's home language while the staff member works toward workplace-level English proficiency. Pooling professional development funds to hire a part-time mentor teacher to provide this necessary coaching and support programwide is often a more effective choice than spending funds on conferences and workshops (Carter and Curtis 2010). In order to enhance actual teaching performance, it is advisable to provide supervision, coaching, and mentoring *within the teaching context* to all teaching staff members.

Accountability to Maintain Program Quality

A successful program is one that accomplishes its mission in ways consistent with its organization's core values, beliefs, and goals. For an early childhood education program with the mission of enabling all children to transition successfully to kindergarten, for example, those values and beliefs will include a clear statement that "all children" truly means all. Its guiding documents will also articulate beliefs about the ways young children learn and grow, the roles of teachers and families in the early learning context, and goals for partnership between the program and its community. Finally, its leadership will translate these guiding values, beliefs, and goals into positive desired outcomes for children and families and a well-outlined plan for accomplishing them.

Integral to this work will be the use of well-respected documents that outline standards for high quality in the field, such as the National Association for the Education of Young Children's (NAEYC's) Early Childhood Program Standards. These standards include specific criteria and indicators that measure quality across 10 broad domains of program functioning. Other widely employed and useful tools are more specifically targeted. The Classroom Assessment Scoring System (CLASS) assesses the quality of interactions between children and classroom adults within three domains: emotional support, classroom organization, and instructional support (Pianta, La Paro, and Hamre 2008). The Early Childhood Environment Rating Scale (ECERS) assesses a program's interactions, activities, and routines, in addition to focusing in detail on the resources of the program's physical environment and their effective use (Harms, Clifford, and Cryer 2006). The revised ECERS 2007 contains inclusive and culturally sensitive indicators for many items. The Program Administration Scale (PAS) measures early childhood program leadership and management (Talan and Bloom 2004).

Each of these tools, used periodically, can provide both assessments of current program quality and goals for continuous program improvement. All are research-based and have been rigorously tested within diverse program settings. As such, they can serve as valid and reliable tools to promote program accountability. In addition, specific tools developed to capture the level of support for dual language learners can be used to supplement the information gathered by general indicators of program quality (e.g., the Early Language and Literacy Classroom Observation [ELLCO] Addendum for dual language learners or the Head Start Program Preparedness Checklist).

Program administrators will also need to select a method for monitoring the amount and quality of overall home language support during different parts of the day and for determining which staff members provide home language support. There are various tools to measure the quality of inclusive practice for children with disabilities or other special needs as well, including the *Early Childhood Inclusion/Universal Design for Learning Checklist and Questions* (Cunconan-Lahr and Stifel 2007) from the Pennsylvania Early Learning Keys to Quality, a program at Northhampton Community College in Pennsylvania. Each selected assessment tool can provide stakeholders with a view of the program's areas of strength and opportunities for growth. In many programs, reports of the results will be required on a regular basis.

NAEYC Early Childhood Program Standards

1. Relationships
2. Curriculum
3. Teaching
4. Assessment of Child Progress
5. Health
6. Teachers
7. Families
8. Community Relationships
9. Physical Environment
10. Leadership and Management

Quality rating processes may also be employed at county and state levels.

Each assessment in a program context can be a valuable starting point for making improvement plans. The use of assessment—with either standardized or individualized tools—can be framed as a collaborative effort when findings are shared and discussed openly with teaching team members and, as appropriate, with families. Viewing the results of an objective measure can often lead to more constructive attention to specific elements of a program's environment or functioning than can a less-formalized critique presented by an administrator.

An ECERS rating showing that a block area should be redesigned to enhance opportunities for collaborative building projects, for example, may prompt creative problem solving by a teaching team. A CLASS score that indicates a classroom's adults need to increase the quality of feedback they provide to children can focus the work of a program's mentor teacher or instructional coach. A PAS rating that indicates budget planning as a weak area may identify something that an administrator needs to bring to the attention of the organization's board. A low score on the ELLCO Addendum may indicate the need to enhance learning centers with more linguistically diverse and culturally authentic materials. The reflective questions from the Pennsylvania Early Learning Keys to Quality checklist may identify the need for more visuals to support transitions.

Effective administrators take the lead in using measures of program quality and also in following up on their findings based on self-assessments and program reviews. Once findings are shared generally within the program community, the next step is to make a plan based on those findings. A plan that encompasses all areas of program quality will most often indicate needs for targeted professional development. It may focus on knowledge, skills, and dispositions of teaching staff members and support staff members who assist with management tasks (e.g., intake specialists, data entry staff, office assistants, and the like). One rating may indicate a need for more knowledge of a specific area of child development, such as the capacity of four-year-olds for perspective taking. Another assessment may show a teaching team's need to improve their skills for working with children with disabilities or other special needs. Perhaps a particular teacher's disposition toward working with families from diverse cultural backgrounds is an issue, or children who do not speak English may need more individual language interactions. In each case, an improvement plan will take a different shape, and the administrator should address the need by using an evidence-based technique, such as targeted professional development or individual mentoring, each coupled with coaching, that has been shown to lead to more changes in teacher behavior than do general requirements for training hours (Pianta et al. 2008).

Maintaining program quality is an ongoing process. Improving program quality requires commitment and intentionality. An administrator leading by example always approaches the day-to-day work of early childhood education with values, beliefs, and goals in mind. A program leader who models commitment to excellence helps others focus on the quality of the experiences they provide to children and families. Such leadership creates a culture of active engagement as the organization works toward its goals. It also strengthens the early childhood program's identity as a community of learners.

Closing Thoughts

The program administrator plays a pivotal role in building and maintaining a high-quality early learning setting. Effective program administration encompasses both leadership and management responsibilities. It is grounded in deep understanding of child development and early childhood best practices, combined with expertise in leading and supervising people and in employing accepted management and business practices.

The leader sets the tone, or organizational climate, of the program for all of its participants. He or she recruits well-qualified teaching staff, provides sufficient resources and guidance to enable them to teach effectively, and gives them the collaborative support and reflective supervision they need to design and implement a program that exemplifies best practices in all areas and is tailored to be responsive to the values and needs of the community it serves. An effective administrator uses ongoing program assessment to ensure that the early learning program continues to accomplish its mission and improve its outcomes in ways consistent with its core values and goals.

References

Bloom, P. J. 2003. *Leadership in Action: How Effective Leaders Get Things Done.* Lake Forest, IL: New Horizons.

———. 2010. *A Great Place to Work: Creating a Healthy Organizational Climate.* Lake Forest, IL: New Horizons.

———. 2011. *Circle of Influence: Implementing Shared Decision Making and Participative Management.* Lake Forest, IL: New Horizons.

Brandon, R., T. Stutman, and M. Maroto. 2009. *The Economic Value of Early Care and Education for Young Children.* Washington, DC: Human Services Policy Center.

California Commission on Teacher Credentialing. 2014. *Child Development Permit Professional Growth Manual.* Sacramento: California Commission on Teacher Credentialing.

California Department of Education (CDE). 2009. *Inclusion Works! Child Care Programs That Promote Belonging for Children with Special Needs.* Sacramento: California Department of Education.

———. 2010. *California Preschool Curriculum Framework, Volume 1.* Sacramento: California Department of Education.

Carter, M., and D. Curtis. 2010. *The Visionary Director: A Handbook for Dreaming, Organizing, and Improvising in Your Center.* 2nd ed. St. Paul, MN: Redleaf Press.

Cunconan-Lahr, R. L., and S. Stifel. 2007. *Early Childhood Inclusion/Universal Design for Learning Checklist and Questions to Consider in UDL Observations of Early Childhood Environments.*

Building Inclusive Child Care Project: Northampton Community College and Pennsylvania Developmental Disabilities Council. http://www.northampton. edu/bicc (accessed July 28, 2014).

Espinosa, L. 1997. "Personal Dimensions of Leadership." In *Leadership in Early Care and Education,* edited by S. L. Kagan and B. T. Bowman. Washington, DC: National Association for the Education of Young Children.

Gilliam, W. S. 2008. *Implementing Policies to Reduce the Likelihood of Preschool Expulsion.* Foundation for Child Development Policy Brief, Advancing PK–3, No. 7. New York: Foundation for Child Development.

Goffin, S. G. 2000. "The Role of Curriculum Models in Early Childhood Education." ERIC Digest EDO-PS-00-8.

Harms, T., R. M. Clifford, and D. Cryer. 2006. *Early Childhood Environment Rating Scale—Revised Edition.* New York: Teachers College Press.

Heffron, M. C., and T. Murch. 2010. *Reflective Supervision and Leadership in Infant and Early Childhood Programs.* Washington, DC: Zero to Three.

Herzenberg, S., M. Price, and D. Bradley. 2005. *Losing Ground in Early Childhood Education: Declining Workplace Qualifications in an Expanding Industry, 1979–2004.* Washington, DC: Economic Policy Institute.

Leana, C., E. Appelbaum, and I. Shevchuk. 2009. "Work Process and Quality of Care in Early Childhood Education: The Role of Job Crafting." *Academy of Management Journal* 52 (6): 1169–92.

McCormick Center for Early Childhood Leadership. 2011. "Quality in Context: How Directors' Beliefs, Leadership, and Management Practices Relate to Observed Classroom Quality." Research Notes. Wheeling, IL: National-Louis University. http://cecl.nl.edu/ research/issues/rnw11.pdf (accessed June 25, 2013).

Paratore, J. R. 2005. "Approaches to Family Literacy: Exploring the Possibilities." *The Reading Teacher* 59:394–96.

Pianta, R. C., K. M. La Paro, and B. K. Hamre. 2008. *Classroom Assessment Scoring System (CLASS) Manual, Pre–K.* Baltimore, MD: Brookes.

Pianta, R. C., A. J. Mashburn, J. T. Downer, B. K. Hamre, and L. Justice. 2008. "Effects of Web-Mediated Professional Development Resources on Teacher-Child Interaction in Prekindergarten Classrooms." *Early Childhood Research Quarterly* 23 (4): 431–51.

Rohacek, M., G. C. Adams, and E. E. Kisker. 2010. *Understanding Quality in Context: Child Care Centers, Communities, Markets, and Public Policy.* Washington, DC: The Urban Institute.

Sciarra, D. J., and A. G. Dorsey. 2009. *Developing and Administering a Child Care and Education Program.* 7th ed. Clifton Park, NY: Thompson Delmar.

State Advisory Council on Early Learning and Care. 2013. *California's Best Practices for Young Dual Language Learners: Research Overview Papers.* Sacramento: California Department of Education. http://www.cde.ca.gov/sp/cd/ce/documents/dllresearchpapers.pdf (accessed April 3, 2014).

Talan, T. N., and P. J. Bloom. 2004. *Program Administration Scale: Measuring Early Childhood Leadership and Management.* New York: Teachers College Press.

United States Bureau of Labor Statistics. http://www.bls.gov (accessed July 29, 2014).

Whitebook, M., and S. Ryan. 2012. *Supportive Environmental Quality Underlying Adult Learning (SEQUAL).* Berkeley, CA: Center for the Study of Child Care Employment (CSCCE).

Further Reading

Alliance for a Better Community. 2012. *Dual Language Learner Teacher Competencies (DLLTC) Report: From Practice to Policy.* http://www.afabc.org/What-we-do/Education/Early-Care---Education/Dual-Language-Learners.aspx (accessed June 12, 2015).

Gifford, J. 2009. "Building Relationships: The Key to Developing Social Competence in Young Children." *PACE: Practical Approaches for Continuing Education* 3 (4) PACE. http://www.highreach.com/highreach_cms/portals/0/pdf/579111.pdf (accessed July 9, 2014).

Warner, P. E. 2009. "Integrating Social Skills and Competence in the Early Childhood Curriculum." *Practical Approaches for Continuing Education (PACE)* 3 (4). http://www.highreach.com/highreach_cms/portals/0/pdf/579111.pdf (accessed July 9, 2014).

Part Two:
Supporting Young Children's Learning and Development

Chapter 5
Use of the California
Preschool Curriculum Framework

Similar to chapter 2, each volume of the *California Preschool Curriculum Framework* opens by focusing on the preschool child. The curriculum framework underscores young children's sense of wonder and love of learning. As the framework states: "[Young children] have an insatiable appetite for knowledge when they have learning experiences that are engaging and enjoyable" (CDE 2011, 2). To help children build their competence and confidence, the framework emphasizes providing them with positive learning experiences in which they can make choices and explore. Along these lines, the framework poses several questions that guide the overall approach to curriculum.

- How can we offer children engaging, enriching, and enjoyable learning experiences that fuel their intellectual engines and build their confidence?

- How can we connect children's fascination with learning to the nine domains covered by the three volumes of the *California Preschool Learning Foundations* (namely Social–Emotional Development, Language and Literacy, English-Language Development, Mathematics, Visual and Performing Arts, Physical Development, Health, History–Social Science, and Science)?

- How can we integrate learning in those nine domains and make the most of children's time in preschool?

The three volumes of the framework address those questions by exploring the meaning of curriculum planning for the nine domains and by presenting how planning in each one connects with planning in the other eight.

Offering children learning opportunities that are attuned to their developing abilities and connected with their experiences at home and in their communities is at the heart of curriculum planning. In the National Association for the Education of Young Children's (NAEYC's) accreditation criteria, it is stated that a curriculum includes the goals for the knowledge and skills to be acquired by children and the plans for learning experiences whereby such knowledge and skills will be acquired (Epstein 2007). A preschool curriculum typically defines a sequence of integrated experiences, interactions, and activities to help young children reach specific learning goals. In contrast to focusing on specific learning sequences, a curriculum framework provides general guidance on planning learning environments and experiences for young children. The *California Preschool Curriculum Framework* (CDE 2010a, 2011, and 2013) provides

- principles for supporting young children's learning;

- an overview of key components of curriculum planning for young children, including observation, documentation, and reflection;

- descriptions of routines, environments, and materials that engage children in learning;

- sample strategies for building on children's knowledge, skills, and interests.

The framework is organized according to the nine domains of the California preschool learning foundations.

The *California Preschool Curriculum Framework* works hand in hand with the California preschool learning foundations, which describe the knowledge and skills that children typically demonstrate with appropriate support. With an integrated approach to planning learning activities and environments, each domain is the focus of a chapter. Volume 1 of the Preschool Learning Foundations (CDE 2008) covers the domains of Social–Emotional Development, Language and Literacy, English-Language Development, and Mathematics. Volume 2 (CDE 2010b) covers the domains of the Visual and Performing Arts, Physical Development, and Health. Volume 3 (CDE 2012) covers History–Social Science and Science.

Thus, each chapter provides a look at integrated curriculum through the lens of a specific domain. For example, in Volume 2, "Foundations in Physical Development" highlights how vocabulary development relates to children's physical development. Information on strategies to support children's learning may appear in more than one domain chapter because the same strategy or similar strategies apply to multiple areas of growth and development. In essence, the curriculum framework is designed to allow the reader to examine the breadth and depth of each domain in the context of integrated learning.

The framework presents ways of setting up environments, encouraging and building upon children's self-initiated play, selecting developmentally appropriate materials, integrating learning experiences across domains, and planning and implementing teacher-guided learning activities. It is based on eight overarching principles that are grounded in early childhood research and practice. Those essential overarching principles emphasize individually, culturally, and linguistically responsive learning experiences and environments (see figure 5.1).

Each domain chapter begins with an overview of guiding principles and strategies for supporting preschool children's learning in a particular domain (e.g., Mathematics) and presents information about environments and materials that promote optimal learning. Each domain is divided into strands that define its scope. Each strand is further divided into substrands, which include

- a brief overview of the substrand;
- sample interactions and strategies (e.g., conversations, activities, experiences, routines) for helping children make progress in the specific area of learning identified by the substrand;
- vignettes that illustrate the strategies in action.

The sample strategies presented range from spontaneous to those that are intentionally planned. Some sample strategies focus on how teachers build on children's interests during interaction and instruction. Some rely on planning and teacher initiation, and others reflect a combination of teacher planning and spontaneous responses to children's learning. Taken together, they offer a range of ways in which early childhood educators can support children's learning and development. The sample strategies are intended to include a broad range of teaching approaches and a variety of ways to address the individual needs of a diverse group of children. However, the sample strategies are neither exhaustive nor meant to be used as recipes to follow. Instead, they serve as starting points, or springboards, to inspire teachers engaged in planning

Figure 5.1. **Eight Overarching Principles**

Relationships are central.
Play is a primary context for learning.
Learning is integrated.
Intentional teaching enhances children's learning experiences.
Family and community partnerships create meaningful connections.
Individualization of learning includes all children.
Responsiveness to culture and language supports children's learning.
Time for reflection and planning enhances teaching.

and implementing their own strategies. The fact that many strategies overlap across domains reflects the integrated nature of young children's learning. The curriculum framework offers rich examples of integrated learning and teaching that support learning.

Each domain chapter includes "Teachable Moments" to address the balance between planning for children's learning and being spontaneous and responsive when a child or a small group of children may be absorbed with solving a problem, excited about a new idea, or show emerging understanding of a concept. Planning creates opportunities for teachable moments. Intentional teaching includes planning interactions, activities, environments, and adaptations. Teachers plan such learning opportunities based on their observations and assessments of children and what they learn from children's families. When teachers plan learning opportunities, they have in mind how the children might respond. But plans need to be flexible so that teachers can be responsive to how the children actually engage in learning. Teachers observe children and listen for teachable moments made possible by the plans.

Integrated Curriculum for Young Dual Language Learners

The curriculum framework addresses the need to give additional, focused support to young dual language learners whose home language is not English. As stated in the first volume of the *California Preschool Curriculum Framework* (CDE 2010a, 178), "Children who are learning English as a second language form a substantial and growing segment of the preschool population in California served by state child development programs."

Children's progress with learning English varies greatly from child to child. Some children entering preschool may have little or no experience with English, while others may be fairly sophisticated in their understanding and use of English. Given the great variation among California's young dual language learners, their knowledge and skills in the English-language development domain of the preschool learning foundations are

described across *beginning*, *middle*, and *later* levels. In other words, the English-language development foundations reflect a continuum of second-language (English) learning regardless of an individual child's age, but based instead on the dual language learner's exposure to and experience with the English language. The continuum shows that, while developing their abilities to use their knowledge and skills in their home language, young dual language learners continue to make progress in all other domains. Dual language learners also vary greatly in their understanding and use of their home language, which, in turn, influences their progress in English-language development.

In an integrated approach to curriculum, the key to supporting all children is to plan learning activities and environments based on an ongoing understanding of each child's interests, needs, and family and cultural experiences. For teachers of young dual language learners, this approach means a focus on each child's experiences in acquiring English and an understanding of how to build on the child's knowledge and skills in the home language. In applying an integrated approach, teachers take advantage of each moment to provide children with opportunities to communicate with greater understanding and skill while engaged in self-initiated learning or in adult-guided learning activities. The curriculum framework's approach to English-language development is based on key considerations for supporting young dual language learners in preschool settings, including the following:

- Young dual language learners possess a home language on which effective teaching strategies can be based.

- Young dual language learners may demonstrate language and literacy knowledge and skills in their home language before they demonstrate the same knowledge and skills in English.

- Young dual language learners may need additional support and time to make progress in all areas that require English knowledge and skills; therefore, the curriculum framework presents strategies to support dual language learners so that teachers can both scaffold children's learning experiences and utilize multiple modes of communication (e.g., nonverbal cues).

- Young dual language learners will demonstrate, in their home language, competence in domains other than English language and literacy.

- An intentional focus on the process of learning English as a second language is necessary at all times in an integrated approach to curriculum in early care and education settings.

The level of additional support and amount of time that dual language learners may need to demonstrate knowledge and skills in domains such as Mathematics, History–Social Science, and Health will be influenced by their development in both their home language and English. The amount of rich experience the child has in the home language will likely affect the amount and type of support the child needs.

The California Department of Education's DVD *A World Full of Language: Supporting Preschool English Learners* (CDE 2007) highlights the importance of a climate of acceptance and belonging as the starting point for giving dual language learners additional support. Children need to feel comfortable with everyone in the preschool setting and with the use of their home language and nonverbal communication to express themselves while learning and trying to use English. As stated in volume 1 of the *California Preschool Curriculum Framework* (CDE 2010a, 181), "Language is a tool of communication used in all developmental domains. Children who are English learners need to be supported not only in activities focused on language and literacy, but across the entire curriculum." Intentional teaching requires an ongoing awareness of the home-language development of each dual language learner as well as an understanding of the child's ability to use the home language and English as tools for learning and communicating.

Universal Design

The guidance in the curriculum framework applies to all young children, including children with disabilities or other special needs. Preschool children with disabilities or other special needs may demonstrate their developmental progress in diverse ways. Recognizing that children follow different pathways to learning, the framework incorporates a concept known as *universal design* for learning. Universal design provides for multiple means of representation, multiple means of engagement, and multiple means of expression (CAST 2007). Although the curriculum framework presents some ways of adapting or modifying an activity or approach, it cannot offer all possible variations to ensure that a curriculum meets the needs of a particular child. Of course, the first and best source of information about any child is his or her family. Some children receive specialized services from a special educator, therapist, or other professional, and the specialist may also contribute ideas and suggestions related to individual curriculum planning, with the permission of the family. Additionally, there are several other resources available to support inclusive practice for young children with disabilities or other special needs. The resources, Web sites, and books listed in appendix D of the *California Preschool Curriculum Framework, Volume 1* (CDE 2010a) and in *Inclusion Works!* (CDE 2009) provide extensive information on adapting to the diverse needs of children in preschool programs.

The Curriculum Planning Process

The curriculum framework provides a detailed explanation of the curriculum planning process. Planning preschool curriculum begins with teachers discovering, through careful listening and observation, each child's developmental level. Observation is an essential teaching skill. When teachers mindfully observe, they discover how individual children make meaning in everyday moments of play and interactions and how to deepen their relationships with children (Jablon, Dombro, and Dichtelmiller 2007). Observation for the purpose of assessing individual children's learning means carefully watching and listening, with thought and reflection. In this process, teachers often find evidence of individual children engaged in making meaning across several developmental domains. The evidence may pertain specifically to individual children's emotional, social, cognitive, or physical development or may pertain to multiple domains simultaneously. If the evidence is clear and significant, teachers hold it in memory with, for example, a note, a photo, or a sample of a child's work. The evidence will often relate to the descriptive levels of the Desired Results Developmental Profile (DRDP), which provides a full range of measures of children's developmental progress.

As teachers observe children's play and interactions, they also discover ways to extend experiences in order to support children in building more complex and coherent ideas. The next steps in curriculum planning emerge as teachers reflect on how they might expand children's thinking, language, and interactions. The process of observation, reflection while observing, documentation, and reflection on the documentation allows teachers not only to gather evidence of children's progress in learning but also generate curriculum plans within ongoing cycles of mindful observation, listening, documenting, and reflecting on what might come next (see figure 5.2). For monolingual English-speaking teachers who have dual language learners in their classrooms, engaging in reflective curriculum planning will mean collaborating with other staff members and volunteers who are fluent in the children's home languages during all phases of the process.

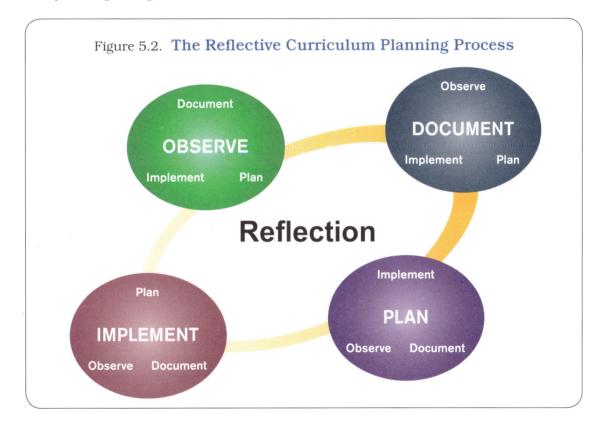

Figure 5.2. **The Reflective Curriculum Planning Process**

Observe, reflect

Observation means being present with children and attentive as they play and interact with others and the environment. This mindful presence is different from participating in children's play or directing their play. Whether for one minute or five, an attentive, mindful presence means waiting to see what unfolds in order to gain a complete picture of children's play. A teacher who observes children as a first step in supporting learning discovers small scientists at work—experimenting, comparing, making assumptions, forming theories about what things are like or what they can do, testing ideas, and, over time, building mastery of a wide range of concepts and skills. While observing, a teacher actively reflects on the children's play and learning and determines what to document.

Document

According to the curriculum framework, documenting means gathering and holding evidence of children's play and interests for future use. A common form of documentation in early childhood settings is a written note, often referred to as an *observation anecdote*. Anecdotal notes, along with other forms of documentation—photos, video recordings, and work samples—serve several purposes. First, they hold memories of a teacher's observations of children's expressions of feelings, thinking, and learning. Second, sharing documentation with the children allows them to revisit and think about an idea or interest and explore it more completely and deeply. Such reflective engagement helps children develop the ability to think about their approaches to making sense of the physical and social worlds and solving problems. Third, documentation can provide a useful guide as teachers determine what might be the next steps in day-to-day curriculum planning. And fourth, anecdotal notes and other evidence can be used to support a teacher's periodic assessment of a child's progress toward reaching competencies measured by the DRDP.

Reflect, discuss, plan

As teachers reflect on the documentation of children's play, they consider ideas for possible next steps in the curriculum—that is, ways to sustain and add complexity to children's learning. Teachers' reflections on the play and interactions that they have observed and documented will suggest several possibilities. Teachers might discuss among themselves what a photo or an anecdote of children's play reveals. They also engage the children's families in thinking about the documentation. At times, teachers also read such stories back to the children, as a way to engage the children in thinking about a possible next step. Reflecting on documentation with children and adults serves as a springboard for developing ways to explore more deeply

a topic that has engaged the interest of the children, the teachers, and the families. Further exploration might include, among other things, materials to add to interest areas, related books to read in either large- or small-group gatherings, or activities to do in small groups. With clear ideas or objectives in mind, teachers plan curriculum that includes strategies to enhance the learning of all children in a group, as well as strategies to support the learning of individual children.

Implement

The next step in the curriculum-planning cycle presented in the framework is implementation. Once a plan is written, teachers implement it, but the planning continues even after the activity or experience is under way. As children encounter the activity or the materials placed in an interest area, the teachers check to find out how the children respond to the materials. To do so, teachers once again observe, reflect, and document. The curriculum-planning cycle that the framework presents is a continuous cycle, as teachers watch to discover children's responses to the planned curriculum and evidence of their developing skills and concepts during the planned learning encounters. As with every phase in the planning cycle, teachers can approach this one with a sense of wonder. They may be surprised and amazed by what children actually do in response once engaged with the materials or activity. To hold in memory significant parts of what they observe, teachers record notes, take a photo, or keep a work sample, labeling and dating each. They can reflect on these documents later, along with parents and even with the children, as a way to assess the impact of the curriculum plans, to generate plans to further support children's learning, and to assess individual children's learning.

Partnering with families in curriculum planning

The curriculum framework describes how families become active participants, along with their children and the teachers, in generating curriculum plans. When teachers share documentation of children's experiences and learning with the children's families, they invite the children's families to reflect together with them on children's learning and on ideas for building the curriculum. Family members offer unique insights and important input for curriculum planning. They also help teachers understand the expectations, values, and beliefs that influence children's behavior and ideas. Discussions among teachers and children's families about class projects and learning experiences add much to the curriculum plans. Such discussions become a conduit for the exchange of resources and ideas, from home to school and from school to home. Projects or investigations jointly planned with families can bridge children's experiences at home and in the community with their experiences at school.

Closing Thoughts

The concepts and strategies described in the preschool curriculum framework require thoughtful planning and implementation. They are grounded in evidence-based practices that have evolved in the early childhood education field over decades. The ability to apply a broad understanding of early learning and development in the preschool setting takes time and experience. For programs and teachers to gain the knowledge and skills necessary to approach curriculum as the framework envisions, opportunities for professional development are essential. The CDE's *California Preschool Learning Foundations* (three volumes) and the *California Preschool Curriculum Frameworks* (three volumes) are well-researched documents informed by practice that can be used for both preservice and in-service professional development. Those two resources are part of the California Early Learning and Development System, along with this publication, *Preschool English Learners: Principles and Practices to Promote Language, Literacy, and Learning—A Resource Guide, the California Early Childhood Educator Competencies*, professional development activities, and the Desired Results assessment system. With appropriate professional development, preschool program administrators and teachers can use the curriculum framework to guide their planning and implementation of environments and experiences that allow all young children to prosper during the preschool years.

References

California Department of Education (CDE). 2007. *A World Full of Language: Supporting Preschool English Learners*. DVD. Sacramento: California Department of Education.

———. 2008. *California Preschool Learning Foundations, Volume 1*. Sacramento: California Department of Education.

———. 2009. *Inclusion Works! Creating Child Care Programs That Promote Belonging for Children with Special Needs*. Sacramento: California Department of Education.

———. 2010a. *California Preschool Curriculum Framework, Volume 1*. Sacramento: California Department of Education.

———. 2010b. *California Preschool Learning Foundations, Volume 2*. Sacramento: California Department of Education.

———. 2011. *California Preschool Curriculum Framework, Volume 2*. Sacramento: California Department of Education.

———. 2012. *California Preschool Learning Foundations, Volume 3*. Sacramento: California Department of Education.

———. 2013. *California Preschool Curriculum Framework, Volume 3*. Sacramento: California Department of Education.

California Department of Education and First 5 California. 2012. *California Early Childhood Educator Competencies*. Sacramento: California Department of Education.

Center for Applied Special Technology (CAST). 2007. Universal Design for Learning. http://www.cast.org/udl (accessed May 3, 2013).

Epstein, A. S. 2007. *The Intentional Teacher: Choosing the Best Strategies for Young Children's Learning*. Washington, DC: National Association for the Education of Young Children.

Jablon, J. R., A. L. Dombro, and M. Dichtelmiller. 2007. *The Power of Observation*. 2nd ed. Washington, DC: National Association for the Education of Young Children.

Further Reading

California Department of Education. Forthcoming. *Overview of the Infant/Toddler and Preschool Curriculum Frameworks*. Sacramento, CA: California Department of Education.

Chapter 6
Support for Young Dual Language Learners

As the number and diversity of preschool dual language learners (DLLs) have grown dramatically during the last decade, so has scientific understanding of how growing up with two or more languages influences development across all domains. Research is illuminating both the challenges and complexities of learning basic concepts through two separate linguistic systems as well as the enormous capacity of young children to learn more than one language during a critical period of cognitive development. In addition, growing research evidence makes clear the linguistic, social, cognitive, academic, cultural, and long-term financial benefits of becoming bilingual.

This chapter presents recommendations on best practices for preschool DLLs based on the latest findings from neuroscience, cognitive psychology, psycholinguistics, educational evaluation, sociocultural research, assessment research, and special education. The recommendations and research conclusions are drawn from six research overview papers written by leading experts across multiple disciplines (State Advisory Council on Early Learning and Care 2013). The papers were commissioned by the California Department of Education (CDE), Early Education and Support Division. The research reviewed in the six papers confirms and updates much of the information in the resource guide *Preschool English Learners: Principles and Practices to Promote Language, Literacy, and Learning* (CDE 2009), and at the same time, provides additional insights into dual language development.[1] Throughout this volume, special considerations related to serving young DLLs are described. This chapter focuses on meeting the needs of young DLLs in preschool across all program areas and considers specific recommendations for program practices.

The CDE has taken clear and consistent positions on the value of linguistic and cultural diversity and the need to promote principles and practices that recognize and build upon every child's linguistic and cultural strengths (see the green box on the next page). In this chapter, 10 Guiding Principles for supporting the learning and development of preschool DLLs offer a framework for interpreting the research findings and provide a rationale for specific practices. Based on the latest findings from the six commissioned research overview papers, these Guiding Principles are adapted and updated from the resource guide *Preschool English Learners: Principles and Practices to Promote Language, Literacy, and Learning* (CDE 2009).

---

1. The full title, as well as a shortened one, and the author(s) of each of the six research overview papers are listed below. The shortened titles are used throughout this chapter in references to each paper.

- "Neuroscience Research: How Experience with One or More Languages Affects the Developing Brain," by Barbara T. Conboy (Paper 1, Neuroscience Research)
- "Cognitive Consequences of Dual Language Learning: Cognitive Function, Language and Literacy, Science and Mathematics, and Social–Emotional Development," by Catherine Sandhofer and Yuuko Uchikoshi (Paper 2, Development Across Domains)
- "Program Elements and Teaching Practices for Young Dual Language Learners," by Claude Goldenberg, Karen Nemeth, Judy Hicks, Marlene Zepeda, and Luz Marina Cardona (Paper 3, Program Elements and Teaching Practices)
- "Family Engagement in Early Childhood Programs: Serving Families of Dual Language Learners," by Linda Halgunseth, Gisela Jia, and Oscar Barbarin (Paper 4, Family Engagement)
- "Assessment of Young Dual Language Learners in Preschool," by Linda Espinosa and Vera Gutiérrez-Clellen (Paper 5, Assessment)
- "Early Intervention and Young Dual Language Learners with Special Needs," by Deborah Chen and Vera Gutiérrez-Clellen (Paper 6, Early Intervention and Special Needs)

"Being exposed to two or more languages at a young age is a gift. It is a gift because children who are able to learn through two or more languages benefit cognitively, socially, and emotionally."

"Exposure to more than one language should be celebrated as a growth opportunity that offers many learning and social advantages. Children who are developing bilingual abilities are developing unique strengths that will add to the cultural and linguistic resources of California."

Source: CDE 2010, 224.

Guiding Principles for Supporting Young Dual Language Learners

1. All young DLLs have the capacity to learn two or more languages and benefit cognitively and socially when they receive instruction that promotes development of their home language as well as English-language development (ELD).

2. High-quality preschool programs benefit all children but are not sufficient for young DLLs to achieve equitable outcomes.

3. Strong and mutually respectful partnerships with families with young DLLs enhance the learning and development of young DLLs.

4. Respect for the culture, values, and language preferences of families with young DLLs will benefit young DLLs' adjustment to preschool.

5. DLLs' knowledge and strengths in their home language need to be recognized and built upon in the preschool curriculum.

6. The learning and development of young DLLs must be supported and assessed across all domains, including ELD.

7. Characteristics of preschool DLLs' language development need to be understood by all program staff:

   a. Young DLLs may take longer to respond to instructional prompts given in English.

   b. Young DLLs will typically progress through several stages of second-language acquisition at different rates depending on their early exposure and usage (see the California Preschool Learning Foundations in English-Language Development for further information)

   c. Young DLLs will likely employ code switching (i.e., combining English and home language words in the same utterance), which is a typical feature of dual language development and should be considered a linguistic strength (see the California preschool learning foundations in English-language development for further information).

8. To individuals without training in dual language learning, some features of language development may appear delayed during the early stages of bilingualism for young DLLs (e.g., vocabulary in each language, grammatical knowledge in second language, expressive abilities in second language), but when provided with a linguistically enriched and balanced program, young DLLs will become proficient in both languages.

9. The executive function abilities of young DLLs can be enhanced through a balanced educational approach to language.

10. All language development activities and interactions should be interesting and engaging for young DLLs and should build upon young children's intrinsic desire to learn language to communicate and participate in their social and educational settings.

Characteristics of Preschool Dual Language Learners

As stated previously in this document, *DLLs are young children learning two or more languages at the same time, as well as those learning a second language while continuing to develop their first (or home) language.* They come from diverse language and cultural backgrounds, a wide range of family circumstances, and many different countries of origin. These children and their families represent the growing diversity in this country and provide a glimpse into the future of this nation's social fabric. Though diverse, young DLLs share a common trait: they all are learning at least two distinct linguistic systems during a period of rapid cognitive, conceptual, and language development. Mastering the fundamentals of one language system during the preschool years is a major developmental accomplishment. Progressing in two is remarkable but achievable when DLLs are appropriately and effectively supported. For the purposes of this chapter, children are considered to be bilingual when they are able to use two languages with comparable proficiency; most young DLLs attending California preschools are not yet equally fluent in both languages and would be considered *emergent bilinguals*.

Research Paper 1 (Neuroscience Research) and Paper 2 (Development Across Domains) indicate that bilingual infants and toddlers show some cognitive advantages during the first year of life as well as enhanced executive control skills by the age of seven months. Conboy's research review (Paper 1: Neuroscience Research) explains that bilingual infants process information in ways that are different from monolinguals. This difference leads to enhanced attention during speech processing, an adaptive strategy that might facilitate further learning. Bilingual preschoolers are also able to detect language switching more quickly than do monolingual children. This finding indicates that a specific language-change response develops when a young child is growing up bilingually. As bilinguals must keep two sets of linguistic rules in mind during speech processing, they most likely develop a heightened sensitivity to distinct patterns of speech and develop increased cognitive functioning. Conboy goes on to say that the particular languages a child is learning, as well as the amount of experience with each language, influence how the brain processes each language.

Sandhofer and Uchikoshi's research review (Paper 2: Development Across Domains) highlights the advantages in executive control tasks that have been

---

What is executive function?

"Enhanced executive function abilities such as working memory, inhibitory control, attention to relevant vs. irrelevant task cues, and mental or cognitive flexibility, as well as improved language skills, have been linked to early bilingualism. These abilities have been portrayed as the biological foundation for school readiness, providing the platform upon which children's capacities to learn (the 'how') educational content (the 'what') depends. It has been found in multiple studies that there is a bilingual advantage when comparing monolinguals and bilinguals on tasks that require selective attention, cognitive flexibility, and certain literacy skills such as decoding when the two languages have similar writing systems. Notably, these advantages have been found across all socio-economic, racial, and ethnic groups."

Source: Espinosa 2013, 54.

---

found during infancy for bilinguals. Seven-month-old bilingual infants were better able to anticipate a switch in learning conditions and respond correctly as compared to monolinguals. This finding indicates that very young bilinguals' showed an advanced ability to inhibit previous learning when the task demands changed. Since these tasks are also associated with speech sounds (syllables), it is possible that the bilingual advantage is related to their enhanced attention during speech processing as described above. Paper 2 (Development Across Domains) further reviews studies that show preschool bilinguals demonstrating even more advantages in executive function than the advantages found for bilingual infants. At the preschool age, bilingual children show advantages in tasks that require selectively attending to competing options and the ability to suppress interfering information. These bilingual benefits have been found across cultural and socioeconomic groups as well as across different language combinations. However, these cognitive advantages depend on the extent to which the child is bilingual. Children who are more balanced in their bilingualism show larger advantages than children who are more strongly dominant in one language. Thus, both papers suggest that when ECE services are provided to young DLLs, the amount of exposure and frequency of experiences in each language is important for programs to consider.

Another conclusion shared by both papers is the scientific consensus that all "children have the capacity to learn two

> "Young children can successfully learn two languages, and do not need to give up their home language in order to learn English if it is the formal language of the preschool setting. Practitioners can enhance the language learning of dual language learners by providing rich learning opportunities in each language. For example, they may support the home language at the same time as the school language through family involvement, bilingual materials, and activities and interactions in the home language with teachers, staff, and peers who speak that language."
>
> *Source:* Paper 1 (Neuroscience Research), 34.

languages from birth and that this early dual language exposure does not confuse children or delay development in either language. In fact, dual language learning provides children with many cognitive benefits" (Paper 2: Development Across Domains, 32). These important findings from cognitive neuroscience underlie the first Guiding Principle for Supporting Dual Language Learners. The fact that preschool DLLs enter programs with some degree of proficiency in their home language and are primed to learn and benefit from learning a second language (i.e., English) provides a compelling rationale for designing programs that support both languages.

Paper 1 (Neuroscience Research), by Barbara T. Conboy, points out that while infants are able to learn two linguistic

systems and keep them separate—and the cognitive processes required to manage this linguistic feat will have long-term cognitive advantages—frequently, when young children are exposed to English, their dominant language shifts to English. Although Conboy's paper did not describe this outcome as home language loss, or a subtractive language experience, other research has documented that in many U.S. preschool settings, young DLLs show home language loss as they become more proficient in English. Because of such effects, Conboy's summary recommends that "it is important for practitioners to look at the long-term outcomes of those effects, and also to consider children's experiences with both of their languages, instead of focusing only on whether second-language performance matches that of native speakers" (p. 38). To summarize, both Papers 1 and 2 cite findings that show preschoolers have the capacity and, indeed are neurologically prepared, to learn more than one language—and they gain cognitively from managing the linguistic processing required when becoming bilingual. However, learning a second language should not come at the expense of continued home language development. The research highlights the importance of sufficient exposure to both languages in order to reap the benefits of bilingualism.

There are additional benefits to knowing two (or more) languages and encouraging children to maintain and develop their home language as they learn English during the preschool years. Children who know more than one language have personal, social, cognitive, and economic advantages throughout their lives. In contrast, children who do not develop and maintain proficiency in their home language may lose their ability to communicate with parents and family members. DLLs who are proficient in their home language are able "to establish a strong cultural identity, to develop and sustain strong ties with their immediate and extended families, and thrive in a global multilingual world" (Espinosa 2006, 2).

Process of Second-Language Acquisition. As preschool children with little or no experience with English progress in their English-language abilities, they typically go through several stages of second-language development. In the *California Preschool Learning Foundations, Volume 1* (CDE 2008), these stages are characterized as follows:

- "Beginning"—Children may continue to use their home language even when no one in the preschool setting speaks or understands them, and over time they start to actively attend to the new language, observing and silently processing the features of the English language.

- "Middle"—During this stage, young dual language learners "typically master the rhythm and the intonation of the second language as well as some key phrases, using telegraphic and formulaic speech to communicate" (CDE 2008, 105).

- "Later"—Children have stronger English comprehension skills and are able to use English to express themselves and engage in most classroom activities in English. However, even during this later stage of English development, the young DLL will most likely not communicate with the same fluency as a native speaker. "The child may mispronounce words as well as make errors in vocabulary choice and grammar. Such errors are indicative of the typical process of learning a language" (CDE 2008, 106).

It is important to remember that the rate at which preschool young DLLs progress through these stages depends on characteristics of the child and the child's language learning opportunities—as with all domains of development, young DLLs progress in their English-language development at different rates.[2]

In other areas of development, preschool bilinguals show either no differences or function slightly less efficiently than do monolingual children. For instance, Sand-

hofer and Uchikoshi's research review (Paper 2: Development Across Domains) points out that studies have consistently indicated bilingual children take longer to recall words from memory. They have slower word retrieval times in picture-naming tasks and lower scores on verbal fluency tasks. These findings underscore the need for teachers to understand the challenges a young DLL experiences when processing language, particularly the nondominant language, and the need to allow sufficient time for the child to come up with a response. Wait time is important for all children, but critical for young DLLs.

Both Paper 1 (Neuroscience) and Paper 2 (Development Across Domains) describe the finding that bilingual preschoolers tend to have smaller vocabularies in each language when compared with English-speaking and Spanish-speaking monolinguals. However, a DLL's vocabulary is distributed across two languages, and when both languages are considered, their vocabulary size is often comparable to monolinguals. Conboy (Paper 1: Neuroscience Research, 25) clearly makes this point: "[B]ilingual lexical learning leads to initially smaller vocabularies in *each separate language* than for monolingual learners of those same languages, but that *total vocabulary sizes* (the sum of what children know in both their languages) in bilingual toddlers are similar to those of monolingual toddlers (Pearson and others 1997)." For more information on this topic, refer to Paper 5 (Assessment) and Paper 6 (Early Intervention and Special Needs).

As vocabulary size is a key goal in preschool and very important to future reading comprehension, this variation in dual language learning is critical for preschool teachers to understand. If a preschool child does not know the English word for *book*, the child often still understands the concept of a book and may know a different word—for example, *libro*. Summing up what is known about this topic, Paper 2 (Development Across Domains) states, "Thus, when examining the vocabulary performance of DLLs, we need to consider a number of factors, including the similarities between the two languages, the

---

2. The California preschool learning foundations in English-language development (see CDE 2008) describe in detail the categories of typical English-language development with multiple examples of children's language and behavior; the *California Preschool Curriculum Framework, Volume 1* (CDE 2010) presents curriculum and instructional adaptations designed to meet the specific needs of young DLLs.

language of the child's school experience, and the quality and quantity of the child's exposure to each language" (p. 63).

Oral language skills (e.g., vocabulary, listening comprehension), grammatical knowledge, and narrative production have received particular attention from both educators and researchers who are trying to meet the learning needs of young DLLs. Research with both monolingual and bilingual populations recognizes that vocabulary is one of the best predictors of reading comprehension, that vocabulary is a complex construct with many components, and that vocabulary is learned in multiple contexts both at home and at school.

Recent research with young Spanish-speaking children from low socioeconomic backgrounds has found that these young DLLs might be at risk for delays in their early literacy development due to their weaker oral language abilities. This research with young DLLs demonstrates the importance of oral language development and supports instructional approaches that focus on developing these skills by providing rich and engaging language environments in both languages, while focusing on building early literacy skills. In light of this research, it is essential for preschool programs to recognize the critical importance of oral language and vocabulary development for young DLLs.

Throughout both Paper 1 (Neuroscience Research) and Paper 2 (Development Across Domains), a common theme is the role of individual factors in predicting second-language outcomes. Individual difference, including the child's home language, cognitive abilities, previous learning experiences, cultural background, and knowledge, can all play an important role in the dynamic process of learning a second language. Thus, preschool programs need to collect information about young DLLs' background, including culture, language(s), knowledge, and skills. Findings on individual factors provide part of the rationale for Guiding Principles 3 (partnerships with families) and 4 (respecting the culture, values, and language preferences of families with young DLLs) referenced earlier in this chapter.

Program Approaches and Teaching Practices

Goldenberg, Nemeth, Hicks, Zepeda, and Cardona's research overview in Paper 3 (Program Elements and Teaching Practices) points out that young children who speak a language other than English in the home make up the fastest-growing segment of the population nationwide. California is one of the most linguistically and culturally diverse states in the country, with about 25 percent of its K–12 population identified as English learners. This sizeable group of children (described as *dual language learners* during the first five years of life and *English learners* during the K–12 years) has historically struggled to become fully proficient in English, lagged behind their native English-speaking peers on most indicators of academic achievement, and had school dropout rates almost twice those of native speakers of English. However, as described above, DLLs have also been shown to demonstrate social–emotional strengths and, when supported in both their languages, they demonstrate many cognitive, linguistic, and social advantages as compared with monolingual children.

These demographic shifts and achievement trends are important to California's preschool programs for the following reasons: (a) the proportion of the population that enters early education programs speaking a language other than English has grown dramatically over the last decade; (b) the educational success of young DLLs is critical to the overall effectiveness of the educational system; (c) increased risk factors associated with poorer school performance have been identified within the DLL/English learner population— particularly children from homes of low socioeconomic status; (d) the preschool years represent a time when children can learn two languages rapidly and effectively and gain the cognitive and social benefits of becoming bilingual; and (e) specific educational approaches that are well implemented during the early years of schooling have the potential to improve the academic achievement and long-term school success of a large and growing group of diverse learners.

Although many influential studies and policy reports have documented the long-term benefits of high-quality preschool on children's development and achievement, very few empirical studies comprehensively describe how to best teach young DLLs. The value of quality preschool and the need to make it available to all young children is based on solid evidence about the long-term impacts on outcomes such as high school completion, reduced juvenile delinquency, reduced crime, and improved labor market participation. Unfortunately, this research offers little guidance on which program elements were most effective for specific groups of children, as it focuses almost exclusively on native English-speaking children.

Because of the growing proportion of children who are DLLs and the role of high-quality preschool practices in promoting young children's school readiness and long-term success, there is an urgent need to carefully define, design, and implement best practices for preschool young DLLs. These recommended program approaches and teaching practices must be based on the most current and valid scientific findings. Paper 3 (Program Elements and Teaching Practices) provides a thorough review of recent research about "the effectiveness of program elements and instructional strategies currently available in California and elsewhere to address the needs of the diverse population of young dual language learners" (p. 3). Thus, the following sections detail specific program elements and strategies to support young DLLs in preschool.

The elements that make up high-quality preschool are important for all children, including young DLLs. However, repeated research studies on both K–12 students and preschool-age children show that young DLLs need additional language supports and instructional adaptations in order to reach a comparable level of academic success. High-quality early childhood programs include such features as the following: intentional teaching and support of integrated learning, positive teacher–child and home–school relationships, play as a context for learning, teacher planning time, qualified teachers, appropriate child–teacher ratios, individu-

alized adult–child conversations that promote language and positive relationships, opportunities for children to learn and practice new vocabulary, frequent assessment that documents individual progress and informs instructional planning, and parent engagement. All of those features are important for young DLLs, but are probably not sufficient for equitable achievement. Goldenberg, Nemeth, Hicks, Zepeda, and Cardona's research overview (State Advisory Council on Early Learning and Care 2013, 96) states this point in the following way:

> Although all children benefit from high-quality preschool, how do we further supplement high-quality environments for young dual language learners in order to support language, cognitive, and other developmental outcomes for these children? The use of children's home language in addition to English—often referred to as bilingual education—is probably the most important and the most controversial issue in the education of dual language learners, whether in preschool or throughout K–12. (Paper 3: Program Elements and Teaching Practices)

A common recommendation across all six research overview papers is to recognize that young DLLs are learning through two languages and that both languages must be supported through intentional instruction, specific language interactions, frequent assessments of children's progress in both languages, and culturally sensitive engagement with families. Increasingly, researchers are also discovering how critical the role of the family is in maintaining the home language (see Paper 4 for a discussion about family engagement of families with young DLLs and the resource guide *Preschool English Learners: Principles and Practices to Promote Language, Literacy, and Learning*, chapter 6, "Code Switching and Language Loss").

The next two sections of this chapter describe recommended program approaches for supporting the integrated learning and development of young DLLs in preschool: (1) balanced English and home language development, and (2) English-language development with home language support.

Balanced-English-and-Home-Language-Development Approach. Programs that serve native speakers of English and children who primarily speak one other home language are able to implement an approach that uses the home language and English in balanced proportions. Research has shown that instructional use of the home language does not hinder or stunt academic progress in English. Goldenberg, Nemeth, Hicks, Zepeda, and Cardona's research reaches the opposite conclusion: "On the contrary, there is evidence that teaching children to read in their home language can support their literacy development in English. In other words, when we systematically provide learning experiences in children's home language along with learning experiences in English, we promote home language development without hampering English development (Lightbown and Spada 2006)" (Paper 3: Program Elements and Teaching Practices, 98).

The balanced approach is intended to maintain and develop the home language while also promoting English-language development. Programs that implement this approach are frequently described as dual language programs. Such programs may provide all instruction and interaction in both languages. The programs have curriculum and language support materials that are of equal quality in both languages. They often have qualified bilingual teachers, but at the least, there are staff members with the capacity to provide high-quality instruction across all learning domains in the home language and English. Of utmost importance is that these programs devote sufficient time in each language to promote bilingualism and early biliteracy.

When programs choose a balanced English-and-home-language approach, careful attention must be paid to the amount of exposure and quality of instruction in each language. There is evidence that if programs do not have a systematic division of time allocated to each language and do not frequently monitor the allocation of time, they often tend to become English-dominant (Paper 3: Program Elements and Teaching Practices, p. 99). Possible methods of balancing class time between the two languages include, but are not limited to, possible program structures described in table 6.1.

Each of those program structures for balancing time between the two languages has been successfully used in different contexts and has led to growth in both the home language and English. The choice of how to balance home language and English may depend on the number of classrooms and children, the availability of qualified bilingual early childhood teachers, and the physical space avail-

Table 6.1. Program Structures for a Balanced English-and-Home-Language Development Approach

Program Structures		Relevant Features
All Spanish in morning or afternoon.	All English in afternoon or morning.	Same bilingual teacher(s), classroom materials, and labeling in both languages
All Spanish day 1	All English day 2	Can use same classroom and same bilingual teacher or alternate between two teachers (one Spanish-speaking, one English-speaking) and classrooms
All Spanish week 1	All English week 2	Children or teachers can alternate between different classrooms: one room for Spanish, one room for English

able. In any case, it will be important for programs to have clear goals in mind for children in both languages throughout their time in preschool and to monitor those goals frequently. In particular, programs will need to assess children's progress with both home language development and English-language development in all developmental and academic areas. Programs will also need to help families understand and support the program philosophy and language goals. Family members can work with program staff to ensure the use of the home language reflects the children's cultural experiences at home and in the community. Finally, if a program has more than one teacher, adequate time must be provided for joint planning and joint professional development on all aspects of the curriculum and assessment methods.

English-Language-Development-with-Home-Language-Support Program Approach. In California and across the country, most young DLLs attend preschool programs that provide instruction in English and little intentional support for home language development. Although a balanced approach that promotes both languages in roughly equal proportions is ideal, many programs are not able to implement such an approach. There are many reasons why programs are not actively integrating the use of children's home languages: teachers are monolingual and speak only English; multiple languages are represented by the children and families, and there is a limited number of bilingual teachers; program resources are inadequate; and community values, program priorities, and possibly parental preferences may differ. However, based on the research summarized above and a growing understanding of how all teachers can intentionally promote home language development, even when teachers are monolingual or bilingual resources are limited, programs can implement a variety of strategies to support young dual language learners appropriately and effectively.

In programs where the only feasible option is for interactions and instruction to be primarily in English, there are many ways that teachers can still bring the home language into the classroom so that young dual language learners can continue to grow in both languages. Some recommended practices adapted from Paper 3 (Program Elements and Teaching Practices) are as follows:

- Read to children from books in the child's home language. This can be done by teachers, families, or community members. Books may be obtained from local libraries or children's homes or made in the classroom and saved from year to year. Parents can record themselves reading or telling a story in their native language, and the audio recording can be available in the listening center. If there are adults in the preschool who speak the child's home language, ensure that there are opportunities for those adults and children to interact.

- Create books that include children's home languages. These can be class books (about animals, for example, where each animal is labeled in all of the classroom's home languages) or individual books (e.g., about children's families, with many words or labels in the home language).

- Teach children rhymes, letters, and numbers in their home language. There are many authentic children's books, compact discs, computer programs, audiotapes, and printed nursery rhymes available in multiple languages that can be used independently in centers or read by an adult. This practice may require community or parental support.

- Teach the entire class the expressions for greetings in all of the home languages in the classroom.

- Summarize or provide key phrases of a story in a book, finger play, or song in the child's home language before introducing it in English. This practice may also require recruiting parents or community volunteers into the classroom.

- Point out cognates (words in two languages that have common roots, such as *elephant* in English and *elefante* in Spanish; *giant* in English and *gigante* in Spanish) and connections between words in the home language and words in English. This may not be possible for some languages, but there are many cognates between Spanish and English, for example, that may be useful for helping young DLLs understand connections between languages and quickly learn new words.

- Let parents know what topics are going to be explored in the classroom (e.g., insects, weather) so that families can build conceptual knowledge in the home language before children are exposed to those concepts in English. For many families, programs will need to use the skills of an experienced interpreter or translator so that information is presented in families' preferred language.

- Allocate classroom time and space for adults who speak the child's home language to interact with children in that language. This can happen during whole-group time to expose English-only children to a new language or during small-group time to reinforce and expand young dual language learners' growth in their home language.

- Display pictures and signs that represent the major languages, cultures, and family practices of the children enrolled in the classroom (include greetings, alphabets, daily schedules and routines and so on).

- Display family posters, cultural artifacts, and "All About My Family" projects (stories that children make describing their family, home activities, favorite foods, and the like) in a designated area throughout the year. Teachers can also share and display their own history and cultural heritage to provide a model, share personal background, and build rapport with children and families.

- Establish a partnership with families and help them understand their role in maintaining the home language. Collaborating with families can help ensure young DLLs hear and use sufficient amounts of their home language outside preschool.

There are important language supports to help young DLLs in English-dominant preschool programs comprehend the meanings of instructional activities and promote English vocabulary growth. As described earlier, when possible, teachers can identify cross-language cognates and intentionally use them to help activate knowledge in the child's home language and apply it to the task of learning English. Young DLLs need to learn complex narrative skills, listening comprehension, academic language, early literacy skills, and the understanding of complex grammatical structures, all of which will contribute to improved reading comprehension in third grade and beyond. As articulated in Paper 3 (Program Elements and Teaching Practices), young DLLs are more likely to comprehend lessons, develop advanced oral language skills, and grow in their English-language development when teachers engage in the following practices:

- Use many types of *pictures of vocabulary words* to illustrate word meanings.

- Use *hand puppets, other realistic props, and gamelike activities* to illustrate concepts and actions and to engage children physically.

- Use *multimedia-enhanced instruction* in the form of videos and computerized animation to enhance vocabulary instruction with nonfiction texts.

- Use books, themes, and resource material with *culturally familiar content* to promote comprehension and facilitate the learning of new concepts and skills.

- Use *pictorial, real-world objects and concrete experiences* to convey the meaning of words and concepts.

- Use *visual cues and physical gestures* and signals linked to specific content vocabulary to imprint meaning.

- *Integrate songs and physical movement* throughout academic instruction.

- Provide some *explicit teaching* (or explanations) of features of English, such as vocabulary and **pragmatics**.

- Teach children *rhymes, poems, and songs*, particularly those with repetitive refrains;
- *Pair children* with different levels of proficiency in English as supports for each other, and occasionally present tasks for those partnerships to complete that do not depend on language proficiency.
- Provide both *safe havens* where children do not have to speak to anyone and spaces in the classroom where children can interact in small groups and one-on-one.

In addition, teachers can meet with families early in the school year to learn critical information about the child and family (see table 6.2 below for an example of a "family languages and interests interview" form). During these one-to-one family conferences, teachers can learn about the child's early language learning experiences as well as the parents' preferences and aspirations for their child's language and academic achievement. Programs have recommended that this interview form be used in a face-to-face discussion with families to avoid potential misunder-

Table 6.2. **Sample Family Languages and Interests Interview**[3]

Child's Name_____ Date_____
First   Middle   Last

Date of Birth_____ Gender: ____Male ____Female
Month   Day   Year

1. How many family members live with you and the child? _____

2. Who are the members of your family? _____

   _____

3. Who is the primary caregiver of your child? _____

4. What language does the primary caregiver speak most often with the child?

   _____

5. What language(s) did your child learn when he or she first began to talk?

   _____

6. Can you tell me what language(s) each of the following people in your household speak to your child?

	Only English	Mostly English, with some other language (identify)	Mostly other language (identify), with some English	Only other language (identify)
Mother (or you)				
Father (or you)				
Older siblings				
Grandmother				
Grandfather				
Aunt/Uncle				
Others, after school, community members				

3. See appendix A of *California's Best Practices for Young Dual Language Learners* (State Advisory Council on Early Learning and Care 2013, 207–8). This family interview form was developed by Espinosa, Matera, and Magruder for the California Transitional Kindergarten program in 2010.

Table 6.2. **Sample Family Languages and Interests Interview** (continued)

7. What are your feelings about maintaining your home language? _____
    _____

8. What special talents or interests does your child have? _____
    _____

9. Who does your child play with most often? _____
    _____

10. What are your aspirations for your child? _____
    _____

11. What are your expectations for the preschool year? _____
    _____

12. Do you have any hobbies or interests that you would like to share with your child's class?
    _____

13. Would you be interested in volunteering in your child's class? _____
    _____

14. If yes, preferred days and times: _____
    _____

standings and encourage ongoing communication. This is also an ideal time to find out if the family has any talents or interests they would like to share with the class and to recruit volunteers for home language support.

Teacher–child relationships. All preschool children thrive academically and socially when their teachers are sensitive, positive, nurturing, and responsive to the children's emotional and social needs. Teacher–child relationships appear to be central to healthy growth and development and important to academic outcomes as well (see chapter 2 for a more complete discussion). Although beneficial for all children, particular benefits of teacher–child relationships have been found for young DLLs. More specifically, young DLL children who speak Spanish and are taught in Spanish in emotionally supportive classrooms make larger gains in math scores than do their peers in less emotionally support-

ive classrooms. Furthermore, low-quality relationships between teachers and young DLLs appear to compromise the benefits of in-school literacy instruction for young DLLs' language and literacy development. Researchers have concluded that positive and nurturing relationships between children and teachers require that teachers establish a number of practices in their classrooms:

- Teachers are physically near to children.

- Teachers engage in social conversation with children.

- Teachers express affection verbally and physically.

- Teachers use a warm, calm voice, make eye contact when appropriate, and use respectful language when talking with children.

- Teachers are flexible with children and allow children to make choices and express themselves.

Other research has also found that teachers who spoke some Spanish to the Spanish-speaking young DLLs viewed the children's behavior in a more positive light than teachers who spoke only English. The research suggests that being in preschool classes taught by English-only teachers may contribute to the achievement gap of young DLLs. The findings of this study highlight the value of home language support not only for academic benefits, but also for social and emotional benefits as well. Thus, for many reasons it is important for programs to recruit both qualified staff and volunteers who are able to provide some level of support for each child's home language. (See Paper 3, Program Elements and Teaching Practices, pp. 102–3, for a discussion of the quality of teacher–child relationships.)

Assessment of Young Dual Language Learners

Preschool teachers and support staff will be asked to accurately assess young DLLs' development and achievement in order to individualize instruction, improve the quality of education, and improve academic school readiness. According to Espinosa and Gutiérrez-Clellen's research overview in Paper 5, assessment is a multistep process that requires all program staff to be knowledgeable about aspects of the linguistic and cultural development of young DLLs (see above discussion) as well as the specific characteristics of the assessment instruments they use. Those responsible for conducting assessments will need to understand the stages of English-language development for young DLLs and the importance of home language development for overall language development and future academic achievement. They also need to be skilled in implementing authentic observational assessment methods that are aligned with curriculum goals and linking ongoing assessment results to individualized instruction (see chapter 8, Guideline 7; and Paper 5, Assessment [State Advisory Council on Early Learning and Care 2013] for further discussion on the types of observation and documentation as represented in the Desired Results Developmental Profile). Paper 5 (Assessment) includes figure 1, a step-by-step diagram, and table 1, a description of the assessment process for a teacher to use with young DLLs.

As consistently stated by the research (Paper 1 [Neuroscience Research], Paper 2 [Development Across Domains], and Paper 5 [Assessment]) and summarized in chapter 8, Guideline 7, it is inappropriate to expect young DLLs to learn and demonstrate knowledge and skills in the same manner as monolingual children. The unique linguistic, social, and cultural characteristics of young DLLs need to be considered when assessments are conducted and the results are interpreted. First, program staff members need to assess the proficiency level of a young DLL in the child's home language and in English-language development by using input from various sources, multiple sources of data collected over time, and a team that includes at least one member who is fluent in the child's home language (Paper 5, Assessment, in State Advisory Council on Early Learning and Care 2013).

When reviewing assessment results, teachers and other staff need to understand the limitations of standardized instruments used with young DLLs and how to use professional judgment when interpreting and applying the assessment results (table 1 in Paper 5, Assessment, includes a matrix for the language and literacy assessment of young DLLs). Assessment in early childhood education is a process that requires teams of individuals who all contribute specialized information about the child; therefore, teachers and other staff must be skilled in team collaboration. Finally, all staff members must be competent in working across cultures to establish effective working relationships with diverse families, who may hold distinct parenting values and beliefs (see Paper 4 for further discussion of collaboration with families with young DLLs).

Family Engagement

In Halgunseth, Jia, and Barbarin's research review in Paper 4, Family Engagement (State Advisory Council on Early Learning and Care 2013), the authors stress the importance of school–family partnerships to improved outcomes for children of all families, including those with DLLs. Although prior research has reported lower levels of school engagement among families with young DLLs, programs can implement several practices that can reduce the "language, cultural, and social networking barriers that keep DLL families from participating in their children's schools" (p. 135).These practices include hiring bilingual staff and translating information into the home language of DLL families (Halgunseth et al. 2009; Ramirez 2003) and helping families to recognize that their language and culture are strengths that should be shared at home and in the program. Because of the mixed messages DLL families may receive about their home language, some DLL family members may adopt the misconception that their children should replace their home language with English (Paper 4, Family Engagement, 136). Preschool program staff members need to emphasize to families with young DLLs that the home language is a strength and should be used in rich language interactions throughout the day and across all kinds of contexts. Further, programs should adopt a strengths-based approach that recognizes the linguistic and cultural contributions families with young DLLs make to their children's learning and development. "The entire program benefits when educators incorporate diverse cultures, languages, and talents of DLL families into the program's learning environment and curriculum" (Paper 4, Family Engagement, 144).

Programs can also work with families of young DLLs in targeted literacy activities in the home language (such as making family books), doing joint or intergenerational reading, purchasing or using books in the home language (if possible), narrating stories, and providing a collection of multilingual books to lend to families. Families can make significant positive contributions to young DLLs' oral language development by talking with their children about everyday experiences, explaining concepts and events, pointing out features of the natural environment, and doing guided television watching. All of these activities should occur in the language in which the family is most dominant or comfortable. Halgunseth and other researchers (State Advisory Council on Early Learning and Care 2013) also

recommend that "Bilingual and bicultural family liaisons, in particular, could serve as an important resource for enhancing communication between DLL families and early childhood programs, and thus maximize learning for young dual language learners" (Paper 4, Family Engagement, 42).

Family engagement practices that have been proven to be effective for DLL families and are recommended by the authors of Paper 4, Family Engagement, and integrated throughout chapter 8, Guideline 4, are as follows:

1. Addressing the bilingual/bicultural needs of DLL families

2. Developing warm and mutually respectful relationships with DLL families

3. Engaging in regular two-way communication

4. Approaching DLL families using a strengths-based framework

5. Engaging families to support their children's development at home

6. Utilizing community resources to support family engagement (see Paper 4, Family Engagement, for further detail and discussion)

Inclusion of Young Dual Language Learners Who Have Special Needs

In Paper 6 (Early Intervention and Special Needs), researchers Chen and Gutiérrez-Clellen (State Advisory Council on Early Learning and Care 2013) discuss recent findings that indicate young children with special needs can also learn more than one language and "there is no available evidence that limiting these children to one language will decrease language difficulties or that dual language learning will increase language delays and problems" (p. 211). Although methodological limitations of current studies and differences across samples make generalizations difficult, the available research suggests, "that speaking one language at home and English at school does not produce language delays or difficulties among children with a range of special needs. Moreover, this research indicates that a bilingual intervention approach actually facilitates these children's language development" (State Advisory Council on Early Learning and Care 2013, Paper 6, Early Intervention and Special Needs, 225).

In addition, research has found that many families of young DLLs value home language maintenance and bilingualism for their children. As with the other DLL research overview papers, Paper 6 (Early Intervention and Special Needs) recommends that programs encourage families to maintain their home language and learn strategies to support their children's language and early literacy development. The most significant conclusion of Paper 6 is "that emerging research suggests that children with a wide range of abilities and language difficulties can learn more than one language. This is a significant message to share with practitioners and families of young dual language learners with special needs" (p. 226). For a more complete discussion of this topic, see State Advisory Council on Early Learning and Care 2013, Paper 6 (Early Intervention and Special Needs).

Support for the Transition to Kindergarten

Young DLLs who benefit from the classroom, family engagement, assessment, and early intervention strategies described in this chapter and the six research overview papers (State Advisory Council on Early Learning and Care 2013) will be better prepared for kindergarten. The important cognitive, social, and language skills promoted by either a balanced English-and-home-language approach or one involving English-language development with home-language support will provide them with the critical foundations for a more academically oriented kindergarten program. Even so, it is also important for programs to carefully plan for successful transitions from preschool to kindergarten.

As with all children, preschool and kindergarten teachers of young DLLs need to schedule joint planning time to share information about the child, services provided, progress made, and any assessment information. In addition, children and families should have opportunities to visit the new setting or classroom and

meet kindergarten teachers. By listening to kindergarten teachers about what is expected and sharing information about their child and their language preferences, families can begin the process of successful transition.

Since a deeper understanding of the language, culture, and family background of young DLLs is critical in designing effective instruction and interactions, these transition activities are essential to the continued learning and achievement of DLLs.

Early Childhood Educator Competencies

The California Early Childhood Educator Competencies (California Department of Education and First 5 California 2012) provide standards for the knowledge, skills, and dispositions that early childhood educators, including those working with young DLLs, need in order to promote young children's learning and development. The Early Childhood Educator Competencies are an integral part of a comprehensive system that includes the early learning foundations for infants, toddlers, and preschoolers and the curriculum frameworks established by the California Department of Education. The competencies inform early childhood educators as they pursue study in institutions of higher education, provide guidance for working toward ECE credentials and certifications, and establish standards for the knowledge, skills, and dispositions that early childhood educators need to support young children's learning and development in all program types. Since qualified and effective teachers are one of the most important features of high-quality early education for young DLLs (and most California preschool classrooms include young DLLs), it is imperative that all early childhood educators in California are qualified to meet the needs of children from culturally and linguistically diverse backgrounds.

As described in chapter 8, Guideline 9, these competencies can be learned through effective preservice or in-service education, professional development activities, and continuous learning experiences such as mentorships, individual consultations, and coaching. A focus on improving practices and outcomes for young DLLs needs to be systematic, continuous, and of the highest priority. Programs need to provide ongoing professional development to staff on features of effective programming for preschool DLLs that is drawn from theory and supported by research. Topics include the following:

- The role of home language development in English-language development during the early years
- Stages of English-language development during the preschool years
- Early literacy development for young DLLs
- Developmental consequences of bilingualism for young children
- Effective teaching strategies for young DLLs
- Early intervention strategies for young DLLs with special needs
- Cross-cultural competence
- Assessment strategies for DLLs
- Interpretation and application of assessment results
- Engaging families from culturally and linguistically diverse backgrounds
- Reflective practices and teaching dispositions

Closing Thoughts

In summary, this chapter highlights the important findings from the six research overview papers to provide specific program and instructional recommendations for preschool DLLs. The research conclusions, as well as, the clearly stated positions of the California Department of Education, reinforce the value of promoting bilingualism during the preschool years. As cited in the opening of this chapter, the *California Preschool Curriculum Framework, Volume 1*, states, "Being exposed to two or more languages at a young age is a gift. It is a gift because children who are able to learn through two or more languages benefit cognitively, socially, and emotionally" (CDE 2010, 224). Paper 3 (Program Elements and Teaching Practices) states that these recommendations "represent the best of the knowledge we possess for educating young dual language learners. Programs designed around these elements are the most likely to provide the strongest possible foundation for children's success in kindergarten and into their schooling careers" (State Advisory Council on Early Learning and Care 2013, 110).

References

California Department of Education (CDE). 2008. *California Preschool Learning Foundations, Volume 1*. Sacramento: California Department of Education.

———. 2009. *Preschool English Learners: Principles and Practices to Promote Language, Literacy, and Learning*. 2nd ed. Sacramento: California Department of Education.

———. 2010. *California Preschool Curriculum Framework, Volume 1*. Sacramento: California Department of Education.

California Department of Education and First 5 California. 2012. *California Early Childhood Educator Competencies*. Sacramento: California Department of Education.

Espinosa, L. M. 2006. "Young English Language Learners in the U.S." *PAT (Parents as Teachers) News*. Fall 2006.

———. 2013. *Challenging Common Myths About Young English-Language Learners*. 2nd ed. (PK–3 Policy Brief No. 8.) New York: Foundation for Child Development.

Halgunseth, L. C., A. Peterson, D. R. Stark, and S. Moodie. 2009. *Family Engagement, Diverse Families, and Early Childhood Education Programs: An Integrated Review of the Literature*. http://www.naeyc.org/files/naeyc/file/ecprofessional/EDF_Literature%20 Review.pdf (accessed July 14, 2014).

Ramirez, F. 2003. "Dismay and Disappointment: Parental Involvement of Latino Immigrant Parents." *The Urban Review* 35 (2): 93–110.

State Advisory Council on Early Learning and Care. 2013. *California's Best Practices for Young Dual Language Learners: Research Overview Papers*. Sacramento: California Department of Education. http://www.cde.ca.gov/sp/cd/ce/documents/dllresearchpapers.pdf (accessed July 14, 2014).

Further Reading

Beltrán, E. 2012. "Preparing Young Latino Children for School Success: Best Practices in Assessments." *Issue Brief 23*. Washington, DC: National Council of La Raza (NCLR).

———. 2012. "Preparing Young Latino Children for School Success: Best Practices in Family Engagement." *Issue Brief 24*. Washington, DC: National Council of La Raza (NCLR).

———. 2012. "Preparing Young Latino Children for School Success: Best Practices in Language Instruction." *Issue Brief 25*. Washington, DC: National Council of La Raza (NCLR).

———. 2012. "Preparing Young Latino Children for School Success: Best Practices in Professional Development." *Issue Brief 22*. Washington, DC: National Council of La Raza (NCLR).

Bridges, M., and N. Dagys. 2012. "Who Will Teach Our Children? Building a Qualified Early Childhood Workforce to Teach English-Language Learners." *New Journalism on Latino Children*. Berkeley: Institute of Human Development, University of California.

Bridges, M., R. Anguiano, and B. Fuller. 2012. "Advancing the Language Skills of Young Latino Children. Fresh Evidence: What Works." *New Journalism on Latino Children*. Berkeley: Institute of Human Development, University of California.

Education Writers Association; National Panel on Latino Children and Schooling. 2009. "The Cultural Strengths of Latino Families: Firm Scaffolds for Children and Youth." *New Journalism on Latino Children*. Berkeley: Institute of Human Development, University of California.

Espinosa, L. M. 2008. "Challenging Common Myths About Young English Language Learners." *Foundation for Child Development Policy Brief, Advancing PK–3*. No. 8.

Killen, M., A. Rutland, and M. D. Ruok. 2011. "Promoting Equity, Tolerance, and Justice in Childhood." *Society for Research in Child Development Social Policy Report* 25 (4): 1–33.

Lopez, M., M. Zepeda, and O. Medina. 2012. *Dual Language Learner Teacher Competencies (DLLTC) Report*. Los Angeles: Alliance for a Better Community.

National Center on Cultural and Linguistic Responsiveness. Office of Head

Start. http://eclkc.ohs.acf.hhs.gov/hslc/tta-system/cultural-linguistic (accessed June 9, 2014).

The Importance of Home Language Series: *The Benefits of Being Bilingual*. http://eclkc.ohs.acf.hhs.gov/hslc/tta-system/cultural-linguistic/docs/benefits-of-being-bilingual.pdf (accessed June 9, 2014). *Las ventajas de ser bilingüe*. http://eclkc.ohs.acf.hhs.gov/hslc/tta-system/cultural-linguistic/docs/benefits-of-being-bilingual-esp.pdf (accessed June 22, 2015).

———. *El lenguaje en el hogar y en la comunidad: para las familias*. The Importance of Home Language Series: *The Benefits of Being Bilingual*. http://eclkc.ohs.acf.hhs.gov/hslc/tta-system/cultural-linguistic/docs/benefits-of-being-bilingual.pdf (accessed June 9, 2014). *Las ventajas de ser bilingue*. http://eclkc.ohs.acf.hhs.gov/hslc/tta-system/cultural-linguistic/docs/benefits-of-being-bilingual-esp.pdf (accessed September 8, 2014).

———. *El lenguaje en el hogar y en la comunidad: para las familias*. http://eclkc.ohs.acf.hhs.gov/hslc/Espanol/aprendizaje/ncclr-esp/docs/language-at-home-families-espanol.pdf (accessed June 22, 2015).

———. *Language at Home and in the Community: For Teachers*. http://eclkc.ohs.acf.hhs.gov/hslc/tta-system/cultural-linguistic/fcp/docs/language-at-home-teachers-8-25.pdf (accessed June 29, 2015). *El lenguaje en el hogar y en la comunidad: para los muestros*. http://eclkc.ohs.acf.hhs.gov/hslc/Espanol/aprendizaje/ncclr-esp/docs/language-at-home-families-espanol.pdf (accessed June 22, 2015).

———. *The Gift of Language: For Families*. http://eclkc.ohs.acf.hhs.gov/hslc/tta-system/cultural-linguistic/docs/gift-of-language.pdf (accessed June 9, 2014) *El don del lenguaje*. http://eclkc.ohs.acf.hhs.gov/hslc/tta-system/cultural-linguistic/docs/gift-of-language-esp.pdf.

National Clearinghouse for English Language Acquisition and Language Instruction Educational Programs (NCELA). 2011. *Key Demographics & Practice Recommendations for Young English Learners, Task 5.3.1. Short Turnaround Report*. Washington, DC: George Washington University.

U.S. Department of Health and Human Services, Office of Head Start, Administration for Children and Families. 2008. *Dual Language Learning: What Does It Take? Head Start Dual Language Report*. Arlington, VA: Office of Head Start, Administration for Children and Families, U.S. Department of Health and Human Services.

———. 2011. *The Head Start Parent, Family, and Community Engagement Framework: Promoting Family Engagement and School Readiness, from Prenatal to Age 8*. Arlington, VA: U.S. Department of Health; and Human Services Administration for Children and Families, Office of Head Start.

Chapter 7
Using Technology and Interactive Media with Preschool-Age Children

Technology and interactive media are integral parts of modern life. The rapid development of technological devices such as computers, smartphones, tablets, and gaming systems has dramatically changed people's daily lives at home and at work. New technologies and **electronic media** provide tools for communication and social-networking, for searching and documenting information, and for learning and entertainment.

Children and Electronic Media

Young children are growing up surrounded by technology and electronic media. At least two-thirds of homes with children (birth to age six) have computers and Internet access (Gutnick et al. 2010; Roberts and Foehr 2008). Moreover, according to a national survey by Common Sense Media in 2011, 52 percent of young children (birth to age eight) have access to smartphones or tablets (Rideout 2011). Young children are active media users (Roberts and Foehr 2008). They acclimate with ease to digital devices and show confidence in using software (Clements and Sarama 2008). With the prevalence of technology and electronic media in their environment, young children are spending an increasing number of hours in front of **screen technologies**, particularly television, but also computers and other devices, with an average of 2.2 hours per day of screen time for children between the ages of two and five (Roberts and Foehr 2008). Children from low-income families, families with less education, and black, Hispanic, and rural families are less likely to have access to the newest technologies and to broadband connections to the Internet (U.S. Department of Commerce 2011). Inequality in access to technology has narrowed over the years, but the "digital divide" still exists (Roberts and Foehr 2008).

The pervasiveness of electronic media in the lives of many young children makes educators, parents, and advocates question the value of technology in children's development. Some electronic media such as certain television programs, videos, and DVDs are noninteractive and involve passive viewing. Other forms of electronic media such as software programs, applications, the Internet, e-books, and certain television programs facilitate active and creative use by young children. These latter forms are referred to as **interactive media** (NAEYC and FRC 2012). There is limited research on the impact of newer technology, such as computer software, handheld devices, interactive applications for mobile devices, and wireless technology, on children's development. Most of the research on the impact of media on young children has focused on television and video. Studies of infants and toddlers suggest that videos have no language benefits for infant and toddlers.

Young children learn much better from real-life experiences than from watching videos. Moreover, excessive exposure to electronic media may have a negative effect on attention development, particularly for children younger than two (Kirkorian, Wartella, and Anderson 2008). Research indicates that the impact of electronic media on older children depends on the age of children, the context in which they use media, the content of the media, and the amount of time they spend with screens (Kirkorian, Wartella, and Anderson 2008; Campaign for Commercial-Free Childhood, Alliance for Childhood, and Teachers Resisting Unhealthy Children's Entertainment 2012).

By age three, children can benefit from well-designed, age-appropriate electronic media, especially when a caring adult views the program with the child and is actively involved in the child's experience

(Bittman et al. 2011). Research emphasizes the importance of developmentally appropriate *content* being offered to children, whether on television or other interactive media software. Educational television programs that were designed around a curriculum with a specific goal to communicate academic or social skills were linked to various cognitive and academic enhancements, with potentially long-lasting effects (Fisch 2004). For example, research demonstrates a positive association between early exposure to *Sesame Street* television episodes and school readiness (Zill 2001). However, television and videos with entertainment content, particularly violent content, were associated with poor cognitive development and lower academic achievement (Kirkorian, Wartella, and Anderson 2008).

Studies of preschool children's computer play demonstrated that young children can use computers and software to support their learning. Children can understand, think about, and learn from their computer activity (Clements and Sarama 2008). Research has shown that in children's computer play with interactive media software there is a period of discovery, which is then followed by involvement, self-confidence, and creativity (Bergen 2008). Computer-play software can offer children various possibilities, including *practice* (self-directed repetition to achieve mastery), *pretense* (symbolic play in a "pretend to be" world), and *games* (challenge and competition, either with a peer, with oneself, or with an imaginary opponent) (Kafai 2006).

There is limited research on how educational computer software may enhance preschool children's academic-readiness skills. Some research suggests that software with an educational curriculum may have a positive influence on learning (Din and Calao 2001). Overall, studies indicate that, when used appropriately, technology and media can enhance children's cognitive and social abilities (Kirkorian, Wartella, and Anderson 2008). Even so, additional research is needed to confirm the positive outcome of technology on children's language and vocabulary, understanding of math concepts, self-regulation, and social-skills development (NAEYC and FRC 2012).

Technology and Interactive Media in the Preschool Environment

Technology has many uses in early childhood settings. On any given day, teachers may use technology to support children's learning, to record and document children's development, to expand their own knowledge in different areas, to maintain ongoing communication with families, and to link homes with school. The focus in this chapter is on the use of technology and interactive media in preschool settings for the purpose of supporting and enhancing children's learning.

A growing number of early childhood educators use technology and interactive media in their programs as tools to support children's learning and development (Wartella et al. 2010). In a recent survey by the Fred Rogers Center (Wartella et al. 2010) about technology in the lives of teachers and classrooms, nearly 60 percent of early childhood teachers reported having a computer, and 45 percent have computers with Internet access in their classrooms. More than half of the early childhood teachers indicated that children should be introduced to technology in the classroom between ages three and four, and about one-third of the teachers reported using computers with children on a daily basis (Wartella et al. 2010). With the increasing interest and use of technology in preschool settings, early childhood educators need guidance on how to use technology and interactive media wisely and effectively. Several important questions come to mind: *Which technology and media tools are effective tools for learning? In which domains of development can the use of technology be most effective? How do early childhood educators appropriately integrate technology and media into preschool settings? How can technology be used to support children's learning?*

A joint position statement issued in 2012 by the National Association for Education of Young Children (NAEYC) and the Fred Rogers Center (FRC) offers guidance. Based on research, the statement addresses both the opportunities and the challenges related to using technology and interactive media in early childhood programs. The following section presents key messages from the NAEYC/FRC posi-

tion statement on technology. A set of strategies consistent with the approach articulated in the position statement is provided to guide administrators and teachers in integrating technology and interactive media into preschool programs.

The Benefits and the Challenges of Using Technology and Interactive Media

Technology and interactive media have the potential to make many contributions to early childhood education. Technology can provide children with additional ways to explore, create, communicate, problem-solve, investigate, and learn. Computer technology, for example, offers young children a range of learning opportunities—from solving math problems to listening to interactive stories, taking a photo, recording a story, creating a digital book, making music, and engaging in other age-appropriate learning activities (Blagojevic et al. 2010). Many educational applications for young children are designed to help children develop skills and knowledge in specific domains, particularly in areas such as language, literacy, and mathematics (Buckleitner 2011). Such programs can provide individualized

learning opportunities for children. In mathematics, computer programs present children with tasks, give feedback, and help young children develop concepts and skills in areas such as counting, number relationships and operations, sorting and patterning, measurement, and geometry (Clements and Sarama 2008; McCarthy, Li, and Tiu 2012). In language and literacy, computer software can enhance vocabulary learning (Segers and Vermeer 2008) and support learning of listening, speaking, writing, and reading skills (Guernsey et al. 2012). Dual language learners can also use computers to enhance their home language and acquire English (Blagojevic et al. 2010; Nemeth 2009).

The use of technology can also enrich the science curriculum. Cameras and recording devices provide valuable educational experiences by allowing children to take photos and videos to document objects and events and track changes in objects and materials. Digital microscopes allow children to save images of objects they explore and to share and discuss such images with their peers. Robotics with manipulative motors and gears engage young children in designing their own robotic creations, providing them

with opportunities both to be creative engineers and to explore abstract mathematical and science concepts in concrete ways (Bers 2008).

The use of technology in preschool settings also creates opportunities for equitable access to technology tools and interactive media experiences for children from different economic backgrounds, including children in families with few resources and little or no access to the latest technologies (NAEYC and FRC 2012). Furthermore, technology has many potential benefits in supporting inclusive practices for children with disabilities or other special needs (Mulligan 2003). A variety of assistive and adaptive technologies (e.g., electronic communication boards, switch-activated toys, recordable devices) enhance children's participation and learning with peers. For example, a child who enjoys playing with bubbles can operate an electronic bubble-blower for other children to chase (Mistrett 2004). Another child can let a peer know which game she wants to play by indicating it on the electronic tablet that has photos taken by her teacher. By using assistive technology, early childhood educators can help children with disabilities or other special needs become more independent. Children with special needs can use tech-

nologies to support their ability to communicate and interact with others, move throughout the environment, manipulate objects, and participate in daily routines and educational activities.

Overall, effective uses of technology and interactive media can enhance and augment children's learning in different domains, extending children's access to new content. However, technology is effective only when used appropriately. Although the use of technology and interactive media provides programs with opportunities to enhance quality and optimize young children's development, early childhood educators should understand the limits of technology and be aware of the challenges of using technology and interactive media in the preschool environment. As stated in the NAEYC/FRC position statement, "Technology and interactive media are tools that can promote effective learning and development when they are used intentionally by early childhood educators, within the framework of developmentally appropriate practice, to support learning goals established for individual children" (NAEYC and FRC 2012, 5).

Technology and interactive media should only supplement, not replace, existing play-based materials and active play, engagement with other children, and face-to-face interactions with adults. Several professional and public health organizations have raised concerns about whether young children should have access to technology and screen media in early childhood programs (e.g., Campaign for a Commercial-Free Childhood, Alliance for Childhood, and Teachers Resisting Unhealthy Children's Entertainment 2012). The American Academy of Pediatrics (2011) recommends that programs limit children's exposure to screen time and discourage any use of screen media for children under the age of two. This chapter follows the recommendations of the NAEYC and the Fred Rogers Center (2012) and is aligned with the public health community in discouraging the use of screen media for children under the age of 24 months in early childhood programs. Such guidance for educators working with infants and toddlers may change in the future as more research on very young children's active use of interactive media and its effect on children's learning and development continues to emerge (e.g., Zack et al. 2013).

Monitoring the content of interactive media is as important as setting limits on the time young children spend with technology. Although there are valuable software, Web sites, and other forms of interactive media for young children, some have limited educational value or may include content that is not safe or appropriate for children. The challenge for early childhood educators is "to make informed choices that maximize learning opportunities for children while managing screen time and mediating the potential for misuse and overuse of screen media" (NAEYC and FRC 2012, 3). Educators should have the knowledge, skills, and experience necessary to select and use technology tools and interactive media that suit the age and developmental level of children and can be integrated effectively in the environment (NAEYC and FRC 2012).

The following guidelines identify key considerations for programs and teachers selecting, evaluating, integrating, and using technology in preschool programs.

Selecting Technology and Interactive Media to Enhance Children's Learning

The rapid development of technology platforms, including computers, laptops, multitouch tablets, and other handheld devices, and the growing selection of available educational applications, Web sites, and software present educators with many choices for integrating technology into the preschool environment. However, technology and media-based products may vary widely in quality. Intentionality is important. Thoughtful, advance planning is essential for a responsible investment in technology in early childhood settings. Early childhood educators should apply their expertise and knowledge of child development in selecting appropriate technology and media for the classroom in the same way that they select any other instructional materials (NAEYC and FRC 2012). Educators should take the time to evaluate and select technology, to observe children's use of the materials, and to make appropriate adoptions based on their observations. The Fred Rogers Center (2012) proposed a framework for quality in digital media (FRC 2012), recommending that educators take into account the *child*, the *content*, and the *context* in the selection of digital media for young children.

- **Consider children's developmental level, interests, abilities, and cultural and linguistic backgrounds.** Teachers must be intentional in selecting the technology and interactive media they offer children in their classroom. In selecting appropriate technology and interactive media, educators make decisions that are informed by developmentally appropriate teaching practices, which means that early childhood educators consider the age, developmental level, needs, interests, linguistic backgrounds, and abilities of individual children in the group (NAEYC and FRC 2012).

- **Ensure equitable access to technology and interactive media experiences.** In selecting technology and interactive media, educators provide opportunities for all children to participate and have access to these learning tools. Educators should consider the cultural and linguistic backgrounds of the children in their classrooms. Technology resources can provide access to children's home language and culture, especially when there are no other ways to obtain such information (NAEYC and FRC 2012). For example, children can listen to electronic books in their home language, record songs and stories, and create digital stories in their home language and English (Blagojevic et al. 2010). Educators can collaborate with family members and colleagues who speak children's home language to gain access to appropriate interactive media in children's home language.

Materials and equipment selected for children with disabilities or other special needs should be evaluated. Adaptive and assistive technologies are available to support individual children in their classrooms. Programs should consider the level of technology necessary and the child's individual needs to ensure that the technology is best suited to the child's unique disabilities and to the demands of the environment (Mulligan 2003). Not all assistive devices are necessarily "high tech" or custom designed for a particular child. In fact, the Individuals with Disabilities Education Act defines an **assistive technology device** as any item, piece of equipment, or product system, whether acquired commercially off the shelf, modified, or customized, that is used to increase, maintain, or improve functional capabilities of a child with a disability (Mistrett 2004).

- **Identify the underlying objectives of the technology.** Most electronic media targeted at preschoolers are intended to entertain rather than to teach. Technology in the preschool environment should be used only for educational activities. In evaluating any software programs, applications, or other forms of interactive media, educators should be able to identify the overall goals or purpose of the product: Is it to educate or to entertain? Is it interactive? Is it to develop particular skills, to introduce children to new information, or maybe a combination

of these (FRC 2012; Campaign for Commercial-Free Childhood, Alliance for Childhood, and Teachers Resisting Unhealthy Children's Entertainment 2012)? Understanding the intent of a digital program and the learning goals for different children in the program should guide educators' intentional decisions in selecting materials of interactive media (FRC 2012).

- **Evaluate the quality of the content.** First and foremost, educators should evaluate the quality of the content to ensure that the use of such materials would not harm young children's overall development or well-being in any way (NAEYC and FRC 2012; FRC 2012). Interactive media products can be used as tools to fulfill the needs of individual children and to expand children's access to new content in areas of interest to them. In the selection process, program administrators and teachers should have information and resources regarding the nature of these tools and the implications for use with children. Program administrators and teachers should also have hands-on opportunities to explore and directly experience the technology that is being considered for use with children. Educators can apply their expertise and knowledge of child development to ensure that digital materials are developmentally and culturally appropriate for the children in the group. They should examine the educational content, format, and features and carefully consider any implicit messages communicated during the use of the software/application. Some undesirable messages (e.g., stereotypes, negative images or actions) may be biased and fail to promote social and emotional understanding in the early years (Tsantis, Bewick, and Thouvenelle 2003).

- **Select technology and interactive media that support children's creativity, exploration, and problem solving.** In selecting activities with technology and interactive media, early educators should ask themselves: *Does it encourage children to explore, to think, to experiment and predict, to be creative, and to problem-*

solve? Does it offer a range of experiences and a high level of interactivity? Is it open-ended or focused on skills? Experiences with technology and other media that engage children in redundant practice and rote learning or involve passive use by children are not desirable. Effective technology and media empower children by giving them control, offering challenges through "leveled" experiences, and providing them with feedback and adaptive scaffolds (Clements and Sarama 2008).

- **Use the best available evidence in the selection process.** More research is needed to understand what young children are able to do with different digital devices and to assess the short- and long-term effects of new technologies on children's learning. Educators are encouraged to make their decisions about the quality of interactive media products based on the best available evidence for any given product (FRC 2012).

Integrating and Using Technology in the Preschool Environment

Once the desired software or appropriate technology devices for the program are selected, educators should apply their expertise and knowledge of child development to make thoughtful decisions on how to introduce and integrate the selected forms of technology into the learning environment. The teacher's role is critical in ensuring that technology is implemented in ways that serve the teaching goals and support children's learning appropriately and effectively.

- **Technology and interactive media are used within the framework of developmentally appropriate practice.** Developmentally appropriate practice encourages hands-on exploration; empowers children to reflect, question, and create; and honors the value of relationships between children and the adults in their lives (NAEYC 2009). Professional knowledge of developmentally appropriate practice informs and guides decision making about how to introduce and integrate any form of technology and

interactive media into early childhood programs. Technology and media should not replace preschool activities such as real-life exploration, physical activity, social interactions, outdoor and indoor play, and arts. Instead, they should be used as additional tools to encourage children's problem solving, exploration, and creativity. They can also support children's relationships with both adults and their peers and foster children's autonomy (NAEYC and FRC 2012; Donohue and Schomburg 2012; Nemeth and Simon 2012), particularly for some children with disabilities (Mistrett 2004).

- **Technology and interactive media are integrated into the environment, curriculum, and daily routines** (NAEYC and FRC 2012). True integration of technology and media into the preschool environment involves the use of different technology resources throughout the classroom. No period is set aside in the daily schedule for "computer time," when technology and media are used as isolated activities. Technology and interactive media are woven into the fabric of the day and are used as tools for learning, rather than as the focus or the goal of a learning activity. Technology is one of many ways to support curriculum goals and needs, and the program offers a balance of activities to support children's development in all domains of learning. In using a particular application or software, teachers should consider how it supports objectives for individual children in the group, how it fits into the classroom's current curriculum project or theme of study, and how it extends other activities in ways not possible otherwise (Nemeth and Simon 2012).

- **Time spent with technology and media is limited.** Setting limits on the time young children spend with technology and interactive media is important. As previously indicated, the public health community discourages the use of passive screen media for children under two years of age and recommends limited screen time daily for children older than two (American Academy of Pediatrics

2011). Some of the public health concern is that the overuse of media takes time away from other activities that involve physical exercise. Sedentary activities are potentially a risk factor for childhood obesity (Wartella and Heintz 2007). The position statement by the NAEYC/FRC points to the following recommendation in the *Early Childhood Obesity Prevention Policies:* "child care [and preschool] settings limit screen time to fewer than 30 minutes per day for children in half day programs or less than one hour per day for those in full day programs (Birch, Parker, and Burns 2011)." Teachers play a critical role in establishing clear boundaries on the use of technology and screen time in the preschool setting. They are also encouraged to share information with families on how to promote children's healthy use of technology at home (Campaign for a Commercial-Free Childhood, Alliance for Childhood, and Teachers Resisting Unhealthy Children's Entertainment 2012).

- **The use of technology and interactive media facilitates social interactions and relationship building.** Effective use of technology and interactive media in the classroom environment allows joint engagement, specifically viewing and participation by both children and adults and children and their peers (NAEYC and FRC 2012). Studies on the social dimension of preschool children's computer play found that preschoolers observe each other while playing, comment on others' actions, share and help with software-related problems, and have conflicts over turn-taking (Heft and Swaminathan 2002). The computer and other digital devices should be located in spaces that allow for joint engagement of a group of children. Some children may select technology such as the computer because it is familiar or even as a way of avoiding interaction. Careful observation is needed to monitor the use of technology and determine individual appropriate use. Effective use of technology and interactive media can promote communication and collaboration

among children (Wright 1994). It often provides the context for information sharing, language development, and collaborative decision making (Tsantis, Bewick, and Thouvenelle 2003). Tech-savvy children may also become computer mentors for their peers (Blagojevic et al. 2010).

- **Teachers provide support while children use technology and interactive media.** As with any learning activities, teachers play an important role in facilitating children's involvement with technology and media. The teachers introduce children to the computer or another device (e.g., digital camera, printer, touch-screen), and explain how it works. They observe what individual children do and learn about children's ability to use technology. Children vary in the ability to use technology and interactive media. Teachers also give children time to freely explore new technology tools, model appropriate use of technology, and help children become familiar with any new software activity. They establish rules and routines with children to guide appropriate handling and use of computer and other technological devices (Blagojevic et al. 2010; Campaign for a Commercial-Free Childhood, Alliance for Childhood, and Teachers Resisting Unhealthy Children's Entertainment 2012). During technology-related activities, teachers carefully observe and document what children do and assess children's learning. Teachers identify problems or opportunities for teachable moments, extending the media experience to other learning opportunities, and facilitating the experience through language-rich interactions. In addition, teachers determine when the child is ready to progress to the next level of knowledge or skill development (FRC 2012). They consider children's varying abilities to control and operate technology and media and support children's "technology-handling" skills, as needed. Teachers make appropriate adaptations, based on their observations, to promote positive outcomes for individual children.

Training and Professional Development Opportunities

Teachers are the key to effective educational use of technology (Clements and Samara 2008; Tsantis, Bewick, and Thouvenelle 2003). They expose children to technology and model appropriate and safe uses of technology. Teachers' knowledge and competence in using technology have a direct impact on how effectively teachers integrate technology and interactive media into the early learning environment. There is evidence that the more support teachers receive in using computers, the more the children learn (Clements and Sarama 2008). Teachers need information and resources about the nature of new technology tools in order to understand how to use them effectively with young children.

It is essential that programs provide teachers with access to training and affordable opportunities for professional development to gain knowledge of technology and related skills (Guernsey 2012). Some features of effective professional development in early childhood educational technology include hands-on training, ample practice, interactions with learning partners (communities of practice), and opportunities for ongoing conversations and reflections about practice with new technology (Clements and Sarama 2008). Teachers can also learn from technology workshops in the community (e.g., local library), online tutorials, and colleagues, a coach or mentor, and other members of their community.

With training and experience, educators develop "digital literacy"—the knowledge and competence to use technology, the ability to think critically about the use of technology and interactive media with young children, and to evaluate technology's impact on children's learning and development (NAEYC and FRC 2012). Two centers that opened recently provide resources to early childhood teachers on integrating technology into preschool settings: the Technology in Early Childhood Center at the Erikson Institute and the Early Learning Environment established by the Fred Rogers Center (http://teccenter.erikson.edu/ [accessed July 29, 2014]). In California the SEEDS Workgroup on Early Education Technology developed training materials and information on infants, toddlers, and preschool children with disabilities (http://www.scoe.net/seeds/resources/at/at.html [accessed July 29, 2014]). Preschool programs should encourage teachers' ongoing professional development to gain skills and knowledge of digital literacy. With such knowledge, teachers become prepared to make informed decisions about how to effectively and appropriately select, evaluate, use, and integrate technology in early childhood programs.

References

American Academy of Pediatrics. 2011. "Policy Statement—Media Use by Children Younger than 2 Years." *Pediatrics* 128 (5): 1–7.

Bergen, D. 2008. "New Technologies in Early Childhood: Partners in Play?" In *Contemporary Perspectives on Science and Technology in Early Childhood Education*, edited by O. N. Saracho and B. Spodek. Charlotte, NC: Information Age.

Bers, M. U. 2008. "Engineers and Storytellers: Using Robotic Manipulatives to Develop Technological Fluency in Early Childhood." In *Contemporary Perspectives on Science and Technology in Early Childhood Education*, edited by O. N. Saracho and B. Spodek. Charlotte, NC: Information Age.

Birch, L. L., L. Parker, and A. Burns, eds. 2011. *Early Childhood Obesity Prevention Policies*. Washington, DC: National Academies Press.

Bittman, M., L. Rutherford, J. Brown, and L. Unsworth. 2011. "Digital Natives? New and Old Media and Children's Outcomes." *Australian Journal of Education*: 5 (2): 161–75.

Blagojevic, B., S. Chevalier, A. MacIsaac, L. Hitchcock, and B. Frechette. 2010. "Young Children and Computers: Storytelling and Learning in a Digital Age." *Teaching Young Children* 3 (5): 1–5.

Buckleitner, W. 2011. "Setting Up a Multi-Touch Preschool." *Children's Technology Review* 19 (3): 5–9.

Campaign for a Commercial-Free Childhood, Alliance for Childhood, and Teachers Resisting Unhealthy Children's Entertainment. 2012. *Facing the Screen Dilemma: Young Children, Technology and Early Education*. Boston: Campaign for Commercial-Free Childhood; New York: Alliance for Childhood.

Clements, D. H., and J. Sarama. 2008. "Mathematics and Technology: Supporting Learning for Students and Teachers. In *Contemporary Perspectives on Science and Technology in Early Childhood Education*, edited by O. N. Saracho and B. Spodek. Charlotte, NC: Information Age.

Din, F. S., and J. Calao. 2001. "The Effects of Playing Educational Video Games on Kindergarten Achievement." *Child Study Journal* 31 (2): 95–102.

Donohue, C., and R. Schomburg. 2012. *Teaching with Technology: Guidelines from the NAEYC/FRC Position Statement*. PowerPoint Presentation at the NAEYC annual conference on November 9. Erikson TEC Center. http:// teccenter.erikson.edu/files/NAEYC_ Position_Statement_slides_11_12.pdf (accessed April 9, 2014).

Fisch, S. M. 2004. *Children's Learning from Educational Television: Sesame Street and Beyond*. Mahwah, NJ: Lawrence Erlbaum Associates.

Fred Rogers Center for Early Learning and Children's Media at Saint Vincent College (FRC). 2012. *A Framework for Quality in Digital Media for Young Children: Considerations for Parents, Educators, and Media Creators*. Latrobe, PA: Fred Rogers Center for Early Learning and Children's Media at Saint Vincent College.

Guernsey, L. 2012. "Technology in Early Education: Building Platforms for Connections and Content that Strengthen Families and Promote Access in School." *The Progress of Education Reform* 13 (4). Education Commission of the States.

Guernsey, L., M. Levine, C. Chiong, and Maggie Severns. 2012. *Pioneering Literacy in the Digital Wild West: Empowering Parents and Educators*. Washington, DC: The Campaign for Grade-Level Reading.

Gutnick, A. V., M. Robb, L. Takeuchi, and J. Kotter. 2010. *Always Connected: The New Digital Media Habits of Young Children*. New York: The Joan Ganz Cooney Center at Sesame Workshop.

Heft, T. M., and S. Swaminathan. 2002. "Computer-Assisted Instruction of Early Academic Skills." *Topics in Early Childhood Education* 20 (3): 145–58.

Kafai, Y. 2006. "Play and Technology: Revised Realities and Potential Perspectives." In *Play from Birth to Twelve: Contexts, Perspectives and Meanings*, 2nd ed., edited by D. P. Fromberg and D. Bergen. New York: Routledge.

Kirkorian, H. L., E. A. Wartella, and D. R. Anderson. 2008. "Media and Young Children's Learning." *Future Child* 18 (1): 39–61.

McCarthy, B., L. Li, and M. Tiu. 2012. *PBS Kids Mathematics Transmedia Suites in Preschool Homes: A Report to the CPB-PBS Ready to Learn Initiative.* San Francisco, CA: WestEd.

Mistrett, S. G. 2004. "Assistive Technology Helps Young Children with Disabilities Participate in Daily Activities." *Technology in Action* 1 (4).

Mulligan, S. A. 2003. "Assistive Technology: Supporting the Participation of Children with Disabilities." *Young Children* 58 (6): 50–51.

National Association for the Education of Young Children (NAEYC). 2009. *Developmentally Appropriate Practice in Early Childhood Programs Serving Children from Birth through Age 8: Position Statement.* Washington, DC: National Association for the Education of Young Children.

National Association for the Education of Young Children (NAEYC) and Fred Rogers Center for Early Learning and Children's Media at Saint Vincent College (FRC). 2012. *Technology and Interactive Media as Tools in Early Childhood Programs Serving Children from Birth through Age 8.* A Joint Position Statement. Washington, DC: National Association for the Education of Young Children; Latrobe, PA: Fred Rogers Center for Early Learning and Children's Media at Saint Vincent College.

Nemeth, K. N. 2009. *Many Languages, One Classroom: Teaching Dual and English Language Learners.* Silver Spring, MD: Gryphon House.

Nemeth, K., and F. Simon. 2012. "Technology DAP-Style! Top Questions Answered–A TEC Track Session." Webinar presentation.

Rideout, V. 2011. *Zero to Eight: Children's Media Use in America.* Los Angeles: Common Sense Media.

Roberts, D. F., and U. G. Foehr. 2008. "Trends in Media Use." *Future Child* 18 (1): 11–37.

Segers E., and A. Vermeer. 2008. "Vocabulary Learning by Computer in Kindergarten: The Possibilities of Interactive Vocabulary Books." In *Contemporary Perspectives on Science and Technology in Early Childhood Education*, edited by O. N. Saracho and B. Spodek. Charlotte, NC: Information Age.

Tsantis, L. A., C. J. Bewick, and S. Thouvenelle. 2003. "Examining Some Common Myths About Computer Use In the Early Years." *Beyond the Journal: Young Children on the Web.* November.

U.S. Department of Commerce. 2011. *Exploring the Digital Nation: Computer and Internet Use at Home.* Washington, DC: Economics and Statistics Administration and the National Telecommunications and Information Administration.

Wartella, E. A., and K. Heintz. 2007. *Young Children and Media: A Snapshot of Public Interest, Public Concerns, and Children's Media Organizations.* Latrobe, PA: Fred Rogers Center for Early Learning and Children's Media at Saint Vincent College.

Wartella, E., R. L. Schomburg, A. R. Lauricella, M. Robb, and R. Flynn. 2010. *Technology in the Lives of Teachers and Classrooms: Survey of Classroom Teachers and Family Child Care Providers.* Latrobe, PA: Fred Rogers Center for Early Learning and Children's Media at Saint Vincent College.

Wright, J. L. 1994. "Listen to the Children: Observing Young Children's Discoveries with the Microcomputer. In *Young Children: Active Learners in a Technological Age*, edited by J. L. Wright and D. D. Shade. Washington, DC: National Association for the Education of Young Children.

Zack, E., P. Gerhardstein, A. N. Meltzoff, and R. Barr. 2013. "15-Month-Olds' Transfer of Learning Between Touch Screen and Real-World Displays: Language Cues and Cognitive Loads." *Scandinavia Journal of Psychology* 54 (1): 20–25.

Zill, N. 2001. "Does Sesame Street Enhance School Readiness? Evidence from a National Survey of Children." In *G Is for Growing: Thirty Years of Re-*

search on Children and Sesame Street, edited by S. M. Fisch and R. T. Truglio. Mahwah, NJ: Lawrence Erlbaum Associates.

Further Reading

Center on Media and Child Health http://www.cmch.tv/ (accessed July 29, 2014). Resources related to understanding and responding to the effects of media on the physical, mental, and social health of children.

Children's Technology Review http://childrenstech.com (accessed July 29, 2014). Summarizes products and trends in children's interactive media.

Fred Rogers Center for Early Learning and Children's Media http://www.fredrogerscenter.org/resources/database/ (accessed July 29, 2014). Key resources related to early learning, early childhood development, and children's media.

Joan Ganz Cooney Center at Sesame Workshop http://www.joanganzcooneycenter.org (accessed July 29, 2014). Advances children's learning in a digital age (research, initiatives, blogs, events).

NAEYC Technology and Young Children Interest Forum http://www.techandyoungchildren.org/children.html (accessed July 29, 2014). Information and resources for using technology with young children in a center or classroom setting.

SEEDS Workgroup on Early Education Technology (SWEET) http://www.scoe.net/seeds/resources/at/principles.html (accessed July 29, 2014). Resources on assistive technology for young children with disabilities, to enhance children's communication and learning.

Tec Center at Erikson Institute: Technology in Early Childhood http://www.teccenter.erikson.edu/ (accessed July 29, 2014). Empowers early childhood educators to use technology thoughtfully and appropriately in early childhood settings.

Part Three:
Program Guidelines

Chapter 8
Guidelines for Operating Preschool Programs

This chapter provides detailed guidance for administrators and teachers in several areas of high-quality preschool programming. After the introduction to each guideline, specific practices of effective programs and teachers are listed. Some redundancy exists across guidelines in the lists of best practices; this redundancy or overlapping content is intentional, as many practices pertain to multiple guideline areas. For a list of all the guidelines, please see appendix F.

In efforts to align the current document with the California Early Learning and Development System, the practices listed are consistent with the content and order of the *California Early Childhood Educator Competencies* (California Department of Education and First 5 California 2012). Please note that the numbering of the guidelines does not indicate an order of importance, as all guidelines are considered essential to high-quality preschool programming.

Guideline 1: Aspiring to Be a High-Quality Program

High-quality preschool programs are thoughtfully designed and carefully implemented to meet the needs of all children in their programs. California's young learners are culturally, linguistically, and socioeconomically diverse. Effective program administrators are responsive to the unique needs of the children and families served in their program by establishing mutually respectful relationships with families and maintaining deep interest in each child and his or her family. They support teachers in efforts to establish collaborative relationships with families so that teachers can organize the preschool environment to be responsive to the unique needs of children in their classrooms. High-quality programs sup-port the full range of abilities and potential of young dual language learners and are intentional about language policies and specific program approaches that support these goals. Responsive programs support teachers in creating the appropriate learning environments for children with disabilities or other special needs. However, because programs are "constantly changing—taking on new children, new families, new teachers, and new leaders"—maintaining program quality is a continually evolving task. Aspiring to be a high-quality preschool program involves engaging in a process of continuous program improvement. Program administrators and teachers might ask the following questions:

- What do we know about our preschool children and families, and how are we responsive to their developmental, linguistic, and cultural strengths and needs?

- How else might we gain feedback from families about how to better meet their needs and the needs of their children?

- How can we use a variety of sources (e.g., teacher observations, teacher–child conversations, samples of children's work/performance, children's reflections on documentation, direct assessment, parent reports, and input from specialized service providers) to inform program planning and improvement?

1.1 High-quality programs engage in continuous program improvement.

High-quality programs are accountable for meeting quality standards; they establish goals to meet quality standards. Many programs must meet specific requirements set by funding or regulatory agencies. They may also be required to document their effectiveness through a designated set of measures. In California, the California Department of Education's Early Education and Support Division (CDE/EESD, formerly the Child Development Division) implements a statewide assessment of children in state-funded programs using the Desired Results System for Children and Families. Frequently, programs on a path of continuous improvement and program excellence will choose a system of accountability, such as accreditation through the National Association for the Education of Young Children (NAEYC) or participation in a quality rating and improvement system, in addition to the required system.

High-quality programs actively engage staff, family members, and community stakeholders, sharing program evaluation information and goals for program improvement with them. Programs set annual goals for program improvement, provide resources and support for meeting objectives, and assess progress toward achieving program goals.

Five key ways in which programs can engage in continuous program improvement are to establish a program philosophy, implement a program-planning process, develop program policies and procedures that are informed by family input, implement a plan for continuous program improvement, and make use of external evaluation to inform program planning.

Program Philosophy

Programs

- Provide leadership to early childhood programs in articulating a statement of philosophy and implementing philosophy-driven practices.

- Recommend elements to include in the program's statement of philosophy regarding child development, learning and curriculum, families, diversity, and inclusion.

- Strive to build staff composition reflective of families and the community.

- Collaborate with staff, colleagues, families, early childhood educators, regula-

tory agencies, and community leaders to regularly review the program's statement of philosophy.

- Lead the program in ongoing analysis of the philosophy and its implications for practice.

- Describe the program's philosophy to prospective staff, colleagues, families, funding agencies, and the community.

Program-Planning Process

Programs

- Develop methods that allow early childhood educators, families, staff, colleagues, regulatory agencies, and community leaders to participate in the program-planning process.

- Provide leadership to early childhood educators on the principles of effective program planning and explain the complex array of funding streams that support early childhood education settings.

- Lead staff, colleagues, families, early childhood educators, regulatory agencies, community leaders, the program's board of directors, funding agencies, and other individuals, as appropriate, in program planning—including the recruitment and enrollment of children.

- Involve staff, colleagues, families, early childhood educators, regulatory agencies, community leaders, the program's board of directors, funding agencies, and others who contribute to the program in setting annual goals for program improvement; provide resources and support for meeting objectives; and assess progress toward achieving program goals.

Program Policies and Procedures

Programs

- Initiate and contribute to discussions with professionals, families, regulatory agencies, policymakers, and other service providers to design policies that support high-quality services in early childhood education settings, including their own.

- Help to develop flexible systems that allow staff, colleagues, and families to participate in the creation of program procedures.

- Promote policies that enhance the quality of program components.

- Develop, document, assess, and monitor program policies and procedures for effectiveness, appropriateness, and compliance with regulations and requirements.

- Collaborate with families, staff, and colleagues to adapt policies and procedures to meet individual child and family requirements, as appropriate.

- Provide professional development to staff and colleagues on policies and procedures.

Continuous Program Improvement

Programs

- Apply organizational theory and leadership styles—as they relate to early care and education settings—to the process of program evaluation.

- Develop policies and standards, including language policies for dual language learners, to promote positive outcomes for all children.

- Examine the effectiveness of policies and procedures for addressing concerns about a child's development, behavior, or other area, such as health.

- Plan and implement a program evaluation and improvement plan to promote positive outcomes for all children and families.

- Maintain a high-quality program based on funding agency requirements and standards.

- Integrate learning and development standards into program planning.

- Promote high-quality standards and practices among staff and colleagues, families, the program's board of directors, local leaders, and other individuals who contribute to the ongoing operation of the program.

- Utilize internal data (staff surveys, parent surveys, child outcomes) in program improvement discussions.

External Program Evaluation

Programs

- Provide resources to colleagues and engage families in conversation about the value of program evaluation and certification for continuous program improvement.

- Analyze the benefit and limitations of pursuing relationships with organizations that offer evaluation services for the purpose of program improvement and certification.

1.2 **Programs and administrators use knowledge of child development to create and implement policies and practices that support children's development in all domains.**

Being informed about child development and using understanding of child development to guide policies and practices are essential to supporting children's positive developmental outcomes. In particular, understanding developmental theory and research, all developmental domains, their interrelatedness, and other factors that contribute to development is important. Additionally, having specific knowledge of preschool development and learning, the importance of learning through play, and individualizing developmental expectations is central to supporting staff members so they can provide appropriate learning experiences for young children in the preschool program.

To make the important instructional enhancements to the learning environment for dual language learners, all staff members will need to understand the layered and culturally rooted influences on children's development. It is important for staff to understand how a child learns a first language and then a second one during the preschool years and how to promote development in both. Knowledge of the similarities and differences between monolingual learners and dual language learners is important when children's rates of progress are considered. Thus understanding general child development and

the variations for dual language learners is an important qualification for staff.

A deep understanding of child development will also contribute to knowledge of individual differences, which will enable administrators to support staff members who are concerned about a child's development or behavior. Screening tools, such as the *Ages & Stages Questionnaire (ASQ)*, can be a great help for programs and teachers in determining when individual variation is outside the expected norms. An early care and education setting is often the one of the first places to identify a child as having a need for more specific assessment. As such, knowledge of child development is critical when children with identified disabilities or other special needs are included in a program. Knowing where the child is on the developmental pathway will also guide the logical next steps and possible adaptations that may be needed.

Context of Developmental Theory and Research

Programs

- Use an understanding of the context of developmental research and theory to inform decisions about policies and practices for diverse groups of children and families.

- Stay current on cross-cultural and dual language developmental theory and research.

- Apply an understanding of the context of developmental theory and research to work with diverse children and families.

Developmental Theory, Research, and Practice

Programs

- Stay informed about current research on children's development, learning, and curriculum and share pertinent information with early childhood educators, demonstrating consideration for their diverse educational, linguistic, and practical experiences.

- Develop program policies and practices that reflect a strong foundation in developmental theory and current research and are supportive of children's growth and development in all domains, within the context of family, home, and cultural considerations.

- Design systems and strategies to help early childhood educators increase their understanding of development in all domains, and of the role of early education settings in supporting child development and learning.

- Introduce, explain, and apply new terms or concepts as appropriate.

- Engage staff, colleagues, and families to discuss development in all domains and in analysis of the cultural sensitivity of developmental theories and research.

Factors That Contribute to Development

Programs

- Stay informed about current research and literature regarding the **ecological perspective** and factors that contribute to child development.

- Interpret, synthesize, or distill research so that it is accessible to teaching staff members and applicable to their teaching practice. Share pertinent information often with staff.

- Provide professional development for staff, colleagues, and families on factors that contribute to child development, including topics such as plasticity, risk and resilience, first- and second-language development, and the importance of relationships.

- Obtain technical assistance and information relevant to the children enrolled, such as methods to increase speech and language skills, or current approaches for inclusion of children who have a disability on the autism spectrum.

Preschool Development and Learning

Programs

- Provide leadership among early childhood educators and community leaders to promote the understanding that

preschool development and learning are integrated across domains and what that means for the design and implementation of curricula and indoor and outdoor learning environments.

- Provide professional development for staff, colleagues, and families to understand that preschool development and learning and the role of nature in children's development are integrated across domains.

- Ensure that resources such as the *California Preschool Learning Foundations* (CDE 2008, 2010b, 2012) and the *California Preschool Curriculum Framework* (CDE 2010a, 2011, 2013) are available to support the planning efforts of staff members.

Learning Through Play

Programs

- Stay informed about research concerning scaffolding, intentional teaching, and play.

- Facilitate collaboration among early education settings, schools, families, and the community to achieve a balance between structured experiences, enrichment activities, and play.

- Provide leadership in creating safe, developmentally appropriate indoor and outdoor play spaces in the neighborhood and communities.

- Provide professional development for staff, colleagues, and families that focuses on play and its implications for child growth and development.

- Take individual family circumstances and cultural preferences into consideration when making recommendations about play. For some families, talking about their relationship and interactions with their child may have more relevance than play.

Individualized Developmental Expectations

Programs

- Guide staff members and families in developmentally appropriate practice that is responsive to the learning strengths, interests, and needs of individual children.

• Create program policies and practices that promote responsiveness to the learning strengths, interests, and needs of individual children.

• Facilitate implementation of developmentally, individually, culturally, and linguistically appropriate early childhood practices.

• Build awareness in the broader community of the importance of developmentally, individually, culturally, and linguistically appropriate early childhood practices.

1.3 Programs and administrators use knowledge about the role of culture in development and the process of dual language development to be responsive to California's young learners.

All children grow and learn in the context of family, school, and community influences. For dual language learners, these contexts include a language other than English as well as cultural practices that may differ from mainstream norms. Culture provides the lens through which young children interpret the world, learning what is expected, what is appropriate, and how to relate to the outside world. Language becomes the essential tool for learning across all contexts. Chapter 6 provides additional information about the dual language learner, current research findings about best practices, and practical recommendations about program approaches, instructional and assessment strategies, and effective family engagement.

Understanding Cultural Perspectives of Self and Others

Programs

• Provide opportunities for early childhood educators to develop awareness of cultural backgrounds, understanding of the influence of culture on their practice, and appreciation of the cultural

perspectives and strengths of children, families, and communities. Promote this awareness, understanding, and appreciation throughout the early childhood profession.

• Design an overall programmatic approach that allows early childhood educators to explore their own cultural perspectives and appreciate the cultural perspectives and strengths of colleagues, children, families, and the community they serve.

Program Strategies

Programs

• Facilitate discussion among staff members, families, and other community leaders about the appropriateness of various educational programs designed to support dual language learners in early education settings.

• Identify and address the need for additional information, research, or support.

• Develop and implement hiring policies and job descriptions for staff that include recruitment and retention of a diverse workforce that reflects the languages and cultures of families and the community.

• Facilitate the articulation of a clear, consistent, evidence-based program approach that is culturally and linguistically appropriate to the site; collaborate with families, staff members, and other community members, as appropriate, to build support for the program approach.

• Conduct ongoing evaluation of the program approach being implemented.

• Support program staff members in learning the language(s) spoken by the children in the program.

Knowledge of Dual Language Development

Programs

• Are knowledgeable about the process of dual language development during the preschool years, including the following topics:

o Simultaneous versus sequential/successive dual language development

o Stages of second-language development during preschool

o Differences in learning and development between dual language learners and monolingual children, including cultural variations

o Developmental and cognitive impacts of learning two languages

o Instructional strategies that support English-language development while also respecting, valuing, and incorporating home language development

o Linguistically and culturally appropriate assessment approaches

o Methods of effective engagement with families of young dual language learners

• Communicate with the larger community about how children develop both their home language and English and how this knowledge applies in early education settings.

• Provide professional development opportunities on dual language development.

• Make available to staff members and families research-based evidence that applies to supporting dual language development.

• Stay current on research and best practices.

• Collaborate with families and colleagues to design an educational program that facilitates continued home language and English-language development.

• Conduct ongoing evaluation of the educational program.

1.4 **Programs participate in efforts to promote a high-quality early care and education system.**

To promote a high-quality early care and education system, program administrators benefit from understanding the early care and education system as well as theories about how systems work and how organizational change takes place.

Systems Knowledge

Programs

• Understand both the shared and divergent interests of early childhood stakeholders, as well as how current policies and proposals for change impact different stakeholders.

• Understand alliances among stakeholders within and outside the early care and education profession.

• Articulate a range of strategies to influence policy and to analyze and evaluate effective strategies for transforming the system to one that is equitable and high quality.

• Develop strategies to overcome barriers to change.

Systems Theory and Organizational Change

Programs

• Use positive, reflective inquiry strategies as a leader when planning professional development.

• Influence others to join in efforts for continuous improvement and change.

• Facilitate the efforts of agencies to develop and apply an understanding of systems theory and factors that influence and impact functions of individual organizations.

• Understand the role of research, data, and storytelling as methods to impact change in organizations, policies, and people.

References

California Department of Education (CDE). 2006. *Infant/Toddler Learning & Development Program Guidelines.* Sacramento: California Department of Education.

———. 2009. *California Preschool Learning Foundations, Volume 1.* Sacramento: California Department of Education.

———. 2010a. *California Preschool Curriculum Framework, Volume 1.* Sacramento: California Department of Education.

———. 2010b. *California Preschool Learning Foundations, Volume 2.* Sacramento: California Department of Education.

———. 2011. *California Preschool Curriculum Framework Volume 2.* Sacramento: California Department of Education.

———. 2012. *California Preschool Learning Foundations, Volume 3.* Sacramento: California Department of Education.

———. 2013. *California Preschool Curriculum Framework Volume 3.* Sacramento: California Department of Education.

California Department of Education and First 5 California. 2012. *California Early Childhood Educator Competencies.* Sacramento: California Department of Education.

Squires, J., and D. Bricker. 2009. *Ages & Stages Questionnaires,* 3rd ed. (ASQ-3). Baltimore, MD: Brookes Publishing. http://agesandstages.com (accessed June 27, 2013).

Further Reading

California Department of Education and State Board of Education. 2011. *Race to the Top—Early Learning Challenge Overview of California's Approach.* Sacramento: California Department of Education.

Guideline 2: Addressing Culture, Diversity, and Equity

Children in California schools come from a wide variety of cultural, religious, ethnic, linguistic, and socioeconomic backgrounds. Encouraging all children to value and respect the differences—and also the similarities—among groups and individuals should be a primary goal of every preschool program.

> Culture is the learned and shared knowledge that specific groups use to generate their behavior and interpret their experience of the world. It comprises beliefs about reality, how people should interact with each other, what they "know' about the world, and how they should respond to the social and material environments in which they find themselves" (Gilbert, Goode, and Dunne 2007). Through culture children gain a sense of identity, a feeling of belonging, and beliefs about what is important in life, what is right and wrong, and how to care for themselves and others. When children are raised only in their home culture, they learn those lessons almost effortlessly. But when they spend some of their formative years in preschool and child care settings with people who were not raised in their culture and who do not necessarily share the same family and community values, the learning of those important early lessons becomes more complex. (CDE 2013, 1)

The Culture of Families and Communities

Effective preschool settings reflect the importance of each child's cultural background, respecting, acknowledging, and building on families' cultural experiences

---

Connecting Cultural Activities to Concrete, Daily Life

"Culture is not an abstraction to young children. It is lived and learned every day through the way family members interact: through language, patterns of communication, family stories, family routines, religious practices, music, household customs, and the responsibilities of family members."

Source: Derman-Sparks and Olsen Edwards 2010, 67.

Anti-Bias Education Activity

Make a class book about "Our Families" for children to take home to share. Make a page for each child and each teacher about who lives with them and what work their family members do in and outside of the home. For the children's pages, get information from family members and from the child. For example, Maurice's page might say: This is Maurice's family. He lives with his dad and his grandma. His aunt and uncle sometimes take care of him. Maurice's dad goes to college to learn to be a teacher, and he cooks dinner for Maurice and puts him to bed. Maurice's grandma brings him to school and works as a secretary. A dog named Gruffy lives with Maurice and his family.

Source: Derman-Sparks and Olsen Edwards 2010, 68–69.

---

and cultural rules for living. Programs and teachers understand the fundamental security that children gain from being a part of a community and use that cultural base to strengthen children's sense of self and feeling of connection to others. Programs and teachers demonstrate an active interest in and acceptance of children's cultural backgrounds and work consciously to integrate the experiences that children have at home and in their community into children's experiences in the classroom.

The Culture of the Early Care and Education Setting

The early care and education setting itself is a small society with its own beliefs, values, and rules for living. The culture of the early care and education setting is always different from that of the home culture, and this difference may be more pronounced if the staff differs from the families in ethnicity, language, social class, or country of birth. When these differences exist, the program should strive to create bridges of understanding, communication, and commonality. Ideally, the cultural, linguistic, and ethnic composition of the staff will reflect the cultural, linguistic and ethnic backgrounds of the children. Although representative staffing may not always be possible, it can contribute significantly to developing a climate in the program that emphasizes appreciation and respect for family diversity. Recruiting new staff members whose cultural, linguistic, and ethnic backgrounds are representative of the children and families should always be a goal that programs actively pursue.

The *California Early Childhood Educator Competencies* (California Department of Education and First 5 California, 2012, 21) states,

> Cultural perspectives of children, families, staff, and colleagues vary widely on issues such as differences in individual children's learning, strengths, and abilities; gender identity and gender-specific roles; family composition and member roles; generational experiences and perspectives; communication styles; regulation and discipline; coordination and physical development; and acquisition and synthesis of information. Early educators who learn to think from a multicultural perspective are better able to provide opportunities that reflect each child's culture and family experiences (Banks 2006, 2008). Learning environments are enriched when diversity among children, families, and peers—as well as children's individual characteristics, values, cultures, and temperaments—are respected and valued in concrete ways.

2.1 Programs encourage and support appreciation of and respect for diversity among individuals and groups.

An attitude of respect for others, whatever their differences, is essential in creating a positive, accepting program environment. This statement applies in culturally, linguistically, and ethnically diverse communities as well as in more homogeneous communities. Families differ in their beliefs and values about child behavior, the role of academics, appropriate discipline methods, school aspirations, and when, how, and with whom young children use language (see State Advisory Council on Early Learning and Care 2013, Paper 4, Family Engagement). These culturally rooted differences influence children's development and behavior. Effective ECE teachers make a commitment to learn from the children's families about the families' values and beliefs to better understand the children and implement culturally responsive practices.

Cultural Diversity of Families

Programs

- Develop and implement policies and practices that promote inclusion of all children and families in the program.

- Facilitate accommodations that address the unique contributions and perspectives, both cultural and generational, of all families.

- Develop a climate statement that expresses the program's appreciation of cultural and linguistic diversity and share the statement with both staff and families.

- Use family information to guide the development of program policies and practices.

- Work with families in need of special assistance and collaborate with culturally and linguistically appropriate support services to ensure that families receive them.

- Provide opportunities for family members to become involved in the program and to learn how to support their child at home.

- Invite family members to plan and carry out large- or small-group activities that reflect the home culture.

- Develop curriculum and classroom practices that create a welcoming atmosphere for all families and children.

Involving Family Members in Planning

Programs

- Encourage the participation of all families and colleagues in curriculum planning throughout a program.

- Collaborate with families and staff members to determine policies that support the inclusion of families and colleagues in planning program services.

Teachers

- Respect and include the contributions of all families in the planning of learning activities.

- Plan curriculum and activities collaboratively with families.

Cultural Diversity of Families

Teachers

- Attend to the culturally diverse attributes of children and families. Work proactively to support children and families as they transition to the early childhood setting.

- Communicate with family members to ensure that they have the support and information necessary to be full participants in the program.

- Embrace each child's culture and see it as an asset.

- Interact with families in a way that encourages their involvement.

- Report family concerns to the supervisor.

- Convey a warm welcome to all families, including during visits and at drop-off and pickup times.

- Communicate regularly with family members to understand each family's current and ongoing concerns.

- Attend to all relevant issues or special circumstances in a responsive and sensitive manner.

- Promote family engagement in the program.

- Gather information about each family's child-rearing practices and goals, and share that information with staff members to support and encourage family engagement and to inform program curriculum planning.

- Understand the importance of providing a learning environment that is welcoming for all families.

2.2 Programs and teachers are responsive to cultural and linguistic diversity.

When teachers follow the form and style of interaction that children experience at home—for example, incorporating familiar ways of using language—those children are likely to feel more secure and comfortable in preschool. At times, cultural consistency between the home and preschool may be difficult to attain, or the teacher may feel that it is beneficial to introduce new strategies and practices. In doing so, culturally sensitive programs support teachers in their efforts to communicate with parents about the preschool's own culture.

Culturally and linguistically responsive programs celebrate each child's cultural and linguistic background as assets to the classroom. All children bring prior knowledge and experiences into the classroom that will shape how they understand concepts and interactions. The ECE teachers' attitude toward these differences is critical in setting the stage for an inclusive, strengths-based, and responsive classroom climate.

Staff Preparation for Communication Practices

Programs

- Provide an orientation for early childhood educators about expressing respect to families through reflective communication; facilitate professional development that reinforces staff members and colleagues' understanding of principles of communication with families.

- Promote policies and practices that invite open communication with all families.

- Promote and seek input from families.

- Ensure that all communications are comprehensible to families when the home language is not English.

Teachers

- Participate in staff orientation sessions that focus on expressing respect to families through reflective communication; develop related skills and knowledge through these sessions.

- Demonstrate understanding of the cultural implications of the roles and expectations for relationships between early educators and families.

- Apply skills and knowledge gained from orientation sessions to communicate respectfully with each family.

- Follow families' culturally based communication practices.

- Implement concepts of intercultural communication, including nonverbal communication.

Family–Teacher Relationships

Programs

- Develop program policies and practices that foster the development of effective family–teacher relationships.

Teachers

- Use multiple strategies for building relationships with families, such as seeking family goals for the child, sharing observations and documentation with families, and being available to meet with family members upon request.

- Attend family–educator meetings and provide information, asking open-ended questions and talking with families about the child's learning.

2.3 **Programs and teachers integrate home culture, language and practices in learning activities, materials, and environments.**

To align the program with the children's family and community cultures, staff members need to ensure that the materials, activities, and visual aids used in the classroom reflect the child's neighborhood and world. Pictures displayed in the classroom or center; artwork created by the children; books housed in the library; music, curricular activities, field trips, and visitors provided for instruction; and the food served in the center should reflect the cultures, languages, and ethnicities of the children. Photographs of the children, families, and their homes; signs in their native languages; and photographs and pictures of their family customs are displayed throughout the classroom. Music, songs, stories, and literature from the cultures and in the languages of the children and families are integrated into instructional activities. Special care is taken to ensure that all materials authentically reflect the cultures and languages of the children and families.

Visual Representation of Diversity

Programs

- Create list of resources that offer developmentally and culturally appropriate recommendations for the visual representation of diversity in early childhood settings.

- Include diversity of abilities.

- Promote the use of materials that authentically reflect the cultures of the children and families and assess the visual representation of diversity in the program.

- Collaborate with early educators and families to design ways of reflecting the families' cultures and languages in governance of the program.

Teachers

- Place photos, pictures, books, signs, and other materials in the learning environment that reflect the authentic cultural, linguistic, ethnicity, ability, and individual diversity of children and families.

- Interact with families formally and informally to ensure that the overall learning environment reflects the cultural, linguistic, and generational diversity of the children and families in the program.

Language Diversity

Programs

- Develop and facilitate the implementation of program policies and practices that honor and promote communication in the home language of children and families

- Implement procedures that strengthen and monitor the support for both home language maintenance and English-language development within the classroom environment (materials, books, displays, and the like) and learning activities and opportunities.

- Promote the effective use of interpreters and translators.

- Ensure that all parents receive complete and accurate information about program options to support children's language development and, in particular, dual language learners.

- Identify tools and services to help communicate with families who speak languages other than English.

Teachers

- Are responsive to children and families who use their home language (including sign language) to communicate.

- Are able to identify when interpreters and/or translators are needed. Create a learning environment that supports children's and families' communication in their home language and in English.

- Articulate the importance of language diversity.

- Use interpreters and translators effectively.

Assessment of Environments

Programs

- Support staff members in the use of assessment data to continually study the environment to ensure it reflects the diverse characteristics, abilities, cultures, and languages of families.

- Individualize assessment procedures and link results to curriculum planning and make adjustments, as necessary, for children with unique needs, including children with disabilities or other special needs, and each dual language learner.

Teachers

- Contribute to the assessment process to determine how environments can be enhanced with an understanding of the cultures, languages, and strengths and abilities of the children and families.

- Articulate to families and colleagues the importance of assessing environments on an ongoing basis to ensure that the cultures and languages of the families are reflected.

2.4 Programs and teachers help children learn strategies to address social injustice, bias, and prejudice.

Whether or not children are able to verbalize about social injustice, bias, and prejudice, they learn about those attitudes at an early age. Many children in preschool are learning about and experiencing cultural differences for the first time and have a natural curiosity about them. In preschool classrooms everywhere, children enact and express the biases of their society—biases related to gender, race, ethnicity, social class, and disability. The early care and education center should be a setting that discourages bias and promotes acceptance of others and respect for diversity.

Social Justice

Programs

- Understand the difference between prejudice and simple curiosity about others.

- Make diversity a part of the ongoing, daily learning environment that is shaped by the cultures of the children and families in the classroom rather than a tourist curriculum in which children "drop in on" strange and exotic people to celebrate their holidays and taste their foods (adapted from Derman-Sparks and Olsen Edwards 2010).

Teachers

- Understand that "it is not human differences that undermine children's development, but rather unfair treatment based upon these differences" (Derman-Sparks and Olsen Edwards 2010, 3).

Children's Identity Development

Programs

- Develop curriculum that promotes children's sense of identity by integrating home culture and language with learning activities and environments.

Teachers

- Actively communicate with children about themselves and their families.

- Conduct activities that promote positive identity development in young children.

- Focus on each child's capabilities and competence when describing the child, particularly when responding to questions from other children. For example, a child asks, "Why does he crawl? Is he a baby?" Teacher responds, "He is four years old, just like you! His legs work differently than yours do, so he crawls to move around when he is not in his wheelchair. Do you want to play with him? He enjoys doing puzzles just like you."

- Use understanding of individual children's life experiences and home culture to promote healthy development.

References

Banks, J. A. 2006. *Race, Culture, and Education: The Selected Works of James A. Banks.* London; New York: Routledge.

———. 2008. *An Introduction to Multicultural Education.* 4th ed. Boston: Pearson Education.

Blanton, R. E. 2013. *Military Families and Child Care Needs in California,* CRB Short Subject, March 2013, S-13-008, Women's Veterans Series, California Research Bureau, California State Library.

California Department of Education (CDE). 2013. *Infant/Toddler Caregiving: A Guide to Culturally Sensitive Care.* 2nd ed. Sacramento: California Department of Education.

California Department of Education and First 5 California. 2012. *California Early Childhood Educator Competencies.* Sacramento: California Department of Education.

Derman-Sparks, L. 1989. *Anti-Bias Curriculum: Tools for Empowering Young Children.* Washington, DC: National Association for the Education of Young Children (NAEYC).

Derman-Sparks, L., and J. Olsen Edwards. 2010. *Anti-Bias Education for Young Children and Ourselves.* Washington, DC: National Association for the Education of Young Children.

Gilbert, J., T. D. Goode, and C. Dunne. 2007. "Cultural Awareness." *Curricula Enhancement Module Series.* Washington, DC: National Center for Cultural Competence, Georgetown University Center for Child and Human Development.

State Advisory Council on Early Learning and Care. 2013. *California's Best Practices for Young Dual Language Learners: Research Overview Papers.* Sacramento: California Department of Education. http://www.cde.ca.gov/sp/cd/ce/documents/dllresearchpapers.pdf (accessed April 3, 2014).

Questions About Differences

When children ask questions about racial and physical characteristics or differences:

- Do not ignore their questions.
- Do not change the subject.
- Do not answer indirectly.

If you are uncomfortable, identify what gets in the way of your responding directly, matter-of-factly, and simply.

Source: Derman-Sparks 1989.

Further Reading

National Association for the Education of Young Children (NAEYC). 2009. *Quality Benchmark for Cultural Competence Project.* http://www.naeyc.org/files/naeyc/file/policy/state/QBCC_Tool.pdf (accessed June 24, 2013).

Office of Head Start. 2010. Revisiting and Updating the Multicultural Principles for Head Start Programs Serving Children Ages Birth to Five. Washington, DC: U.S. Department of Health and Human Services, Administration for Children and Families, Office of Head Start.

Office of Head Start, Office of the Administration for Children and Families, Early Childhood Learning & Knowledge Center (ECLKC). *Multicultural Principles for Head Start Programs.* http://eclkc.ohs.acf.hhs.gov/hslc/tta-system/cultural-linguistic/Dual%20Language%20Learners/pdm/responsiveness/manage_pub_00602a1_092305.html (accessed June 24, 2013).

Guideline 3: Supporting Relationships, Interactions, and Guidance

The quality of relationships children develop with adults and peers is central to children's successful learning and development. As stated in the *California Early Childhood Educator Competencies* (California Department of Education and First 5 California 2012), whether children's development is supported or compromised by their participation in early care and education programs is determined in large part by the quality of their social–emotional experiences in those settings, including their relationships with both adults and peers (National Research Council and Institute of Medicine 2000). Increasing evidence suggests that efforts to promote children's school readiness should focus on supporting children's social–emotional development as well as their cognitive development.

Clearly, all preschool children thrive academically and socially when their teachers are sensitive, positive, nurturing, and responsive to their emotional and social needs. Teacher–child relationships appear to be central to healthy growth and development as well as important to academic outcomes. Although teacher–child relationships are generally beneficial for all children, the benefits for dual language learners have been found to be significant. In particular, Spanish-speaking dual language learners who receive instruction in their home language in emotionally supportive classrooms make larger academic gains than their peers in less emotionally supportive classrooms. Furthermore, low-quality relationships between teachers and dual language learners appear to compromise the benefits of in-school literacy instruction for dual language learner language and literacy development.

Thus, a fundamental part of the learning environments and curricula of early childhood programs includes relationships, interactions, and guidance (Center on the Social and Emotional Foundations for Early Learning [CSEFEL] 2009 and 2010, adapted from the California Department of Education and First 5 California 2012, 29). Fostering relationships at all levels—adults with individual children, adult with groups of children, between or among children and adults, and adults (e.g., teachers) with other adults (e.g., colleagues, family members)—is central to a child and family's sense of confidence and competence in the early childhood setting.

3.1 Programs and teachers collaborate with families to create a supportive emotional climate for children.

Children learn best in environments where they feel safe and cared about. Creating early childhood programs that are supportive of children's social and emotional well-being depends on how the overall program is designed, the child's role in the learning environment, and the kind of social interactions that occur there (adapted from CDE 2011, 39–40). Through the ongoing, daily interactions that teachers have with children and their families, children develop a sense of security and safety. Effective preschool teachers communicate with family members regularly about children's experiences at home, so they can connect the children's home experiences with those in the classroom. When children feel secure in their relationships with consistent, caring preschool teachers, they feel safe to learn through play and exploration.

Thus, children need consistent relationships with teachers. In addition, early healthy emotional development depends on adults' alertness to children's feelings. Children benefit when adults acknowledge those feelings as valid and respond with empathy and compassion. A child who displays fear, anger, or excitement has difficulty engaging in learning unless her emotional needs are met first. Emotional support from caring adults helps children resolve troubled feelings so that they can reconnect in productive ways with peers and adults and engage more fully in learning experiences in the classroom.

Supportive Emotional Climate

Programs

- Provide professional development, including reflective supervision, mentorship, and coaching, to staff members on the relationship between the social–emotional climate and the overall learning environment.

- Ensure that assessments of program quality include family input and the evaluation of the social–emotional climate, providing access to interpreters for families with dual language learners when needed.

- Develop staffing policies that help to maintain stability and consistency in the program environment.

- Provide professional development opportunities to staff and resources to families about the importance of relationships, attachment, responsiveness, and respect.

- Work to promote staff retention to ensure continuity of relationships with teachers for children and families.

- Work to hire, retain, and support staff members who represent the children and families' cultural and linguistic backgrounds.

- Provide professional development opportunities to staff about the ways young children express their feelings about separation and transitions, as well as the importance of supporting families during times of separation and transition.

- Establish program policies to minimize the number of separations or transitions that children experience and the distress those occurrences may cause.

Teachers

- Work with colleagues to plan a positive social–emotional climate in the learning environment based on the individual strengths, cultures, languages, and interests of the children in the group.

- Provide a responsive and sensitive social–emotional climate to support all children.

- Respond to children's emotional needs by providing individual attention in the child's home language to each child in the group on a daily basis.

- Organize the learning environment to reflect the importance of consistency, continuity, and responsiveness in supporting children's emotional development.

- Understand that it is important for children to have stable relationships with adults.

- Oversee day-to-day transitions, being sensitive to each child's responses to separations and transitions, and working with families to develop effective support to children during transitions.

Expression of Emotions

Teachers

- Use a variety of terms to describe children's individual emotional experiences.

- Respond appropriately to children's expression of emotion and facilitate communication about emotional experiences according to each child's development, language, and culture.

- Model appropriate expression of emotions and understand how adults' emotions affect children.

- Establish an environment in which children and adults feel safe to explore their emotional experiences and to receive support as needed, incorporating throughout the day discussions about feelings with adults and other children.

- Develop, in close collaboration with the families, appropriate ways for children to express strong emotions appropriately.

- Incorporate materials that help children identify feelings.

3.2 Programs support teachers' implementation of strategies to establish warm, nurturing relationships with all young children.

Nurturing relationships are essential to children's successful social and academic learning in preschool. Ample research now suggests that positive teacher–child relationships are linked to positive developmental outcomes for young children. In particular, positive teacher–child relationships positively impact children's ability to get along with peers and children's ability to pay attention and engage in cognitive tasks. Importantly, children whose teachers establish warm, nurturing relationships with them are also less likely to display behavior problems (Peisner-Feinberg et al. 2001; NICHD ECCRN 2001).

Nurturing Collaborative Relationships Support Mindful Teaching

"A mindful approach . . . to education involves a shift in our attitude toward the individuals with whom we work. The active involvement of the student in the learning process enables the teacher to join as a collaborative explorer in the journey of discovery that teaching can be: We can embrace both knowledge and uncertainty with curiosity, openness, acceptance, and kind regard."

Source: Siegel 2007, 20.

Teachers who are able to speak the home language to dual language learners tend to view children's behavior in a more positive light (Chang et al. 2007). These findings have led researchers to suggest that being in preschool classes taught by English-only teachers may contribute to the achievement gap of dual language learners. The ability of the staff to provide home language support to dual language learners is important for social and emotional benefits as well as academic achievement.

Establishment of Warm, Nurturing Relationships

Programs

- Provide professional development opportunities to staff and colleagues and resources to families about the principles of relationship-based practice.

Teachers

- Model positive relationships with each other and other program staff and with children and families, and encourage children to develop and maintain positive relationships.

- Work with colleagues and families to support positive relationships among early childhood educators, between early childhood educators and children, and among children.

- Ensure that each child has developmentally and individually appropriate opportunities to interact with adults and peers in meaningful ways.

- Implement strategies that establish warm, nurturing relationships with all young dual language learners.

3.3 Programs and teachers collaborate with families to identify challenges that may affect children's social–emotional development and offer resources to address those challenges.

Both daily and ongoing experiences in the family and community can affect children's social–emotional development. Program administrators and teachers need to work closely with families and one another to identify stressors and any other factors at home or in the child's community that may be negatively impacting children's social–emotional development. Once stressors are identified, programs and teachers can collaborate with families to share knowledge and resources that are supportive of children's health and well-being.

When program staff members do not speak a dual language learner's home language, they may misinterpret or misunderstand the child's behavior. It is important for staff to enlist a native speaker of the child's home language to assist with the assessment of a dual language learner's behavior and contribute appropriate responses.

Collaboration to Address Family Challenges

Programs

- Work with families to identify family challenges that may affect children's emotional development.

- Work with families to identify family resources that support children's emotional development.

- Establish ties with community agencies that may meet the needs of families in the program.

- Provide professional development for colleagues and families related to the impact of family stress on children's emotional development.

Teachers

- Understand that daily occurrences and family and community stress may affect children's emotional development, and respond to the needs of individual families as appropriate, referring concerns to other staff when necessary.

- Respect the confidentiality of children and families with regard to stress and other family circumstances.

- Plan with colleagues to adapt the program and its environment to meet the needs of all children and families.

- Share knowledge and resources with families to support their health and well-being.

3.4 Programs ensure teachers have ample time to engage in supportive, responsive interactions with each child.

A preschool teachers' job is multifaceted. Preschool teachers juggle many responsibilities, including scaffolding children's learning experiences, assessing children's learning and development, re-

flecting on and planning learning environments and experiences to meet children's individual needs, debriefing with staff and colleagues, and meeting with parents. It is the role of the program administrator to ensure teachers have the "release time" needed to engage in activities outside the classroom that are necessary to success on the job, while still having sufficient time in the classroom. It is not reasonable to expect teachers to hold staff meetings or meetings with family members during classroom time if appropriate substitutes are not provided for teachers. Program administrators and teachers need to think collaboratively and creatively about how to ensure that teachers have ample time to engage in supportive relationships with each child in their program while still holding meetings, assessing children's learning, and planning for their learning experiences.

Time to Engage Children

Programs

- Develop program policies and practices that allow early childhood educators to have ample time for quality interaction with each child in the child's home language.

- Develop procedures to monitor the quality and frequency of interactions between staff and children.

- Work collaboratively and intentionally to plan meetings with families during times that would be least disruptive to children.

3.5 Programs and teachers provide positive guidance to promote social–emotional competence and prevent challenging behaviors.

In the preschool years, children are actively working on a variety of skills that contribute to their growing sense of social–emotional competence, such as developing an understanding of other people's feelings and needs, empathizing with others, and learning to manage their own behavior. Preschool children are starting to learn about the reciprocal nature of friendships and how to negotiate conflict successfully. However, in all their social–emotional learning, preschool children rely on guidance from preschool teachers to practice and eventually master the complex skills required to navigate social interactions with peers and adults. With guidance from caring adults in their environment, preschool children can develop a sense of competence, learn developmentally appropriate ways to socialize with peers, and resolve conflicts.

Social–Emotional Competence

Programs

- Collaborate with families to create a program environment that supports the emotional experiences of children and adults.

- Provide resources to colleagues and families about emotional development in early childhood, including information about variability in individual preferences and cultural expectations for the expression of emotion.

Strategies for Socialization and Guidance

Programs

- Facilitate sharing of observations of children among appropriate staff members, encouraging peer reflection of observations to inform planning.

- Facilitate communication with families to ensure that the program implements appropriate strategies to promote healthy social–emotional development.

- Seek input from outside resources and specialists and share it with program staff and families.

- Provide guidance to other adults about individual children's temperament, language, culture, communication skills, and abilities that contribute to learning and development.

- Explain individual and typical child development to adult family members.

Teachers

- Implement, with family input, a variety of developmentally appropriate strategies for socialization and guidance.

- Plan experiences that incorporate a variety of developmentally appropriate, evidence-based strategies for supporting children's social–emotional development, based on observations of children's behavior and family input.

Challenging Behaviors

Programs

- Provide support and professional development on the practices that are most likely to prevent challenging behavior in young children, including strong relationships, supportive environments (including carefully planned transitions, schedules, and grouping), and teaching social–emotional skills to children.

- Provide professional development opportunities to staff and resources to families on the use of strategies to respond to challenging behaviors, including support from behavioral or developmental specialists, early interventionists, and mental-health professionals as necessary.

Teachers

- Observe and identify the emotions underlying challenging behaviors.

- Gather input from colleagues, other program staff members, and families to gain a greater understanding of the function or purpose behind children's challenging behaviors and to develop strategies—including self-reflection and peer-reflection—for addressing those behaviors.

- Share observations appropriately and respect confidentiality when discussions involve children and families.

- Implement strategies designed by colleagues, families, and other specialists to address children's challenging behaviors.

- Develop, modify, and adapt schedules, routines, and the program environment to positively affect challenging behaviors.

Conflict Resolution

Programs

- Provide professional development opportunities to staff and resources to families on the development of conflict-

resolution strategies, communication skills, and factors that may influence behavior in young children.

Teachers

- Support children in expressing their emotions and negotiating conflict in developmentally appropriate ways.

- Model appropriate behavior for resolving conflicts.

- Refine and implement developmentally appropriate strategies to help children learn how to express emotions, negotiate conflict, and solve problems.

- Work with coworkers to utilize a similar and consistent process with children in the same classroom or environment.

- Engage colleagues and other program staff, children, and families in discussions around conflict resolution.

Appropriate Expectations for Behavior

Teachers

- Respond adaptively to individual children, considering each child's age, temperament, language, communication skills, culture, interests, and abilities.

- Examine their own expectations of "appropriate" and "safe" behavior, looking for potential bias toward gender or developmental skills.

References

California Department of Education (CDE). 2010. *California Preschool Curriculum Framework, Volume 1*. Sacramento: California Department of Education.

———. 2011. *California Preschool Curriculum Framework, Volume 2*. Sacramento: California Department of Education.

California Department of Education and First 5 California. 2012. *California Early Childhood Educator Competencies*. Sacramento: California Department of Education.

Chang, F., G. Crawford, D. Early, D. Bryant, C. Howes, M. Burchinal, O. Barbarin, R. Clifford, and R. Pianta. 2007. "Spanish Speaking Children's Social and Language Development in Pre-Kindergarten Classrooms." *Early Education and Development* 18 (2): 243–69.

National Research Council and Institute of Medicine, Committee on Integrating the Science of Early Childhood Development. 2000. *From Neurons to Neighborhoods: The Science of Early Childhood Development*. J.P. Shonkoff and D.A. Phillips, eds. Washington, DC: National Academies Press.

NICHD Early Child Care Research Network (ECCRN). 2001. "Nonmaternal Care and Family Factors in Early Development: An Overview of the NICHD Study of Early Child Care." *Journal of Applied Developmental Science* 22 (5): 457–92.

Peisner-Feinberg, E.S., M. R. Burchinal, R. M. Clifford, M. L. Culkin, C. Howes, S. L. Kagan, and N. Yazejin. 2001. "The Relation of Preschool Child-Care Quality to Children's Cognitive and Social Developmental Trajectories through Second Grade." *Child Development* 72 (5): 1534–53.

Siegel, D. J. 2007. *The Mindful Brain: Reflection and Attunement in the Cultivation of Well-Being*. New York: W. W. Norton & Company.

Further Reading

TEACHER–CHILD RELATIONSHIPS

Buyse, E., K. Verschueren, S. Doumen, J. Van Damme, and F. Maes. 2007. "Classroom Problem Behavior and Teacher–Child Relationships in Kindergarten: The Moderating Role of Classroom Climate." *Journal of School Psychology* 46 (4): 367–91.

DeMulder, E. K., S. Denham, M. Schmidt, and J. Mitchell. 2000. "Q-Sort Assessment of Attachment Security During the Preschool Years: Links From Home to School." *Developmental Psychology* 36 (2): 274–82.

Hamre, B. K., and R. C. Pianta. 2001. "Early Teacher–Child Relationships and the Trajectory of Children's School Outcomes through Eighth Grade." *Child Development* 72 (2): 625–38.

Howes, C. 2008. "Teacher Sensitivity, Children's Attachment and Play with Peers." *Early Education & Development* 8 (1): 41–49.

Howes, C., and C. E. Hamilton. 1992. "Children's Relationships with Child Care Teachers: Stability and Concordance with Parental Attachments." *Child Development* 63 (4): 867–78.

Howes, C., and S. Ritchie. 1999. "Attachment Organizations in Children with Difficult Life Circumstances." *Development and Psychopathology* 11:251–68.

Howes, C., C. E. Hamilton, and C. C. Matheson. 1994. "Children's Relationships with Peers: Differential Associations with Aspects of the Teacher–Child Relationship." *Child Development* 65 (1): 253–63.

Howes, C., L., C. Phillipsen, and E. Peisner-Feinberg. 2000. "The Consistency of Perceived Teacher–Child Relationships Between Preschool and Kindergarten." *Journal of School Psychology* 38 (2): 113–32.

La Paro, K. M., and R. C. Pianta. 2000. "Predicting Children's Competence in the Early School Years: A Meta-Analytic Review." *Review of Educational Research* 70 (4): 443–84.

Mashburn, A. J., and R. C. Pianta. 2006. "Social Relationships and School Readiness." *Early Education & Development* 17 (1): 151–76.

Mindsight Institute. https://www.mindsightinstitute.com/ (accessed June 24, 2013).

National Scientific Council on the Developing Child. 2004. "Young Children Develop in an Environment of Relationships, Working Paper No.1." Cambridge, MA: Center on the Developing Child, Harvard University.

O'Connor, E., and K. McCartney. 2006. "Testing Associations between Young Children's Relationships with Mothers and Teachers." *Journal of Educational Psychology* 98 (1): 87–98.

———. 2007. "Examining Teacher–Child Relationships and Achievement as Part of an Ecological Model of Development." *American Educational Research Journal* 44 (2): 340–69.

Ostrosky, M. M., and E. Y. Jung. 2003. "Building Positive Teacher–Child Relationships." *Center on the Social and Emotional Foundations for Early Learning, What Works Briefs* 12.

Pianta, R. C., C. Howes, M. Burchinal, D. Bryant, R. Clifford, D. Early, and O. Barbarin. 2005. "Features of Pre-Kindergarten Programs, Classrooms, and Teachers: Do They Predict Observed Classroom Quality and Child–Teacher Interactions?" *Applied Development Science* 9 (3): 144–59.

Pianta, R. C., S. L. Nimetz, and E. Bennett. 1997. "Mother–Child Relationships, Teacher–Child Relationships, and School Outcomes in Preschool and Kindergarten." *Early Childhood Research Quarterly* 12: 263–80.

Pianta, R. C., and M. W. Stuhlman. 2004. "Teacher–Child Relationships and Children's Success in the First Years of School." *School Psychology Review* 33 (3): 444–58.

Rimm-Kaufman, S. E., D. M. Early, M. J. Cox, G. Saluja, R. C. Pianta, R. H. Bradley, and C. Payne. 2002. "Early Behavioral Attributes and Teachers' Sensitivity as Predictors of Competent Behavior in the Kindergarten Classroom." *Applied Developmental Psychology* 23 (4): 451–70.

Siegel, D. J. 2010. *Mindsight: The New Science of Personal Transformation.* New York: Random House. http://drdansiegel.com (accessed June 24, 2013).

Siegel, D. J., and T. P. Bryson. 2011. *The Whole Brain Child: 12 Revolutionary Strategies to Nurture Your Child's Developing Mind, Survive Everyday parenting Struggles, and Help Your Family Thrive.* New York: Random House. http://drdansiegel.com (accessed June 24, 2013).

Tran, H., and M. Weinraub. 2006. "Child Care Effects in Context: Quality, Stability, and Multiplicity in Nonmaternal Child Care Arrangements During the First 15 Months of Life." *Developmental Psychology* 42 (3): 566–82.

"A growing body of research suggests that meaningful engagement of families in their children's early learning supports school readiness and later academic success" (NAEYC 2009; Henrich and Gadaire 2008; Weiss, Caspe, and Lopez 2006). Programs and teachers who strive to build genuine partnerships with the parents, guardians, and other primary caregivers at home and encourage families to become active participants in their child's early learning and development help families to become advocates for their children. "High levels of engagement often result from strong program–family partnerships that are co-constructed and characterized by trust, shared values, ongoing bidirectional communication, mutual respect, and attention to each party's needs (Lopez, Kreider, and Caspe 2004; NAEYC 2009, 6).

In addition, ECE programs have learned that when they can effectively partner with families, young children benefit and families are more likely to maintain involvement with school settings across the years. By strengthening family engagement during the preschool years, particularly with families from diverse backgrounds, families that have children with disabilities or other special needs, and families with dual language learners, early childhood education (ECE) programs can help to reduce the achievement gap. (See State Advisory Council on Early Learning and Care 2013, Paper 4, Family Engagement, for a comprehensive discussion on the research and recommendations on engaging families with dual language learners.)

Ways to Engage Parents

Effective preschool programs and teachers strive to develop respectful relationships with families by recognizing their goals and values. Such relationships give families confidence that their own goals for their children's development will be valued. Thus, instead of conveying information in one direction from the teacher to the family member, the teacher makes the effort to foster respectful two-way communication (NAEYC 2009).

Researchers have identified six components to family engagement: joint decision making, regular two-way communication, collaboration and exchange of knowledge, learning in the home and in the community, joint family–program goal setting, and professional development (see State Advisory Council on Early Learning and Care 2013, Paper 4, Family Engagement). In essence, family engagement means that families and ECE programs agree to share responsibility for the well-being and education of the children. They work collaboratively to bring elements of the home into the preschool and elements of the preschool into the home.

4.1 Programs and teachers build trusting collaborative relationships with families.

When programs strive to build trusting, open, and collaborative relationships with families and genuinely seek the family's input to inform program planning, family members receive the message that they play a key role in their child's development and learning. In efforts to establish strong links between home and the early care and education setting, programs and teachers focus on developing strategies for family collaboration and being responsive to each family's home language.

It is well documented that positive interactions between the dual language learner family and the school are important for promoting dual language learners' development and well-being and that mutual respect is essential to fostering collaborative relationships. Programs need to make their centers warm and welcoming for all families, so that families with dual language learners feel comfortable, welcome, and enthusiastic about getting involved in school activities.

Engaging and Collaborating with Families

Programs

- Develop and implement program policies that give families and staff members opportunities to observe and discuss children's development and behavior.

- Support families by providing tools and resources that help them contribute to their children's learning.

- Invite families to participate formally and informally in the development, governance, and evaluation of program services and policies, as appropriate.

Teachers

- Recognize that working with families promotes children's development.

- Build relationships with families to ensure meaningful two-way collaboration, supporting the children's learning and development and helping families to understand child development.

- Attentively greet family members when they arrive and depart from the program setting, and use those opportunities to exchange information about the family's child.

- Contribute ideas and resources to promote each child's learning and development in the home and community.

- Collaborate formally and informally with families and colleagues to share observations, describe children's accomplishments, plan for children individually and as a group, and address concerns about children.

- Support families as decision makers for and educators of their children.

- Actively solicit and listen to families' goals, aspirations, and concerns about their children's development.

Home Language

Programs

- Create strategies to engage family members from diverse linguistic and cultural backgrounds and invite family members to share goals and strategies for supporting children's home languages in the group or classroom. This may require the use of interpreters and translators (please see table 6.2, "Sample Family Languages and Interests Interview," in chapter 6 as a way to gather important information from families).

Teachers

- Learn a few words in each child's home language, such as greetings, names of family members, words of comfort, and important objects or places. Parents and other family members can be good resources for learning their language.

- Seek and use resources to facilitate communication with family members in their home language, ensuring that all families are included.

4.2 Programs and teachers value the primary role of families in promoting children's development.

The family is central in children's lives, as it is through their experiences with their families that children learn about themselves and the world around them (adapted from CDE 2006, 56). In this publication, *family member* is used to define the people who are primarily responsible for a child, including extended family members, teen parents, or foster families (text adapted from CDE 2006,

56). Programs support the healthy growth and development of the child within the context of the family by creating continuity between the home and the early care and education setting. Programs are responsible for learning about the children's home life through communication with family members and, when possible, home visits. As part of this process, programs will learn to work with diverse family structures, including those headed by grandparents, foster families, same-sex parents, and teen parents. An essential aspect of high-quality programs is finding ways to support the growing relationship between the child and the family, and adapting to the strengths and needs of each child–family relationship (CDE 2006, 57). By getting to know families and understanding the importance of children's relationships with caregivers at home, programs and teachers can support the primary role of the family in children's learning and development.

Knowledge of Families

Programs

- Develop or adapt program policies, based on knowledge of the families and on their input and feedback, to support family engagement in the program.

Teachers

- Gather information from family members and engage in direct, effective communication to learn about family composition, values, and traditions to support the primary role of families in their children's care and education and to engage families in the early education setting.

- Learn about each family's values, beliefs, and practices by observing and engaging family members in conversation or by communicating with other staff members as appropriate.

- Find out about each family's language preferences and language goals for their child.

- Refer to and use pertinent family information when responding to needs of children and families.

Parent–Child History and Relationships

Programs

- Develop program policies that support children's relationships with their adult caregivers at home.

- Provide professional development for staff on facilitating parent–child relationships and identifying areas of concern.

- Provide resources or consultation as appropriate to address concerns related to children's relationships with adult caregivers at home.

Teachers

- Understand that all children develop in the context of relationships and that the quality of children's interactions with adult caregivers at home has an impact on child outcomes.

- Follow program policies or practices designed to support relationships between children and adult family members.

- Use a variety of techniques to facilitate and reinforce positive interaction between children and adult family members and support each adult family member's capacity to be responsive and sensitive to the child.

- Understand that culture influences approaches to nurturing young children.

- Identify concerns related to children's relationships with adult family members and follow up as appropriate.

4.3 Programs create a climate in which family members feel empowered and comfortable as advocates for their children.

When programs and teachers engage in open, respectful communication with family members and strive to develop positive, collaborative relationships with them, family members feel included and empowered. The experience of authentically contributing to their children's experiences in preschool helps family members become advocates for their children both within the program and in interactions with other service providers. For example, they are more likely to seek or request services for their children, such as referrals to special education, when needed or appropriate.

Programs can help families with dual language learners recognize their families' cultural and linguistic strengths and learn the skills to ask for the types of services that they think will benefit their children. Families should be encouraged to share their strengths with the program and be asked to participate in joint goal setting and decision making about their children's education. The entire program benefits when educators incorporate diverse cultures, languages, and talents of families with dual language learners into the program's learning environment and curriculum. Once family members feel their contributions and opinions are valued, programs will benefit from their knowledge and experience.

Empowerment of Families

Programs

- Develop an open-door policy that encourages family members to visit the classroom or center at any time.

- Encourage families to offer recommendations for the program's structure and curriculum and to observe the ways in which their contributions are used in the setting.

- Invite families to share their areas of expertise with the teacher, other families, and the children in the program.

- Ensure all families have the opportunity to participate in a policymaking capacity or leadership role (e.g., as members of a board of directors or advisory board).

- Develop a climate statement that expresses the program's appreciation of cultural and linguistic diversity and share the statement with both staff and families.

- Invite families with young dual language learners to participate formally as part of groups that contribute to decisions for the program (e.g., boards, committees, and the like), and to share on an ongoing basis their ideas on how to support and engage with families.

Teachers

- Solicit help from family members in solving problems their child may be having in an early care and education setting.

- Invite families to volunteer regularly in the class and to participate in activities.

- Hold conferences regularly, not just when there is a problem with the child.

4.4 Programs support teachers' responsiveness to the families' goals for their children's development and school readiness.

The most successful opportunities for parent engagement are those that address the ideas of parents about their roles in their children's education and their sense of efficacy in helping their children to succeed in school (Hoover-Dempsey and Sandler 1997). Working with parents to define shared goals helps to strengthen the home–school partnership. In particular, when programs and teachers work to integrate school and family experiences, implement school-readiness practices, and identify strategies for school readiness and transitions, both families and their children benefit.

Researchers have found that preschoolers achieved at higher levels when families and teachers shared similar child-centered beliefs and practices. Thus, it is important that programs ask all families to collaborate and participate in joint goal setting for their children, and to ask families with dual language learners and those families who have children with disabilities or other special needs, about effective strategies and the contexts in which their children learn best.

Integrating School and Family Experiences

Programs

- Explain the program's philosophy on school readiness to classroom staff and families, with consideration for each child's level of development.

- Incorporate the role of family members in facilitating their children's transition from preschool to kindergarten.

- Ensure that families with young dual language learners are included as partners in their children's education. Families should be consulted regarding their children's early language learning experiences, their educational goals for their children, and the educational progress of their children.

- Ensure that families of young children with disabilities or other special needs are included as partners in their education. Families should be consulted regarding their children's unique learning needs, their educational goals for their children, and the educational progress of their children.

- Invite families to collaborate with program staff on long-term language development and learning goals for their children. Actively recruit families to participate in classroom activities.

Teachers

- Respond to children and family members in ways that encourage them to share family experiences.

- Share information about children's experiences in the early education setting with families.

- Support each child's home language and culture at home and at school.

- Maintain confidentiality of family and child information as appropriate.

- Design early education environments that reflect the diverse experiences of children and families.

Implementation of School-Readiness Practices

Programs

- Collaborate with local transitional kindergarten and kindergarten programs, schools, and support staff in preparing children and families for upcoming transitions.

- Provide professional development activities for staff on school-readiness issues,

including developmentally appropriate practice, communication with families, and social–emotional competence.

Teachers

- Describe the program's philosophy on school readiness and transitions.

- Engage in discussions with families about children's experiences in the group or classroom as the experiences relate to school readiness and transitions.

- Respond to questions from families or refer them to appropriate staff for inquiries related to school readiness.

- Articulate that school entry is one milestone in the context of a developmental and educational continuum.

- Include all families as partners in the education of their children with attentiveness to families whose home language is not English.

Strategies for School Readiness and Transitions

Programs

- Coordinate developmentally appropriate experiences to support children's school readiness in all developmental domains, anticipating upcoming transitions to new programs or schools.

Teachers

- Know the previous early care and education experiences of children in the group and plan for upcoming transitions to new programs or schools.

- Identify indicators of school readiness and developmental precursors of school readiness, as appropriate, for the ages of the children served.

4.5 Programs and teachers use effective communication strategies that reflect the diversity of families served.

Honoring diversity strengthens relationships with families and children, thereby enhancing the quality of care and education for preschool children (adapted from

CDE 2006, 57–58). Being responsive to cultural, linguistic, and economic differences and how these differences affect the ways in which programs and teachers communicate with families demonstrates a program's commitment to each family's unique strengths. Programs and teachers can work to enhance their communication strategies, attending carefully to individual differences in family preferences for communication.

Two-way communication strategies have been found to be particularly effective with families with dual language learners who may otherwise feel disconnected from the program. Two-way communication allows both parties to share information about the learning progress and well-being of the dual language learner and to collaborate on ways to help the child reach important learning goals. This type of communication works well during one-on-one meetings with the teacher or in a more informal setting such as in the community or in a group setting with other families with dual language learners of similar linguistic backgrounds. Regular two-way communication may be the first step toward increasing family engagement and key to developing strong dual language learner family–program partnerships.

Communication Strategies

Programs

- Provide professional development for staff on the principles of and strategies for effective communication with families.

- Ensure confidentiality and privacy in communications throughout the program.

- Develop a language and communication policy that informs families with young dual language learners on the possible modes to communicate with staff.

Teachers

- Respect each family's style and preferred method of communication and interact with families in a transparent, accountable manner.

- Interact with families in a timely and professional manner to establish relationships that encourage mutual, two-way exchange of information about children.

- Maintain confidentiality and ensure privacy in communications regarding children, families, and staff and colleagues.

Family Preferences for Communication

Programs

- Interpret and apply communication policies (as appropriate) to ensure that diverse families are included and complex situations are addressed.

- Help staff to understand and apply communication styles based on each family's expressed needs and preferences.

- Ensure that all communications are accessible and comprehensible to families (i.e., in the family's preferred language).

Teachers

- Use various ways to communicate with families (e.g., active listening, e-mail and telephone contact, text messaging), depending on each family's preferences and on the situation.

- Model for families effective strategies for communicating with children, adapt strategies for communicating with children, and adapt strategies (as needed) to meet diverse language and literacy needs.

4.6 **Programs provide a welcoming space in the environment for communication between staff and family members.**

Establishing a welcoming environment is an important aspect of fostering family engagement. "A welcoming environment implies that a program has focused efforts on maintaining an atmosphere that is inviting to families and honors their presence" (Constantino 2008, 25). In a welcoming environment, families feel that they belong and seek ways to contribute to the program. They become comfortable with exchanging information with their children's teachers and open to exploring ways to bring learning activities from the preschool program to home. An essential part of a welcoming environment for families with dual language learners is the program ensuring that they have opportunities to communicate in their home language. Encouraging communication between families with dual language learners who share a home language, hiring staff members (when possible) who are able to communicate in the families' home language, and providing translations help the families to feel welcome in the preschool setting.

A welcoming environment also benefits the children. The family members' presence strengthens the children's sense of comfort and belonging in the preschool setting. For young dual language learners, seeing that the program makes it possible for family members to communicate in the home language helps the children value their home language and culture and appreciate the importance of communicating in their home language.

Creating a Welcoming Space

Programs

- Express a warm welcome by having staff and teachers greet families at the door.

- Offer a family room, where family members can mingle with one another and find information on child development.

- Make a private space available for families and staff to communicate with one another.

- Arrange for support so families with dual language learners can use the home language to communicate with teachers and other program staff members.

4.7 Programs regularly provide family members with information about their children's learning and development, well-being, and everyday experiences.

A key to building successful partnerships with parents is to make them true partners by sharing with them the same kinds of educational information and ideas that are important to the teacher and staff. In a high-quality program, there is ongoing communication between the home and the early care and education center. As much as possible, what the children learn in the program should be supported and reinforced at home.

Family practices in the home are also important for young dual language learners to learn, practice, and reinforce concepts in their home language that were initially introduced in school, such as literacy-building skills. Recent research suggests the use of families' home language is a protective factor for children of immigrant families. When some amount of the family's native language is used regularly in the home, young dual language learners show improved cognitive and social development. Thus, it is important for preschool programs to encourage learning at home in dual language learners' home languages. This may be particularly beneficial in the realm of reading and literacy-building skills.

Information about Learning

Programs

- Offer regular workshops for adult family members that family members helped to design and implement.

- Provide resources for educating the children's family members in various media (print, audio, video) and in the home languages of the families served by the early care and education setting, if appropriate to do so.

- Provide current information about the role of the family in maintaining home language skills.

Teachers

- Inform parents regularly about the purpose and benefits of the activities in the program for their children.

- Provide information regularly to families with dual language learners about the benefits of developing both of the child's languages and promoting bilingualism.

4.8 Programs support and are advocates for strong families.

The better that families are able to meet their children's basic need for shelter, food, and clothing, the more that family members will be available to support their child's learning. Effective preschool programs provide support to families who want it, usually by linking families with resources in the community through referrals. To support family functioning and promote resilience in families and young children, programs and teachers can establish community partnerships and identify key resources for families, connecting them to those resources considered appropriate. In particular, services that help families become self-sufficient and prevent risk of stress or at least reduce ongoing, intense stress, allow family members to become sources of support for each other. Services that promote positive, nurturing relationships among family members enable families to become more resilient and strengthen the children's capacity for learning. Once working relationships with other service providers in the community are established, preschool programs can work to ensure that families receive needed services and children experience continuity in their learning and development.

Family Functioning

Programs

- Collaborate with staff, families, and social service providers to develop policies and procedures related to family support.

- Respond to questions or concerns from staff members or other adults and act as a professional resource.

> ### Strengthening Families: Five Protective Factors
>
> Five protective factors are the foundation of the Strengthening Families Approach: parental resilience, social connections, concrete support in times of need, knowledge of parenting and child development, and social and emotional competence of children. Research studies support the commonsense notion that when these protective factors are well established in a family, the likelihood of child abuse and neglect diminishes. Research shows that these protective factors are also "promotive" factors that build family strengths and a family environment that promotes optimal child and youth development.
>
> *Source:* Center for the Study of Social Policy, n.d.

- Provide professional development opportunities to staff on family functioning, protective and risk factors, and community resources.

Teachers

- Articulate an understanding that families function in a variety of ways and that children or families may require support outside the program.

- Demonstrate an understanding of risk, stress, and resiliency factors related to family functioning and how to support all families appropriately.

- Take steps for further inquiry when concerns arise based on observations of a child or family.

- Communicate daily with families about children's well-being.

- Refer questions or concerns to other staff members when appropriate.

- Work with colleagues to respond to signs of risk or stress in children, as developmentally appropriate and individually meaningful.

Community Partnerships

Programs

- Establish effective relationships with partners to ensure continuity of children's learning and development.

- Maintain professional connections to community and state partners.

Teachers

- Understand the importance of community partnerships in meeting children's needs.

- Forms effective partnerships and collaborations with families, professionals, and community representatives.

- Support the needs of children, their success, and their well-being by maintaining professional connections to community and state partners.

Connecting Families with Resources

Programs

- Support staff and families in the referral process as appropriate.

- Work with community resources to conduct outreach or provide services to program families as appropriate.

- Anticipate families' needs for support based on knowledge of the families' circumstances or of current events that may affect them (e.g., economic climate, natural disasters).

- Identify key community resources that support program practices and family needs, including services that support families with dual language learners' communication with the program.

- Share information with colleagues and develop connections to the program.

Teachers

- Demonstrate familiarity with community resources to support children and families.

- Respond to requests from families about community resources and refer questions to appropriate staff members.

- Protect the confidentiality and privacy of families.

- Engage in conversations with families about referrals to community resources and assist in identifying or gaining access to services as needed, with consideration for the diverse linguistic and cultural experiences of families.

- Identify signs that children or families may require support outside the program, maintain documentation, and initiate closer observation or further inquiry, collaborating with families as appropriate.

- Provide resources linked to classroom instructions to assist families in supporting continued development and maintenance of the home language.

Use of Community Resources

Teachers

- Gain knowledge about the importance of community resources that can enhance professional expertise and children's learning experiences.

- Use community resources routinely to enhance their knowledge about families and services and classroom learning activities.

4.9 Programs and teachers engage families in supporting continued development and maintenance of the home language.

Programs and families with dual language learners are critical to children's language development as the sheer amount of words children hear and the richness of the speech they hear is strongly linked to their future language and literacy abilities. Thus, it is critical that programs communicate to families with dual language learners the importance of speaking to children in their home language and suggest that families seize as many opportunities as possible to engage children in conversation. Parents need to help families understand the importance of dual language learning concepts in their home language and engaging in extended language interactions in their home language. In addition, preschool programs can provide families with dual language learners with the necessary provisions and resources to teach new concepts at home in dual language learners' first language.

Home Language

Programs

- Collaborate with families and colleagues to provide a variety of ways throughout the program for young dual language learners and their families to participate.

- Model one-on-one, group, and unstructured peer-to-peer activities.

- Collaborate with families and colleagues to design an educational program that incorporates each child's home language(s).

- Encourage families, colleagues, and community members to use children's home languages and provide training or support as needed.

- Conduct ongoing evaluation of programmatic support for children's home language(s) and use data to guide program improvements.

Teachers

- Assist in offering a variety of developmentally appropriate, individually meaningful, and culturally responsive ways for young dual language learners to participate in the group (CDE 2009).

- Work with colleagues to create various opportunities for young dual language learners and their families to participate in the group throughout the day.

- Demonstrate understanding that the early education setting is often the first place where young dual language learners encounter English and that honoring each child's home language fosters positive social–emotional development and the child's development and learning in all other areas.

- Support home language development.

- Plan with families, colleagues, community members, and others who support children's development and learning.

- Incorporate practices that honor the role of the home language as a vital foundation in English language development.

References

California Department of Education (CDE). 2006. *Infant/Toddler Learning & Development Program Guidelines.* Sacramento: California Department of Education.

———. 2009. *Preschool English Learners: Principles and Practices to Promote Language, Literacy, and Learning—A Resource Guide.* 2nd ed. Sacramento: California Department of Education.

Center for the Study of Social Policy. n.d. Parental Resilience: Protective and Promotive Factors. Washington, DC: Center for the Study of Social Policy. http://www.cssp.org/reform/strengthening-families/2013/SF_All-5-Protective-Factors.pdf (accessed July 21, 2014).

Constantino, S. M. 2008. *101 Ways to Create Real Family Engagement.* Galax, VA: ENGAGE! Press.

Henrich C., and D. Gadaire. 2008. "Head Start and Parental Involvement." *Infants and Young Children* 21 (1): 56–69.

Hoover-Dempsey, K. V., and H. M. Sandler. 1997. "Why Do Parents Become Involved in Their Children's Educations?" *Review of Educational Research* 67 (1): 3–42.

Lopez, M. E., H. Kreider, and M. Caspe. 2004. "Co-Constructing Family Involvement." *Evaluation Exchange* X (4): 2–3.

National Association for the Education of Young Children (NAEYC). 2009. National Standards for Early Childhood Professional Preparation Programs, Position Statement. Washington, DC: NAEYC.

State Advisory Council on Early Learning and Care. 2013. *California's Best Practices for Young Dual Language Learners: Research Overview Papers.* Sacramento: California Department of Education. http://www.cde.ca.gov/sp/cd/ce/documents/dllresearchpapers.pdf (accessed April 3, 2014).

Further Reading

Halgunseth, L. C., A. Peterson, D. R. Stark, and S. Moodie. 2009. "Family Engagement, Diverse Families, and Early Childhood Education Programs: An Integrated Review of the Literature." *NAEYC* and *Pre-K Now.*

Mendez, J. L. 2010. "How Can Parents Get Involved in Preschool? Barriers and Engagement in Education by Ethnic Minority Parents of Children Attending Head Start." *Cultural Diversity and Ethnic Minority Psychology* 16 (1): 26–36.

Guideline 5: Including Children with Disabilities or Other Special Needs

This section provides a broad framework for early childhood educators to help in planning and implementing quality educational programs for the inclusion of young children with disabilities or other special needs in regular early care and education settings. Program approaches for children who do not qualify for special educational services but who have such special needs as behavioral or communication issues are also offered.

For an overview of California's system for delivering services to children with disabilities or other special needs, see appendix E and appendix G. For additional resources related to core concepts and recommended practices in early childhood special education, please refer to the Early Childhood Special Education Series developed by the Special Education Division—SEEDS—in collaboration with the California Department of Education (http://www.scoe.net/seeds/resources/handbooks.html [accessed July 21, 2014]).

Inclusion as a Program Goal

Over the past 40 years, changes in both state and federal laws and in public policies and attitudes have resulted in growing numbers of young children with disabilities or other special needs participating with peers who are typically developing in early care and education settings. Federal laws, such as the Individuals with Disabilities Education Act **(IDEA)** and Americans with Disabilities Act (ADA), protect the rights of children with disabilities or other special needs. The IDEA states that children should be educated in the least restrictive environment. The ADA prohibits discrimination and ensures equal opportunity for persons with disabilities. Additionally, national associations such as the Division for Early Childhood and the National Association for the Education of Young Children (DEC and NAEYC) (2009) have developed position statements to address inclusion in early childhood settings. In their joint position statement on inclusion, the DEC and NAEYC state:

Early childhood inclusion embodies the values, policies, and practices that support the right of every infant and young child and his or her family, regardless of ability, to participate in a broad range of activities and contexts as full members of families, communities, and society. The desired results of inclusive experiences for children with and without disabilities and their families include a sense of belonging and membership, positive social relationships and friendships, and development and learning to reach their full potential. The defining features of inclusion that can be used to identify high quality early childhood programs and services are access, participation, and supports. (DEC and NAEYC 2009, 1)

Inclusion as an overarching program goal supports the growth and development of all children. This statement is particularly true when educators hold themselves accountable for the progress of all children, including those with diverse learning or developmental needs. When thoughtfully planned and implemented, inclusive programs contribute to a sense of community in early childhood settings by creating places where all families and children belong. Research indicates that the most effective programs are those in which all collaborators (families, early childhood educators, special educators, and administrators) have shared values and goals for including children with disabilities or other special needs. Inclusion is understood to benefit all children, families, and communities.

> "When inclusive [practice] is fully embraced, we abandon the idea that children have to become 'normal' in order to contribute to the world. Instead, we search for and nourish the gifts that are inherent in all people. We begin to look beyond typical ways of becoming valued members of the community, and in doing so, begin to realize the achievable goal of providing all children with an authentic sense of belonging."
>
> *Source:* Kunc 1992.

Universal Design for Learning

To support inclusive practices, preschool programs should employ the principles of a **universal design for learning** (UDL) in the design of environments and curriculum approaches.

> UDL provides considerations for the widest diversity of learners possible so that all children benefit. These include children with varying disabilities, linguistic diversities, and varied learning styles. The concept of UDL facilitates inclusive early childhood environments by ensuring equitable access and meaningful participation through flexible and creative approaches within a developmentally appropriate setting . . . Curriculum design must be responsive to diverse classrooms. Educators must share a commitment that all children participating will be successful in their development and learning. Successful outcomes for all children are characterized by diversity and individualization. (Cunconan-Lahr and Stifel 2007)

Services for Children with Other Special Needs

Some preschool-age children have special needs that do not meet the eligibility criteria for special education services, but that nonetheless require modifications or adaptations to the environment, curriculum, or instructional strategies so that those children may function successfully in the classroom. Such adaptations may include providing a footrest so that a child's feet are flat on the ground (providing stability when the child is seated), offering choices between two objects for a child with delays in language skills, preparing a child to use a replacement skill such as a gesture to request help, or providing visual cues to prepare a child for transitions.

Nearly two-thirds of children (65 percent) identified by special education as having a disability, have delays in communication (see appendix C). There are fewer children with more significant disabilities like intellectual disability (formerly mental retardation), physical and mobility impairments, or multiple disabilities. When children do have significant disabilities, they are likely to be receiving specialized services to support success in the preschool setting. Eligible children who receive special education services

have individualized education programs (IEPs) that outline the goals and strategies for preschool teachers to use.

An additional area that continues to be of concern to early educators is providing responsive and caring educational settings for children with behavioral concerns. Young children's behavior is their primary method of communicating. Behavior communicates what they want to express, obtain, or avoid through their actions. Challenging behavior often indicates that a child is experiencing stress from a number of factors: internal stress from fatigue, poor nutrition, illness, pain or discomfort; external stress from a mismatch in the classroom environment or expectations, poor relationships with the teachers or children, overly difficult or overly simple tasks, limited social skills, trauma in the home environment; or a combination of these factors. A consistent and supportive teacher or other important adult can provide support for the child during short periods of stress. If challenging behavior continues over longer periods of time, it may be necessary to examine possible contributors to the behavior in the classroom and from other sources. A tiered intervention framework such as Response to Intervention and Instruction (RtI[2]), or the Teaching Pyramid, may be an appropriate response to challenging behavior (see the box below).

Unfortunately, many children may have challenges to or risks for their development, but are not eligible for specialized services. Early childhood educators have two general goals for such children: (1) to provide an environment where the child feels safe, secure, and cared for; and (2) to help the child develop coping skills to decrease stress and promote learning and development. As is the case with children with disabilities, children with other types of special needs must be assessed systematically and regularly so that staff members are aware of each child's progress toward goals and provide timely intervention if problems or concerns arise. In high-quality early care and education programs, staff members receive professional development and training in areas of disabilities and other special needs. Staff members are also aware of community resources available to children with disabilities or other special needs and their families.

Recommended Practices: Program Practices for Promoting the Development of Young Children and Addressing Challenging Behavior

"Early education environments should be structured to provide universal, secondary, and indicated prevention and intervention practices. There are promising data indicating that the adoption of this model as a program-wide approach results in positive outcomes for children, families, and the programs that support them (Dunlap, Fox, & Hemmeter, 2004).

• At the universal level, all children should receive sufficient density of positive feedback from their caregivers (Shores, Gunter, & Jack, 1993; Shores, Jack, Gunter, Ellis, Debrine, & Wehby, 1993). Early educators should maintain a predictable schedule, minimize transitions, provide visual reminders of rules, give time and attention for appropriate behavior, use positive reinforcement to promote appropriate behavior, provide choices where appropriate, and maximize child engagement to minimize problem behaviors (Laus, Danko, Lawry, Strain, & Smith, 1999; Lawry, Danko, & Strain, 1999; Strain & Hemmeter, 1999).

• At the secondary level, a social-skills curriculum should be adopted and implemented. Research indicates that systematic efforts to promote children's social competence can have both preventive and remedial effects (Walker et al. 1998; Webster-Stratton & Reid 2004).

• At the tertiary (or intervention) level, assessment-based interventions that are developed through the process of Positive Behavior Support (PBS) have been shown to be effective (Blair, Umbreit, & Bos, 1999; Blair, Umbreit, & Eck 2000; Dunlap & Fox, 1999; Galensky, Miltenberger, Stricker & Garlinghouse, 2001; Moes & Frea 2000; Reeve & Carr, 2000). In PBS, early educators team with families to determine the function of problem behavior through functional behavior assessment and then develop a behavior support plan that is implemented across all environments."

Source: Fox 2006.

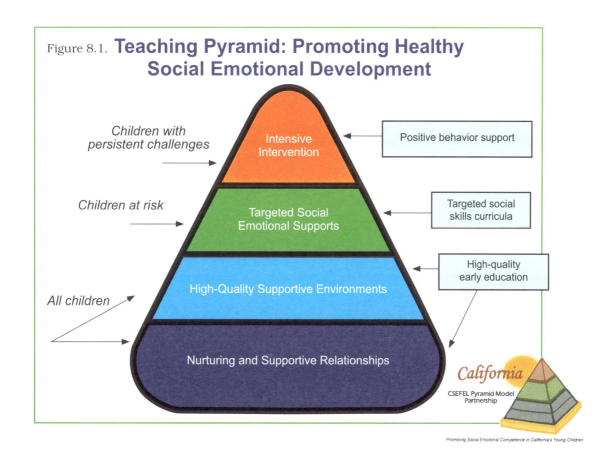

Figure 8.1. **Teaching Pyramid: Promoting Healthy Social Emotional Development**

According to the California Collaborative on Social and Emotional Foundations for Early Learning (CA CSEFEL), fundamental to promoting social and emotional competence in young children is guiding children in their efforts to build positive relationships with adults and peers and creating supportive social and emotional learning environments for all children. For children at risk of developing behavior problems, targeted social and emotional strategies may be necessary, and for those children who display very persistent and severe challenging and behavior problems, individualized intensive interventions are required, when the children do not respond to typical preventive practices, child guidance procedures, or social–emotional teaching strategies that would normally work with most children (CA CSEFEL Teaching Pyramid, Promoting Social and Emotional Competence, Module 3a, 2013).

Addressing Children's Challenging Behavior	
Old Way	*New Way*
• General intervention for all behavior problems	• Intervention matched to purpose of the behavior
• Intervention is reactive	• Intervention is proactive
• Focus on behavior reduction	• Focus on teaching the child new skills
• Quick fix	• Long-term interventions

5.1 Programs and teachers ensure a sense of belonging and support full participation of children with disabilities or other special needs.

Teachers in high-quality preschool programs regard children with disabilities or other special needs as *children first* and as children with disabilities or other special needs second. The child's individual personality, learning strengths, needs, and interests are taken into account in setting learning goals and planning activities. Likewise, families of children with disabilities or other special needs are viewed as having the same kinds of concerns for their child's well-being and progress as do families of typically developing children.

Being rated as a high-quality preschool program may not be sufficient for adequately meeting the individual learning needs of children with disabilities or other special needs. Successful inclusion involves collaboration among professionals, specialized instruction, and organizational supports such as ongoing coaching and mentoring to ensure that inclusion is of high quality. When these supports are in place, teachers can successfully include children with disabilities or other special needs seamlessly and thus contribute to children's positive social and academic outcomes such as the development of peer relationship and engagement in learning (Odom, Buysse, and Soukakou 2011). Inclusion provides benefits not only for children with disabilities or other special needs and their families, but also for typically developing children in the program, who learn about acceptance and appreciation of individual differences (Diamond and Huang 2005; Odom et al. 2006).

Sense of Belonging

Programs

- Welcome and support children with disabilities or other special needs.

- Develop program guidelines to inform developmentally appropriate practice; collaborate with families and staff to assess the program's educational practices.

- Offer professional development opportunities to staff, in collaboration with **specialized service providers**, on meeting the needs of diverse learners through multiple approaches to learning.

- Communicate with families about the program's approach to understanding and meeting the needs of diverse learners.

- Develop program policies to support the use of *people-first language.*

- Provide professional development opportunities to staff and families on *people-first language.*

Teachers

- Actively encourage acceptance of children with disabilities or other special needs and positive social interactions among all children through adaptation of the environment, curriculum, and instructional practices.

- Follow guidance from specialized service providers and parents to support the learning and development of all children, according to developmental theory and program philosophy and practices.

- Respond to children's cues and preferences such as sensory processing needs.

- Follow guidance to support all children's active participation in learning opportunities through the use of easily adaptable materials, strategies, and techniques.

- Use *people-first language* by referring to the child first, not the disability or special need. For example, refer to a *child with special needs* rather than a *special-needs child.*

Research Synthesis Points on Early Childhood Inclusion

1. *Inclusion* has multiple meanings but is essentially about belonging, participating, and reaching one's full potential in a diverse society.

2. Inclusion takes many different forms.

3. Universal access to inclusive programs is not yet a reality for all children (from birth to age five) with disabilities.

4. A wide variety of factors such as attitudes and beliefs about inclusion, child and adult characteristics, policies, and resources can influence how inclusion is implemented and viewed by families and practitioners.

5. Collaboration is a cornerstone of high-quality inclusion.

6. Specialized instruction, interventions, and supports are key components of high-quality inclusion and essential in reaching desired outcomes for children and their families.

7. Children in inclusive programs generally do at least as well as children in specialized programs.

8. Inclusion can benefit children both with and without disabilities.

9. Professional development is necessary to ensure that practitioners acquire the knowledge, skills, and ongoing supports for effective inclusion practices.

Sources: Early Childhood Research Institute on Inclusion (Odom 2002), National Professional Development Center on Inclusion 2009, Buysse and Hollingsworth 2009, and Odom, Buysse, and Soukakou 2011.

- Regularly provide children with disabilities or other special needs with opportunities to develop friendships with other children in the classroom (see appendix H).

5.2 Programs and teachers work closely with families in an educational partnership and provide them with appropriate community resources, information, and support as it relates to the child's disability or special needs.

Collaboration with families is key to successful inclusion in early childhood settings. Features of collaboration that have been associated with successful inclusion have been identified by Lieber et al. (1997) as "joint participation in planning, shared philosophies, shared "ownership" of (i.e., responsibility for) all children, communication, professional roles, stability of relationships, and administrative support" (Odom et al. 2011, 348). Although some effective inclusive models may include coaching and mentoring with the specialized professional (e.g., speech pathologist, physical therapist), providing ongoing guidance and support to the lead teacher, other models might have preschool teachers and early childhood special education teachers engage in a co-teaching model together. In all cases, intervention that focuses on collaboration among professionals and between professionals and families working in an equal, respectful partnership to assess a child's strengths and needs, to make decisions, and to set goals for the child's learning and development is likely to be the most successful approach.

Partnership with Families of Children with Disabilities or Other Special Needs

Programs

- Express openness, sensitivity, and caring in response to initial contact by the family of a child with disabilities or other special needs.

- Establish trust with the families of a child with disabilities or other special needs by being consistently available, maintaining confidentiality, sharing significant information, maintaining a safe environment, and demonstrating that the child is valued and liked (CDE 1996).

- Provide staff members with information and ongoing mentoring, coaching, and reflective supervision that help them address special or individual needs of children in the programs.

Teachers

- Engage in ongoing daily communication with families. For example, teachers might exchange a notebook with information about the child between the preschool setting and home.

- Work closely with specialized professionals to meet children's individual needs.

- Build relationships with community resources available to families of children with disabilities or other special needs.

- Ask open-ended questions about children and engage in active listening to gain information about children with disabilities or other special needs.

- Operate within the bounds of professional knowledge and experience when assessing the strengths or needs of a child with disabilities or other special needs, referring parents to appropriate specialized service providers when the child's needs are beyond teachers' expertise.

- Offer families opportunities to explore with other families the common interests and concerns about child development, parenting, or concerns specific to special needs.

- Explore and respect cultural preferences in communicating with families about children with disabilities or other special needs.

5.3 Programs meet legal requirements related to the care and education of children with disabilities or other special needs.

Federal legislation such as the Individuals with Disabilities Education Act (the IDEA 2004) and the Americans with Disabilities Act (ADA), along with state specific mandates are in place to protect the rights of children with disabilities or other special needs. At a very minimum, programs need to meet the legal requirements related to the care and education of children with disabilities or other special needs in their programs. However, programs should strive to develop policies that extend beyond the bare minimum requirements in federal and state legislation and move toward honoring policies such as the position statement developed by the Division of Early Childhood of the Council for Exceptional Children and the National Association for the Education of Young Children (DEC/NAEYC 2009).

Early Childhood Inclusion: A Joint Position Statement of the Division for Early Childhood (DEC) and the National Association for the Education of Young Children (NAEYC)

Recommendations for using this position statement to improve early childhood services:

1. *Create high expectations for every child to reach his or her full potential.*

2. *Develop a program philosophy on inclusion.*

3. *Establish a system of services and supports.*

4. *Revise program and professional standards.*

5. *Achieve an integrated professional development system.*

6. *Influence federal and state accountability systems.*

IDEA and ADA

Programs

- Develop program policies and practices that meet legal requirements related to the care and education of young children with disabilities or other special needs, communicating these to families and staff.

- Develop program policies and practices that meet the requirements of the IDEA and ADA, and state law related to parents' rights.

- Conduct ongoing monitoring of program procedures to ensure compliance.

- Provide professional development opportunities to staff and families on parents' rights.

Teachers

- Plan the environment and learning experiences in consultation with specialized service providers to meet the legal requirements as well as children's individual needs and interests.

- Follow requirements regarding parents' rights under the IDEA, ADA, and state law.

- Refer questions to appropriate staff as needed.

- Respect the confidentiality of children and families.

5.4 Programs provide sufficient release time, training, information, and support for teachers to plan and consult regarding children with disabilities or other special needs.

Including children with disabilities or other special needs sometimes requires additional teacher time. To promote the success of such efforts, high-quality programs provide release time and opportunities for training and reflection so that teachers can gain the skills and information they need. Teachers report that one of their most common needs to help make inclusion effective is regular access to consultants (Scruggs and Mastropieri

1996). Early childhood teachers need information about specialized resource agencies and professionals, and they need the time and support necessary to work with such specialized service providers. Information to support collaboration with specialized service providers is included in chapter 5, "Collaborating for Inclusion," of *Inclusion Works!* (CDE 2009b).

Time to Support Inclusion

Programs

- Provide professional development activities and staff support sessions so that teachers have ample time to meet and to discuss the best ways to help children with disabilities or other special needs.

- Encourage staff to discuss assessments or IEPs, plan instructional strategies, and monitor individual children's progress.

- Make meeting with parents and family members a high priority and accommodate parents' schedules by making special arrangements, if necessary.

Inclusion Skills

Teachers

- Engage in professional development opportunities provided by programs and in the community.

- Are open to ongoing coaching and mentoring, working with specialized professionals to learn more about effective ways to meet the needs of children in their care.

- Use their knowledge and experience of individualizing activities for children to support inclusive practice and develop questions for specialized service providers or coaches.

5.5 Programs ensure teachers' participation on an educational team that develops and implements individualized education programs (IEPs) for children eligible to receive special education services.

Children over the age of three who qualify for special education must have an IEP developed by an interdisciplinary team. As required by federal and state laws, the IEP contains clearly identified goals and objectives that are regularly monitored (see appendix E for more information). This team includes the child's parents or guardians; the preschool teacher, as required by the federal IDEA; special education professionals; and the child. The team approach has numerous potential benefits, including mutual support and communication. Regular classroom and curricular routines and activities for many children with disabilities will require a minimal degree of modification. For example, the program might already be serving children who have a language delay or a learning disability.

The team can support the early childhood staff in helping to meet the goals and individual needs of the child within the early care and education setting. Cooperative teams can also help establish a practice of staff planning and implementing curricula to meet the needs of all children. (See also chapter 3.)

IEP Participation

Programs

- Partner with families and specialized service providers to assess and build staffing capacity to support children with disabilities or other special needs and their families.

- Facilitate participation of program staff members on teams with families and specialized service providers.

- Use the *California Preschool Learning Foundations* (CDE 2008, 2010b, 2012b) and *California Preschool Curriculum Framework* (CDE 2010a, 2011, and 2013) since the primary goal of the IEP

is to ensure access to the general curriculum. For children with developmental delays, programs should be familiar with the *California Infant/Toddler Learning & Development Foundations* (CDE 2009) and the *California Infant/Toddler Curriculum Framework* (CDE 2012a) as that information may be useful.

- Coordinate with other agencies or specialized service providers to ensure effective delivery of services to children in the program who have disabilities or other special needs.

- Participate in individualized education program (IEP) teams and monitor implementation of recommendations at the program level.

- Adopt an interdisciplinary team approach (i.e., teachers and specialized service providers related to the child's learning needs) to address the complexity of facilitating the language development of young dual language learners with disabilities and to provide coordinated and comprehensive intervention.

Teachers

- Gather input from colleagues and families to inform the work of the team.

- Engage in two-way communication with team members (inside and outside the program) to ensure effective delivery of services for children with disabilities or other special needs and their families.

- Understand the range of services available to children with disabilities or other special needs, the roles of specialized service providers, and different models of support.

- Listen to and implement recommendations from specialized service providers.

- Understand the underlying goals of the curriculum in order to provide appropriate access to the curriculum for children with different abilities.

- As much as possible, integrate approaches for helping children with disabilities or other special needs into their regular daily classroom routines and practices. For example, a child's IEP may include regular peer interaction as a means to promote the development of language skills. In this case, adults might introduce strategies that promote child-to-child communication throughout the day, such as extending conversation, asking questions, or helping to interpret children's communication.

- Other parts of the IEP may consist of the teacher following an instructional approach that is used with all children in the classroom. For example, for children with low vision, a teacher needs to provide spoken directions and information instead of requiring children to rely on visual information. This strategy is helpful for all children's understanding because it provides additional information and direction.

5.6 Programs promote teachers' collaborative work with specialized service providers in implementing appropriate modifications in the curriculum, instructional methods, or classroom environment.

Children with disabilities or other special needs may require modifications in educational environments or instructional activities in order to support full participation. Some children may also receive specialized therapeutic services. Sometimes these services are delivered directly by a specialized service provider—such as a speech–language pathologist, an occupational therapist, or a physical therapist—who can offer ideas to support the child's use of skills in the preschool setting.

Sometimes classroom and instructional modifications are recommended by family members or other consultants. The most effective practice results when staff, family members, and specialized service providers work together.

Early childhood educators bring skills, expertise, and knowledge about children and contribute to an effective team effort involving teachers, families, and specialized service providers.

Accommodation

Programs

- Plan the physical environment to support access for children who move differently or who use mobility equipment such as wheelchairs. Ensure that toys and materials are accessible, and all activities can be accomplished in similar positions—for example, sitting on the floor, standing at the sensory table, or sitting in a chair.

- Ensure that strategies to enhance learning and autonomy take into consideration the degree of visual and sound stimulation present in the learning environment.

- Plan work areas and learning materials to promote children's interactions and

Related Services

Related services means transportation and such developmental, corrective, and other supportive services as are required to assist a child with a disability in order to benefit from special education. These related services are identified in a child's individualized education program (IEP) and may include the following:

- Speech–language pathology and audiology services
- Interpreting services
- Psychological services
- Physical and occupational therapy
- Recreation, including therapeutic recreation
- Early identification and assessment of disabilities in children

- Counseling services, including rehabilitation counseling
- Orientation and mobility services
- Medical services for diagnostic or evaluation purposes
- School health services and school nurse services
- Social-work services in schools
- Parent counseling and training

play so that children can participate in meaningful and relevant ways independently, partially assisted, or totally assisted.

Teachers

- Collaborate with family members and specialized service providers to modify activities in the curriculum to maximize participation and learning. For example, include modified materials or equipment, or break down an activity into smaller steps.

- Are sensitive to the level and degree of help required by each child. For instance, teachers attend responsively and consistently to children who require more cues or prompting to interact with materials, participate in activities, or persist with activities.

5.7 Programs, teachers, and specialized service providers (e.g., special educators and therapists) support dual language learning in preschool children with disabilities or other special needs.

"Despite concern that dual language input will confuse or delay the language acquisition of young children with special needs, emerging research indicates that these children can learn and benefit from learning more than one language. Moreover, there is no available evidence that limiting these children to one language will decrease language difficulties or that dual language learning will increase language delays and problems (Kohnert and Medina 2009)." (State Advisory Council on Early Learning and Care 2013, Paper 6, 211) for a comprehensive research review and discussion of ECE for young dual language learners with disabilities or other special needs). Research on the bilingual development of children with autism, intellectual disabilities, and deaf children with cochlear implants suggests that children with a wide range of abilities and language and communication challenges can learn more than one language. Just as with typically developing preschoolers, classroom use of the home language provides the child with various social situations that support understanding of how to interact with others and how to apply **pragmatics** when communicating with others (see chapter 6 for a full discussion of classroom strategies). The scientific findings suggest that speaking the home language facilitates social interactions and, in turn, language and social development.

Recent research also underscores the positive effects of a bilingual intervention approach for children who have limited English-language development. In addition, based on the most current research findings, a bilingual approach is recommended for children with severe disabilities. There does not appear to be any research evidence for limiting exposure to a single language when children have disabilities. Furthermore, the need to support the home language for these children is critical: for many children, the home language, rather than English, is the only language in which the family can communicate.

Research indicates that many families of preschoolers with disabilities or other special needs value home language maintenance and bilingualism for their children. Given the significance of the culture of a family, parent–child interactions, a child's sense of identity and belonging, and the parents' sense of competence and confidence, families who speak a language other than English should be encouraged to maintain their home languages with their children. Therefore, all teachers, even those who are monolingual, will need to develop collaborative relationships with family members, intervention specialists, and other colleagues to provide intervention that includes the use of both the home language and English.

To effectively implement a bilingual early intervention for young dual language learners, bilingual teachers and staff will need to be recruited and trained. As the State Advisory Council on Early Learning and Care (2013, 225) made special evident in Paper 6 (Early Intervention and Special Needs):

[T]eachers and other practitioners should be trained to facilitate the language development of all young dual language learners, including those with special needs. This is an important area for professional development. There is also a critical need to recruit and train bilingual teachers and speech–language pathologists. In addition, an interdisciplinary team approach (i.e., teachers and specialized service providers related to the child's learning needs) is required to address the complexity of facilitating the language development of young dual language learners with disabilities and to provide coordinated and comprehensive intervention.

Dual Language Learners with Disabilities or Other Special Needs

Programs

- Collaborate with specialized professionals to develop an understanding of emerging research that suggests children with a wide range of abilities and patterns of language development can learn more than one language.

- Understand that speaking one language at home and English at school does not produce language delays or difficulties among children with a range of disabilities or other special needs.

- Collaborate with specialized service professionals to develop a shared understanding of the fact that families of preschoolers with disabilities or other special needs value home language maintenance and bilingualism for their children.

- Encourage families to maintain their home languages with their children as the culture, family, parent–child interactions, children's sense of identity and belonging, and the parents' sense of competence and confidence contribute significantly to children's learning and development.

- Involve families in their children's learning experience and provide parent education opportunities when

serving young dual language learners with disabilities or other special needs. Family members benefit from learning strategies that support their children's language development through home visits, coaching, and modeling. For example, family members can be taught to use interactive storybook reading strategies such as dialogic reading and responsive language interactions in their home languages.

Teachers

- Understand that recent research findings indicate that the use of the home language in intervention does not slow the second-language acquisition of dual language learners who have various disabilities or other special needs.

- Recognize that children with language and communication disorders can apply their home language skills when learning a second language and, in many cases, this results in a greater rate of English-language development.

- Recognize that dual language learners with a range of disabilities or other special needs, including autism spectrum disorders or intellectual disabilities and deaf children with cochlear implants, can learn more than one language, and when the first language is not stimulated, these children are likely to experience limited potential for growth in the second language.

- Collaborate with family members and other interdisciplinary team members to implement interventions that support maintenance of the child's home language and English-language development.

- Participate in ongoing professional development to learn specific language strategies and instructional adaptations that support bilingual development.

References

California Department of Education (CDE). 1996. *Project EXCEPTIONAL: A Guide for Recruiting Child Care Providers to Serve Young Children with Disabilities*, Vol. 1. Sacramento: California Department of Education.

———. 2008. *California Preschool Learning Foundations, Volume 1*. Sacramento: California Department of Education.

———. 2009a. *California Infant/Toddler Curriculum Framework*. Sacramento: California Department of Education.

———. 2009b. *Inclusion Works! Creating Child Care Programs That Promote Belonging for Children with Special Needs*. Sacramento: California Department of Education.

———. 2010a. *California Preschool Curriculum Framework, Volume 1*. Sacramento: California Department of Education.

———. 2010b. *California Preschool Learning Foundations, Volume 2*. Sacramento: California Department of Education.

———. 2011. *California Preschool Curriculum Framework, Volume 2*. Sacramento: California Department of Education.

———. 2012a. *California Infant/Toddler Curriculum Framework*. Sacramento: California Department of Education.

———. 2012b. *California Preschool Learning Foundations, Volume 3*. Sacramento: California Department of Education.

———. 2013. *California Preschool Curriculum Framework, Volume 3*. Sacramento: California Department of Education.

California Collaborative on the Social and Emotional Foundations for Early Learning (CA CSEFEL). 2013. Teaching Pyramid in *Promoting Social and Emotional Competence, Module 3a*. Individualized Intensive Interventions: Determining the Meaning of Challenging Behavior. www.CAinclusion.org/teachingpyramid.

Cunconan-Lahr, R. L., and S. Stifel. 2007. *Early Childhood Inclusion/Universal Design for Learning Questions to Consider and Checklist*. Building Inclusive Child Care (BICC) Project, Northampton Community College and Pennsylvania Developmental Disabilities Council.

Diamond, K. E., and H. Huang. 2005. "Preschoolers' Ideas about Disabilities." *Infants and Young Children* 18:37–46.

Division for Early Childhood (DEC) and the National Association for the Education of Young Children (NAEYC). 2009. *Early Childhood Inclusion: A Joint Position Statement of the Division for Early Childhood (DEC) and the National Association for the Education of Young Children (NAEYC)*. Chapel Hill: The University of North Carolina, FPG Child Development Institute.

Fox, L. 2006. "Recommended Practices: Program Practices for Promoting the Social Development of Young Children and Addressing Challenging Behavior." Handout 4.5 Leadership Strategies. Available from Center on the Social and Emotional Foundations for Early Learning (CSFEL). http://challengingbehavior.fmhi.usf.edu/do/resources/handouts.htm (accessed July 31, 2014).

Hemmeter, M. L. 2001. *Recommended Practices Program Assessment: Improving Practices for Young Children with Special Needs and Their Families*. Missoula, MT: Division for Early Childhood.

Kunc, Norman. 1992. "The Need to Belong: Rediscovering Maslow's Hierarchy of Needs." In *Restructuring for Caring and Effective Education*, edited by R. Villa, J. Thousand, W. Stainback, and S. Stainback. Baltimore, MD: Paul Brookes. http://www.broadreachtraining.com/articles/indxarti.htm (accessed May 13, 2014).

Lieber, J., P. J. Beckman, M. J. Hanson, S. Janko, J. M. Marquart, E. Horn, and S. L. Odom. 1997. "The Impact of Changing Roles on Relationships between Professionals in Inclusive Programs for Young Children." *Early Education and Development* 8:67–83.

National Association for the Education of Young Children (NAEYC). 2009. *Early Childhood Inclusion*. A Joint Position Statement of the Division for Early Childhood (DEC) and the National Association for the Education of Young Children (NAEYC). Washington, DC: NAEYC. http://www.naeyc.org/files/naeyc/file/

positions/DEC_NAEYC_ECSummary_A.pdf (accessed July 31, 2014).

Odom, S. L. 2000. "Preschool Inclusion: What We Know and Where We Go From Here." *Topics in Early Childhood Special Education* 20 (1): 20.

Odom, S. L., C. Zercher, S. Li, J. Marquart, and S. Sandall. 2006. "Social Acceptance and Social Rejection of Young Children with Disabilities in Inclusive Classes." *Journal of Educational Psychology* 98:807–23.

Odom, S. L., V. Buysse, and E. Soukakou. 2011. "Inclusion for Young Children with Disabilities: A Quarter Century of Research Perspectives." *Journal of Early Intervention* 33 (4): 344–56.

Scruggs, T.E., and M. A. Mastropieri. 1996. "Teacher Perceptions of Mainstreaming/Inclusion, 1958–1995: A Research Synthesis." *Exceptional Children* 63:59–74.

Soukakou, D. P. 2012. "Measuring Quality in Inclusive Preschool Classrooms: Development and Validation of the Inclusive Classroom Profile (ICP)." *Early Childhood Research Quarterly* 27:478–88.

Guideline 6: Promoting Health, Safety, and Nutrition

Children's health includes not only the absence of illness or injury, but also encompasses children's overall fitness and well-being. Equally important is the acknowledgment that children's health is related to family functioning as well as the sociocultural context and the emotional, social, and physical environments in which children live. Therefore in promoting children's health, safety, and nutrition, preschool programs attend to policies and regulations as well as a relationship-based approach to supporting child and family well-being through health promotion and prevention. Promotion and prevention, such as following sound health and safety practices, providing nutritious meals and snacks, and offering several periods of outdoor play each day, are important aspects of health, safety, and nutrition.

While prevention is the primary focus of this set of guidelines, interventions (including emergency response and administration of medication) are considered essential components of promoting health and safety in early childhood settings. To implement health, safety, and nutrition guidelines effectively, program administrators and preschool teachers should consider ways to adapt health, safety, and nutrition practices that are sensitive and responsive to families' cultural, linguistic, and socioeconomic backgrounds (adapted from California Department of Education and First 5 California 2012, 79). Being sensitive and responsive begins by building trust with children and families through nurturing and supportive relationships. Respectful, two-way relationships with young children and families developed over time lead to feelings of safety and a sense of belonging. Such relationships promote well-being and become an important base for children's learning and development.

6.1 Programs and teachers promote the physical health and well-being of all children and families.

Children and families' physical health and well-being is important to their overall day-to-day functioning. Promoting the physical health and well-being of children and families includes implementing routine health checks, encouraging regular physical activity in the classroom and at home, and attending carefully to each child's special health-care needs. See Title 5 and Title 22 of the *Health and Safety Code* for related regulatory requirements.

Routine Health Checks

Programs

- Collaborate with staff to develop program policies and procedures related to daily health checks.

- Interpret and apply illness policies, as needed, to ensure they are appropriate for complex situations.

- Identify and respond to programwide issues regarding illness or injury (e.g., lice) and report to a regulatory agency as required.

- Monitor program requirements for certification in child cardiopulmonary resuscitation (CPR) and pediatric first aid, providing professional development to staff on CPR and pediatric first aid on a regular basis.

Teachers

- Conduct daily individual health checks for signs of illness or injury in children.

- Maintain documentation and respond accordingly.

- Recognize and respond to sign of illness or injury in children or alert other staff as appropriate.

- Implement illness policies that include following universal precautions to reduce the spread of infection and disease.

- Understand the criteria for excluding children when they are ill.

Physical Activity

Programs

- Provide professional development to staff on the importance of physical activity and how to promote the development of movement skills.

- Plan and implement program services, events, and regular assessment of the outdoor space to promote physical activity in children.

- Ensure that the daily classroom schedule includes a balance of quiet and active times each day.

- Provide adequate equipment (e.g., tricycles, scooters, and the like) and materials that promote small and large motor development.

Teachers

- Plan schedules, environments, and experiences to provide children with ample opportunities for physical activity, including a variety of developmentally appropriate and noncompetitive games, making adaptations as necessary to meet individual requirements.

- Promote child health by ensuring that children go outside for physical activity, feel connected with nature, and follow their own curiosity and interests during child-initiated play in the outdoors.

- Encourage children to engage in physical activities. For children with disabilities or other special needs, including health issues, discuss with the family and specialized service providers (if available) ways to encourage physical activity appropriately.

Special Health-Care Requirements

Programs

- Provide supervision and professional development—including information about community resources and use of referrals—on how to support children with special health-care requirements and their families.

- Ensure that staffing policies are designed to meet children's special health-care requirements, create and maintain a fully inclusive program setting, and

protect the privacy and confidentiality of children and families.

- Collaborate with families and community service providers (as appropriate) to develop individualized daily plans for children with identified special health-care requirements.

- Inform relevant staff about children's plans and requirements.

- Adapt the environment as necessary to meet children's special health-care requirements.

- Ensure that staff members receive professional development on the storage and administration of medications, regulatory requirements, and related topics.

- Work with families to develop individualized plans for children who require medication.

Teachers

- Know individual children's identified special health-care requirements and locate documentation as needed.

- Refer concerns about children's health status to appropriate staff and participate in the referral discussions as appropriate.

- Protect the privacy and ensure the confidentiality of children and families.

- Support children's understanding of special health-care requirements, as developmentally appropriate and individually meaningful.

- Know individual children's current use of medication and follow procedures to label, store, and administer medication.

- Locate and maintain documentation as needed.

Knowledge of Health Practices

Teachers

- Communicate with families daily about children's well-being.

- Work with colleagues and families to plan opportunities to support children's learning about health, as developmentally appropriate.

- Maintain certification in child CPR and pediatric first aid, and respond accordingly to children's injuries or illnesses.

6.2 Programs and teachers ensure the safety of all children.

One of the highest priorities for families in selecting a preschool program is to have the environment meet high standards for health and safety. California has its own licensing requirements to ensure the safety of children in early childhood programs. However, many programs go beyond minimum state requirements to ensure children's safety and the prevention of accidents and injuries.

Child Safety

Programs

- Provide ongoing professional development for health and safety policies and practices, identifying and addressing potential barriers to compliance.

- Report program-related injuries to regulatory agencies as required.

- Anticipate, investigate, and resolve complex health and safety problems in the immediate and broader environments (e.g., using monthly inventories or checklists).

- Facilitate development of a programwide plan to ensure that children will be adequately supervised at all times, including procedures for safe drop-off and pickup of children.

- Collaborate with staff on the development of programwide emergency plans.

- Regularly review emergency plans, including first-aid and CPR training, to ensure they are current and effective.

- Maintain current emergency contact information for families and staff.

- Implement emergency plans and assign roles using systematic exchange of information with families and staff to ensure everyone is prepared to respond.

- Conduct emergency drills, maintain documentation as required by regulatory agencies, and engage in ongoing evaluation of the program's emergency preparedness.

Teachers

- Stay updated on policies and practices that address indoor and outdoor environmental health and safety and ensure program compliance.

- Respond quickly to accidents involving children and inform appropriate family members, providing documentation as appropriate.

- Model safe behavior.

- Engage children in learning about safety in indoor and outdoor environments, as developmentally appropriate.

- Collaborate with staff and colleagues to provide adequate supervision that supports safe, fun, and challenging play and prevents the intrusion of unauthorized visitors.

- Provide direction to children and adults during emergency drills.

6.3 Programs and teachers ensure that children are well nourished and enjoy mealtimes.

Children's nutritional needs change as they develop and grow. In some cases, the program provides meals; in others, family members bring their child's meals. Either way, close communication with family members about the child's daily nourishment is necessary to ensure a balanced diet for each child. How meals are provided is also important. Mealtimes can be wonderful opportunities for teachers to nurture their relationships with children and also to support developing peer relationships. Eating together in a pleasant environment contributes to a sense of community, especially when mealtimes reflect the practices and preferences of the families. Mealtimes offer opportunities for teachers to support the development of healthful habits and attitudes toward food and help to ensure that children receive the nutrition they need to grow (adapted from CDE 2006, 68–69).

Nutrition

Programs

- Provide professional development for staff on healthful food choices and habits and food preparation within the family and cultural context.

- Identify barriers to healthful behaviors.

- Provide resources and support to families regarding healthful food choices and habits and fresh foods, such as information on outdoor green spaces for families and farmers markets.

- Ensure program policies address issues such as schedules, staffing patterns, and how the program's food service supports children's learning during mealtimes.

- Collaborate with families and staff to develop and implement specialized plans to meet the dietary requirements for individual children.

Teachers

- Follow principles of healthy food choices and habits, including offering appropriate portion sizes and a healthy selection of fresh foods.

- Facilitate conversations about healthful food choices and habits, taking into account individual family and cultural preferences.

- Plan opportunities for children to learn about healthful food choices and habits, as developmentally appropriate, and invite families to share strategies and suggestions for selecting and preparing healthful foods.

- Promote and adhere to policies regarding celebrations, foods brought from home, making sure healthful foods are offered.

- Help to create a positive climate during meals.

- Support children's learning and social development during mealtimes, as developmentally, linguistically, and culturally appropriate.

- Adopt feeding practices that respect children's internal cues of hunger and fullness.

- Know and meet children's individual dietary requirements (e.g., regarding food allergies) and locate information in children's records.

6.4 Programs and teachers promote children's positive mental health.

A child's mental health is affected by social and emotional experiences; in particular, the emotional responses the child receives from other people. A child's mental health is inextricably linked to the mental health of the family members who are primary attachment figures, whether they are parents, grandparents, or others. From the child's perspective, mental health is a sense of well-being: Does the child feel safe and comfortable? Does the child trust that her needs will be met? Social–emotional development and a child's progress in increasing self-regulatory skills depend on the experience the child has in personal relationships.

Programs that support early childhood mental health as a health and safety issue provide emotional as well as physical safety and security for preschoolers. A collaborative relationship with the family members helps program staff members understand the values that influence the family's interactions, expectations, and beliefs. Social–emotional well-being is necessary for a child to be mentally healthy and is foundational to children's learning in all other developmental domains (adapted from CDE 2006). Additional information can be found in chapter 2 and Guideline 5.

Mental Health

Programs

- Take steps to reduce staff turnover in the program and encourage positive relationships between children and teachers and among teachers.

- Maintain contacts with mental health consultants and other mental health professionals who can provide advice or services when children, family members, or staff members appear to be especially sad, under stress, unpredictable, or short-tempered over a period of time.

- Understand that the way children and families express and manage emotions is influenced by their culture.

- Collect information on mental health services and offer referrals to families or staff members as appropriate.

- Promote reflective practice and reflective supervision as a vehicle to support teachers in their efforts to make sense of their own emotional responses or reactions to children and respond intentionally rather than reactively.

Teachers

- Observe and reflect upon children's emotional responses to the day's experiences and take these responses into consideration in all planning processes.

- Guide and support children's efforts to engage in satisfying relationships with adults and peers.

- Discuss with family members children's emotional responses and family members' related interpretations.

- Recognize the emotional nature of early care and education, taking time to reflect on one's own emotional responses (both positive and negative) to particular children, interactions, or events.

- Take a break or talk with a supervisor or colleague, when needed, to avoid immediately acting on difficult feelings.

- Seek help when experiencing mental health problems, such as depression or anxiety.

- Recognize cultural differences in understanding mentally healthy behavior.

6.5 Programs and teachers protect all children from abuse and neglect.

To protect children and prevent abuse and neglect, programs should offer support to families to help lessen the stress they may be experiencing. A positive relationship with the family opens the door for providing assistance. This support can come in the form of conversations, referrals to services, or information on education or job opportunities. In addition, program leaders need to foster an environment in which teachers feel comfortable engaging in confidential discussions with designated staff members about concerns for a child, and, as appropriate, with the child's family members. Program leaders and staff members must also comply with requirements for reporting child abuse and neglect (adapted from CDE 2006, 71).

Child Abuse Prevention

Programs

- Develop programwide policies and practices to reduce the risk of child abuse and neglect.

- Assess complex situations involving concerns about child abuse or neglect, making recommendations for action and collaborating with personnel on specific cases as appropriate.

- Provide professional development and ensure that staff members understand the role of a mandated reporter.

- Provide community resources for children, families, and staff in situations involving abuse and neglect.

Teachers

- Identify signs of child abuse or neglect, addressing concerns about child abuse or neglect according to regulation and law; refer concerns to supervisor(s), as necessary.

- Adhere to the role of a mandated reporter.

- Respond to stress and trauma experienced by children, families, colleagues, or staff members, seeking support from colleagues or mental health consultants, as appropriate.

- Honor the confidentiality of children, colleagues, and families.

References

California Department of Education (CDE). 2006. *Infant/Toddler Learning & Development Program Guidelines.* Sacramento: California Department of Education.

California Department of Education and First 5 California. 2012. *California Early Childhood Educator Competencies.* Sacramento: California Department of Education.

Further Reading

Child Care Law Center. n.d. *Overview of Preschool Licensing in California.* San Francisco: Child Care Law Center. http://childcarelaw.org (accessed June 24, 2013).

Children's Environmental Health Network. 2012. *Child Care Fact Sheets.* Washington, DC: Children's Environmental Health Network. http://www.cehn.org/resources (accessed June 26, 2013).

Seltenrich, N. 2013. "Environmental Exposures in the Context of Child Care." *Environmental Health Perspectives* 121: A160-A165. http://ehp.niehs.nih.gov/121-a160/ (accessed June 27, 2013).

Guideline 7: Assessing Children's Development and Learning

Assessment is the process of obtaining information about various areas of children's development, learning, and progress. A primary purpose of ongoing assessment in early childhood settings is to provide feedback to teachers about children's progress and guide instructional decisions. Assessment for the purposes of curriculum planning, planning of environments, and planning of other early learning experiences is essential to ensuring high quality in early childhood programs (see Snow and Van Hemel 2008 for a review). Screening, observations, and frequent documentation are important methods that teachers can use to understand individual children and groups of children.

Engaging in some form of ongoing assessment is essential for helping the family and teacher know whether a child is making progress and helps teachers to set goals for learning and plan effective instructional approaches for the program. It is particularly important that early childhood assessments used by programs are developmentally appropriate, culturally and linguistically sensitive, and fully cover the diverse learning needs of children with disabilities or other special needs. Informed assessment systems provide teachers and families with valuable information about what children know and are able to do and contribute to the overall quality of a preschool program. However, when assessment systems are not informed by considerations of developmental appropriateness or are not sensitive to the diverse learning needs of individuals, or groups of children, there is a risk of making children uncomfortable and generating insufficient and perhaps inaccurate information.

At the preschool level, assessment should be broadly focused, including children's knowledge, skills, behaviors, personality, and health. As described in this section, assessment is distinct from program evaluation because it focuses on *children*, not on programs or services.

Purposes of Assessment

Assessments can be used for a variety of purposes (Snow and Van Hemel 2008). In the *Principles and Recommendations for Early Childhood Assessments* (National Education Goals Panel 1998), four broad purposes for early childhood assessment were established:

- To promote learning and development of individual children
- To identify children who may have special needs and health conditions
- To monitor trends in programs and evaluate program effectiveness
- To obtain benchmark data for accountability purposes at the local, state and national level

One of the most important assumptions underlying effective assessment of young children is that their development is continuing and complex. Although a one-shot, easily administered assessment may offer some information about children's development, it is better to use a variety of instruments and methods over a period of time to gain a more comprehensive picture.

NAEYC Program Standard

The program is informed by ongoing systematic, formal, and informal assessment approaches to provide information on children's learning and development. These assessments occur within the context of reciprocal communications with families and with sensitivity to the cultural contexts in which children develop. Assessment results are used to benefit children by informing sound decisions about children, teaching, and program improvement.

Source: NAEYC 2008.

The Need for Formal Assessments and Documentation

Teachers frequently assess children, but often these assessments may not be done formally or documented systematically. Carefully maintaining detailed records of assessments provides a basis for well-considered judgments about children's progress in learning and development. The records enable teachers to analyze children's strengths and areas that may need improvement. Assessments may be conducted through an array of tools and a variety of processes, including collections of children's representative work, records of teachers' observations or interviews with children, and teachers' summaries of children's progress both individually and in groups (NAEYC 1995).

The Time for an Assessment

When to do an assessment depends on the purpose and functions. For example, if a teacher wants to find out whether a child has a disability or developmental problems, a developmental screening should be done when the child enters the program and annually thereafter. In contrast, if the purpose of the assessment is to document how well children are learning and progressing in the program, the staff will want to use a continuous, systematic assessment and recordkeeping tool throughout the year.

7.1 Programs engage in authentic, ongoing observational assessment to document each child's learning and developmental progress.

As much as possible, assessment should reflect the natural settings and the types of activities with the people children are familiar with in daily life. Assessment procedures that occur outside the typical boundaries or context of a child's experiences may produce misleading information. When the assessment process is completed in this way, it may also frighten or inhibit the child from behaving naturally. For more information on effective strategies, please see appendix I.

Engaging in authentic assessment means choosing assessment tools that

The Desired Results Developmental Profile

The Desired Results Developmental Profile (DRDP) is an observation-based assessment designed for teachers to observe, document, and reflect on the learning, development, and progress of children in the preschool years. The assessment results are used to plan curriculum for individuals and for groups of children.

Teachers using the DRDP:

- **Observe children.** Teachers observe the child in his/her regular environment during daily routines, interactions, and activities.

- **Document evidence of children's development.** Teachers regularly take anecdotal notes, gather samples of children's work, and take photos to document children's progress.

- **Reflect and rate.** After organizing and reflecting on the documented evidence, teachers assign a rating to each measure. They may do this by hand on a paper copy of the DRDP or within DRDPtech©, a Cloud-based application available for teachers and programs.

- **Analyze and plan.** After compiling the DRDPs, teachers analyze the information and use the results to plan for an individual and groups of children.

rely on tasks that are close to the real-life experiences of the young children assessed and are used in everyday real-life contexts (McAfee, Leong, and Bedrova 2004). For all young children, authentic assessment allows children to reveal their knowledge and skills as they naturally engage in learning in the preschool setting. For dual language learners who typically use their home language to communicate, authentic assessment must include assessment in their home language as well as in English. See State Advisory Council on Early Learning and Care 2013, Paper

5 (Assessment), for a fuller discussion of assessing dual language learners in their home languages).

Ongoing observational assessment is essential if it is to be used to inform the planning of curriculum, activities, and interactions. Throughout the preschool day, there are many opportunities for teachers to observe children's play, exploration, problem solving, language, interests, and behaviors and to document indicators of progress. When assessment is an ongoing practice, teachers and program administrators can make effective instructional adaptations that build on children's prior knowledge and support new learning for each child and for groups of children.

Child Assessment

Programs

- Evaluate and select child observational assessments that are reliable, valid, and culturally, linguistically, and developmentally appropriate.

- Develop policies on how to conduct assessments in settings that are natural and familiar to the child (such as the home or early care and education setting) rather than unfamiliar, artificial settings structured exclusively for the purpose of assessment.

- Set up assessments to engage the child and have assessments conducted primarily by people who are familiar with the child and who understand the child's unique behavioral traits. Strangers may intimidate the child.

- Identify procedures for the monitoring of language interactions of young dual language learners to ensure that rich learning opportunities are provided in both English and the home language.

- Establish procedures on how to assess young dual language learners in both languages to understand each child's overall language development and determine whether there is a need for further language evaluation.

- Individualize assessment procedures and link results to curriculum planning and make adjustments as necessary

for each child, with particular attention to dual language learners and children with disabilities or other special needs.

- Observe and document young children's behaviors and interactions in the preschool setting continually in order to complete the DRDP-PS© instrument, including the English-language development measures for young dual language learners, at least twice per year.

- Enlist native speakers of the home languages of young dual language learners so they can assist in completing the DRDP-PS© measures in all domains of development. See State Advisory Council on Early Learning and Care 2013, Paper 5 (Assessment).

Teachers

- Meet together and with families regularly to gather information about children's behavior in the home and discuss different approaches to assessment and children's progress.

- Implement procedures for the monitoring of language interactions of young dual language learners to ensure rich learning opportunities are provided in both English and the home language.

- Engage in observation regularly, as it is one of the most important and useful forms of assessment in preschool settings. Observation allows teachers to learn about children by carefully watching them, listening to them, and studying their work. When using observation as an assessment method, teachers should

  o ask questions that encourage children to describe their thinking;

  o listen to children as they describe how they made decisions and solved problems;

  o watch children as they play and work with materials and other children;

  o hold conversations with children about their work;

  o listen as children talk with others informally and during group discussions;

  o study the children's work (e.g., projects, writing, drawings).

Examples of Documentation, Artifacts, and Evidence

- Teacher's description and overview of an event/experience/skill development, such as photographs and descriptions of a field trip

- Photographs of children at work— for example, conducting a science experiment

- Samples of children's work, like a writing sample from the beginning of the year

- Children's comments, such as "All the rocks have sparkles in them," in writing or as recorded by the teacher

- Teacher or parent comments about a classroom event (e.g., "It was really fun helping the children measure the ingredients for play dough.")

- Teacher transcriptions of conversations during small-group time when children are exploring a new topic, such as why snow melts indoors

- Important items or observations relating to an event/experience/development, such as "Johnny can now write his own name on his work"

Source: Seitz 2008.

7.2 Programs use child assessments that are evidence-based, reliable, valid, and culturally, linguistically, and developmentally appropriate.

In preschool programs, special care should be taken with assessments that require significant linguistic processing or language-based responses. Child assessment instruments should be culturally, linguistically, and developmentally fair and unbiased. Observational or nonverbal approaches should also be used. For dual language learners, assessments should be conducted in both the home language and in English.

Appropriate Assessment

Programs

- Provide professional development opportunities to staff members on the benefits and limitations of various assessment instruments, taking into account developmental, linguistic, or cultural considerations and whether gathering information from families is included.

- Evaluate and select assessment instruments that are valid, reliable, and developmentally, culturally, and linguistically and contextually appropriate for the children served. See State Advisory Council on Early Learning and Care 2013, Paper 5 (Assessment).

- Ensure that staff members are qualified to administer assessment instruments, as appropriate.

- Interpret results of all assessments cautiously, particularly in the area of vocabulary and language development, making only tentative conclusions about the development of each young dual language learner and understanding the limitations of assessment instruments considered.

7.3 Programs use a formalized system of screening with all young children, making referrals when appropriate.

Screening often is one of the first steps in the assessment process. A valid and reliable screening of a child's health and development includes speech, hearing, and vision. Although screening plays an important role in helping to identify whether a child needs further evaluation, screening alone is not sufficient to determine that a child has a disability or developmental delay (adapted from Head Start Performance Standard 1308.6 b [http://eclkc.ohs.acf.hhs.gov/hslc/standards/hspps/] accessed October 6, 2014.)

Developmental Screening

Programs

- Develop guidelines related to screening and collaborate with qualified service providers to administer and interpret screenings.

- Provide information to staff and family members regarding the use, benefits, and limitations of screening instruments; also offer follow-up recommendations for assessment or intervention as appropriate.

- Evaluate and select screening instruments that are reliable, valid, and developmentally, culturally, linguistically, and contextually appropriate for the children served.

- Develop program policies regarding referrals and supervise implementation.

- Support staff and family members in the referral process.

- Include qualified bilingual assessors in the screening process when dual language learners are screened.

- Identify what screening is appropriate for children already identified as having disabilities or having an individualized education program (IEP). For example, a child with a diagnosis of speech and language delays with mild hearing loss may benefit from screening in other developmental areas such as vision, social–emotional, and physical development, but would not need "screening" in speech and language or hearing.

Teachers

- Review the results of screening and initiate discussions with staff, colleagues, and family members regarding the universal or targeted screening.

- Contribute information (including input from staff, colleagues, and family members) to the screening process.

- Identify the need for referral for further evaluation based on observations, information from staff, colleagues, and family members, for dual language learners (including adults who are familiar with the child's home culture and language); and screening assessment tools.

- Assist family members in identifying or gaining access to further evaluation or other services as needed, with consideration for their diverse linguistic and cultural experiences.

7.4 **Programs provide sufficient time, training, information, and guidance to support ongoing assessment of all children and appropriate interpretation and use of assessment results.**

Support Child Assessment

Programs

- Provide professional development opportunities to staff on the appropriate use of screening results, observational data, and documentation for assessment.

- Provide professional development opportunities regarding appropriate assessment instruments and procedures and how to interpret the results in order to conduct valid assessments of the development and achievement of all children, with particular attention to young dual language learners and children with disabilities or other special needs.

- Ensure that staff members have the guidance needed to appropriately analyze and interpret both formative and summative assessment data.

- Develop or modify program policies on the interpretation, application, and dissemination of observation and assessment information.

- Provide adequate time for family members and staff members to reflect individually and consult in teams regarding observation and assessment information.

- Adopt an interdisciplinary team approach (i.e., teachers and specialized service providers related to the child's learning needs) to address the complexity of facilitating the language development of young dual language learners with disabilities and to provide coordinated and comprehensive intervention.

Use of Child Assessments

Teachers

- Understand that assessment includes ongoing child observations as well as the use of specific assessment instruments for different purposes.

- Use assessment instruments appropriately with individual children or groups of children.

- Engage in discussions with staff and family members about the meaning of observation, screening, documentation, and assessment data to support children's learning and development.

- Understand the role of child assessment to guide curriculum development and focus areas.

7.5 Child assessment considers multiple sources of information and covers all early learning domains.

To fully understand a child's development, educators need information from many sources: teacher observations, parent reports, samples of children's work/performance, or direct assessment (Snow and Van Hemel 2008). Gathering information from multiple sources helps provide a balanced view and helps to reduce the chances of underestimating children's abilities. While applicable to all children, this is especially important in the case of assessing children with disabilities or other special needs.

Sources of Information

Programs

- Ensure that assessment procedures regularly involve family members as highly relevant sources of information regarding their children.

- Use an approach called *triangulation*, in which several sources of information are gathered to answer the same questions about the child's development.

Teachers

- Use a variety of assessment methods regularly and consistently to understand and document what children do, both individually and in groups.

- Use assessments as a basis for planning and developing new curricular and instructional approaches and for helping children to build their knowledge and skills.

- Collect information about each child's early language learning experiences from family members so that the unique linguistic, social, and cultural characteristics of young dual language learners are considered when conducting assessments and interpreting the results.

- For children receiving services from other sources (such as therapy through insurance, or special education through an IEP), work with family members to gather input from specialized service professionals. With the families' permission, the specialized service professional may send reports to or talk directly with the teacher.

Triangulation: An Example of a Multiple-Sources Approach to Assessment

Ms. Rojas, a preschool teacher, is interested in understanding more fully why David is behaving aggressively with his peers. She obtains information from a variety of sources, beginning with observation of David in the preschool setting. She observes, for example, the frequency of his aggressive behavior and the activities and persons that provoke it. She also speaks with his parents about his behavior at home. And she uses a structured checklist that provides indicators of social behavior for children who are David's age. She combines all this information into a summary report, which she uses as a basis for planning ways to help David gain self-control and find positive outlets for his aggression.

Source: CDE 2000, 51.

- Assess young dual language learners in both the home language and English to understand each child's overall language development and determine whether further language evaluation is needed. See State Advisory Council on Early Learning and Care 2013, Paper 5 (Assessment).

7.6 Family members are aware of the program's approach to assessment (including screening, observation, and documentation) and contribute to activities that support the assessment process.

Family members need to be fully informed and aware of the different kinds of assessments being done in the preschool setting. Information about the child's behavior at home and in other places outside the preschool program should be sought from family members because this knowledge can be helpful in the assessment process. Enlisting the assistance of families in the assessment process is important for all children, especially when program staff members do not speak the home languages of the children.

Collaborating Regarding Child Assessment

Programs

- Collaborate with family members to clarify differences in the interpretation of observation or assessment information.

- Provide concrete examples of the behavior or activity that is being assessed to support understanding and clarity.

- Request family members' input, data, and interpretation, when needed.

- Collaborate with colleagues and family members, as appropriate, to analyze observation and assessment data for program planning, community outreach, and professional development.

- Gather information about each child's early language learning experiences from family members so that the unique linguistic, social, and cultural characteristics of young dual language learners are considered when conducting assessments and interpreting the results.

- Communicate with family members about a program's approach to assessment and the specific assessment activities.

Communicating about Assessment of Data

Teachers

- Communicate with family members in their home language about the interpretation of observation or assessment data, as appropriate.

- Maintain confidentiality and ensure privacy when sharing assessment information with family members and specialized service providers.

- Collaborate with family members and service providers to adapt learning experiences or the environment based on observation or assessment.

- Identify the need for additional assessment, evaluation, or follow-up and assist family members in identifying or gaining access to services, sensitively considering the diverse linguistic and cultural experiences of families.

References

California Department of Education (CDE). 2000. *Prekindergarten Learning and Development Guidelines*. Sacramento: California Department of Education.

Dichtelmiller, M. L. 2001. *The Work Sampling System: Work Sampling in the Classroom (A Teacher's Manual)*. New York: Rebus.

Head Start Program Performance Standard. 45 CFR 1308.6b. Assessment of children. http://eclkc.ohs.acf.hhs.gov/hslc/standards/hspps/ (accessed October 6, 2014).

McAfee, O., D. J. Leong, and E. Bodrova. 2004. *Basics of Assessment: A Primer for Early Childhood Educators*. Washington, DC: National Association for the Education of Young Children.

National Association for the Education of Young Children (NAEYC). 1987. *Testing of Young Children: Concerns and Cautions*. Washington, DC: NAEYC.

———. 1995 *School Readiness: A Position Statement of the NAEYC*. Washington, DC: NAEYC.

———. 2008. *Overview of the NAEYC Early Childhood Program Standards*. Washington, DC: National Association for the Education of Young Children. http://www.naeyc.org/files/academy/file/OverviewStandards.pdf (accessed July 21, 2014).

National Education Goals Panel. 1998. Principles and Recommendations for Early Childhood Assessments. Washington, DC: The National Education Goals Panel. http://govinfo.library.unt.edu/negp/reports/prinrec.pdf (accessed April 8, 2014).

Seitz, H. 2008. *The Power of Documentation in the Early Childhood Classroom*. Washington, DC: National Association for the Education of Young Children (NAEYC).

Snow, C. E., and S. B. Van Hemel. 2008. *Early Childhood Assessment: Why, What, and How?* Washington, DC: National Research Council of the National Academies.

State Advisory Council on Early Learning and Care. 2013. *California's Best Practices for Young Dual Language Learners: Research Overview Papers*. Sacramento: California Department of Education. http://www.cde.ca.gov/sp/cd/ce/documents/dllresearchpapers.pdf (accessed April 3, 2014).

Further Reading

Early Learning Standards Task Force, Kindergarten Assessment Work Group, Pennsylvania BUILD Initiative, and Pennsylvania's Departments of Education and Public Welfare. 2005. *Early Childhood Assessment for Children from Birth to Age 8 (Grade 3): Pennsylvania Early Learning Standards*. Harrisburg PA: Early Learning Standards Task Force, Kindergarten Assessment Work Group, Pennsylvania BUILD Initiative, and Pennsylvania's Departments of Education and Public Welfare.

National Association for the Education of Young Children (NAEYC). 2008. *Overview of the NAEYC Early Childhood Program Standards*. Washington, DC: NAEYC.

National Association for the Education of Young Children (NAEYC), and the National Association of Early Childhood Specialists in State Departments of Education (NAECS/SDE.) 2003. *Position Statement with Expanded Resources. Early Childhood Curriculum, Assessment, and Program Evaluation: Building an Effective System in Programs for Children Birth through Age 8*. Washington, DC: NAEYC and NAECS/SDE.

Guideline 8: Planning the Learning Environment and Curriculum

The environment has an impact on every facet of the early childhood program. Research conducted with the Early Childhood Environment Rating Scale (ECERS) (Sylva et al. 2010; Peisner-Feinberg et al. 2001) and the Classroom Assessment Scoring System (CLASS) (Howes et al. 2008; Mashburn et al. 2008) indicates that both the physical environment and the social and emotional climate of a program influence its overall quality. High-quality physical and social environments enhance young children's well-being and development and help them become ready for school.

All environments communicate messages. In an early childhood program, these messages may convey program staff members' beliefs and values about young children, ways in which children learn, the role of families, and the importance of community. The environment makes a strong impression on young children and their families when they enter the program. It should convey to all children that they belong and they will be safe and cared for. When well designed and organized, the environment can help support appropriate developmental goals for children. For preschoolers, this support includes social–emotional knowledge and skills described in the first volume of the *California Preschool Learning Foundations* (CDE 2008), such as the development of self-awareness, self-regulation, social and emotional understanding, empathy and caring, initiative in learning, cooperation and responsibility, and relationships with adults and peers.

Designing a High-Quality Environment

Preparing the environment (for both children and adults) in high-quality programs involves responding to a fundamental question: *How does it feel to live, play, and work here every day?* Personal preferences and experiences—what is pleasing, energizing, soothing, and comforting—may vary among individuals. Similarly, many different factors influence an individual's response to the environment:

1. **Physical space.** Many considerations influence decisions about the use of physical space. For example, are there opportunities for children to move easily into and out of a busy room? Do pathways provide clear directions to children, encouraging safe and unencumbered movement from one area to another? Are routes leading to different learning centers clear? Are there places for two or three children to play apart from the larger activity? Are there places for a child to step back and observe?

2. **Lighting and color.** Lighting and color can add warmth to a room or cool it down. Is there a variety of lighting that supports focused learning in different parts of the environment? Is there plenty of natural light? Do the colors create a peaceful feeling and allow children to focus on teachers and learning materials?

3. **Display areas.** Children's art can be displayed in ways that communicate, "This is a child's place" and "You belong and what you create is valued." Displays of children's art should be aesthetically pleasing yet not make the environment overstimulating or filled with visual clutter.

4. **Texture.** Children are responsive to environments that offer variety. Floor coverings, play materials, furniture, animals, and foods all contribute to heightening children's awareness of the world around them.

5. **Auditory surroundings.** How do children experience the sound levels in a room? Are quiet activities planned in proximity to one another, or is the reading area next to the manipulatives area? Some children may be highly sensitive to noise, and the amount of background noise, including music, may make it difficult for them to concentrate or to listen attentively. Children need opportunities to experiment with sound, to express themselves with exuberance, and to experience the power of sound to soothe, relax, or make a transition to other activities.

The learning environment requires thoughtful planning by preschool teachers. A well-designed learning environment appropriately provides organization for children's learning experiences and supports children's learning during routines throughout the day. The teacher's intentional design of the learning environment increases opportunities for children to have engaging and meaningful interactions with adults and peers. In essence, the environment can support children's progress with the learning and development that is described in California's preschool learning foundations. Along with interactions, instruction, learning activities, and routines, the learning environment is a central part of preschool teachers' planning and implementation of curriculum.

> "In the Reggio Emilia approach, the importance of the environment lies in the belief that children can best create meaning and make sense of their world through environments which support 'complex, varied, sustained, and changing relationships between people, the world of experience, ideas and the many ways of expressing ideas.'"
>
> *Source:* Caldwell 1997, 93.

The play environment as curriculum: Interest areas to support children's play and child-initiated learning

The play environment of a preschool setting is the primary source of early childhood curriculum. Well-stocked play areas, often called interests areas or learning centers, provide young children with a vast array of possibilities for learning. Driven to explore novel objects, people, and events, young children relate to well-planned play and learning environments just as scientists relate to their laboratories or artists relate to their studios. When teachers thoughtfully organize the space into small, well-stocked interest areas, young children use such spaces like mini-laboratories or studios. In each interest area, children find familiar materials and novel materials, the latter added as a way to pique new interest or to add challenge and complexity to the learning within children's play.

Children enter these play areas and explore what they might do with the easily accessible materials. As children play, they form theories about what they can make the items do. They experiment, invent, and devise theories to make sense of their experiences, all embedded in their play. Play-based interest areas, both indoors and outdoors, each with a distinct focus, are designed to offer a basic inventory of materials with which children can apply emerging skills and develop concepts while they play.

As teachers plan curriculum, they consider ways to provoke more complex and coherent ideas by adding materials to an area. When adapting the curriculum to support all learners, teachers modify the play space or the materials available in the play space to make sure that each child in the program has access. Such ongoing additions and changes to the play spaces are essential to curriculum planning. By thoughtfully planning and arranging the interest areas with specific learning goals in mind and allocating long blocks of uninterrupted time for self-initiated play, teachers provide children with important opportunities to develop many fundamental concepts and skills. Examples of interest areas in a preschool environment include the following:

- Dramatic play area
- Block area
- Art area
- Book area
- Writing area
- Math area
- Science area
- Family display area
- Music, movement, and meeting area

The environment as a context for curriculum includes interest areas that are both indoors and outdoors. Interest areas not only hold novel items added as part of an ongoing small-group project, but they also provide resource materials for children's exploration and investigation.

8.1 The environment is safe and comfortable for all children, teachers, and family members.

One of the highest priorities for families in selecting a preschool program is that the environment meets high standards for health and safety. As a baseline, California has licensing requirements to ensure the safety of children in early childhood programs. Many programs go beyond minimum state requirements to ensure children's safety and the prevention of accidents and injuries. Safety guidelines are readily available and should be used routinely because circumstances may change within a program and recommendations from leading organizations continually evolve (American Academy of Pediatrics, American Public Health Association, National Resource Center for Health and Safety in Child Care and Early Education 2011).

Planning, implementing, and monitoring programs to ensure the well-being of children includes establishing routines and procedures that take into account the age and developmental status of the children. Evaluation of the environment also considers children's individual needs. For example, program staff may address the following concerns: *Do some children have special health or developmental issues? Are modifications required in setting up a room or establishing routines?* In some cases, the staff may need training on the specialized procedures for the health care needs of a child or on making special physical accommodations.

Considerations of health and safety are embedded in every aspect of a preschool program. Programs must attend to routine care practices (e.g., washing hands, using gloves, washing toys), the provision of safe and age-appropriate play materials, and the creation of program policies and procedures to address various health concerns (e.g., coping with sick children, infectious diseases, lice). Of particular note is the monitoring of safety in the outdoor environment. Because young children are active explorers and enjoy the challenges of practicing new motor skills and competencies, all equipment should be carefully inspected and in good repair. In some areas, the air quality may influence outdoor time for children with asthma or compromised health. Staff should engage in periodic review of the environment and the program's routines and procedures to identify safety issues and prevent injuries and accidents. Even well-designed environments that meet the highest standards still require an attentive, thoughtful approach to health and safety. Teachers always need to supervise three- through five-year-olds and provide ongoing guidance in the safe use of play materials and equipment.

Safe Environment

Programs

- Facilitate development of a program-wide plan to ensure that children will be adequately supervised at all times.

- Ensure that areas and furnishings in the environment support full participation of all children and adults in the program, including persons with disabilities or other special needs.

- Provide a staff lounge for relaxation and storage of personal belongings, as well as for lunch and breaks.

Teachers

- Comply with policies and practices addressing environmental health and safety indoors and outdoors.

- Collaborate with other staff and colleagues to provide adequate supervision that supports safe, fun, and challenging play that excludes unauthorized visitors.

- Maintain a safe environment to support children's learning and to prevent accidents.

8.2 The environment promotes a supportive social–emotional climate and sense of belonging and community for everyone.

Preschool children develop special relationships with teachers and rely on these relationships for security and support in the learning environment. Teachers recognize the importance of these close relationships to a young child's self-confidence and feelings about preschool. Teachers actively nurture those relationships when they affirm the child's initiative, convey enthusiasm for his accomplishments, are responsive to her needs for assistance or comfort, and seek to develop a friendly, cooperative relationship with the child's primary family members (adapted from CDE 2010a, 81).

Young children spend many hours in the preschool setting; therefore, it should become a home away from home. For teachers, other staff members, and children's family members, the preschool program should become a place of community and togetherness. Providing comfortable furnishings (e.g. adult-sized and child-sized chairs) where adults and children can relax together and creating an atmosphere that conveys both emotional and physical safety are essential for this type of setting. A comfortable and safe environment that everyone can enjoy contributes greatly to the quality of a preschool program (adapted from CDE 2006, 74).

Supportive Climate

Programs

- Provide professional development, including reflective supervision, mentoring, and coaching to staff and colleagues on the relationship between the social–emotional climate and the overall learning environment.

- Provide professional development opportunities to staff and colleagues, and resources to families, about the principles of relationship-based practice.

- Ensure that a private area is made available for sharing sensitive information with family members.

- Ensure that classrooms contain both safe havens where young children, including dual language learners, can take a break and do not have to speak to anyone as well as spaces in the classroom where children can interact in small groups and one-on-one.

Teachers

- Respond to children's interests by reflecting, expanding on, or demonstrating enthusiasm for their ideas.

- Work with staff to plan a positive social–emotional climate in the learning environment based on the individual strengths and interests of the children in the group.

- Provide responsive and sensitive care to support children's early learning experiences.

- Work with staff and families to support positive relationships among early childhood educators, between early childhood educators and children, and among children.

- Ensure that each child has developmentally and individually appropriate opportunities to interact with adults and peers in meaningful ways.

- Implement strategies that establish warm, nurturing relationships and foster a sense of belonging for all children, with particular attention to dual language learners, children with disabilities or other special needs, and children receiving services from child protective services.

- Encourage positive peer interactions among children and positive interactions among families enrolled in the program to ensure the program environment is welcoming. Positive interactions are particularly important for dual language learners and children with disabilities or other special needs and their families. The interactions will establish a culture of inclusion where families can connect and share experiences, resources, and so on.

8.3 The indoor and outdoor environments are organized and prepared to support children's learning interests and focused exploration.

High-quality indoor and outdoor learning environments set the stage for social–emotional exploration and growth. When children are presented with a friendly, inviting, and culturally familiar environment, they feel comfortable and secure. For young dual language learners and culturally diverse populations, it is especially important for materials to reflect the families' histories, culture, and familiar customs. For example, this might mean incorporating authentic materials from the children's homes and communities. The attractive spaces adults prepare for children communicate expectations of responsibility and cooperative care. Preparing a variety of learning areas with open-ended materials encourages each child to participate in meaningful play experiences that match their individual temperaments, knowledge, and skills. Incorporating elements from the home and community creates a feeling of belonging by reflecting the cultures, languages, familiar traditions, and histories of the children and families served (adapted from CDE 2010a, 42–43).

Inviting Learning Spaces

Programs

- Ensure that resources such as the *California Preschool Learning Foundations* (CDE 2008, 2010b, and 2012) and *California Preschool Curriculum Framework* (CDE 2010a, 2011, and 2013) are available to staff in planning for children.

- Provide professional development for staff on the environmental elements of developmentally appropriate, culturally responsive program design and philosophy.

- Ensure that staff members have access to a wide variety of materials and equipment that are safe, engaging, open-ended, aesthetically pleasing, developmentally appropriate, and reflective of diverse experiences.

- Plan indoor and outdoor environments that are developmentally appropriate, aesthetically pleasing, and reflective of children's cultural and linguistic experiences and the program's philosophy.

- Collaborate with staff to gather information from children and families to guide the selections of safe, developmentally appropriate, engaging, open-ended, and aesthetically pleasing materials and equipment that reflect diverse experiences and encourage play, exploration, and learning in all domains.

Teachers

- Use *California Preschool Learning Foundations* (CDE 2008, 2010b, and 2012) and *California Preschool Curriculum Frameworks* (2010a, 2011, and 2013) to inform the curriculum planning process for preschool children.

- Adapt the environment as necessary to meet the interests and requirements of children in the group.

- Plan opportunities for all children to engage with materials and equipment, including objects from nature, making adaptations as necessary to meet the interests and needs of children in the group; include materials in children's home languages as needed.

8.4 The environment and materials reflect the cultural and linguistic diversity of the children and families served.

Authentic, meaningful connections to the young children's experiences in their homes and communities enhance learning and a sense of belonging, especially for culturally diverse children and dual language learners. Preschool programs need to create a climate of respect for each child's culture and language. Programs and teachers regularly communicate with family members to get to know the cultural strengths each child brings to the program. An essential part of being culturally and linguistically responsive is to value and support each child's home language. Also important are interactions with children and their families in which programs and teachers learn about the cultural history, beliefs, values, ways of communicating, and practices of children and families, so connections can be made between the children's family and community life and the preschool setting. Sometimes making connections between families' cultures and languages requires working through differences in perspectives. Programs and teachers have the responsibility to recognize tension with sensitivity, honor families' perspectives, and work with families to resolve or manage differences.

All aspects of the preschool setting should reflect or represent the families' culture, customs, and language, including the teachers, other staff, and volunteers. Families' artifacts and pictures of the family members' special talents (e.g., musical or artistic) should be displayed prominently throughout the setting. Environmental print that reflects the languages of the children, as well as English, should also be incorporated into learning activities and classroom routines. High-quality books in both English and the children's home languages should be readily accessible (adapted from CDE 2010, 183).

Reflection of the Community

Programs

- Communicate in the philosophy statement or handbook the importance of connecting a child's cultural or linguistic experience at home with the early care and education setting.

- Develop outreach efforts to achieve representative staffing (culture, language, race and ethnicity, gender) at all staffing levels within the program.

- Encourage volunteers from the children's cultural and linguistic communities to participate in program activities.

- Invite extended family members to participate in program events.

- Provide program information and announcements in the home languages of the families.

- Provide an interpreter or someone representative of the family's culture, when necessary to help in communication with the family.

- Initiate discussions with families about cultural preferences and practices and how these preferences may be incorporated into the learning environment and curriculum.

Teachers

- Value the role of culture and home language in child-rearing and discuss its influence with families and other staff members.

- Support a family's cultural style and respond positively to a child's expressions of cultural identity (for instance, a child may hug or kiss his father rather than wave "bye-bye").

- Ensure that play materials, family photos, room decorations, and celebrations reflect the various backgrounds of the children in the program as well as other racial and ethnic groups in the community.

- Ensure that classrooms have linguistically and culturally representative materials. Expand the listening library to include texts in both English and the home language(s) of the children.

- Choose classrooms materials that reflect the cultures and languages of children and families enrolled by

  o displaying photographs of the children and families, to reflect families' homes and everyday lives;

  o incorporating music, songs, poetry, and literature that authentically reflect the cultures and languages of the children enrolled;

  o using culturally and linguistically authentic materials as part of intentional teaching strategies.

- Speak a child's home language frequently or, if not proficient, learn simple, essential phrases of a child's home language and use them in daily communication with the child.

- Discuss regularly with family members their children's needs and preferences and use this information to create continuity between the home and the program.

- Acknowledge any tension that may arise over differing cultural practices and work with families to resolve or manage it.

8.5 The environment is organized and prepared to support full participation by children and adults with disabilities or other special needs.

Learning materials should be accessible to all children in the setting, including those with physical or sensory disabilities. When young children are allowed to move any way they can, they learn about themselves and the environment through movement and sensory exploration. Like all children, those who need support to move learn from movement and exploration (adapted from CDE 2011, 134).

As discussed in Guideline 5.5, "Including Children with Disabilities or Other Special Needs," using a universal design for learning (UDL) approach will ensure maximum access. The environment should support the learning of all children and be adapted to allow for **multiple means of representation**, **multiple means of engagement**, and **multiple means of expression**. *Multiple means of representation* refers to providing information in a variety of ways so the learning needs of all children are met. For example, it is important to speak clearly to children with auditory disabilities in an area with little or no background noise while also presenting information visually (such as with objects and pictures). *Multiple means of expression* refers to allowing children alternative ways to communicate or demonstrate what they know or what they are feeling, such as through gestures, sign language, or pictures. And *multiple means of engagement* refers to providing choices in the environment that facilitate learning by building on children's interests, experiences, knowledge, and skills; for example, providing a chair for a child who is interested in the sensory table and uses a therapeutic walker (adapted from CDE 2010a, 13; 2011, 14; and 2013, 14).

Program leaders should turn to family members and specialized service providers for guidance on appropriate ways to make adaptations in the environment to support full participation of all children. The environment, materials, and teaching methods can be modified to facilitate participation and skill development for all children. All children in the preschool program benefit when provided with opportunities to play alongside peers with diverse abilities; they learn the important values of inclusion, empathy, respect, and acceptance (adapted from CDE 2011, 134).

Family members may have disabilities or special needs as well. Be prepared to make adjustments, and accommodate adults as needed. The same UDL principles can apply. For example, a parent may have difficulty reading materials sent home or completing paperwork. Including photos and offering to assist family members to complete paperwork will provide multiple means of representation. Providing an adult chair for a grandmother who uses a cane or listening carefully to an aunt with speech difficulties provides multiple means of engagement and expression.

Inclusion

Programs

- Provide appropriate support, accommodations, or adaptations so that every child may participate fully in the program.

- Celebrate and enjoy each child for the unique individual he or she is.

- Acknowledge and support a child's emerging abilities.

- In collaboration with specialized service providers, offer professional development opportunities to staff on meeting the needs of diverse learners through multiple approaches to learning.

- Communicate with families about the program's approach to understanding and meeting the needs of diverse learners.

- Provide information to staff members about working closely with specialists who may be involved with a child or family.

- Share information regarding local resources that offer support groups or information for family members of children with disabilities or other special needs.

Teachers

- Plan developmentally appropriate environments, interactions, and experiences for the learning environment.

- Represent ability diversity in the classroom even if there are no children with identified special needs enrolled (e.g., include children and adults with disabilities in photos, books, and other materials as it exposes children to a wide range of abilities and sets a welcoming climate for all people).

- Find meaningful ways for children with disabilities or other special need to be leaders or helpers or take on other roles shared by classroom members.

- Facilitate child-to-child interaction within the group and help children develop relationships with each other.

- Facilitate visits by specialists who support individual children with disabilities or other special needs.

- Adapt to children's approaches to learning and interacting with people.

- Celebrate and enjoy each child for the unique individual he or she is.

- Work with families, other teachers, and specialists to create a plan for inclusion.

8.6   The materials in the environment are developmentally appropriate and encourage play, exploration, and learning in all domains.

In supporting children's multiple approaches to learning, programs and teachers may use a variety of strategies (e.g., interactions, scaffolding, explicit instruction, modeling, demonstration, changes in the environment and materials, and adaptations, which are especially important for children with disabilities or other special needs). By adapting the physical environment, materials, and the curriculum in developmentally and individually appropriate ways, teachers gain a better sense of individual children's diverse strengths, abilities, interests, and experiences, and how best to support their play, exploration, and learning.

Whole-Child Learning

Programs

- Create an environment that is safe for free movement and exploration.

- Provide developmentally appropriate play equipment that offers opportunities for invigorating and challenging large-muscle movement both indoors and outdoors.

- Provide a variety of objects and materials for children to explore with their small muscles.

- Provide professional development for staff and families that focus on play and its implications for child growth and development.

- Initiate discussions with staff and reinforce with families that indoor and outdoor play throughout the early childhood period is important for child development and learning while being sensitive to individual family circumstances and cultural preferences.

- Create program policies and practices that promote responsiveness to the learning strengths, interests, and needs of individual children.

- Facilitate implementation of developmentally, individually, culturally, and linguistically appropriate early childhood practices.

Teachers

- Design and maintain the indoor and outdoor environments to support children's participation during play, including the provision of open-ended, developmentally appropriate materials and activities that engage children based on observations of their development.

- Schedule ample time for child-initiated and adult-facilitated play.

- Give children time to solve problems they encounter.

- Plan opportunities for families to observe and engage their children in play.

- Consider individual family circumstances and cultural values when making recommendations about play.

8.7 Programs support teachers in selecting, using, and integrating appropriate technology into everyday experiences to enhance curriculum.

Technology is an ever-present, powerful tool in people's daily lives. Many young children come to preschool with considerable experience using technology, and others have limited experience with it. Technology in the preschool environment can support learning in different ways. Of course, preschool programs' use of technology should be consistent with the principles of curriculum set forth in the *California Preschool Curriculum Framework*, volumes 1–3. Teachers can use technology effectively as additional modes of learning that augment children's learning through interaction, collaboration, constructive manipulation of materials, physical movement, and their senses. Technology can be an important tool for introducing or designing adaptations that address the individual needs, interests, and abilities of children, especially children with disabilities or other special needs. At all times, technology should support children's integrated exploration and learning and allow children to engage in actively making meaning in collaboration with others.

Technology

Programs

- Support teachers in selecting technology and interactive media products that are developmentally appropriate and are consistent with the abilities, interests, needs, and cultural and linguistic backgrounds of individual children in the program.

- Support teachers in evaluating the quality of content, overall goals, format, and features of any software program or other forms of interactive media they may use with children in the program.

- Ensure equitable access to technology and interactive media experiences to all children in the program, making accommodations for children with disabilities or other special needs.

- Provide guidance to teachers on how to introduce and integrate technology and interactive media into the learning environment appropriately and effectively.

- Provide teachers with training and professional development to gain the knowledge and competence to use technology, to think critically about the use of technology and interactive media with young children, and to evaluate the impact of technology on children's learning and development.

Teachers

- Apply knowledge of developmentally appropriate practice to guide and inform decision making about how to integrate technology and interactive media into the learning environment.

- Use technology and interactive media as tools to intentionally support curriculum goals and to promote learning of individual children in the group.

- Establish with children rules and routines to guide appropriate handling and use of computers and other technological devices, setting limits on the time children spend with technology and interactive media (i.e., screen technologies).

- Observe and support children while they use technology and interactive media, identifying opportunities for teachable moments and making appropriate adaptations to promote positive outcomes for individual children.

- Ensure that the use of technology and interactive media allows for joint engagement between children (or between children and adults) and promotes communication and collaboration among children.

8.8 Programs support both home language maintenance and English-language development in the learning environment.

Young dual language learners bring a wealth of ability and knowledge as well as varied cultural backgrounds to preschool programs. Young dual language learners require curricular adaptations beyond what are usually considered high-quality early childhood practices to make the most of their abilities while they progress toward English proficiency. Current knowledge, based on successful practices and sound research, strongly suggests that specific teaching strategies, individualized interaction approaches, and enhanced environments are critical to the long-term success of young dual language learners.

Intentional teaching of dual language learners requires ongoing awareness of the home-language development of each child as well as the child's ability to use English to engage in learning. Preschool programs and teachers need to be knowledgeable about both the role of home language in the process of early learning and the stages of second-language development for dual language learners. Continued use and development of the home language will benefit dual language learners as they acquire English. Language is a tool of communication used in all developmental domains. Young dual language learners need to be supported in the use and development of both the home language and English not only in activities focused on language and literacy, but across the entire curriculum, especially in integrated ways (adapted from CDE 2010a).

Language Support

Programs

- Facilitate the articulation of a clear, consistent, evidence-based program approach for young dual language learners at the site; collaborate with families, staff, and other community members as appropriate to build support for the program approach.

- Support second-language acquisition by adult learners.

- Develop and implement hiring policies and job descriptions for staff that comply with regulations or other requirements and that consider the diverse linguistic experiences of children and families.

- Implement procedures that enhance and monitor support for both home-language maintenance and English-

language development (ELD) within the classroom environment (materials books, display, and the like) and learning activities and opportunities.

- Encourage family members, colleagues, and community members to use children's home languages and provide training or support as needed.

- Conduct ongoing evaluation of program support for children's home language and use data to make program improvements.

Teachers

- Collaborate with families, staff, and others who support children's development and learning.

- Incorporate practices that honor the role of the home language as a vital foundation in English-language development.

- Honor each child's home language in order to foster positive social–emotional development and the child's development and learning in all other areas.

- Systematically and intentionally implement strategies that promote English-language development, including supporting the English proficiency of all staff members who provide English-language support for dual language learners.

- Actively recruit native speakers of the home languages of children in the class to participate in classroom activities (e.g., read and tell stories, help with child dictation, connect young dual language learners to background information that is familiar to them, help with translations, and so on).

8.9 The environment reflects the program's philosophy and beliefs about how children develop and learn.

The overarching principles and strategies articulated in the *California Preschool Curriculum Framework* (CDE 2010a) offer a general approach to adapting or designing the learning environment and curriculum for young children. In particular, the program's curriculum should define an approach to supporting integrated learning and be developmentally, individually, culturally, and linguistically appropriate. Widely used approaches to preschool curriculum fit within this framework. In addition, some preschool programs may decide to create their own curriculum in a manner aligned with the curriculum framework. Whether adapted or designed by the program, the curriculum should reflect the program's philosophy and beliefs about how children learn and develop in all domains, including approaches to guidance and discipline.

The program's policies and practices should be consistent with the educational philosophy reflected in its curriculum. The program should provide learning opportunities to staff and families about the beliefs underlying its approach to curriculum. Written information about the program's philosophy should be available to everyone, and conversations about the curriculum should occur regularly. Young children will likely gain the most from preschool when all of the adults responsible for them have a shared understanding of how to support and enhance early learning and development.

California Preschool Curriculum Framework publications (CDE 2010a, 2011, and 2013) and DVDs are available to support the planning efforts of all staff and colleagues.

- Engage staff and families in discussing curricular goals for children along a broad developmental continuum and for specific developmental stages.

Program Philosophy and Curriculum

Programs

- Develop program policies and a **pedagogical philosophy** that support children's learning and development in all domains.

- Provide professional development to staff and families about the goals, features, strengths, and limitations of all curricula used in the program.

- Provide professional development for staff and families to understand that preschool development and learning are integrated across domains.

- Collaborate with staff in selecting or developing appropriate curricula and consider ways curricula might be adapted to meet the developmental and individual needs of children in the program.

- Ensure that resources such as the *California Preschool Learning Foundations* (CDE 2008, 2010b, and 2012) and

Curriculum

Teachers

- Use knowledge of development to inform planning for individual children in the indoor and outdoor learning environments, including support for relationships and the development of emotion regulation.

- Plan experiences that support preschool development and learning in all domains and content areas.

- Use the *California Preschool Learning Foundations* (CDE 2008, 2010b, and 2012) and *California Preschool Curriculum Framework* publications (CDE 2010a, 2011, and 2013) to inform the curriculum-planning process for preschool children.

- Demonstrate understanding that preschool development and learning can be described with regard to the developmental domains and content areas of social-emotional development, language and literacy, mathematics, English-language development, visual and performing arts, physical development, health, history–social science, and science and that children learn in an integrated way across domains.

8.10 Teachers observe, document, and reflect on children's learning and development on a daily basis as part of the curriculum planning process.

Planning preschool curriculum begins with teachers discovering, through careful listening and observation, each child's interests, abilities, and needs on a daily basis. Observation is an essential teaching skill. When teachers mindfully observe, they discover how individual children make meaning in everyday moments of play, exploration, and interactions. Observation for the purpose of assessing individual children's learning means mindfully watching and listening, with thought and reflection. As teachers observe children's play and interactions each day, children reveal evidence of their emerging skills and ideas. Such evidence, recorded as a written observation, photo, or video clip, is used in a child's portfolio to demonstrate developmental progress. As teachers observe, they also discover ways to extend learning experiences in order to support children in building more complex and coherent ideas.

Documentation means gathering and holding evidence of children's play and interests for future use. Documentation supports teachers in planning the next steps in the curriculum. Teachers reflect on how they might expand children's thinking, exploration, language, and interactions. Teachers might discuss among themselves what a photo or an anecdote of children's play reveals. They also engage the children's families in thinking about the documentation. Just as important, teachers share their documentation with the children and create opportunities for

the children to participate in the process of documentation as a way to engage children in thinking about ideas and problems they are exploring or have previously explored. Such reflection on documentation by teachers, families, and children serves as a springboard for developing ways to explore more deeply a topic that has engaged the interest of the children. Further exploration might include, among other things, materials to add to interest areas, related books to read in either large- or small-group gatherings, or activities to do in small groups. With clear ideas or objectives in mind, teachers plan curriculum that includes strategies to enhance the learning of all children in a group, as well as strategies to support the learning of individual children (adapted from CDE 2010a, 21; 2011, 29–30; and 2013, 33).

Curriculum Planning

Programs

- Develop program policies to facilitate observations of children that are conducted over time, across settings, and that include input from multiple observers.

- Regularly assesses with colleagues how systems of observation are working to enhance a learning community.

- Coordinate documentation and data gathering, storage, and management to ensure accuracy, thoroughness, confidentiality, and timeliness.

- Collaborate with staff and families to develop documentation policies that support children's learning and development and link directly to curriculum planning.

- Provide tools and strategies to support objective, clear, and timely documentation.

Teachers

- Plan the daily schedule to facilitate observation of children by appropriate staff.

- Explain to families principles of curriculum planning that are based on observation, documentation, interpretation, planning, and implementation and clarifies the goals and features of curricula used in the learning environment.

- Know that ongoing observation of children, individually and in groups, is an important part of the curriculum-planning process.

- Plan opportunities for children to participate in documentation of their experiences, as developmentally appropriate.

- Collaborate with fellow teachers, engaging in dialogue about observations and documentation of individual children to gain a deeper understanding of each child's development and learning.

- Engage children in activities and experiences designed to be responsive to their interests and needs as understood through collaborative reflection on documentation of their play, exploration, and learning.

- Collaborate with family members and specialized service providers in documenting the learning and development of children with disabilities or other special needs and in planning learning experiences for them.

- Implement systematic, ongoing procedures to document the learning and development of young dual language learners in all domains, in both the home language and English.

- The three principles of universal design serve as the foundation for intervention planning for all children. For children with disabilities that need additional support, various accommodations can be made. Teachers, in collaboration with family members and specialized service providers, can

  o provide social supports (e.g., peer-mediated intervention strategies, cooperative learning);

  o use visual, auditory, and kinesthetic methods (e.g., use pictures and models when explaining);

  o use a range of reinforcers (e.g., smiles, hugs, acknowledgment, provision of desired toy/object, continuing play);

  o adapt toys/materials to allow children

to use a variety of movements in different positions;

  o alter the physical, social, or temporal environment;

  o alter the schedule of activities and routines;

  o adjust the amount and type of support provided;

  o divide an activity into smaller steps (DEC 2007).

- Share observations with families in an objective, timely, private, and confidential manner.

- Maintain current documentation of children's development, including information gathered from staff, families, and children.

- Contribute to the curriculum planning process by helping to gather artifacts for use in documentation, including samples of children's work and other materials involving children, as developmentally appropriate.

8.11 Teachers plan and implement learning experiences based on multiple forms of assessment and collaborative planning.

Screening, observation, and documentation are all assessment processes for gathering, interpreting, applying, and sharing information that build upon children's previous experiences. They are important tools for understanding children individually and in groups, and for the purposes of planning learning environments, curriculum, and other learning experiences. For example, to support effective assessment practice, the CDE has developed the Desired Results Developmental Profile (DRDP), which is aligned with the preschool learning foundations.

A key concern for programs is ensuring that teachers and other staff responsible for supporting children's learning possess the necessary knowledge and skills to conduct responsible, ethical, and effective assessments for supporting children's learning and development, and when appropriate, for identifying children who may have disabilities or other special needs. Staff members need to understand the purposes, uses, benefits, and limitations of various assessment approaches. In addition, it is important to collaborate with families when assessing preschool children's learning and development.

The program's assessment approaches should be consistent with developmentally appropriate practice, be culturally and linguistically sensitive, and provide individually meaningful information. Programs should clearly articulate how assessment methods used inform decision making and planning and program evaluation. Assessment policies and practices should ensure confidentiality and protect the privacy of children and families. Well-understood policies and practices should also be in place for collaborating with special education providers who are qualified to administer and interpret assessments that inform an individualized education program (IEP) for children with disabilities or other special needs as well as for collaborating with families and qualified service providers in the IEP process (adapted from the California Department of Education and First 5 California 2012, 51, 54).

Differentiated Planning

Programs

- Develop program policies that encourage staff and families to engage in an intentional planning process—one that is based on knowledge of child development and information about the children served.

- Individualize assessment procedures and link results to curriculum planning, making adjustments as necessary for each young dual language learner.

- Ensure that assessment procedures are appropriately inclusive of children with disabilities or other special needs, including children with IEPs.

Teachers

- Engage families in discussions about the role of observation, documentation, interpretation, and reflection in planning.

- Synthesize information gathered through the planning process, including input from families, in planning for individual children and for the group, with consideration for diverse cultural and linguistic experiences.

- Solicit ideas from families to meet children's learning and developmental goals; to inform the planning of activities, experiences, and interactions; and to inform the selection of materials for both indoor and outdoor spaces.

- Respond to children's interests by selecting materials, expanding on the children's ideas, or planning activities and experiences, engaging children in planning as developmentally appropriate.

8.12 Programs and teachers engage in curriculum planning that includes an integrated approach to all domains of learning and development.

As learning engages young children in holistic ways, the *California Preschool Curriculum Framework* (CDE 2010a, 2011, and 2013) emphasizes taking an integrated approach to supporting early learning and development. Young children continually use all their senses and competencies to relate new experiences to prior experiences and to understand things and create meaning. Their learning is integrated while having a specific focus. For example, during book reading, children use their knowledge and thinking abilities, emotional responses, understanding of language, physical skills, and the full range of experiences at home and in the community to make new connections and expand their understanding about themselves and the world around them.

Children come to preschool as experts about many things—particularly their families, their home language(s), and their belongings. Of most value to them are experiences that support their inclination to explore (for example, mathematics, language, literacy, art, and science) within meaningful moments of play and interaction. When learning builds on what children know and allows them to expand their skills playfully, they are happy to participate in any learning experience or activity, to recite any rhyme, to count any set, and to take on any new, developmentally appropriate physical challenge. That is why it is so important for preschool programs to offer children experiences that are personally meaningful and connected or integrated. In addition, since children learn using all of their sensory modalities in an integrated way, strengthening the modalities in which individual children need special help and building upon their areas of strength is essential (adapted from CDE 2011, 7).

Integrated Learning

Programs

- Provide time for staff and colleagues to reflect individually and in teams to support an integrated curriculum-planning process that includes observation, documentation, and reflection.

- Monitor program practices for consistency with principles of integrated curriculum planning that is developmentally, linguistically, and culturally appropriate.

Teachers

- Plan regular opportunities for staff and colleagues to meet and discuss information about children in the group and how to use it in curriculum planning.

- Contribute to staff discussions about the significance of observations and documentation for understanding children individually and in groups and for informing curriculum planning.

- Implement curriculum according to collaboratively developed plans.

- Arrange or use indoor and outdoor materials and space in accordance with the curriculum-planning process.

References

American Academy of Pediatrics, American Public Health Association, and the National Resource Center for Health and Safety in Child Care and Early Education. 2011. *Caring for Our Children: National Health and Safety Performance Standards: Guidelines for Early Care and Education Programs.* 3rd ed. Elk Grove Village, IL: American Academy of Pediatrics; Washington, DC: American Public Health Association. http://nrckids.org (September 15, 2014).

Caldwell, L. 1997. *Bringing Reggio Emilia Home: An Innovative Approach to Early Childhood Education.* New York: Teachers College Press.

California Department of Education (CDE). 2006. *Infant/Toddler Learning and Development Program Guidelines.* Sacramento: California Department of Education.

———. 2008. *California Preschool Learning Foundations, Volume 1.* Sacramento: California Department of Education.

———. 2010a. *California Preschool Curriculum Framework, Volume 1.* Sacramento: California Department of Education.

———. 2010b. *California Preschool Learning Foundations, Volume 2.* Sacramento: California Department of Education.

———. 2011. *California Preschool Curriculum Framework, Volume 2.* Sacramento: California Department of Education.

———. 2012. *California Preschool Learning Foundations, Volume 3.* Sacramento: California Department of Education.

———. 2013. *California Preschool Curriculum Framework, Volume 3.* Sacramento: California Department of Education.

California Department of Education and First 5 California. 2012. *California Early Childhood Educator Competencies.* Sacramento: California Department of Education.

Division for Early Childhood of the Council for Exceptional Children (DEC). 2007. *Promoting Positive Outcomes for Children with Disabilities: Recommendations for Curriculum, Assessment, and Program Evaluation.* Missoula, MT: DEC.

Howes, C., M. Burchinal, R. Pianta, D. Bryant, D. M. Early, R. M. Clifford, and O. Barbarin. 2008. "Ready to Learn? Children's Pre-Academic Achievement in Pre-Kindergarten Programs." *Early Childhood Research Quarterly* 23 (1): 27–50.

Mashburn, A. J., R. C. Pianta, B. K. Hamre, J. T. Downer, O. A. Barbarin, D. Bryant, M. Burchinal, D. M. Early, and C. Howes. 2008. "Measures of Classroom Quality in Prekindergarten and Children's Development of Academic, Language, and Social Skills." *Child Development* 79 (3): 732–49.

National Professional Development Center on Inclusion. 2009. Research Synthesis Points on Early Childhood Inclusion. Chapel Hill: The University of North Carolina, FPG Child Development Institute, Author. http://npdci. fpg.unc.edu/sites/npdci.fpg.unc.edu/ files/resources/NPDCI-ResearchSynthesisPoints-10-2009_0.pdf (accessed January 8, 2015).

Peisner-Feinberg, E. S., R. M. Clifford, M. L. Culkin, C. Howes, S. L. Kagan, and N. Yazejian. 2001. "The Relation of Preschool Child Care Quality to Children's Cognitive and Social Developmental Trajectories through Second Grade." *Child Development* 72:1534–53.

Pianta, R. C., K. M. La Paro, and B. K. Hamre. 2007. *Classroom Assessment Scoring System* (CLASS). Baltimore, MD: Brookes.

Sylva, K., E. Melhuish, P. Sammons, and I. Siraj-Blatchford, eds. 2010. *Early Childhood Matters: Evidence from the Effective Pre-school and Primary Education Project.* Oxford: Routledge.

Further Reading

Dodge, D. T. 2004. "Early Childhood Curriculum Models: Why, What, and How Programs Use Them." *Child Care Information Exchange* January/February: 71–75.

Guideline 9: Supporting Professionalism and Continuous Learning

Supporting professional development and continuous learning is essential to ensure that preschool teachers are well prepared to support the learning and development of the preschool children in their programs. As defined by the NAEYC, "Professional Development is a continuum of learning and support activities designed to prepare individuals for work with and on behalf of young children and their families, as well as ongoing experiences to enhance this work. These opportunities lead to improvements in the knowledge, skills, practices, and dispositions of early childhood professionals" (NAEYC, n.d.). Professional development includes both formal (e.g., community college course work) and informal (e.g., workshops, mentorship) learning experiences that take place prior to becoming a preschool teacher (preservice training), as well as in learning experiences throughout a teaching career (in-service training). Research suggests that both preservice and in-service training significantly predict program quality (Ackerman 2005).

Across the country, states have put in place professional development systems (PDS) in efforts to prepare the early childhood workforce. The PDS state licensing or regulations may determine who is qualified to teach, yet those requirements tend to vary by state. For instance, in one state early childhood educators may need to have a bachelor's degree in an early childhood related field, while in another state, they may need 12 units in early childhood education. More recently, however, states have begun to focus on developing quality rating and improvement systems, early childhood educator competencies, and career ladders as a more comprehensive way to ensure that early childhood educators are well prepared to be effective in the early childhood setting (Howes et al. 2008).

In California, the California Early Childhood Educator Competencies (California Department of Education and First 5 California 2012) provide coherent structure and content to

- foster the professional development of California's early childhood workforce;
- inform the course of study that early childhood educators follow in institutions of higher education;
- provide guidance about ECE credentials and certifications;
- establish standards for the knowledge, skills, and dispositions needed by educators to support young children's learning and development across program types.

The competencies aim at supporting young children's overall development by preparing the early childhood workforce to provide learning experiences that are "developmentally, culturally, and linguistically appropriate" (California Department of Education and First 5 California 2012, 2). The Early Childhood Educator Competencies are grounded in a comprehensive system that includes the early learning and development foundations for infants, toddlers and preschoolers and the curriculum frameworks.

Each competency area includes key concepts derived from theory and research. Two competency areas are especially relevant to young dual language learners: "Culture, Diversity and Equity" and "Dual Language Development." The "Culture, Diversity, and Equity" competency area underscores the concept that there is no knowledge base, skill set, teaching practice, or curriculum for early development and learning that is applicable to all children. Instead, learning environments are enriched when children's individual characteristics, values, cultures, and temperaments—as well as diversity among children, families, and peers—are respected and valued in concrete ways (CDE 2010). Effective early childhood educators, including preservice and in-service teachers, demonstrate competencies in areas such as supporting the development of children's home language as well as their English. The "Dual-Language Development" competency area addresses the knowledge and skills that early childhood educators need in order to support the optimal development and learning of young dual language learners as well as the relatively small number of young children who experience learning more than two languages (CDE 2010).

In a literature review prepared for the U.S. Department of Education, Office of Planning, Evaluation and Policy Development and Program Studies Service, Zaslow and her colleagues (2010b) outline key features of effective professional development practices in the field of early childhood. The authors suggest that professional development strategies for early childhood educators may be more effective when the following conditions are in place:

- There are specific and articulated objectives for professional development.

- Practice is an explicit focus of the professional development, and attention is given to linking the focus on early educator knowledge and practice.

- There is collective participation of teachers from the same classrooms or schools in professional development.

- The intensity and duration of the professional development is matched to the content being conveyed.

- Educators are prepared to conduct child assessments and interpret their results as a tool for ongoing monitoring of the effects of professional development.

- Professional development is appropriate for the organizational context and is aligned with standards for practice (Zaslow et al. 2010b).

In addition to the strategies named above, appropriate, continuous learning experiences for early childhood professionals, including mentorship, consultation, and coaching, are likely to positively contribute to children's high-quality learning experiences in the areas of language and literacy, English-language development, social-emotional development, and cognitive development (including math) (Wayne et al. 2008; Grace et al. 2008; Hamre et al. 2012; Virmani et al. 2012; Rudd et al. 2009).

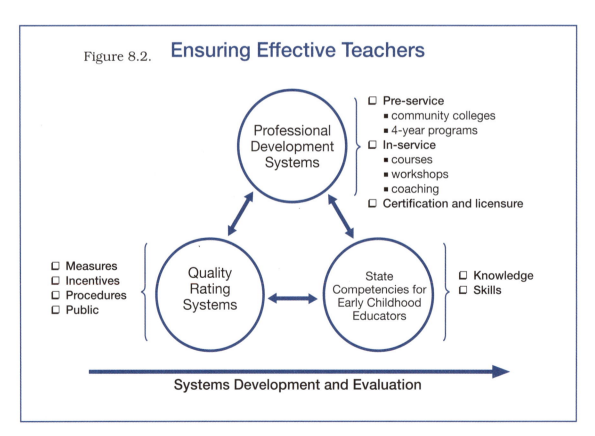

Figure 8.2. **Ensuring Effective Teachers**

Professional Development Systems

□ Pre-service
  ■ community colleges
  ■ 4-year programs
□ In-service
  ■ courses
  ■ workshops
  ■ coaching
□ Certification and licensure

Quality Rating Systems

□ Measures
□ Incentives
□ Procedures
□ Public

State Competencies for Early Childhood Educators

□ Knowledge
□ Skills

Systems Development and Evaluation

Source: Howes et al. 2008.

9.1 Programs develop and implement a comprehensive, ongoing plan for staff development.

A comprehensive staff development plan should be actively supported and implemented by the program's administrators and should also have the support of the staff and parents. The plan should be based on the assumption that early childhood educators, like all other professionals, need continual professional renewal. The staff development plan should allow for a continuing cycle of knowledge acquisition, review of research, reflection, practice, and assessment of results. The plan should provide a coherent series of staff development experiences that build from one to the next, offering opportunities for teachers to practice and reflect on what they learn, including on-site follow-up and peer support.

The staff development plan should be linked to the program's approach to maintaining, building, and strengthening program quality. For instance, if the administrator assessing the needs of the program learns that interactions between staff and children need improvement, the professional development plan would need to consider establishing a systematic way to provide training, coaching, and mentorship to staff to yield improvements in this area. Identifying the professional skills and knowledge of staff is key to knowing where to best invest time and resources to achieve overall program improvements. As the staff improves in targeted areas, the program can shift efforts around training, coaching, and mentoring to other priority areas. Often there will be multiple areas of potential focus for a program, and the administrator will need to set priorities, taking into account the needs of the program, available resources, and the community context.

In addition to incorporating the preceding principles, the plan for professional development and training should contain the following elements:

- Be based on the identified needs of the staff both as a group and individually.

- Reinforce staff capabilities in such areas of the curriculum as language and literacy, English-language development, mathematical and scientific thinking, social and emotional development, the arts, creative play, and appropriate uses of technology.

- Allow time for regular review and reflection to be built into the weekly schedule.

- Include staff relations and conflict management.

- Include coaching and mentoring.

- Include training on the inclusion of children with disabilities or other special needs and on community resources available to children and their families.

- Include training on cultural and linguistic responsiveness.

- Incorporate continual evaluation and revision.

- Include a thorough orientation for new staff and volunteers.

- Include multiple strategies that promote teachers' development of self awareness and reflection about their teaching, such as video and audio records, and providing discussion groups, action research, peer observation, and visits to other programs or sites.

Professional Development Plans

Programs

- Collaborate with staff to develop individualized professional development plans that fill gaps in knowledge and include mentoring and coaching.

- For teachers working on their Child Development Permit, facilitate teacher participation in the Teacher Credentialing Professional Growth Plan (see appendix J).

- Support the long-term professional development of staff by collaborating, sharing responsibilities, and following professional code of ethics established by one of the field's respected organizations (e.g., NAEYC).

- Provide professional development regularly to all staff members on how to implement best practices for young dual language learners, focusing on program approaches that are effective for dual language learners and address key considerations, including home language development, English-language development, development across all curriculum domains, cross-cultural competence, and collecting and interpreting valid assessment information.

- Provide learning opportunities in formal and informal contexts.

- Inform and consult with family members about continuing professional development opportunities for teachers and program leaders.

- Encourage staff to attend off-site trainings or courses that cover the domains of preschool learning and development, children with disabilities or other special needs, influences of family, cultural and linguistic responsiveness, and curriculum.

- Present and help implement strategies, concepts and recommendations based on current research on early childhood development and program improvement.

Teachers

- Plan professional development opportunities with the program administrator.

- Participate in needs assessment activities.

- Participate in opportunities to develop pedagogical knowledge and skills.

- Take advantage of opportunities to meet with mentors, either within the program or through connections with other teachers.

9.2 Programs allocate resources to support individual staff members' participation in professional development and education.

Recognizing that staff time for professional development is limited, program administrators should offer a wide va-

riety of opportunities for staff members to enhance their professional knowledge and skills. Providing adequate paid time to attend in-service trainings, classes, and conferences is an important part of ensuring staff members' participation in professional development and education.

Finding and making time for staff development activities can be a major challenge in the busy day of all early childhood program staff. Some programs occasionally schedule a shortened day to release staff for professional development activities or hire a part-time substitute to release certain staff members for individual coaching or mentoring. Adequate time for planning, meeting, talking to one another, taking courses in early childhood education, and sharing ideas in both formal and informal ways must be provided for the staff to grow professionally and for the program to improve. Ideally, some staff development will include early childhood professionals from other settings, such as elementary schools, or neighboring public or private programs to provide diverse perspectives on a topic. Staff development activities should not be something teachers must only do on their own time or without pay.

In addition to making time for staff to engage in professional development activities, providing access to resources such as particular books, periodicals, DVDs, CDs, and other electronic media such as the Internet and e-mail is likely to help facilitate teacher engagement in continuous learning.

Professional Development Support

Programs

- Provide adequate paid time and incentives for staff members to attend in-service training, classes, and conferences.

- Provide easy access to California Department of Education (CDE) materials referenced in this document, professional journals, and other publications related to early childhood education.

- Support additional professional development opportunities that may be available through membership in professional organizations such as local affiliates of the NAEYC, the National Association of Family Child Care, and through Local Child Care Planning Councils, and local First 5 agencies.

9.3 Programs employ staff members who meet the requirements for education, experience, knowledge, and skills for their positions and encourage advancement along a planned career pathway.

There is growing recognition in California of the need to systematically improve the quality of early care and education. The CDE has invested in the creation of an early learning and development system. The Governor, through a Race to the Top Early Learning Challenge Grant, has initiated an effort to establish a local quality improvement rating and improvement system; higher education is aligning undergraduate curriculum in early care and education; and several child care and development organizations and networks receive quality improvement funding to conduct statewide training. Training, combined with incentives for education and retention, is designed to build up the early childhood workforce. These professional development efforts draw from the same research base and share an overall vision of quality. The *California Early Childhood Educator Competencies* (California Department of Education and First Five California 2012) was developed to create a well-designed, coordinated framework for guiding the preparation and professional development of early childhood educators.

All ECE teachers in California must also be prepared to meet the needs of children from culturally and linguistically diverse backgrounds. The proportion of preschool children in California who are dual language learners has grown rapidly during the last decades to the extent that almost all classrooms contain children who speak a language other than English in the home. Teachers and staff members who are fluent in languages other than English and familiar with families' cultural practices are better able to provide the linguistic and behavioral support many dual language learners need. In order to be effective with young dual language learners, early care and education teachers will also need to understand first- and second-language acquisition, the impact of bilingualism on a child's overall development, the consequences of home language loss, teaching practices that promote English-language development while also supporting home language development, effective family engagement strategies, and appropriate assessment approaches. Recent research indicates that young dual language learners need specific language supports and instructional adaptations to thrive in preschool classrooms (see chapter 6); all teachers have both the capacity and the potential to learn these skills and become effective teachers of young dual language learners.

Career Pathway

Programs

- Provide a clear career ladder for teachers and administrators within the program, including opportunities for teachers to grow professionally while remaining in the classroom.

- Inform staff of professional development activities and opportunities.

- Encourage staff to establish professional development and career goals.

- Recruit bilingual, bicultural staff members who are familiar with the cultures of children served and speak their home languages.

- Recruit and train bilingual and bicultural early childhood special education teachers, speech-language pathologists, and other intervention specialists.

- Promote credit-bearing educational opportunities as a main means for staff members to become eligible to accept greater levels of responsibility in early care and education settings or to find employment in other related positions over the course of their careers.

9.4 Programs ensure that professional development activities promote awareness and understanding of children's cultural and linguistic backgrounds and provide strategies for culturally and linguistically responsive practices.

Cultural competence is the ability to know and understand diverse cultures and cultural points of view. It is based on a deliberate effort to know, respect, and understand cultures that are different from one's own. A well-designed professional development program offers opportunities for program staff to develop cultural competence. For example, teachers may be encouraged through professional development activities to recognize that their values and cultural predispositions are based on childhood experiences and current cultural influences in addition to professional training and experiences. By becoming aware of their cultural "lens," teachers can gain insight into their practices and their responses to the children and families.

In chapter 6, there is a compelling research rationale for supporting home language development while promoting English-language development with specific instructional and language interaction strategies. For many teachers, those strategies are new since most ECE teachers have not received training or preparation to meet the needs of dual language learners. Therefore, programs will need to carefully design a professional development approach that systematically prepares all the staff members to understand and meet the needs of preschool dual language learners who are at different stages of English-language development.

Cultural and Linguistic Competence

Programs

- Promote professional development activities that encourage teachers to reflect on how their cultural perspectives and experiences affect how they relate to diverse children and families.

- Plan with all staff to provide professional development on how to implement best practices for young dual language learners.

- Provide professional development regularly to all staff members on effective programming for dual language learners and addressing key considerations including home language development, English-language development, development across all domains, cross-cultural competence, and collecting and interpreting valid assessment information.

- Recruit and train bilingual and bicultural early childhood special education teachers, speech-language pathologists, and other intervention specialists.

Teachers

- Explore with each other during meetings and discussions the ways in which their approaches to teaching are affected by their own experiences and cultural backgrounds.

- Engage in teacher mentoring and support in efforts to develop a better understanding of the values of the children's communities and cultures and to address conflicts in values between the school and families when they occur.

9.5 Programs promote professionalism and ethical behavior.

The program should continually support the staff members' sense of professionalism and appropriate, ethical behavior. The work of the ECE profession is becoming increasingly recognized by policymakers throughout the country. The impact of high-quality early childhood education is well established. To advance the profession and to be effective in extending the benefits of high-quality preschool services to young children and families, it is important for all early childhood educators to conduct themselves in a professional manner. Moreover, programs need to uphold professional and ethical standards and support teachers and staff to carry out their work according to those standards.

A Professional Code of Ethics

Ethical responsibilities to children. Childhood is a unique and valuable stage in the human life cycle. Our paramount responsibility is to provide care and education in settings that are safe, healthy, nurturing, and responsive for each child. We are committed to supporting children's development and learning; respecting individual differences; and helping children learn to live, play, and work cooperatively. We are also committed to promoting children's self-awareness, competence, self-worth, resiliency, and physical well-being.

Ethical responsibilities to families. Families* are of primary importance in children's development. Because the family and the early childhood practitioner have a common interest in the child's well-being, we acknowledge a primary responsibility to bring about communication, cooperation, and collaboration between the home and early childhood program in ways that enhance the child's development.

Ethical responsibilities to colleagues. In a caring, cooperative workplace, human dignity is respected, professional satisfaction is promoted, and positive relationships are developed and sustained. Based upon our core values, our primary responsibility to colleagues is to establish and maintain settings and relationships that support productive work and meet professional needs. The same ideals that apply to children also apply as we interact with adults in the workplace. (Note: Section III includes responsibilities to co-workers and to employers. See the "Code of Ethical Conduct: Supplement for Early Childhood Program Administrators" for responsibilities to personnel (employees in the original 2005 Code revision), online at http://www.naeyc.org/files/naeyc/file/positions/PSETH05_supp.pdf [accessed July 21, 2014].)

Ethical responsibilities to community and society. Early childhood programs operate within the context of their immediate community made up of families and other institutions concerned with children's welfare. Our responsibilities to the community are to provide programs that meet the diverse needs of families, to cooperate with agencies and professions that share the responsibility for children, to assist families in gaining access to those agencies and allied professionals, and to assist in the development of community programs that are needed but not currently available.

As individuals, we acknowledge our responsibility to provide the best possible programs of care and education for children and to conduct ourselves with honesty and integrity. Because of our specialized expertise in early childhood development and education and because the larger society shares responsibility for the welfare and protection of young children, we acknowledge a collective obligation to advocate for the best interests of children within early childhood programs and in the larger community and to serve as a voice for young children everywhere.

The ideals and principles in this section are presented to distinguish between those that pertain to the work of the individual early childhood educator and those that more typically are engaged in collectively on behalf of the best interests of children—with the understanding that individual early childhood educators have a shared responsibility for addressing the ideals and principles that are identified as "collective."

---

*The term *family* may include those adults, besides parents, with the responsibility of being involved in educating, nurturing, and advocating for the child.

Source: National Association for the Education of Young Children 2005 (the complete text of the NAEYC Code appears in appendix K).

Professionalism

Programs

- Set clear expectations for professionalism and ethical behavior, such as those presented in the NAEYC Code of Ethical Conduct (see appendix K).

- Facilitate and model program practices that balance a productive workplace, with a safe, supportive environment.

- Establish and model appropriate behavioral and attitudinal standards for staff.

- Encourage personal and professional growth in staff.

- Engage in professional responsibility and remain dedicated to the success of children, families, and the agency or program.

- Establish professional relationships with families and children, and support staff in maintaining professional relationships with families and children.

Teachers

- Follow expectations for professionalism and ethical behavior, such as those presented in the NAEYC Code of Ethical Conduct (appendix K).

- Seek support from healthy role models who successfully maintain a work–life balance.

- Model health and well-being for children and families.

- Arrive at work on time each day, prepared to engage with children, families, and staff in a professional manner.

- Maintain professional boundaries related to establishing close relationships with children and families outside the work environment.

9.6 **Programs support ongoing reflective practice, adult learning, coaching, and mentoring.**

Providing ongoing experiences for adult learners that include reflective practice, coaching, and mentorship is essential for high-quality preschool teaching. This type of support applies to teachers' efforts to provide high-quality learning experiences across all developmental domains. Much of the professional development literature makes clear that ongoing coaching and mentoring is an important component of enhancing the skills of early childhood teachers. Reflective supervision is particularly important in helping teachers nurture children's social–emotional development. Relationships between teachers and young children and the children's capacity to use those relationships as a base for learning are enhanced when teachers have opportunities to explore their responses to children and families. In addition, reflective supervision has been demonstrated to decrease teacher burnout and contribute to greater understanding of children's behavior.

Ongoing Adult Learning and Reflective Practice

Programs

- Provide regular opportunities for teachers to meet individually with their supervisor to reflect and plan children's learning experiences.

- Set aside time during staff meetings for teachers to reflect on their practice.

- Help individual staff members reflect on their emotional responses to children, interactions, attitudes, and behaviors, and become mindfully aware of their own biases.

- Provide consistent opportunities for each teacher to meet with mentors, either through the program or by connecting them with teachers outside the program.

- Provide opportunities to staff members to engage in ongoing coaching and mentorship to address their needs according to their professional development plan.

- Provide professional development in the language most easily understood by the teachers.

Teachers

- Engage in professional development provided by program administrator.

- Practice self-assessment and shared reflective dialogue.

- Participate in reflective dialogue with the aim of better understanding how to meet the unique needs of the children in their program.

9.7 Programs offer professional development activities on how to support children with disabilities or other special needs.

Providing ongoing professional development activities on how to support children with disabilities or other special needs is essential to teachers feeling prepared to meet the needs of all young children in their classrooms. "The biggest barrier to including a child with a disability or other special need seems to be fear—fear not *of* children with special needs but *for* the children. [Teachers] are afraid of physically hurting a child, of not meeting perceived needs, and of having to tell a parent 'I do not know how to care for your child.' With knowledge, however, this fear fades and competence blooms" (CDE 2009, viii–ix). When teachers focus on the child, and not the disability or other special need, they can capitalize on their knowledge of child development and learning. The majority of children with disabilities or other special needs will progress through the various domains in a similar fashion to children who are typically developing. They may need more time, focused teaching, or more opportunities for guided practice in the skills. Teachers find that the adaptations and modifications they make for a child with special needs are simply extensions of individualizations they have been doing with other children. The key to the adaptation is what is important for good teaching: observation, reflection, and understanding of development. Teachers who have included children with disabilities and who are focused on providing access, support, and participation report increased skills as teachers for all children.

As stated in Guideline 5, the vast majority of children receiving special education services are those with delays in the area of speech and language. Implementing the universal design for learning approach for multiple methods of representation, engagement, and expression will go a long way in supporting the progress of children with speech and language delays. Also, given the information shared in chapter 6, it is clear that some children may be misidentified due to differences in the way that dual language learners who are typically developing acquire language. The increased emphasis on understanding the language-acquisition process of dual language learners and implementing intentional teaching strategies should be of great help in working with all young children. A better understanding of the process of second-language development for young dual language learners will promote more responsive and targeted services for all children.

Professional Development in Inclusion

Programs

- Provide professional development opportunities to staff members and families on inclusive practice and related policies.

- Facilitate discussion among staff and families about applying the principles of *people-first language* in the program.

- Collaborate with specialized service providers to offer professional development opportunities to staff members and family members on how to support children's understanding of disabilities and other special needs, and on developmentally appropriate strategies for engaging children with disabilities or other special needs.

Teachers

- Follow guidance from families and specialized service providers to support the learning and development of each child, according to developmental theory and program philosophy and practices.

- Follow guidance to support each child's active participation in learning opportunities through the use of easily adaptable materials, strategies, and techniques.

- Explore the role of values, beliefs, and perceptions when viewing and responding to children's behavior, developmental skills, and learning approaches.

References

Ackerman, D. J. 2005. "Getting Teachers from Here to There: Examining Issues Related to an Early Care and Education Teacher Policy." *Early Childhood Research & Practice* 7 (1).

California Department of Education (CDE). 2009. *Inclusion Works! Creating Child Care Programs That Promote Belonging for Children with Special Needs.* Sacramento: California Department of Education.

——. 2010. *California Preschool Curriculum Framework, Volume 1.* Sacramento: California Department of Education.

California Department of Education and First 5 California. 2012. *California Early Childhood Educator Competencies.* Sacramento: California Department of Education. Sacramento: California Department of Education.

Grace, C., D. Bordelon, P. Cooper, R. Kazelskis, C. Reeves, and D. G. Thames. 2008. "Impact of Professional Development on the Literacy Environments of Preschool Classrooms." *Journal of Research in Childhood Education* 23 (1): 52–81.

Hamre, B. K., R. C. Pianta, A. J. Mashburn, and J. T. Downer. 2012. "Promoting Young Children's Social Competence through the Preschool PATHS Curriculum and MyTeachingPartner Professional Development Resources." *Early Education & Development* 23 (6): 809–32.

Howes, C., R. Pianta, D. Bryant, B. Hamre, J. Downer, and S. Soliday-Hong. 2008. "Ensuring Effective Teaching in Early Childhood Education Through Linked Professional Development Systems, Quality Rating Systems and State Competencies: The Role of Research In an Evidence-Driven System." White Paper from the National Center for Research on Early Childhood Education 2008 Leadership Symposium.

Kagan, S. L., and M. J. Neuman. 1996. "The Relationship Between Staff Education and Training and Quality in Child Care Programs." *Child Care Information Exchange* 107: 65–70.

National Association for the Education of Young Children (NAEYC). n.d. Professional Development. http://www.naeyc.org/ecp (accessed May 7, 2013).

——. 2005. *NAEYC Code of Ethical Conduct and Statement of Commitment.* Washington, DC: NAEYC.

Rudd, L. C., M. Lambert, M. Satterwhite, and C. Smith. 2009. "Professional Development + Coaching = Enhanced Teaching: Increasing Usage of Math Mediated Language in Preschool Classrooms." *Early Childhood Education Journal* 37 (1): 63–69.

Sharpe, P. 1997. "Teaching and Learning at Home: Features of Parental Support for the Bilingual Competence of Preschoolers." *Early Child Development and Care* 130: 75–83.

Virmani, E. A., K. E. Masyn, R. A. Thompson, N. A. Conners-Burrow, and L. Whiteside-Mansell. 2012. "Early Childhood Mental Health Consultation: Promoting Change in the Quality of Teacher-Child Interactions." *Infant Mental Health Journal* 34 (2): 156–72.

Wayne, A. J., K. S. Yoon, P. Zhu, S. Cronen, and M. S. Garet. 2008. "Experimenting with Teacher Professional Development: Motives and Methods." *Educational Researcher* 37 (8): 469–79.

Zaslow, M., K. Tout, T. Halle, J. Vick Whittaker, and B. Lavelle. 2010a. "Emerging Research on Early Childhood Professional Development." *In Preparing Teachers for the Early Childhood Classroom: Proven Models and Key Principles.* Edited by S. B. Neuman, M. L. Kamil, and D. Strickland. Baltimore, MD: Brookes.

——. 2010b. *Toward the Identification of Features of Effective Professional Development for Early Childhood Educators: Literature Review.* Alexandria, VA: Office of Planning, Evaluation and Policy Development. Produced for the U.S. Department of Education.

Further Reading

California Early Learning Quality Improvement System (CAELQIS) Advisory Committee. 2010. *Dream Big for Our Youngest Children: California Early Learning Quality Improvement System Advisory Committee Final Report.* Sacramento: California Department of Education.

National Association for the Education of Young Children (NAEYC). 2011. *Position Statement: Code of Ethical Conduct and Statement of Commitment.* A Position Statement of the National Association for the Education of Young Children.

Burchinal, M. 2008. *Competencies and Credentials for Early Childhood Educators: What Do We Know and What Do We Need to Know?* Irvine: University of California.

Burchinal, M., M. Hyson, and M. Zaslow. 2008. "Competencies and Credentials for Early Childhood Educators: What Do We Know and What Do We Need to Know?" *NHSA Dialog:* 11 (1): 1–7.

Castle, K. 2012. "Professional Development through Early Childhood Teacher Research." *Voices of Practitioners* 7 (2): 1–8.

Howes, C., and R. C. Pianta. 2011. *Foundations for Teacher Excellence: Connecting Early Childhood Quality Rating, Professional Development, and Competency Systems in States.* Baltimore, MD: Brookes Publishing Co.

Howes, C., R. Pianta, D. Bryant, B. Hamre, J. Downer, and S. Soliday-Hong. 2008. *Ensuring Effective Teaching in Early Childhood Education through Linked Professional Development Systems, Quality Rating Systems and State Competencies: The Role of Research in an Evidence-Driven System.* A National Center for Research in Early Childhood Education White Paper. Charlottesville, VA: National Center for Research in Early Childhood Education.

Kinzie, M. B., S. D. Whitaker, K. Neesen, M. Kelley, M. Matera, and R. C. Pianta. 2006. "Innovative Web-Based Professional Development for Teachers of At-Risk Preschool Children." *Educational Technology and Society* 9 (4): 194–204.

Landry, S. H., P. R. Swank, K. E. Smith, M. A. Assel, and S. B. Gunnewig. 2006. "Enhancing Early Literacy Skills for Preschool Children: Bringing a Professional Development Model to Scale." *Journal of Learning Disabilities* 39 (4): 306–324.

National Association for the Education of Young Children (NAEYC). 2007. "Professional Development: Educational Qualifications of Program Administrators and Teaching Staff, Building Better Futures for Children and the Profession." *Beyond the Journal: Young Children on the Web.*

———. 2011. *Code of Ethical Conduct and Statement of Commitment.* Washington, DC: NAEYC.

———. n.d. *What Is Professional Development in Early Childhood Education?* Washington, DC: NAEYC.

Pennsylvania Office of Child Development and Early Learning. 2012. *Early Childhood Education Teacher Quality: Recognizing High Quality Core Content in Pennsylvania.* July. Office of Child Development and Early Learning, Commonwealth of Pennsylvania.

PROFESSIONAL DEVELOPMENT

Pianta, R. C., A. J. Mashburn, J. T. Downer, B. K. Hamre, and L. Justice. 2008. "Effects of Web-Mediated Professional Development Resources on Teacher–Child Interactions in Pre-Kindergarten Classrooms." *Early Childhood Research Quarterly* 23:431–451.

Powell, D. R., K. E. Diamond, M. R. Burchinal, and M. J. Koehler. 2010. "Effects of an Early Literacy Professional Development Intervention on Head Start Teachers and Children." *Journal of Educational Psychology* 102 (2): 299–312.

Wasik, B. A., M. A. Bond, and A. Hindman. 2006. "The Effects of a Language and Literacy Intervention on Head Start Children and Teachers." *Journal of Educational Psychology* 98 (1): 63–74.

Guideline 10: Administering Programs and Supervising Staff

Two critical components of high-quality early care and education are effective administrative practices and continuous program improvement; both of them allow early childhood professionals to better serve young children and their families and to meet short- and long-term program goals. Research shows that effective administrative practices are crucial for ensuring high-quality outcomes for children and families (Talan and Bloom 2004) and indicates that high-quality interactions and learning environments cannot be sustained in the long term without these administrative systems and practices in place.

Effective administrators of early childhood programs display key dispositions toward their work that include valuing high quality and high expectations; valuing inclusion and diversity in early education settings; considering multiple perspectives in the contexts of planning and decision making; and emphasizing continuous program improvement based on both assessment and collaboration. They exhibit skills and knowledge in the areas of program planning, development, and operations; human resources; and organizational systems, policies, and procedures.

A program's administrator provides leadership in establishing the practices and systems that enable the program to fulfill its mission and serve the community well. The program's other early childhood professionals also play key administrative roles. In a collaborative organization, they work as a team with the administrator to plan for and assess program operations; contribute to policy- and procedure-related decisions, ongoing monitoring, and documentation to meet standards; and maintain the systems that ensure smooth day-to-day program functioning.

Many practices of effective program administrators to support staff are discussed in the recommended program guidelines that follow. To avoid repetition, each recommended practice generally appears only within one guideline. Administrators can find a full list of practices in the Administration and Supervision section of the *California Early Childhood Educator Competencies* (California Department of Education and First 5 California 2012). The following practices are addressed:

- Fostering positive, effective communication between and among staff and colleagues
- Addressing conflict resolution between and among staff and colleagues
- Supporting positive relationships among staff members to foster a team environment and to contribute to continuous program improvement
- Ensuring the staff compensation is a program priority and that salary scales are commensurate with qualifications and education
- Supporting reflective practice and reflective supervision
- Supporting ongoing adult learning, coaching, and mentoring

10.1 Programs have a compensation schedule that acknowledges and validates the required training and experience of each staff member by providing a living wage, as well as wage increases based on additional education and professional activities.

The California Department of Education, Early Education and Support Division (CDE/EESD), reaffirms its endorsement of the principle of providing pay and benefits for preschool teachers that are at parity with that of their counterparts in the K–12 school system. Most teaching staff members in California preschools still earn very low wages and minimal benefits, including many teachers with substantial college training who barely earn a living wage. Better compensation attracts better-qualified staff and leads to less staff turnover. This leads to higher program quality and better outcomes for children and families (Whitebook and Ryan 2011).

Compensation

Programs

- Prioritize compensation that is comparable to that of the K–12 system for all staff members as a primary concern of the program's administrators, families, board of directors, and sponsoring organization.

- Implement an equitable compensation schedule, with regular increments, as a key program tool for staff development and retention.

- Base salary increases upon advancement along a planned career pathway aligned with articulated education and credentialing, mentor-recommended professional development activities, demonstrated mastery of skills as documented in annual performance evaluations, assumption of program leadership roles and responsibilities.

- Establish equitable health and retirement plans and benefits.

- Ensure that salary schedules are commensurate with qualifications and education.

- Follow the recommended guidelines for an equitable salary schedule (Burton and Whitebook 1998, 10):

  o The basic structure of the salary guidelines establishes a floor for entry-level staff and benchmarks for highly trained staff in teaching and administrative roles.

  o An Aide's salary, which marks the floor of the guidelines, is indexed to the self-sufficiency wage required for single adults in their county.

  o The benchmark for a Master Teacher with a bachelor's degree plus a supervised practicum is a salary equivalent to that of a beginning public school teacher in the local school district.

  o The Program Director's salary is indexed to that of a more-experienced public school teacher in the local school district.

Teachers

- Know the program's policies that relate to salaries, benefits, and advancement and seek clarification from appropriate staff as needed.

- Seek and pursue educational and professional development pathways that will lead to advancement along the program's career pathway and on the salary schedule.

10.2 Programs create working conditions that support job satisfaction.

The workplace climate is an important contributor to teachers' job satisfaction, and staff members' positive or negative ratings of an organization's overall climate are usually widely shared (Bloom 2010). In addition to fair and adequate compensation, good administrative practices can also support teachers' sense of job satisfaction and can reduce staff turnover, contributing to the staffing stability that helps an early childhood program succeed in improving quality.

Program Planning and Personnel Policies

Programs

- Invite staff, families, and others to participate in program planning.

- Involve staff in setting annual goals for program improvement, provide resources and support for meeting objectives, and assess progress toward achieving program goals.

- Be aware of issues related to collective bargaining and labor contracts.

Teachers

- Participate in program planning, including decisions about curriculum and, as appropriate, contribute ideas from the teaching team.

- Know the expectations of the job description and become familiar with other personnel policies, including those that involve salaries, benefits, and volunteer or internship agreements.

- Seek mentorship with more-experienced early childhood educators and offer assistance to less-experienced colleagues.

Performance Evaluation and Professional Development

Programs

- Conduct private, formal performance reviews at least annually.

- Ensure that staff members understand the role of formal performance evaluations in continuous professional improvement.

- Ensure that a climate of continuous improvement is provided so that individuals can seek educational and professional certification.

Facilities

Programs

- Set and evaluate facility design policies and practices that reflect the program's philosophy of providing a high-quality environment that meets the ever-changing requirements of families and staff members.

- Facilitate staff members' access to the equipment and materials needed to furnish a high-quality early education environment and funds or procedures to replace and replenish them as needed.

Teachers

- Participate in adapting and maintaining the facility and environment as needed to support adult needs, interests, and comfort as well as children's interests, learning, and development.

Performance Evaluation

Teachers

- Provide timely and objective feedback to staff and colleagues.

- Conduct or contribute to formal performance reviews, including review of supervisor performance, at least annually, based on clearly defined job descriptions, expectations, and direct observations, incorporating input from others as appropriate.

- Maintain confidentiality and protect privacy in the supervision and evaluation of staff and colleagues.

Professional Development

Teachers

- Seek opportunities to attain educational and professional improvement and learn how to establish a professional development plan.

- Develop core competencies as detailed in the California Early Childhood Educator Competencies (California Department of Education and First 5 California 2012).

10.3 Programs foster respectful, collaborative relationships among staff.

An administrative leader sets the tone for respectful, collaborative work within a program. The leader sets policies supportive of positive staff relationships; models constructive, respectful interaction styles; and affirms, through words and actions, the diverse strengths of each person to the program.

Personnel Policies

Programs

- Support positive relationships among staff members to foster a team environment.

Teachers

- Communicate proactively with staff and colleagues about personnel changes.

Communication Between and Among Staff

Programs

- Interpret and apply communication policies, as appropriate, to ensure effectiveness for diverse staff members or in complex situations.

- Adapt communication strategies to meet the diverse language and literacy abilities of staff members.

- Establish a time in staff meeting agendas to ensure regular sharing of information.

Teachers

- Determine the communication styles and preferences of staff and colleagues and use this information when communicating.

- Maintain transparency and accountability in interactions.

- Provide timely and accurate communication.

- Establish relationships with other staff that encourage mutual exchange of information and ideas.

- Model appropriate methods of communication with consideration for the communication preferences of colleagues.

- Maintain confidentiality and professionalism in communications with staff.

- Adapt communication strategies to meet the diverse language and literacy abilities of staff and colleagues.

Conflict Resolution Among Staff Members

Programs

- Engage staff members in the development of protocols or resolution of specific conflict situations, as appropriate.

- Provide staff members with professional development and support on conflict resolution that incorporates cultural considerations.

- Invite outside consultant or facilitator to coach staff on relationship-based problem solving, reflective communication, and conflict-resolution skills.

Teachers

- Facilitate the use of conflict-resolution strategies among staff and colleagues.

- Initiate discussions to inform a clear understanding of cultural and individual considerations in conflict resolution.

- Anticipate areas of potential conflict between and among staff and colleagues and proactively address identified area(s) of concern with staff in advance to avoid potential conflicts.

- Use a professional code of ethics established by a respected national early childhood education organization (such as the NAEYC).

- Refer complex conflict situations to the supervisor or other staff/colleagues, as appropriate.

10.4 Programs collaborate with staff in making decisions.

Participatory decision making is one of the hallmarks of a truly collaborative program. This democratic leadership model recognizes that job satisfaction increases when teachers have a voice in making decisions that affect their lives (Bloom 2011). Having regular opportunities to make positive, recognized contributions to improving their program's effective functioning reinforces early childhood educators' perceptions of themselves as valued professionals.

Program Philosophy

Programs

- Collaborate with staff members and others to review the program's statement of philosophy and its implications for practice.

Program-Planning Process, Policies, and Procedures

Programs

- Involve staff members in program planning and evaluation—including setting annual goals for program improvement, planning, and evaluation of the program's curriculum, and recruiting staff and enrolling children.

Teachers

- Gather information about children from families, staff, and colleagues to contribute to the planning process.

- Participate in program planning (including curriculum), recruitment and enrollment of children, and procedures for meeting individual child and family needs, as appropriate.

- Participate in hiring processes as appropriate.

Program Policies and Procedures

Programs

- Collaborate with families and staff members to adapt policies and procedures to meet individual child and family requirements, as appropriate.

Fiscal Procedures

Programs

- Collaborate with staff members, families, and other stakeholders to develop short- and long-term financial goals for the program.

Facilities

Teachers

- Identify resources available to resolve facility problems and issues, such as utility companies and repair services, and act efficiently to resolve problems.

- Adapt the facility and environment as needed to support adult needs, interests, and comfort as well as children's interests, learning, and development.

10.5 Programs establish and implement policies regarding reflective practice and reflective supervision.

An administrator who structures the early childhood program as a learning community for its adults as well as its children views staff supervision through the lens of a mentor and coach. The goal is to encourage **reflective practice**—approaching the educational setting with the intention to observe mindfully, respond thoughtfully, and take time to share reflections, thereby deepening one's own understanding and improving one's own practice (Heffron and Murch 2010). **Reflective supervision** is a way of guiding teachers to draw lessons from their own experiences that is likely to enhance interactions with children in their care (Howes, James, and Ritchie 2003).

Reflective Practice

Programs

- Provide professional development opportunities and establish program policies on reflective practice and reflective supervision.

- Invite an outside coach or facilitator to guide staff on how to increase authentic communication and refine reflective communication skills.

- Develop an environment in which adults can be engaged in continuous learning and development.

- Use teachable moments with adults through coaching practices.

- Actively seek professional development opportunities for staff members to make early childhood educators' work meaningful, challenging, and engaging.

- Cultivate the development of mentorship skills through leadership that is characterized by openness, honesty, care, and encouragement and demonstrates strong, reflective communication skills.

Teachers

- Demonstrate and apply an understanding of the principles of reflective practice.

- Use the learning environment to incorporate principles of adult learning and of children's learning and development.

- Seek mentorship opportunities with experienced early childhood educators and, in turn, become a mentor to less-experienced educators.

- Understand that adult learning opportunities outside the classroom enhance the work with children.

10.6 Programs develop staff policies and systems to maintain stability and consistency in program quality.

Stable, consistent staffing over time is crucial to an early childhood program's ability to achieve and maintain high quality. Continuous program improvement depends on building a stable, committed, professional learning community of educators who will actively engage with a board of directors (or community advisory board or committee), administrators and school community members to work toward achieving the program's long-term goals. A framework of supportive staff policies and systems can help achieve this stability.

Program-Planning Process and Personnel Policies

Programs

- Involve others in setting annual goals for program improvement, provide resources and support for meeting objectives, and assess progress toward achieving program goals.

- Develop and implement hiring policies and job descriptions (for staff members) that comply with regulations or other requirements, consider the diverse linguistic and cultural experiences of children and families, and includes individuals with disabilities.

- Develop a process for informing new staff and colleagues, including substitute teachers, volunteers, and interns, about program policies, procedures, and supports.

Teachers

- Participate in program planning by contributing ideas from the teaching team.

- Inform new staff and colleagues, including volunteers and interns, about policies, procedures, and supports.

- Communicate proactively with families, staff, and colleagues about personnel changes.

- Participate in hiring processes as appropriate.

- Know the expectations of their job descriptions and are familiar with other personnel policies, including those that involve salaries, benefits, and volunteer or internship agreements.

Continuous Program Improvement

Programs

- Plan and implement a program evaluation and improvement plan to promote positive outcomes for children and families.

- Collaborate with a board of directors or community advisory board or committee to develop a strategic plan or framework for continuous program improvement.

- Maintain a high-quality program based on agency standards.

- Integrate standards into program planning.

- Promote high-quality standards and practices among staff members, and others who contribute to the ongoing operation of the program.

Teachers

- Engage with staff, colleagues, and families in reflective practice and self-study and implement action plans for strengthening relationships with families and community partners.

- Participate in program improvement activities.

- Assist in maintaining a high-quality program based on agency standards.

Performance Evaluation

Teachers

- Assess and document the performance of staff and colleagues based on clearly defined job descriptions, expectations, and direct observation, incorporating input from families or other staff and colleagues as appropriate.

- Contribute to performance reviews of themselves and the supervisor.

Professional Development

Teachers

- Encourage colleagues to set professional and educational goals related to individual certification.

- Seek opportunities to attain educational and professional improvement and to establish a professional development plan.

10.7 Programs engage in sound business practices.

One component of a high-quality program is the presence of sound business practices. Although less visible than classroom work with children, sound business practices enable a program to operate smoothly and efficiently while avoiding disruptions due to uncertainties about regulation compliance, budget accuracy, and the capacity to pursue short- and long-term financial goals. The ability to improve facilities and equipment, increase staff compensation, and enhance services for children and families depends on competent long-term and day-to-day management of procedures and resources.

Recordkeeping

Programs

- Analyze data in records and apply information to programwide planning, decision making, evaluation, and

monitoring to ensure compliance with requirements.

- Provide professional development activities on record requirements and establish program policies or procedures to facilitate recordkeeping.

Teachers

- Implement timely recordkeeping that meets the requirements of regulatory, funding, or accrediting agencies.

- Explain recordkeeping requirements to staff, colleagues, and families, as appropriate.

- Gather information from staff, colleagues, and families to guide recordkeeping processes, as appropriate.

Program Policies and Procedures

Programs

- Develop, document, and assess program policies and procedures for effectiveness, appropriateness, and compliance with regulations and requirements.

Teachers

- Explain program policies and procedures to adults as needed.

- Keep inventory of all supplies, materials, and equipment, as needed.

- Follow program policies and procedures.

Regulatory Agencies

Programs

- Serve as liaison between the program and regional and national regulatory agencies.

- Ensure compliance with laws and regulations through monitoring and provide regular and timely reports.

Teachers

- Become familiar with and comply with requirements of applicable regulatory agencies (e.g., licensing bodies, health departments, fire marshal).

Fiscal Procedures

Programs

- Collaborate with staff members, families, and other stakeholders to develop short- and long-term financial goals for the program.

- Identify multiple funding sources.

- Meet reporting requirements.

Teachers

- Manage the budget for materials, supplies, and related documentation to meet reporting obligations.

- Know the program's funding sources and requirements (e.g., tuition, state and/or federal funding, private foundations).

- Use and care for resources in an appropriate manner.

Loss and Liability

Programs

- Assess the program's insurance requirements and maintain adequate coverage for loss and liability.

- Develop program policies and ensure professional development opportunities on strategies to prevent loss and reduce liability.

Teachers

- Maintain current and accurate documentation related to risk management.

- Refer loss and liability-related questions or report alleged violations to appropriate staff.

Facilities

Programs

- Understand how the facility operates and is managed, contribute design ideas, and become familiar with all aspects of the use of the facility, including accessibility and accommodation issues specified by the Americans with Disabilities Act.

Teachers

- Identify resources available to resolve facility problems and issues, such as utility companies or repair services.

- Maintain awareness of facility requirements and report maintenance issues to the supervisor.

References

Bloom, P. J. 2003. *Leadership in Action: How Effective Leaders Get Things Done.* Lake Forest, IL: New Horizons.

———. 2010. *A Great Place to Work: Creating a Healthy Organizational Climate.* Lake Forest, IL: New Horizons.

———. 2011. *Circle of Influence: Implementing Shared Decision Making and Participative Management.* Lake Forest, IL: New Horizons.

Bloom, P. J., and M. Sheerer. 1992. "The Effect of Leadership Training on Child Care Program Quality." *Early Childhood Research Quarterly* 7 (4): 579–94.

Brandon, R., T. Stutman, and M. Maroto. 2009. *The Economic Value of Early Care and Education for Young Children.* Washington, DC: Human Services Policy Center.

Bueno, M., L. Darling-Hammond, and D. Gonzales. 2010. *A Matter of Degrees: Preparing Teachers for the Pre-K Classroom.* Education Reform Series. Pew Center on the States. http://www.childinst.org/images/stories/resource_center_docs/A_Matter_of_Degrees.pdf (April 10, 2104).

California Department of Education and First 5 California. 2012. *California Early Educator Competencies.* Sacramento: California Department of Education.

Carter, M., and D. Curtis. 2010. *The Visionary Director: A Handbook for Dreaming, Organizing, and Improvising in Your Center.* 2nd. ed. St. Paul, MN: Redleaf Press.

Committee on Early Childhood Care and Education Workforce. 2012. *The Early Childhood Care and Education Workforce: Challenges and Opportunities: A Workshop Report.* Washington, DC: The National Academies Press.

Espinosa, L. 1997. "Personal Dimensions of Leadership." In *Leadership in Early Care and Education,* edited by Sharon L. Kagan and Barbara T. Bowman. Washington, DC: National Association for the Education of Young Children.

———. 2010. *Getting It Right for Young Children from Diverse Backgrounds: Applying Research to Improve Practice.* Upper Saddle River, NJ: Prentice Hall.

Gilliam, W. S. 2008. *Implementing Policies to Reduce the Likelihood of Preschool Expulsion* (Foundation for Child Development Policy Brief, Advancing PK-3, No. 7). New York: Foundation for Child Development.

Harms, T., R. M. Clifford, and D. Dryer. 2005. *Early Childhood Environment Rating Scale, Revised Edition.* New York: Teachers College Press.

Heffron, M. C., and T. Murch. 2010. *Reflective Supervision and Leadership in Infant and Early Childhood Programs.* Washington, DC: Zero to Three.

Herzenberg, S., M. Price, and D. Bradley. 2005. *Losing Ground in Early Childhood Education: Declining Workplace Qualifications in an Expanding Industry, 1979–2004.* Washington, DC: Economic Policy Institute.

Howes, C., J. James, and S. Ritchie. 2003. "Pathways to Effective Teaching." *Early Childhood Research Quarterly* 18:104–20.

Leana, C., E. Appelbaum, and I. Shevchuk. 2009. "Work Process and Quality of Care in Early Childhood Education: The Role of Job Crafting." *Academy of Management Journal,* 52 (6): 1169–92.

McCormick Center for Early Childhood Leadership. 2011. "Quality in Context— How Directors' Beliefs, Leadership, and Management Practices Relate to Observed Classroom Quality." *Research Notes.* Wheeling, IL: National Louis University.

National Association for the Education of Young Children. 2006. *NAEYC Accreditation Standards and Criteria.* Washington, DC: National Association for the Accreditation of Young Children.

Paratore, J. R. 2005. "Approaches to Family Literacy: Exploring the Possibilities." *The Reading Teacher* 59:394–96.

Pianta, R. C., K. M. La Paro, and B. K. Hamre. 2008. *Classroom Assessment Scoring System.* Baltimore: Brookes Publishing Co. http://www.cehd.umn.edu/ceed/projects/atc/resources/CLASSOverview.pdf (accessed July 31, 2014).

Pianta, R. C., A. J. Mashburn, J. T. Downer, B. K. Hamre, and L. Usatice. 2008. "Effects of Web-Mediated Professional Development Resources on Teacher–Child Interaction in Prekindergarten Classrooms." *Early Childhood Research Quarterly* 23 (4): 431–51.

Rohacek, M., G. C. Adams, and E. E. Kisker. 2010. *Understanding Quality in Context: Child Care Centers, Communities, Markets, and Public Policy.* Washington, DC: The Urban Institute.

Sciarra, D. J., and A. G. Dorsey. 2009. *Developing and Administering a Child Care and Education Program.* 7th ed. Clifton Park, NY: Thompson Delmar.

Talan, T. N., and P. J. Bloom. 2004. *Program Administration Scale: Measuring Early Childhood Leadership and Management.* New York: Teachers College Press.

Whitebook, M., and S. Ryan. 2011. "Degrees in Context: Asking the Right Questions about Preparing Skilled and Effective Teachers of Young Children." *Preschool Policy Brief.* New Brunswick, NJ: National Institute for Early Education Research.

———. 2012. "More Than Teachers: The Early Care and Education Workforce." In *Handbook of Early Childhood Education,* edited by R. C. Pianta, 92–110. New York: Guilford Press.

Further Reading

Bueno, M., L. Darling-Hammond, and D. Gonzales. 2010. *A Matter of Degrees: Preparing Teachers for the Pre-K Classroom.* Washington, DC: The Pew Center on the States, Education Reform Series.

Heffron, M. C., and T. Murch. 2012. Finding the Words, *Finding the Ways: Exploring Reflective Supervision and Facilitation.* San Francisco, CA: WestEd.

Zero to Three. 2013. *PCAN: Curriculum.* Washington, DC: Zero to Three. http://www.zerotothree.org/about-us/areas-of-expertise/training-and-professional-development/pcan-curriculum.html (accessed June 24, 2013).

Appendixes

Appendixes

Appendix A
Resources for Early Care and Education Programs

 **All About Young Children** provides family-focused, multimedia products aimed at families and describes the California infant/toddler and preschool foundations. Products available in eight languages. http://allaboutyoungchildren.org (accessed June 12, 2015).

 Beginning Together is a project designed to move inclusive experiences for young children with disabilities or other special needs and their families from theory to practice. http://www.CAinclusion.org/bt (accessed August 29, 2014).

 CDE/ECE Faculty Initiative Project aligns and integrates essential content and competencies of key CDE/EESD materials and initiatives with core early childhood education curriculum of the California Community College and the California State University systems. http://www.facultyinitiative/wested.org (accessed August 29, 2014).

 **The California Collaborative on the Social and Emotional Foundations for Early Learning (CA CSEFEL)** is a project that connects early childhood programs with trainers and coaches versed in the CA CSEFEL Teaching Pyramid Framework. The CA CSEFEL Teaching Pyramid Framework is an approach based on evidence from research. CA CSEFEL practices are intended to emphasize universal practices that promote healthy social–emotional development; practices that help prevent behaviors that are challenging in group settings; and intervention to address individual behaviors in infants and young children. CA CSEFEL trainers and coaches maximize collaboration to enhance linkages and methods for local agencies to deliver services and connect families to appropriate interventions, including children's mental health, Early Start, special education, and medical services. http://www.cainclusion.org/camap/cacsefel.html (accessed August 29, 2014).

 **The California Early Childhood Mentor Program** provides resources and support to aspiring and experienced teachers and administrators in programs serving children birth to five and before- and after-school programs. http://www.ecementor.org/ (accessed August 29, 2014).

 **California Early Childhood Online (CECO):** These online overview modules cover CDE publications and resources and other key state-approved content. Get free one-hour overviews of the foundations, frameworks, Desired Results, ERS, Healthy and Active Preschoolers, California CSEFEL, Strengthening Families, and the 3Rs of Early Childhood Education. Registered participants receive certificates upon successful completion of each module. http://www.caearlychildhoodonline.org/ (accessed June 12, 2015).

 The **California Inclusion and Behavior Consultation (CIBC) Network** is a professional development resource that includes on-site consultation, reflective practice conversations, and resources regarding challenging behavior and special needs. http://www.cibc-ca.org/ (accessed August 29, 2014).

California Map to Inclusion and Belonging: Making Access Possible (MAP) develops materials and serves as a clearinghouse of resources and information for individuals, organizations, and child care providers in the state about inclusive practices, including current information on successful state and local initiatives. http://www.CAinclusion.org/camap (accessed August 29, 2014).

 **California Preschool Instructional Network (CPIN).** Training is based on publications by the Early Education and Support Division: primarily the *California Preschool Learning Foundations, the California Preschool Curriculum Framework, the Preschool English Learner (PEL) Guide*, and *Inclusion Works!* http://www.cpin.us/ (accessed August 29, 2014).

 The **California School-Age Consortium (CalSAC)** mission is to enhance the performance of California out-of-school program providers by building connections, competence, and community. http://www.calsac.org/ (accessed August 29, 2014).

 The **Child Care Initiative Project (CCIP)** works through local Child Care Resource and Referral (CCR&R) agencies to recruit, train, and retain licensed family child care providers. http://www.rrnetwork.org/ccip-quality (accessed February 27, 2015).

 The **Child Development Training Consortium** provides financial and technical assistance to students and professionals in the early care and education field. Its Web site includes the training portal for professional development and course work that allows the user to locate trainings across the state, the Mapping Tool (which enables training systems to map the course content to the ECE Competencies), and the Curriculum Alignment Project that establishes an alignment of required

core course work for ECE degrees. It also houses information about California's Professional Growth Matrix and a list of Professional Growth Advisers. https://www.childdevelopment.org (accessed June 29, 2015).

 CompSAT–Competencies Self-Assessment Tool is an online, professional development Web site filled with interactive and self-reflective activities and videos highlighting research-based guidance on the California Early Childhood Educator Competencies. http://ececompsat.org/index.html (accessed August 29, 2014).

 Desired Results Training and Technical Assistance Project provides training and technical assistance in the implementation of the Desired Results system, including assessing children with the Desired Results Developmental Profile©. http://www.desiredresults.us (accessed June 12, 2015).

 **Family Child Care at Its Best** provides high-quality education on child development to thousands of licensed and license-exempt family child care providers throughout California. http://humanservices.ucdavis.edu/ChildDev/Programs/FamilyChildCare.aspx?unit=CHLDEV (accessed August 29, 2014)

 The **Program for Infant Toddler Care (PITC)** is CDE's training system for professionals who work with infants and toddlers (birth to age three). PITC seeks to ensure that America's infants get a safe, healthy, emotionally secure and enriching start in life. http://www.pitc.org/ (accessed August 29, 2014).

For more information on EESD Resources, visit http://www.cde.ca.gov/sp/cd/re/cddprofdevtrain.asp

ORGANIZATIONS

The following organizations provide resources that cover a wide range of topics in early childhood education.

California Child Care Health Program (CCHP) Healthline

1322 Webster St., Suite 402
Oakland, CA 94612
Telephone: 800-333-3212
Web site: http://www.ucsfchildcarehealth.org/html/healthline/healthlinemain.htm (accessed August 29, 2014).

The Healthline provided consultation on concerns dealing with special needs, behavioral health, nutrition, car seat safety, and infant and toddler behavior. Funding for the CCHP Healthline was discontinued; however, resources developed as part of this project are still available on the CCHP Web site. They include frequently asked health-related questions, health and safety tips, and multilingual resources.

California Child Care Resource and Referral Network

111 New Montgomery St., 7th Floor
San Francisco, CA 94105
Telephone: 415-882-0234
Web site: http://www.rrnetwork.org (accessed August 29, 2014).

The California Child Care Resource and Referral Network was founded in 1980 as an association of resource and referral (R&R) agencies throughout the state. These R&Rs help parents find child care and provide a well-developed system that supports parents, providers, and local communities in finding, planning for, and providing affordable, quality child care. R&Rs have grown into comprehensive agencies equipped to provide information, training, and support for parents, caregivers, other community-based agencies, employers, and government policymakers.

California Department of Education

CDE Press, Sales Office
1430 N Street, Suite 3705
Sacramento, CA 95814
Telephone: 800-995-4099
Fax: 916-323-0823
Web site: http://www.cde.ca.gov/re/pn/rc (accessed August 29, 2014).

The CDE Press Web site contains information about publications such as model curriculum standards; child development materials, quality review, school-age care, special needs, and infant/toddler caregiver and parent resources.

California Learning Resource Network (CLRN)

1100 H Street
Modesto, CA 95354
Telephone: 209-238-1420
Fax: 209-238-4223
E-mail: info@clrn.org

The network identifies and reviews supplemental electronic learning resources such as software, video, and Internet resources and provides descriptions and ratings of these resources by age group. The network also identifies learning units aligned with the resources and the state academic content standards.

The California Reading Association

638 Camino De Los Mares
San Clemente, CA, CA 92673
Telephone: 714-435-1983
Web site: http://www.californiareads.org (accessed August 29, 2014)

This professional organization offers publications, professional development and networking, and updated information on policy issues.

California Tomorrow

PO Box 99664
Emeryville, CA 94662
Telephone: 510-496-0220
Web site: http://www.californiatomorrow.org (accessed August 29, 2014).

California Tomorrow, a nonprofit organization, conducts research, provides technical assistance, and produces publications on building a more equitable, inclusive, and multicultural society.

Child Care Law Center
445 Church St.
San Francisco, CA 94114
Telephone: 415-558-8005
E-mail: info@childcarelaw.org
Web site: http://www.childcarelaw.org
(accessed August 29, 2014).

The Child Care Law Center uses legal expertise to secure good, affordable child care for low-income families and communities.

Children Now
Headquarters
1404 Franklin St., Suite 700
Oakland, CA 94612
Telephone: 510-763-2444
E-mail: info@childrennow.org
Web site: http://www.childrennow.org

Children Now is a national organization that promotes community action and policy changes to improve children's quality of life, with special emphasis on poor and at-risk children. Each year Children Now publishes a "report card" on family economics, health, education, and safety. A branch of this organization is located in the following city:

> Sacramento Office
> 1510 J Street, Suite 115
> Sacramento, CA 95814
> Telephone: 916-379-5256
> Fax: 916-443-1204
> E-mail: info@childrennow.org

Council for Exceptional Children
CEC Publications
2900 Crystal Drive, Suite 1000
Arlington, VA 22202
Telephone: 888-232-7733
Web site: http:www.cec.sped.org (accessed August 29, 2014).

The Council for Exceptional Children (CEC) is an international organization dedicated to improving the educational success of individuals with disabilities and/or gifts and talents. The CEC is an advocate for appropriate governmental policies and persons with disabilities and special needs, sets professional standards, provides professional development, and helps provide the resources necessary for effective professional practice.

The CEC publishes journals, newsletters, and special education materials.

Disability Rights of California
1831 K Street
Sacramento, CA 95811
Telephone: 916-504-5800
Web site: http://www.disabilityrightsca.org
(accessed August 29, 2014).

This organization is an advocate for Californians with disabilities, educates the public, conducts investigations, and litigates to advance and protect their rights.

ERIC Clearinghouse on Elementary and Early Childhood Education
Early Childhood and Parenting Collaborative
Children's Research Center
University of Illinois at Urbana-Champaign
51 Gerty Drive
Champaign, IL 61820
Telephone: 217-333-1386 or 877-275-3227
Web site: http://ecap.crc.illinois.edu/eecearchive/index.html (accessed August 29, 2014).

The ERIC Clearinghouse provides resources for educators in early childhood and elementary education. It maintains an archive of research articles and papers on theory, practice, and policy for early childhood and elementary education and provides, at no cost, digests of useful articles for parents and teachers.

Institute of Education Sciences (IES)
The IES is the research arm of the U.S. Department of Education. The IES disseminates information and resources to practitioners, researchers, and policymakers through the What Works Clearinghouse, the ERIC database, the Regional Educational Laboratories, and the National Research and Development Centers.

• **What Works Clearinghouse (WWC)**

  The WWC identifies studies that provide credible and reliable evidence of the effectiveness of a given practice, program, or policy, and disseminates summary information and reports on the WWC Web site. http://ies.ed.gov/ncee/wwc/ (accessed August 28, 2014).

- **Education Resources Information Center (ERIC)**

  ERIC is an online digital library of education research and information. ERIC provides ready access to education literature to support the use of educational research and information to improve practice in learning, teaching, educational decision-making, and research. http://www.eric.ed.gov/ (accessed August 29, 2014).

- **National Education Research and Development Centers (R&D Centers)**

  The R&D Centers develop, test, and disseminate new approaches to improve teaching and learning, and student achievement. Each center conducts education research in its topic area. In addition, each center works cooperatively with the National Center for Education Research, conducts supplemental research within its broad topic area, and provides national leadership in defining research and development directions within its topic area. http://ies.ed.gov/ncer/randd/ (accessed August 29, 2014).

- **Regional Educational Laboratory Program**

  The 10 Regional Educational Laboratories (RELs) serve the educational needs of designated regions, using applied research, development, dissemination, and training and technical assistance to bring the latest and best research and proven practices into school improvement efforts. http://ies.ed.gov/ncee/edlabs/ (accessed August 29, 2014).

National Association for the Education of Young Children

1313 L Street NW, Suite 500
Washington, DC 20005
Telephone: 202-232-8777 or 800-424-2460
Web site: www.naeyc.org (accessed August 29, 2014).

The NAEYC is a professional organization that promotes excellence in early childhood education. It publishes materials and resources covering all topics included in the *California Preschool Program Guidelines*.

STANDARDS AND ASSESSMENT TOOLS

Standards can help to guide programs in their aim to ensure high-quality preschool programming. Additionally, specific assessment tools, used periodically, can provide assessments of current program quality as well as support a program's aim to engage in continuous program improvement.

The resources listed below are geared to support program administrators in their efforts to maintain program quality.

STANDARDS

National Association for the Education of Young Children Accreditation System

The National Association for the Education of Young Children (NAEYC), the nation's largest organization of early childhood educators, has established an accreditation program through its NAEYC Academy for Early Childhood Program Accreditation. Since 1985, the NAEYC's national accreditation system has set professional standards for early childhood education programs, allowing families to find high-quality programs for their children.

The NAEYC Accreditation of Programs for Young Children seeks to enhance children's well-being and early learning by improving the quality of early childhood programs serving children birth through kindergarten. The NAEYC Academy for Early Childhood Program Accreditation sets and monitors standards for high-quality programs for young children and accredits programs that meet these standards—the mark of quality in early childhood education.

This program is a national voluntary accreditation system for all types of preschools, kindergartens, child care centers, and school-age child care programs.

More information on the NAEYC's accreditation program is available from the NAEYC Web site: http://www.naeyc.org (accessed August 28, 2014).

California Commission on Teacher Credentialing

Since its inception in 1970, the California Commission on Teacher Credentialing has supported and encouraged the professional development of all educators. An educator's growth is valued as a mark of professional stature and as a source and a stimulant of student growth and achievement. The Commission believes that "learning students" are most likely to be found in the presence of "learning teachers" and other educators.

The manual titled The Child Development Permit Professional Growth Manual (2012) is available from the Commission on Teacher Credentialing. This document provides information for holders of the Child Development Permit on how to renew a permit. It also provides information for professional growth advisers, defined as an individual who advises permit holders regarding their professional growth and development. It includes information on all levels of the permit, renewal requirements, selection of a professional growth adviser, and the stages in the professional growth cycle.

Common Core State Standards

Educational standards describe what students should know and be able to do in each subject in each grade. In California, the State Board of Education decides on the standards for all students, from kindergarten through high school.

Since 2010, 45 states have adopted the same standards for English and math. These standards are called the Common Core State Standards (CCSS). Having the same standards helps all students get a good education, even if they change schools or move to a different state. Teachers, parents, and education experts designed the standards to prepare students for success in college and the workplace.

The California Common Core State Standards publications include:

California's Common Core State Standards for English Language Arts & Literacy in History/Social Studies, Science, and Technical Subjects (Spanish translation available).

California Common Core State Standards: Mathematics

More information is available from the California Common Core State Standards Web site: http://www.cde.ca.gov/re/cc/ (accessed August 29, 2014).

Content Standards for Kindergarten Through Grade Twelve

Subject-specific content standards for kindergarten through grade twelve have been developed to ensure high quality in curriculum and instruction. Preschool teachers and staff should be aware of these content standards so that their daily planning will support the development of needed skills and provide opportunities for practice. These publications are listed as follows:

California English Language Development Standards: Kindergarten Through Grade Twelve. Forthcoming. Sacramento: California Department of Education.

History–Social Science Standards for California Public Schools, Kindergarten Through Grade Twelve. 2000. Sacramento: California Department of Education.

Science Content Standards for California Public Schools, Kindergarten Through Grade Twelve. 2000. Sacramento: California Department of Education.

Health Education Content Standards for California Public Schools: Kindergarten Through Grade Twelve. 2008. Sacramento: California Department of Education.

Physical Education Model Content Standards for California Public Schools, Kindergarten Through Grade Twelve. 2006. Sacramento: California Department of Education.

Visual and Performing Arts Content Standards for California Public Schools: Prekindergarten Through Grade Twelve. 2001. Sacramento: California Department of Education.

More information is available from the California Department of Education Content Standards Web site: http://www.cde.ca.gov/be/st/ss/

More information is available from California Commission on Teacher Credentialing Website: http://www.ctc.ca.gov (accessed August 29, 2014).

ASSESSMENT TOOLS

Ages and Stages Questionnaire

The Ages and Stages Questionnaire (ASQ) is a series of questionnaires designed to screen the developmental performance of children in the areas of communication, gross motor skills, fine motor skills, problem solving, personal-social skills, and overall development across time. The age-appropriate scale is completed by the parent or caregiver. The items on the scale represent behaviors that the child should be able to perform at that age.

More information is available from the Ages and Stages Questionnaire Web site: http://agesandstages.com (accessed August 28, 2014).

The Classroom Assessment Scoring System (CLASS)

The Classroom Assessment Scoring System™ (CLASS™) is an observational instrument developed at the Curry School Center for Advanced Study of Teaching and Learning to assess classroom quality in PK-12 classrooms. It describes multiple dimensions of teaching that are linked to student achievement and development and has been validated in over 2,000 classrooms. The CLASS™ can be used to reliably assess classroom quality for research and program evaluation and also provides a tool to help new and experienced teachers become more effective.

More information is available from the CLASS Web site: http://curry.virginia.edu/research/centers/castl/class (accessed August 28, 2014).

Desired Results for Children and Families

The Desired Results for Children and Families Web site provides an overview of the background, purpose, and components of the Desired Results System. The system includes the Desired Results Developmental Profile (DRDP), which is

an observational assessment of children's progress in development and learning; the Environment Rating Scale (ERS), which assesses program quality through a broad definition of environment that includes the arrangement of space, the materials and activities, interactions, daily schedule, and support given to families and staff; and the Desired Results Parent Survey.

More information is available from the Desired Results Web site: http://www.desiredresults.us/ (accessed August 29, 2014).

The Early Language and Literacy Classroom Observation (ELLCO)

ELLCO Pre-K is designed specifically for early childhood settings, focusing on important preliteracy activities like storybook reading, circle time conversations, and child-originated storywriting. ELLCO Pre-K helps programs: get a complete picture of classrooms' literacy environment, meet NAEYC and IRA recommendations for print-rich preschool environments, and give teachers explicit guidance on ways to strengthen the quality of teaching practices in positive, supportive ways.

More information is available from the Brooke's Publishing Company Web site: http://www.brookespublishing.com/resource-center/screening-and-assessment/ellco/ellco-pre-k/ (accessed August 29, 2014).

Environment Rating Scale (ERS)

The Environment Rating Scale (ERS) is a widely used program quality assessment instrument designed for use with children aged two through five in infant-toddler programs (ITERS-R), preschool and kindergarten programs (ECERS-R), and family child care programs (FCCERS-R). Developed at the Frank Porter Graham Child Development Center at the University of North Carolina, Chapel Hill, the ERS was revised and updated in 1998 and 2005 to include greater emphasis on cultural diversity, family concerns, and individual children's needs.

The ECERS-R, to be used in preschool and kindergarten programs addresses the following content areas: space and furnishings, personal care routines, language-reasoning, activities, interactions, program structure, and parents and staff.

Both the reliability and the validity of the ECERS-R are well established; therefore, the instrument can be used with confidence that positive results indicate good program quality. The instrument is self-administering, meaning that a program director can assess his or her own program, or it can be used by outside observers of the program.

A video training package for the ECERS-R is available from Teachers College Press for use in self-instruction or as part of group training.

> Harms, T.; R. M. Clifford; and D. Cryer. *Early Childhood Environment Rating Scale* (Revised edition). 2005. New York: Teachers College Press.

More information is available from the Environment Rating Scale Institute Web site: http://www.ersi.info (accessed August 29, 2014).

Head Start Program Preparedness Checklist (Version 5)

Head Start Program Preparedness Checklist (Version 5) helps Head Start and Early Head Start programs to promote school readiness for dual language learners (DLLs) by examining the systems and services for children and families who speak languages other than English. This revised comprehensive document features indicators drawn from the Head Start Program Performance Standards, the research, and recommended practices.

More information is available from the ECLKC Web site: http://eclkc.ohs.acf.hhs.gov (accessed August 29, 2014).

Inclusive Classroom Profile (ICP)

The Inclusive Classroom Profile (ICP) is a structured observation rating scale designed to assess the quality of provisions and daily classroom practices that support the developmental needs of children with disabilities in early childhood settings.

Ratings on the items indicate the extent to which "classroom practices intentionally adapt the classroom's environment, activities and instructional support in ways that encourage access and active participation in the group, through adjustments that might differ from child to child."

More information is available from the National Professional Development Center on Inclusion at Frank Porter Graham Child Development Institute Web site: http://fpg.unc.edu/node/2880

The Program Administration Scale (PAS)

The *Program Administration Scale* (PAS) is a valid and reliable instrument designed to measure the leadership and management practices of early childhood programs. The PAS provides valuable information to directors about the quality of their administrative practices and can be used for program improvement efforts.

More information is available from the McCormick Center Web site: http://mccormickcenter.nl.edu/program-evaluation/program-administration-scale-pas/ (accessed August 28, 2014).

Questions to Consider in Universal Design Learning (UDL) Observations of Early Childhood Environments - Building Inclusive Child Care (BICC)

Individuals conducting early childhood environment observations can use these questions and checklist to discover how to increase UDL policies and practices and to identify those that already exist.

More information is available from the North Hampton Community College Web site: http://www.northampton.edu/bicc (accessed August 29, 2014).

Appendix B
Books and Media on Early Education by the California Department of Education

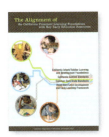

The Alignment of the California Preschool Learning Foundations with Key Early Education Resources (2012)
Delineates how California's preschool foundations are aligned with the California Infant-Toddler Learning & Development Foundations, California Content Standards, Common Core State Standards, and Head Start Child Development & Early Learning Framework. Includes color graphics. Online digital format only. http://www.cde.ca.gov/sp/cd/re/documents/psalignment.pdf

California Early Childhood Educator Competencies (2012)
This important professional resource describes the knowledge, skills, and dispositions that early childhood educators need in order to provide high-quality care and education to young children and their families. The California Early Childhood Educator Competencies (2012) is divided into the following overlapping areas: (1) Child Development and Learning; (2) Culture, Diversity, and Equity; (3) Relationships, Interactions, and Guidance; (4) Family and Community Engagement; (5) Dual-Language Development; (6) Observation, Screening, Assessment, and Documentation; (7) Special Needs and Inclusion; (8) Learning Environments and Curriculum; (9) Health, Safety, and Nutrition; (10) Leadership in Early Childhood Education; (11) Professionalism; and (12) Administration and Supervision. The California ECE Competencies are research-based and are aligned with the California Preschool Learning Foundations

and the California Infant/Toddler Learning & Development Foundations to guide professional development and related quality improvement activities. Available as a free download and as a binder-ready publication.

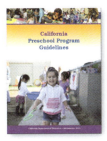

The **California Preschool Program Guidelines (2015)** is designed for administrators, directors, supervisors, college faculty, and policymakers. This comprehensive publication includes effective approaches for creating high-quality preschool programs. Special chapters include "Support for Young Dual Language Learners" and "Using Technology and Interactive Media with Preschool-Age Children." Companion DVD set available.

California's Best Practices for Young Dual Language Learners: Research Overview Papers (2013)
This series of research overviews spans the disciplines of neuroscience, cognitive science, and developmental psychology as well as assessment, educational research, family engagement, and special needs. They provide insight into how young dual language learners learn two languages and how they learn and develop in other domains. This online publication gives guidance to early childhood educators on how to support the learning and development of young dual language learners in preschool programs. http://www.cde.ca.gov/sp/cd/ce/documents/dllresearchpapers.pdf

Curriculum Frameworks

Aligned with the foundations, the curriculum frameworks guide early childhood educators working in programs serving children birth to five years of age. The frameworks provide guidance on the implementation of high-quality curriculum and instruction practices that optimize children's potential to acquire the knowledge and skills necessary to ensure that children are ready for kindergarten entry.

Desired Results Developmental Profile© (DRDP©)

The DRDP is an observation-based assessment instrument used to assess children's developmental progress. The DRDP was developed for the following four age groups:

- Infant Toddler (I/T)—Birth to 36 months
- Preschool (PS)—Three years to kindergarten entry
- School Age (SA)—Kindergarten through twelve years
- School Readiness (SR)—Transitional Kindergarten (TK) and Traditional Kindergarten (K)

Versions in English and Spanish are available for download on the Desired Results Web site.

The **Guidelines for Early Learning in Child Care Home Settings** Recognizing the importance of home-based child care settings in today's society, this publication provides guidance to help home-based child care providers offer high-quality early care and learning experiences to children. The book covers topics such as the roles and relationships involved in home-based child care; how to create safe, inclusive environments that foster early learning and development; ideas for implementing appropriate curriculum; professional development for home-based providers; and things to consider when infants and toddlers receive care in mixed-age group settings. http://www.cde.ca.gov/sp/cd/re/documents/elguidelineshome.pdf

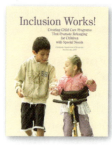

Inclusion Works! Creating Child Care Programs That Promote Belonging for Children with Special Needs (2009) is a handbook for early care and education programs. It provides guidance and resources on ways to include young children who have disabilities or other special needs. Strategies on how to adapt the environment, create family-friendly approaches to inclusion, and engage and use inclusion resources are discussed.

The **Infant/Toddler Learning and Development Program Guidelines** publication complements the preschool version. It takes a family-focused approach and presents research-based guidelines on early care and education that help ensure the healthy development and learning for very young children ages birth to three years old.

Learning Foundations

At the center of the California Early Learning & Development System are two sets of learning foundations: Infant/Toddler Learning and Development Foundations and California Preschool Learning Foundations (Volumes 1, 2, & 3). The entire set of foundations describe competencies—knowledge and skills—that all young children typically learn with appropriate support. DVD sets covering all domains of the foundations are available.

PITC Publications

The Program for Infant/Toddler Care (PITC) has developed high-quality training materials based on sound theoretical principles and research. Developed for trainers, program administrators, and teachers of infants and toddlers, these materials spell out a responsive, relationship-based approach to early care in which teachers learn to understand children's cues, interests, and skills and use them as the basis for an integrated curriculum that includes cognitive, language, perceptual–motor, and social–emotional development. The importance of forming a close, caring relationship with each child and family is emphasized throughout all PITC materials. http://www.pitc.org/pub/pitc_docs/products4.html

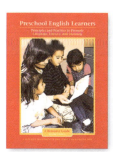

Preschool English Learners (PEL) Guide

The *Preschool English Learners Guide: Principles and Practices to Promote Language, Literacy, and Learning* was developed by experts with strong academic and research backgrounds. This publication presents the specific knowledge and tools needed to promote language, literacy, and learning for these young English learners. It is available in English and Spanish.

The **Transitional Kindergarten Implementation Guide (2013)** focuses on the essential components of a comprehensive transitional kindergarten (TK) program. The first chapter discusses considerations for the structure and design of TK programs. Chapters 2–8 provide in-depth discussions of effective instructional and curricular approaches. Family and community partnerships and systems of support are crucial for TK. Links to videos are embedded in this online guide. http://www.cde.ca.gov/ci/gs/em/documents/tkguide.pdf

Watching My Child Grow

is an introduction to the Desired Results system. It is dubbed in English, Spanish, and Mandarin.

A World Full of Language: Supporting Preschool English Learners DVD

This DVD and booklet provide information on how young children acquire English as a second language. Research-based strategies are featured to guide teachers on how to support English learners. The DVD is closed-captioned and formatted so that viewers can see it in its entirety or in sections. Companion DVD for *Preschool English Learners: Principles and Practices to Promote Language, Literacy, and Learning*. This DVD is available in English and Spanish on one disc.

Link for CDE Educational Resources catalog: http://www.cde.ca.gov/re/pn/rc/
Link for CDE/EESD Publications: http://www.cde.ca.gov/sp/cd/re/cddpublications.asp

To order CDE/EESD publications and DVDs, call toll-free at 800-995-4099, e-mail sales@cde.ca.gov, or mail a request to CDE Press Sales Office, 1430 N Street, Suite 3705, Sacramento, CA 95814.

Appendix C
California Preschool Children Enrolled in Special Education

The percentage of California children (ages three to five years) enrolled in special education was provided by the Special Education Division of the California Department of Education as of December 2011. The proportion in each of the categories is represented below.

Special Education Category	Total Number	Percentage
Speech & language impairment	47,863	64.92
Autism	13,163	17.85
Mental retardation	4195	5.69
Other health impairment	2732	3.72
Orthopedic impairment	1896	2.57
Hard of hearing	1066	1.45
Specific learning disability	817	1.12
Multiple disabilities	801	1.09
Deaf	499	.67
Visual impairment	473	.64
Traumatic brain injury	98	.13
Emotional disturbance	95	.12
Deaf-blindness	22	.03
Total	73,720	100.00

Source: California Department of Education DataQuest Web site at http://data1.cde.ca.gov/dataquest/.

Appendix D
Desired Results for Children and Families

The Desired Results (DR) system designed by the Early Education and Support Division (EESD) of the California Department of Education is designed to improve the quality of programs and services provided to all children, birth through twelve years of age, who are enrolled in early care and education programs and before-and after-school programs, and their families. Desired Results are defined as conditions of well-being for children and families. Each Desired Result defines an overall outcome. The DR system was developed based on six Desired Results—four for children and two for their families.

Desired Results for Children and Families:

DR1: Children are personally and socially competent

DR2: Children are effective learners

DR3: Children show physical and motor competence

DR4: Children are safe and healthy

DR5: Families support their child's learning and development

DR6: Families achieve their goals

The DR system implemented by the California Department of Education is a comprehensive approach that facilitates the achievement of the Desired Results identified for children and families. California is one of the very few states in the nation that has developed its own system designed specifically for measuring child progress toward desired outcomes. The system is aligned with both the state's learning and development foundations for early care and education programs and the California Common Core State Standards for English Language Arts & Litera-cy in History/Social Studies, Science, and Technical Subjects for kindergarten.

Components of the DR System

The DR system consists of the following components:

1. Desired Results Developmental Profile© (DRDP©) assessment instruments

2. Desired Results Parent Survey

3. Environment Rating Scales (ERS)

4. Program Self Evaluation

1. Desired Results Developmental Profile© Assessment Instruments

The DRDP© assessment instruments are designed for teachers to observe, document, and reflect on the learning, development, and progress of children, birth through twelve years of age, who are enrolled in early care and education programs, kindergarten programs and before-and after-school programs. The assessment results are intended for use by the teacher to plan curriculum for individual children and groups of children and to guide continuous program improvement.

2. Desired Results Parent Survey

The Parent Survey is designed to assist programs in gathering information from families about (1) the family members' satisfaction with their child's program and how it supports the child's learning and development; and (2) family members' perceptions of their children's progress toward reaching the two Desired Results identified for families. Families in the program are asked to complete the Parent Survey once a year and return it to their classroom. Families complete this survey anonymously to ensure that their opinions and concerns are kept confidential.

3. Environment Rating Scales

The Environmental Rating Scales (ERS) are used to measure the quality of the program environment (e.g., child–teacher interactions, children's interactions and activities, use of language, health and safety practices, space, and materials). The ERS are required instruments for yearly program self-evaluation and used for the reviews conducted CDE/CDD program staff.

4. Program Self-Evaluation

The Program Self-Evaluation addresses family and community involvement; governance and administration; funding; standards, assessment, and accountability; staffing and professional growth; opportunity and equal educational access; and approaches to teaching and learning. Program quality is assessed annually through the required self-evaluation and the reviews conducted by the CDE/EESD program staff.

Figure D1, the Desired Results System, depicts the system as a set of four concentric circles. The innermost circle represents the "heart" of the system: **the individual child's developmental progress**. Progress is assessed through the use of the Desired Results Developmental Profile© (DRDP©).

The next circle represents agencies' support for **families' goals**. Parent satisfaction is determined through the distribution and collection of Parent Surveys.

The third circle represents **classroom or family child care home environments**. The appropriateness of children's environments is assessed by using the Environment Rating Scale (ERS) instrument.

The last circle represents the **program** or agency. Program quality is assessed using the Categorical Program Monitoring/Categorical Monitoring Review (CPM/CMR).

Figure D1. **Desired Results Model**

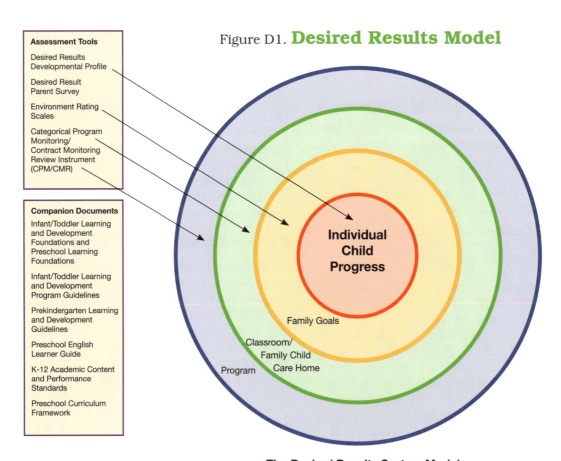

Assessment Tools

Desired Results Developmental Profile

Desired Result Parent Survey

Environment Rating Scales

Categorical Program Monitoring/ Contract Monitoring Review Instrument (CPM/CMR)

Companion Documents

Infant/Toddler Learning and Development Foundations and Preschool Learning Foundations

Infant/Toddler Learning and Development Program Guidelines

Prekindergarten Learning and Development Guidelines

Preschool English Learner Guide

K-12 Academic Content and Performance Standards

Preschool Curriculum Framework

Individual Child Progress

Family Goals

Classroom/ Family Child Care Home

Program

The Desired Results System Model

The following publications address components of the system: the *California Infant/Toddler Learning and Development Foundations, California Preschool Learning Foundations, Infant/Toddler Learning and Development Program Guidelines, Califor-nia Preschool Program Guidelines, Standards and the California Preschool Curriculum Framework* (three volumes) and *Preschool English Learners: Principles and Practices to Promote Language, Literacy, and Learning.*

Appendix E
State and Federal Laws Regarding People with Disabilities

State and federal laws provide protection for people with disabilities.

California's Unruh Civil Rights Act

Every state has the option of enacting provisions that provide more protection than the federal Americans with Disabilities Act (ADA). California has the Unruh Civil Rights Act, California Civil Code Section 51, which is much more expansive than the ADA and offers even broader protection for children with special needs. Unlike the ADA, it provides protection from discrimination by all business establishments in California, including housing and public accommodations. California's law may even apply to religious entities, although there have not been published legal opinions where that has been tested.

The Americans with Disabilities Act

The Americans with Disabilities Act (ADA) is federal legislation that was passed in 1990. The ADA guarantees civil rights protections to people with disabilities in areas such as employment, transportation, and public accommodations, including child care. Both child care centers and family child care homes must comply with the ADA, whether they are privately or publicly funded. The only exemptions allowed are for religious organizations operating child care programs. The ADA provides protection to a child or adult who meets one of the following criteria:

- Has a physical or mental impairment that substantially limits one of the "major life activities"

- Has a record of such an impairment

- Is regarded as having an impairment

- Is associated with an individual with a disability

The ADA mandates that "reasonable accommodations" be made for children with disabilities in child care. In most cases, the accommodations needed are quite simple and inexpensive to implement. For instance, a child with diabetes may need a snack at a different time or more frequently than other children; or a child who has difficulty making the transition to different activities may need a little extra time and support to do so. The ADA also makes it clear that the child care program may not charge families of children with disabilities higher fees than other families pay.

The ADA also mandates that architectural barriers to entering or using facilities be removed when this is "readily achievable." This phrase means that those necessary changes that do not place "an undue burden" on a provider need to be made ("an undue burden" is defined as a "significant difficulty or expense"). Examples of readily achievable designs may involve rearranging furniture for a child with visual impairments, installing a handrail in the bathroom for a child who uses a walker, changing door hinges, or other similarly minor accommodations. By making these relatively simple accommodations, a child care provider complies with the ADA.

However, accommodation, in some instances, may involve more significant changes. Fortunately, tax credits and other resources can help offset the cost of more extensive alterations to the child care setting.

The ADA also acknowledges that a child may not be admitted to the child care program if the child would pose a direct threat to others, if the modification would fundamentally alter the program itself, or if the accommodation needed would be an undue hardship to the program. These exceptions are considered on an individual basis, and the law expects child care providers to work hard to include children with disabilities as often as possible.

The Individuals with Disabilities Education Act

The Individuals with Disabilities Education Act is federal legislation mandating special education for all eligible children.[17] The Individuals with Disabilities Education Improvement Act of 2004 (IDEA 2004) is the most recent reauthorization of the statute. The IDEA guarantees children with disabilities a free, appropriate public education (FAPE); an education in the least restrictive environment; related services; and fair assessment in the delivery of those special education services to children, from birth to age twenty-two. The law has four parts: Part A covers the general purpose of the law and definitions; Part B addresses the requirements for the education of all children with disabilities from age three through age twenty-one; Part C covers the specific requirements for services to infants and toddlers (children from birth to thirty-six months) with disabilities and their families; and Part D authorizes national activities to improve special education services (research, personnel development, technical assistance, and state improvement grants).

The IDEA makes it possible for states and localities to receive federal funds to assist in the education of infants, toddlers, preschoolers, children, and youth with disabilities. Essentially, in order to remain eligible under the law for federal funds, states must ensure the following:

- All children and youths with disabilities, regardless of the severity of their disability, will receive a free, appropriate public education (FAPE) at public expense.

- The education of children and youths with disabilities will be based on a complete and individual evaluation and assessment of the specific, unique needs of each student.

- An individualized education program (IEP) or an individualized family services plan (IFSP) will be drawn up for every child or youth found eligible for early intervention or special education, stating precisely what types of early intervention services or what kinds of special education and related services or each infant, toddler, preschooler, child, or youth will receive.

- To the maximum extent appropriate, all children and youths with disabilities will be educated in the regular education environment. Children and youths receiving special education have the right to receive the related services they need to benefit from special education instruction.

- Parents have the right to participate in every decision related to the identification, evaluation, and placement of their child or youth with a disability.

- Parents must give consent for any initial evaluation, assessment, or placement; they must be notified of any change in placement that may occur; they must be included, along with teachers, in conferences and meetings held to draw up IEPs; and they must approve these IEPs before they go into effect for the first time.

- The right of parents to challenge and appeal any decision related to the identification, evaluation, and placement—or any issue concerning the provision of FAPE—of their child is fully protected by clearly spelled-out due process procedures.

- Parents have the right to have information kept confidential. No one may see a child's records unless the parents give written permission. Once a child has an IFSP or IEP, parental consent is needed for anyone to discuss the child with others. (The exception to this is school personnel who have legitimate educational interests.)

Services for Children Three to Twenty-Two Years of Age

As briefly discussed, Part B of the IDEA applies to children three to twenty-two years of age who qualify for special education services. The California Department of Education oversees the implementation of Part B services in the state, as do departments of education in other states across the country.

There have been several revisions to the IDEA over the years, and the latest strengthens provisions concerning "least restrictive environments." This term means that, to whatever extent possible, children should be in the same classes as their typically developing peers. For children ages three to five, this means that specialized services are ideally provided in settings such as the home, child care center, or family child care home. For this age group, services are provided through the local school district, county office of education, or special education local planning area (SELPA).

Special education provides specific early education programs for children between the ages of three and five who have disabilities. These programs include individual and group services in a variety of typical, age-appropriate environments for young children, such as regular child care programs, the home, and special education preschool programs. Services are based upon ongoing consultations with the family, include related support services for the child and family, and are provided in the least restrictive environment.

IDEA and Child Care

Part B of the IDEA strongly emphasizes a collaborative relationship between parents and teachers/providers in the development of services. Parents may invite child care providers to participate in the development and implementation of IEPs. Participation in this process is an excellent opportunity for child care providers to share knowledge about the child in their care and to assist in coordinating services for that child. Families can also request that consultation or direct services from early intervention and special education programs be provided in the child care setting.

For information about laws, consult the resources named below.

Americans with Disabilities Act (ADA)
Web site: http://www.usdoj.gov/crt/ada/adahom1.htm
Child care page: http://www.ada.gov/childq&a.htm
Disability Rights Section of ADA mailing address:

U.S. Department of Justice
Civil Rights Division
Disability Rights Section-NYAV
950 Pennsylvania Avenue, NW

Washington, DC 20530
ADA Information Line: 800-514-0301

Commonly Asked Questions About Child Care Centers and the Americans with Disabilities Act is a 13-page publication that explains how the requirements of the ADA apply to child care centers. It also describes some of the Department of Justice's ongoing enforcement efforts in the child care area, as well as a resource list on sources of information on the ADA. This document is available at the Web site listed above and can also be requested by fax. To order a publication by fax, call the ADA Information Line and follow the directions for placing a fax order. When prompted, enter the document number: 3209.

Child Care Law Center
221 Pine Street, Third Floor
San Francisco, CA 94104
Telephone: 415-394-7144
Fax: 415-394-7140
E-mail: info@childcarelaw.org
Web site: http://www.childcarelaw.org

The Child Care Law Center (CCLC) is a national, nonprofit legal services organization founded in 1978. The CCLC's primary objective is to use legal tools to foster the development of high-quality, affordable child care for every child, every parent, and every community. The CCLC works to expand child care options, particularly for low-income families, and to ensure that children are safe and nurtured in care outside the home. It is the only organization in the country that focuses exclusively on the complex legal issues surrounding the establishment and provision of child care.

Disability Rights Education & Defense Fund
2212 Sixth Street
Berkeley, CA 94710
Telephone: 800-348-4232 (v/tty)
Telephone: 510.644.2555 (v/tty)
Fax: 510-841-8645
E-mail info@dredf.org
Web site: http://www.dredf.org/

The Disability Rights Education and Defense Fund, founded in 1979, is a leading national civil rights law and policy center directed by individuals with disabilities and parents who have children with disabilities.

Appendix F
Summary of the California Preschool Program Guidelines

Guideline 1: Aspiring to Be a High-Quality Program

Guideline 2: Addressing Culture, Diversity, and Equity

Guideline 3: Supporting Relationships, Interactions, and Guidance

Guideline 4: Engaging Families and Communities

Guideline 5: Including Children with Disabilities or Other Special Needs

Guideline 6: Promoting Health, Safety, and Nutrition

Guideline 7: Assessing Children's Development and Learning

Guideline 8: Planning the Learning Environment and Curriculum

Guideline 9: Supporting Professionalism and Continuous Learning

Guideline 10: Administering Programs and Supervising Staff

Appendix G
Resources on Early Childhood Inclusive Practice

The following resources were compiled in April 2009, and the information was accurate as of that time.

California MAP to Inclusion and Belonging: Making Access Possible

Web site: www.cainclusion.org/camap/

This comprehensive Web site for the California MAP to Inclusion and Belonging Project operates under the Center for Child and Family Studies at WestEd and is funded by the California Department of Education's Early Education and Support Division. A portion is funded by the federal Child Care Development Fund Quality Improvement Allocation. This wide-ranging Web site is devoted to inclusion and disabilities.

CALIFORNIA STATE AGENCIES

California Department of Developmental Services

1600 9th Street
Sacramento, CA 95814
P.O. Box 944202
Sacramento, CA 94244
Telephone: (916) 654-1690
Web site: http://www.dds.ca.gov

The California Department of Developmental Services (DDS) is the state agency that provides services and supports to children and adults with developmental disabilities. These disabilities include mental retardation, cerebral palsy, epilepsy, autism, and other conditions. The DDS is California's lead agency for services for children birth to three years of age, as defined under Part C of the Individuals with Disabilities Education Act (IDEA '04). There are several Web links for agencies and services related to Early Start:

- California Early Start: http://www.dds.ca.gov/earlystart/home.cfm

- Family Resource Center/Network: http://www.dds.ca.gov/earlystart/familyresources.cfm

- Regional Centers: http://www.dds.ca.gov/RC/Home.cfm

California Department of Education Early Education and Support Division

1430 N Street, Suite 3410
Sacramento, CA 95814
Telephone: 916-322-6233
Fax: 916-323-6853
Web site: http://www.cde.ca.gov/sp/cd/

The Early Education and Support Division's mission is to provide leadership and support to all individuals and organizations concerned with children and families by promoting high-quality child development programs. The division works to educate the general public about developmentally appropriate practices for infants, toddlers, preschoolers, and school-age children in a variety of safe and healthy child care and child development environments. It measures its success by the preponderance of children ready to learn when entering school and the number of school-age children who successfully continue their education. The goal is to have the combined efforts result in children and families being balanced, lifelong learners.

California Department of Education Special Education Division

1430 N Street, Suite 2401
Sacramento, CA 95814
Telephone: 916-445-4613
Fax: 916-327-3706
Web site: http://www.cde.ca.gov/re/di/or/sed.asp

The home page for the California Department of Education, Special Education Division, links to current information about services and programs provided by the department.

California Department of Education After School Division
1430 N Street, Suite 3400
Sacramento, CA 95814
Telephone: 916-319-0923
Web site: http://www.cde.ca.gov/ls/ba/as/contactaspo.asp

The home page for the California Department of Education's After School Division includes links to program and fiscal resources to build, implement, and sustain quality after school programs, including school-age care and other out-of-school opportunities for children and youths.

California Department of Health Care Services, Children's Medical Services Branch, California Children's Services
MS 8100
P.O. Box 997413
Sacramento, CA 95899
Telephone: 916-327-1400
Web site: http://www.dhcs.ca.gov/

California Children's Services (CCS) Web site: www.dhcs.ca.gov/formandpubs/publications/Pages/CMSC

The Children's Medical Services Branch (CMS) provides a comprehensive system of health care for children through preventive screening, diagnoses, treatment, rehabilitation, and follow-up services. CMS is a full-scope management system for California Children's Services (CCS) Program.

California Department of Social Services
744 P Street
Sacramento, CA 95814
Telephone: 916-651-8848
Web site: http://www.cdss.ca.gov

Community Care Licensing Division
Web site: http://www.ccld.ca.gov

The mission of the California Department of Social Services is to serve, aid, and protect needy and vulnerable children and adults in ways that strengthen and preserve families, encourage personal responsibility, and foster independence.

First 5 California (California Children and Families Commission)
2389 Gateway Oaks Drive, Suite 260
Sacramento, CA 95833
Telephone: 916-263-1050
Fax: 916-263-1060
Web site: http://www.ccfc.ca.gov

The California Children and Families Act of 1998 was also known as Proposition 10 and is now called First 5 California. Many of its activities include children with special needs, and its Web site has links to local county CCF commissions and much more.

CALIFORNIA TRAINING AND TECHNICAL ASSISTANCE ORGANIZATIONS

The organizations in this section provide technical assistance and/or training that may be useful to child care providers, preschool staff, afterschool staff, specialists, or families who are developing or supporting an inclusive setting for children. State organizations are listed here. Information about local training and technical assistance may be available through a local child care resource and referral agency or a local Early Start family resource center (see below).

Beginning Together: Caring for Infants and Toddlers with Disabilities or Other Special Needs in Inclusive Settings
Telephone: 760-682-0200
Fax: 760-471-3862
E-mail: beginningtogether@wested.org
Web site: http://www.cainclusivechildcare.org/bt/

Beginning Together was created in collaboration with the California Department of Education, Early Education and Support Division (EESD) and WestEd, Center for Child and Family Studies as an inclusion support to the Program for Infant/Toddler Caregivers (PITC). The purpose of Beginning Together is to ensure that children with special needs are included, appropriate inclusive practices are promoted in the training and technical assistance provided by the existing cadre of CDE/WestEd certified trainers in the PITC, and inclusion of other infants and toddlers is supported.

Family Resource Center Network of California
E-mail: info@frcnca.org
Web site: http://www.frcnca.org

The Family Resource Center Network of California (FRCNCA) is a coalition of California's 47 Early Start Family Resource Centers. Staffed by families of children with special needs, the resource centers offer parent-to-parent support and help parents, families, and children locate and use needed services. They offer resources in many languages, which may include newsletters, resource libraries, Web sites, and support services such as parent-to-parent groups, sibling support groups, warmlines, and information and referral for parents and professionals.

Other California Parent Organizations
Web site: http://www.cde.ca.gov/sp/se/qa/caprntorg.asp

Lists California agencies providing resources for families of children with disabilities including Parent Training & Information Centers, California Community Parent Resource Centers, and Family Empowerment Centers.

California Preschool Instructional Network (CPIN)
Telephone: 800-770-6339
E-mail: cpin@wested.org
Web site: http://www.cpin.us/

California Preschool Instructional Networks (CPIN) provides professional development and technical assistance to preschool teachers and administrators to ensure that preschool children are ready for school. The CPIN is divided into the 11 regions designated by the California County Superintendents Educational Services Association (CCSESA). There is a regional lead and an English learner lead stationed in each of 11 regions throughout the state of California.

California Services for Technical Assistance and Training
Fax: 707-586-2735
E-mail: info@calstat.org
Web site: http://www.calstat.org

CalSTAT (California Services for Technical Assistance and Training) is a special project of the California Department of Education, Special Education Division. It is located at the Napa County Office of Education. It is funded through the Special Education Division and a California State Personnel Development Grant (SPDG). The SPDG, a federal grant, supports and develops partnerships with schools and families by providing training, technical assistance, and resources to both special education and general education.

Center for Prevention & Early Intervention
Telephone: 800-869-4337
Fax: 916-492-4002
E-mail: cpei@wested.org
Web site: http://www.wested.org/about-us/programs/center-for-prevention-early-intervention

WestEd's Center for Prevention and Early Intervention (CPEI) in Sacramento provides statewide high-quality training, technical assistance and resource development, dissemination services, and support to state agencies and community programs that administer or provide prevention and early intervention services. The state agencies have included the California departments of Education, Developmental Services, Health Services, Social Services, Mental Health, and Drug and Alcohol Programs.

Desired Results *access* Project
Telephone: 800-673-9220
E-mail: info@draccess.org
Web site: http://www.draccess.org

Desired Results *access* Project assists the California Department of Education's Special Education Division in implementing the Desired Results Developmental Profile (DRDP) assessment system to measure the progress of California's preschool-age children who have individualized education programs. The Desired Results access Project Web site offers information and resources to assist special educators, administrators, and families with participation in the Desired Results assessment system.

Kids Included Together National Training Center on Inclusion
Telephone: 858-225-5680
Fax: 619-758-0949
E-mail: info@kitonline.org
Web site: http://www.kitonline.org/ntci/home.html

Kids Included Together (KIT) National Training Center on Inclusion (NTCI) was established to support the overall mission of Kids Included Together through training, technical assistance, and resources of the highest quality for staff in out-of-school-time programs at all levels of experience and interest. KIT's National Training Center on Inclusion utilizes a combination of the latest technology coupled with live presentations by dynamic and experienced trainers and practitioners to support providers in welcoming children with disabilities.

Least Restrictive Environment Resources Project
Telephone: 916-492-4000
E-mail: dmeinde@wested.org
Web site: http://www.wested.org/cs/cpei/view/pj/204

The Least Restrictive Environment (LRE) Resources Project, operated by WestEd for the California Department of Education, develops resources for use by school districts and sites to improve services for all students. To achieve this goal, the project is establishing a network of leadership sites and consultants that focus on teacher training, mentoring, facilitating, technical assistance, and specialized materials.

Supporting Early Education Delivery Systems Project
Telephone: 916-228-2379
Fax: 916-228-2311
E-mail: rryan@scoe.net
Web site: http://www.scoe.net/SEEDS

The Supporting Early Education Delivery Systems (SEEDS) Project assists the California Department of Education in providing technical assistance to early childhood special education programs. Under the Department's direction, SEEDS has established a network of consultants and visitation sites to assist local educational agencies in providing quality services

PROFESSIONAL ORGANIZATIONS

American Speech-Language-Hearing Association
2200 Research Boulevard
Rockville, MD 20850
Telephone: (Voice or TTY) 800-638-8255
E-mail: actioncenter@asha.org
Web site: http://www.asha.org

The American Speech-Language-Hearing Association (ASHA) is the professional, scientific, and credentialing association for more than 103,000 audiologists, speech-language pathologists, and speech, language, and hearing scientists. ASHA's mission is to ensure that all people with speech, language, and hearing disorders have access to quality services to help them communicate more effectively.

The Division for Early Childhood
3415 So. Sepulveda Blvd., Suite 1100
Los Angeles, CA 90034
Telephone: 310-428-7209
Fax: 855-678-1989
E-mail: dec@dec-sped.org
Web site: http://www.dec-sped.org

The Division for Early Childhood (DEC) is an organization designed for individuals who work with—or on behalf of—children with special needs, birth through age eight, and their families. DEC, a subdivision of the Council for Exceptional Children (CEC), is dedicated to promoting policies and practices that support families and enhance the optimal development of children. Children with special needs include those who have disabilities or developmental delays, are gifted/talented, or are at risk of future developmental problems.

Infant Development Association of California
P.O. Box 189550
Sacramento, CA 95818
Telephone: 916-453-8801
Fax: 916-453-0627
E-mail: mail@idaofcal.org
Web site: http://www.idaofcal.org

The Infant Development Association of California (IDA) is a multidisciplinary organization of parents and professionals committed to optimal developmental and positive social and emotional outcomes for infants, birth to three, with a broad range of special needs and their families. IDA advocates improved, effective prevention and early intervention services while providing information, education, and training to parents, professionals, decision makers, and others.

National Association for the Education of Young Children
1313 L Street NW, Suite 500
Washington, DC 20005
Telephone: 202-232-8777 or 800-424-2460
Fax: 202-328-1846
E-mail: naeyc@naeyc.org
Web site: http://www.naeyc.org

The National Association for the Education of Young Children (NAEYC) is the nation's largest organization of early childhood professionals and others dedicated to improving the quality of early childhood education programs for children birth through age eight. NAEYC's primary goals are to improve professional practice and working conditions in early childhood education and to build public understanding and support for high-quality early childhood programs.

Zero to Three
1255 23rd Street, NW, Suite 350
Washington, DC 20037
Telephone: 800-899-4301
Web site: http://www.zerotothree.org

Zero to Three is a national, nonprofit organization dedicated solely to advancing the healthy development of babies and young children. Zero to Three disseminates key developmental information, trains providers, promotes model approaches and standards of practice, and works to increase public awareness about the significance of the first three years of life.

NATIONAL DISABILITY AND INCLUSION RESOURCES

Center for Inclusive Child Care
Telephone: 651-603-6265
Web site: http://www.inclusivechildcare.org

The mission of the Center for Inclusive Child Care (CICC) is to create, promote, and support pathways to successful inclusive care for all children. The program is a comprehensive resource network for inclusive early childhood practitioners, school age programs, and providers. The CICC provides leadership, administrative support, training, and consultation to early care and education providers, school-age care providers, parents, and professionals in the field.

Child Care Aware (formerly National Child Care Information and Technical Assistance Center)
Telephone: 800-424-2246
Fax: 703-341-4101
TTY: 866-278-9428
Web site: http://childcareaware.org

The National Child Care Information and Technical Assistance Center (NCCIC), a project of the Child Care Bureau, Administration for Children and Families (ACF), U.S. Department of Health and Human Services, is a national resource that links information and people in order to complement, enhance, and promote child care delivery systems. The organization works to ensure that all children and families have access to the highest-quality comprehensive services.

Disability Is Natural
Telephone: 210-320-0678
Web site: http://www.disabilityisnatural.com

This Web site created by Kathie Snow includes her widely used article on "people-first language" and other resources to support inclusion. She challenges outdated ways of thinking and helps parents, people with disabilities, and professionals acquire new perceptions and attitudes— the first rung on the ladder of change.

Early Childhood Technical Assistance Center
Telephone: 919-962-2001
TDD: 919-843-3269
Fax: 919-966-7463
E-mail: ectacenter@unc.edu
Web site: http://www.ectacenter.org

The Early Childhood Technical Assistance Center supports the implementation of the early childhood provisions of the Individuals with Disabilities Education Act (IDEA). The center's mission is to strengthen service systems to ensure that children with disabilities (birth through five) and their families receive and benefit from high-quality, culturally appropriate, and family-centered supports and services.

Fathers Network
Telephone: 425-653-4286
Web site: http://www.fathersnetwork.org

The Fathers Network is a nonprofit organization that serves as an advocate for men and believes they are crucial to the lives of their families and children. The network provides supports and resources to fathers and families of children with developmental disabilities and chronic illness, as well as to the professionals who serve them.

Individuals with Disabilities Education Act
IDEA Partnership
Web site: http://www.ideapartnership.org

This site is part of a federal project to support the implementation of the Individuals with Disabilities Education Act (IDEA

'04). The site answers questions about the IDEA and makes available the full text of the law and its regulations.

National Dissemination Center for Children with Disabilities
Telephone (Voice/TTY): 800-695-0285
Fax: 202-884-8441
E-mail: nichcy@aed.org
Web site: http://www.parentcenterhub.org

The Center for Parent Information and Resources provides information on disabilities and related issues to families, educators, and other professionals. One special focus is children and youths (birth to age twenty-two). Many publications are available in Spanish.

National Professional Development Center on Inclusion
Frank Porter Graham Child Development Institute
E-mail: community@mail.fpg.unc.edu
Web site: http://npdci.fpg.unc.edu/

The National Professional Development Center on Inclusion (NPDCI) works with states to ensure that early childhood teachers are prepared to educate and care for young children with disabilities in natural settings with their typically developing peers.

teacher(s):   classroom: date:

member of the class: teachers guide

Teachers:

Use this checklist to guide your classroom inclusion practices. These indicators will help you think about and plan for ways to promote membership in your classroom. Answer the questions from the perspective of a child with special needs.

QUESTION	CIRCLE BELOW	IF NO, WHAT IS THE PLAN?
Do I have a cubby or place to put my coat and backpack just like my classmates?	yes no	
Do I have a seat at circle that includes all the items my classmates have like a carpet square and name tag?	yes no	
Do I have a classroom job just as my classmates?	yes no	
Do I get to take a turn during group activities?	yes no	
Do I have the opportunity to participate in "messy" activities when available, even though I may be a little messier than others?	yes no	
During regular activities am I in a similar position to my classmates (i.e. my classmates are standing-I am standing, etc.)?	yes no	
Can I physically get to all the activities in the classroom (reach into the sensory table, get toys from shelves)?	yes no	
Is there something I know how to use and can use independently in each learning center?	yes no	
Do I have the opportunity to sometimes be in the front and middle of the line during transitions?	yes no	
Am I usually participating in the same or similar activities as my classmates (though they might be adapted)?	yes no	
Do I have the chance to be the "helper" on occasion?	yes no	
Am I an active participant in classroom activities (not just an observer)?	yes no	
Do my teachers and classmates talk to me, ask me questions, play with me?	yes no	
Do I have friends in my class?	yes no	

HEAD START CENTER FOR INCLUSION FUNDED BY THE OFFICE OF HEAD START DEPARTMENT OF HEALTH AND HUMAN SERVICES

This material was developed by the Head Start Center for Inclusion with federal funds from the U.S. Department of Health and Human Services, Office of Head Start (Grant No. 90YD0270). The contents of this publication do not necessarily reflect the views or policies of the U.S. Department of Health and Human Services, nor does mention of trade names, commercial products, or organizations imply endorsement by the U.S. Government. You may reproduce this material for training and information purposes.

Appendix I
Effective Strategies for Observing Children's Learning and Behavior

The Desired Results system involves direct observation of children, using an instrument called the Desired Results Developmental Profile (DRDP). Developmental assessment is designed to deepen understanding of a child's strengths and to identify areas where a child may need additional support. Teachers and other child development professionals are encouraged to complete the developmental profiles through observation, a method of gathering information by carefully and systematically observing children in their early care and education environments.

Conducting Effective Observations

The process of systematically observing the development of children in the context of day-to-day family and early care and education activities is the initial step in finding and planning appropriate strategies to support the continuing development of children and families. Information gathered through observations can help teachers in arranging the environment and in developing curricular plans and materials.

There are a variety of ways of gathering information through observations: video and digital recordings; photographs; portfolios; anecdotal records, diaries, and logs; activity lists; time sampling and event recording; and checklists and rating scales.

Effective observation of children requires training and practice on the part of observers. It also requires an environment that is conducive to documenting children's activities and interactions with minimal effort or interruption to the natural flow of typical daily routines.

Using Observation

When using observation to complete the DRDP, educators need to consider several points:

1. Use skilled observers.

Observation is a complex, essential skill that can be developed through systematic training and practice. Observers completing the DRDP must be the teacher or caregiver who is the most familiar with the child.

Effective observers . . .

- Are familiar with the tools, measures, and indicators for the developmental levels being observed.

- Have an in-depth understanding of child development, including cultural variations expressed in children's behavior.

- Identify behaviors or signals that may indicate possible disabilities or other special needs.

- Understand the child's cultural context. Family and community cultures influence the child's access to multiple approaches to literacy and are related to expectations regarding a child's educational accomplishments.

- Consider the child's experience and family history: Was the child born premature, full-term? Does the child have an existing medical condition or any other health-related concerns that you are aware of? Is the child living in an economically secure and supportive household that affords ample opportunities for play and discovery?

- Are aware of how performance styles, motivational factors, and environmental variables influence the judgments made about children's strengths and weaknesses.

- Refrain from labeling children and avoid the tendency to place stereotypical expectations on children.

- Are aware of a child's total performance (across developmental domains), even when focusing on a single aspect of behavior.

2. Set up the environment to support effective observations of children.

Observers can do the following to provide an appropriate environment:

- Arrange activities so that observers can watch from a place where they can hear children's conversations.

- Plan activities that do not require the full assistance of teachers or caregivers when they wish to observe a child.

- Seat the observer unobtrusively near children's activities.

- Scatter "observation chairs" at strategic locations throughout the program, if possible. Children who are accustomed to having observers present who are "writing" are more likely to behave naturally, which allows the observer to take notes without interruption.

- Carry a small notepad in a pocket. In several places on the wall, hang clipboards with lined paper and an attached pencil.

3. Keep a few specific points in mind.

The following strategies improve observers' effectiveness:

- Focus on observing exactly what the child does. Be as objective as possible. Opinions or stereotypes must not influence judgment.

- Record observations as soon as possible. Details may be important and can be easily forgotten.

- Observe in a variety of settings and at different times during the day.

- Be realistic in scheduling observations. Haphazard or incomplete observations will not present an accurate or comprehensive picture of the child's behavior.

Child Development Permit Matrix - *with Alternative Qualification Options Indicated*

Permit Title	Education Requirement (Option 1 for all permits)	Experience Requirement (Applies to Option 1 Only)	Alternative Qualifications (with option numbers indicated)	Authorization	Five Year Renewal
Assistant (Optional)	*Option 1:* 6 units of Early Childhood Education (ECE) or Child Development (CD)	None	*Option 2:* Accredited HERO program (including ROP)	Authorizes the holder to care for and assist in the development and instruction of children in a child care and development program under the supervision of an Associate Teacher, Teacher, Master Teacher, Site Supervisor or Program Director.	105 hours of professional growth*****
Associate Teacher	*Option 1:* 12 units ECE/CD including core courses**	50 days of 3+ hours per day within 2 years	*Option 2:* Child Development Associate (CDA) Credential.	Authorizes the holder to provide service in the care, development, and instruction of children in a child care and development program, and supervise an Assistant and an aide.	Must complete 15 additional units toward a Teacher Permit. Must meet Teacher requirements within 10 years.
Teacher	*Option 1:* 24 units ECE/CD including core courses** plus 16 General Education (GE) units*	175 days of 3+ hours per day within 4 years	*Option 2:* AA or higher in ECE/CD or related field with 3 units supervised field experience in ECE/CD setting	Authorizes the holder to provide service in the care, development and instruction of children in a child care and development program, and supervise an Associate Teacher, Assistant and an aide.	105 hours of professional growth*****
Master Teacher	*Option 1:* 24 units ECE/CD including core courses** plus 16 GE units* plus 6 specialization units plus 2 adult supervision units	350 days of 3+ hours per day within 4 years	*Option 2:* BA or higher (does not have to be in ECE/CD) with 12 units of ECE/CD, plus 3 units supervised field experience in ECE/CD setting	Authorizes the holder to provide service in the care, development and instruction of children in a child care and development program, and supervise a Teacher, Associate Teacher, Assistant and an aide. The permit also authorizes the holder to serve as a coordinator of curriculum and staff development.	105 hours of professional growth*****
Site Supervisor	*Option 1:* AA (or 60 units) which includes: • 24 ECE/CD units with core courses** plus 6 administration units plus 2 adult supervision units	350 days of 3+ hours per day within 4 years including at least 100 days of supervising adults	*Option 2:* BA or higher (does not have to be in ECE/CD) with 12 units of ECE/CD, plus 3 units supervised field experience in ECE/CD setting; **or** *Option 3:* Admin. credential *** with 12 units of ECE/CD, plus 3 units supervised field experience in ECE/CD setting; **or** *Option 4:* Teaching credential**** with 12 units of ECE/CD, plus 3 units supervised field experience in ECE/CD setting	Authorizes the holder to supervise a child care and development program operating at a single site; provide service in the care, development, and instruction of children in a child care and development program; and serve as a coordinator of curriculum and staff development.	105 hours of professional growth*****
Program Director	*Option 1:* BA or higher (does not have to be in ECE/CD) including: • 24 ECE/CD units with core courses** plus 6 administration units plus 2 adult supervision units	One year of Site Supervisor experience	*Option 2:* Admin. credential *** with 12 units of ECE/CD, plus 3 units supervised field experience in ECE/CD setting; **or** *Option 3:* Teaching credential**** with 12 units of ECE/CD, plus 3 units supervised field experience in ECE/CD setting, plus 6 units administration; **or** *Option 4:* Master's Degree in ECE/CD or Child/Human Development	Authorizes the holder to supervise a child care and development program operating in a single site or multiple sites; provide service in the care, development, and instruction of children in a child care and development program; and serve as coordinator of curriculum and staff development.	105 hours of professional growth*****

NOTE: All unit requirements listed above are *semester* units. All course work must be completed with a grade of C or better from a regionally accredited college. Spanish translation is available.

*One course in each of four general education categories, which are degree applicable: English/Language Arts; Math or Science; Social Sciences; Humanities and/or Fine Arts.

**Core courses include child/human growth & development; child/family/community or child and family relations; and programs/curriculum. You must have a minimum of three semester units or four quarter units in each of the core areas.

***Holders of the Administrative Services Credential may serve as a Site Supervisor or Program Director.

****A valid Multiple Subject or a Single Subject in Home Economics.

*****Professional growth hours must be completed under the guidance of a Professional Growth Advisor. Call (209) 572-6080 for assistance in locating an advisor.

This matrix was prepared by the Child Development Training Consortium. To obtain a permit application visit our website at www.childdevelopment.org or call (209) 572-6080.

Permit Matrix 7-10

7/10

Code of Ethical Conduct and Statement of Commitment

**Revised April 2005,
Reaffirmed and Updated May 2011**

A position statement of the National Association for the Education of Young Children

Endorsed by the Association for Childhood Education International

Adopted by the National Association for Family Child Care

Preamble

NAEYC recognizes that those who work with young children face many daily decisions that have moral and ethical implications. The **NAEYC Code of Ethical Conduct** offers guidelines for responsible behavior and sets forth a common basis for resolving the principal ethical dilemmas encountered in early childhood care and education. The **Statement of Commitment** is not part of the Code but is a personal acknowledgement of an individual's willingness to embrace the distinctive values and moral obligations of the field of early childhood care and education.

The primary focus of the Code is on daily practice with children and their families in programs for children from birth through 8 years of age, such as infant/toddler programs, preschool and prekindergarten programs, child care centers, hospital and child life settings, family child care homes, kindergartens, and primary classrooms. When the issues involve young children, then these provisions also apply to specialists who do not work directly with children, including program administrators, parent educators, early childhood adult educators, and officials with responsibility for program monitoring and licensing. (Note: See also the "Code of Ethical Conduct: Supplement for Early Childhood Adult Educators," online at www.naeyc.org/about/positions/pdf/ethics04. pdf. and the "Code of Ethical Conduct: Supplement for Early Childhood Program Administrators," online at http://www. naeyc.org/files/naeyc/file/positions/PSETH05_supp.pdf)

Core values

Standards of ethical behavior in early childhood care and education are based on commitment to the following core values that are deeply rooted in the history of the field of early childhood care and education. We have made a commitment to

• Appreciate childhood as a unique and valuable stage of the human life cycle

• Base our work on knowledge of how children develop and learn

• Appreciate and support the bond between the child and family

• Recognize that children are best understood and supported in the context of family, culture,* community, and society

• Respect the dignity, worth, and uniqueness of each individual (child, family member, and colleague)

• Respect diversity in children, families, and colleagues

• Recognize that children and adults achieve their full potential in the context of relationships that are based on trust and respect

---

* The term *culture* includes ethnicity, racial identity, economic level, family structure, language, and religious and political beliefs, which profoundly influence each child's development and relationship to the world.

Conceptual framework

The Code sets forth a framework of professional responsibilities in four sections. Each section addresses an area of professional relationships: (1) with children, (2) with families, (3) among colleagues, and (4) with the community and society. Each section includes an introduction to the primary responsibilities of the early childhood practitioner in that context. The introduction is followed by a set of ideals (I) that reflect exemplary professional practice and by a set of principles (P) describing practices that are required, prohibited, or permitted.

The **ideals** reflect the aspirations of practitioners. The **principles** guide conduct and assist practitioners in resolving ethical dilemmas.* Both ideals and principles are intended to direct practitioners to those questions which, when responsibly answered, can provide the basis for conscientious decision making. While the Code provides specific direction for addressing some ethical dilemmas, many others will require the practitioner to combine the guidance of the Code with professional judgment.

The ideals and principles in this Code present a shared framework of professional responsibility that affirms our commitment to the core values of our field. The Code publicly acknowledges the responsibilities that we in the field have assumed, and in so doing supports ethical behavior in our work. Practitioners who face situations with ethical dimensions are urged to seek guidance in the applicable parts of this Code and in the spirit that informs the whole.

Often "the right answer"—the best ethical course of action to take—is not obvious. There may be no readily apparent, positive way to handle a situation. When one important value contradicts another, we face an ethical dilemma. When we face a dilemma, it is our professional responsibility to consult the Code and all relevant parties to find the most ethical resolution.

Section I

Ethical Responsibilities to Children

Childhood is a unique and valuable stage in the human life cycle. Our paramount responsibility is to provide care and education in settings that are safe, healthy, nurturing, and responsive for each child. We are committed to supporting children's development and learning; respecting individual differences; and helping children learn to live, play, and work cooperatively. We are also committed to promoting children's self-awareness, competence, self-worth, resiliency, and physical well-being.

Ideals

I-1.1—To be familiar with the knowledge base of early childhood care and education and to stay informed through continuing education and training.

I-1.2—To base program practices upon current knowledge and research in the field of early childhood education, child development, and related disciplines, as well as on particular knowledge of each child.

I-1.3—To recognize and respect the unique qualities, abilities, and potential of each child.

I-1.4—To appreciate the vulnerability of children and their dependence on adults.

I-1.5—To create and maintain safe and healthy settings that foster children's social, emotional, cognitive, and physical development and that respect their dignity and their contributions.

I-1.6—To use assessment instruments and strategies that are appropriate for the children to be assessed, that are used only for the purposes for which they were designed, and that have the potential to benefit children.

I-1.7—To use assessment information to understand and support children's development and learning, to support instruction, and to identify children who may need additional services.

I-1.8—To support the right of each child to play and learn in an inclusive environment that meets the needs of children with and without disabilities.

I-1.9—To advocate for and ensure that all children, including those with special needs, have access to the support services needed to be successful.

I-1.10—To ensure that each child's culture, language, ethnicity, and family structure are recognized and valued in the program.

I-1.11—To provide all children with experiences in a language that they know, as well as support children in maintaining the use of their home language and in learning English.

I-1.12—To work with families to provide a safe and smooth transition as children and families move from one program to the next.

---

* There is not necessarily a corresponding principle for each ideal.

Principles

P-1.1—Above all, we shall not harm children. We shall not participate in practices that are emotionally damaging, physically harmful, disrespectful, degrading, dangerous, exploitative, or intimidating to children. *This principle has precedence over all others in this Code.*

P-1.2—We shall care for and educate children in positive emotional and social environments that are cognitively stimulating and that support each child's culture, language, ethnicity, and family structure.

P-1.3—We shall not participate in practices that discriminate against children by denying benefits, giving special advantages, or excluding them from programs or activities on the basis of their sex, race, national origin, immigration status, preferred home language, religious beliefs, medical condition, disability, or the marital status/family structure, sexual orientation, or religious beliefs or other affiliations of their families. (Aspects of this principle do not apply in programs that have a lawful mandate to provide services to a particular population of children.)

P-1.4—We shall use two-way communications to involve all those with relevant knowledge (including families and staff) in decisions concerning a child, as appropriate, ensuring confidentiality of sensitive information. (See also P-2.4.)

P-1.5—We shall use appropriate assessment systems, which include multiple sources of information, to provide information on children's learning and development.

P-1.6—We shall strive to ensure that decisions such as those related to enrollment, retention, or assignment to special education services, will be based on multiple sources of information and will never be based on a single assessment, such as a test score or a single observation.

P-1.7—We shall strive to build individual relationships with each child; make individualized adaptations in teaching strategies, learning environments, and curricula; and consult with the family so that each child benefits from the program. If after such efforts have been exhausted, the current placement does not meet a child's needs, or the child is seriously jeopardizing the ability of other children to benefit from the program, we shall collaborate with the child's family and appropriate specialists to determine the additional services needed and/or the placement option(s) most likely to ensure the child's success. (Aspects of this principle may not apply in programs that have a lawful mandate to provide services to a particular population of children.)

P-1.8—We shall be familiar with the risk factors for and symptoms of child abuse and neglect, including physical, sexual, verbal, and emotional abuse and physical, emotional, educational, and medical neglect. We shall know and follow state laws and community procedures that protect children against abuse and neglect.

P-1.9—When we have reasonable cause to suspect child abuse or neglect, we shall report it to the appropriate community agency and follow up to ensure that appropriate action has been taken. When appropriate, parents or guardians will be informed that the referral will be or has been made.

P-1.10—When another person tells us of his or her suspicion that a child is being abused or neglected, we shall assist that person in taking appropriate action in order to protect the child.

P-1.11—When we become aware of a practice or situation that endangers the health, safety, or well-being of children, we have an ethical responsibility to protect children or inform parents and/or others who can.

Section II

Ethical Responsibilities to Families

Families* are of primary importance in children's development. Because the family and the early childhood practitioner have a common interest in the child's well-being, we acknowledge a primary responsibility to bring about communication, cooperation, and collaboration between the home and early childhood program in ways that enhance the child's development.

Ideals

I-2.1—To be familiar with the knowledge base related to working effectively with families and to stay informed through continuing education and training.

I-2.2—To develop relationships of mutual trust and create partnerships with the families we serve.

I-2.3—To welcome all family members and encourage them to participate in the program, including involvement in shared decision making.

---

* The term *family* may include those adults, besides parents, with the responsibility of being involved in educating, nurturing, and advocating for the child.

I-2.4—To listen to families, acknowledge and build upon their strengths and competencies, and learn from families as we support them in their task of nurturing children.

I-2.5—To respect the dignity and preferences of each family and to make an effort to learn about its structure, culture, language, customs, and beliefs to ensure a culturally consistent environment for all children and families.

I-2.6—To acknowledge families' childrearing values and their right to make decisions for their children.

I-2.7—To share information about each child's education and development with families and to help them understand and appreciate the current knowledge base of the early childhood profession.

I-2.8—To help family members enhance their understanding of their children, as staff are enhancing their understanding of each child through communications with families, and support family members in the continuing development of their skills as parents.

I-2.9—To foster families' efforts to build support networks and, when needed, participate in building networks for families by providing them with opportunities to interact with program staff, other families, community resources, and professional services.

Principles

P-2.1—We shall not deny family members access to their child's classroom or program setting unless access is denied by court order or other legal restriction.

P-2.2—We shall inform families of program philosophy, policies, curriculum, assessment system, cultural practices, and personnel qualifications, and explain why we teach as we do—which should be in accordance with our ethical responsibilities to children (see Section I).

P-2.3—We shall inform families of and, when appropriate, involve them in policy decisions. (See also I-2.3.)

P-2.4—We shall ensure that the family is involved in significant decisions affecting their child. (See also P-1.4.)

P-2.5—We shall make every effort to communicate effectively with all families in a language that they understand. We shall use community resources for translation and interpretation when we do not have sufficient resources in our own programs.

P-2.6—As families share information with us about their children and families, we shall ensure that families' input is an important contribution to the planning and implementation of the program.

P-2.7—We shall inform families about the nature and purpose of the program's child assessments and how data about their child will be used.

P-2.8—We shall treat child assessment information confidentially and share this information only when there is a legitimate need for it.

P-2.9—We shall inform the family of injuries and incidents involving their child, of risks such as exposures to communicable diseases that might result in infection, and of occurrences that might result in emotional stress.

P-2.10—Families shall be fully informed of any proposed research projects involving their children and shall have the opportunity to give or withhold consent without penalty. We shall not permit or participate in research that could in any way hinder the education, development, or well-being of children.

P-2.11—We shall not engage in or support exploitation of families. We shall not use our relationship with a family for private advantage or personal gain, or enter into relationships with family members that might impair our effectiveness working with their children.

P-2.12—We shall develop written policies for the protection of confidentiality and the disclosure of children's records. These policy documents shall be made available to all program personnel and families. Disclosure of children's records beyond family members, program personnel, and consultants having an obligation of confidentiality shall require familial consent (except in cases of abuse or neglect).

P-2.13—We shall maintain confidentiality and shall respect the family's right to privacy, refraining from disclosure of confidential information and intrusion into family life. However, when we have reason to believe that a child's welfare is at risk, it is permissible to share confidential information with agencies, as well as with individuals who have legal responsibility for intervening in the child's interest.

P-2.14—In cases where family members are in conflict with one another, we shall work openly, sharing our observations of the child, to help all parties involved make informed decisions. We shall refrain from becoming an advocate for one party.

P-2.15—We shall be familiar with and appropriately refer families to community resources and professional support services. After a referral has been made, we shall follow up to ensure that services have been appropriately provided.

Section III

Ethical Responsibilities to Colleagues

In a caring, cooperative workplace, human dignity is respected, professional satisfaction is promoted, and positive relationships are developed and sustained. Based upon our core values, our primary responsibility to colleagues is to establish and maintain settings and relationships that support productive work and meet professional needs. The same ideals that apply to children also apply as we interact with adults in the workplace. (Note: Section III includes responsibilities to co-workers and to employers. See the "Code of Ethical Conduct: Supplement for Early Childhood Program Administrators" for responsibilities to personnel (*employees* in the original 2005 Code revision), online at http://www.naeyc.org/files/naeyc/file/positions/PSETH05_supp.pdf.)

A—Responsibilities to co-workers

Ideals

I-3A.1—To establish and maintain relationships of respect, trust, confidentiality, collaboration, and cooperation with co-workers.

I-3A.2—To share resources with co-workers, collaborating to ensure that the best possible early childhood care and education program is provided.

I-3A.3—To support co-workers in meeting their professional needs and in their professional development.

I-3A.4—To accord co-workers due recognition of professional achievement.

Principles

P-3A.1—We shall recognize the contributions of colleagues to our program and not participate in practices that diminish their reputations or impair their effectiveness in working with children and families.

P-3A.2—When we have concerns about the professional behavior of a co-worker, we shall first let that person know of our concern in a way that shows respect for personal dignity and for the diversity to be found among staff members, and then attempt to resolve the matter collegially and in a confidential manner.

P-3A.3—We shall exercise care in expressing views regarding the personal attributes or professional conduct of co-workers. Statements should be based on firsthand knowledge, not hearsay, and relevant to the interests of children and programs.

P-3A.4—We shall not participate in practices that discriminate against a co-worker because of sex, race, national origin, religious beliefs or other affiliations, age, marital status/family structure, disability, or sexual orientation.

B—Responsibilities to employers

Ideals

I-3B.1—To assist the program in providing the highest quality of service.

I-3B.2—To do nothing that diminishes the reputation of the program in which we work unless it is violating laws and regulations designed to protect children or is violating the provisions of this Code.

Principles

P-3B.1—We shall follow all program policies. When we do not agree with program policies, we shall attempt to effect change through constructive action within the organization.

P-3B.2—We shall speak or act on behalf of an organization only when authorized. We shall take care to acknowledge when we are speaking for the organization and when we are expressing a personal judgment.

P-3B.3—We shall not violate laws or regulations designed to protect children and shall take appropriate action consistent with this Code when aware of such violations.

P-3B.4—If we have concerns about a colleague's behavior, and children's well-being is not at risk, we may address the concern with that individual. If children are at risk or the situation does not improve after it has been brought to the colleague's attention, we shall report the colleague's unethical or incompetent behavior to an appropriate authority.

P-3B.5—When we have a concern about circumstances or conditions that impact the quality of care and education within the program, we shall inform the program's administration or, when necessary, other appropriate authorities.

Section IV

Ethical Responsibilities to Community and Society

Early childhood programs operate within the context of their immediate community made up of families and other institutions concerned with children's welfare. Our responsibilities to the community are to provide programs that meet the diverse needs of families, to cooperate with agencies and professions that share the responsibility for children, to assist families in gaining access to those agencies and allied professionals, and to assist in the development of community programs that are needed but not currently available.

As individuals, we acknowledge our responsibility to provide the best possible programs of care and education for children and to conduct ourselves with honesty and integrity. Because of our specialized expertise in early childhood development and education and because the larger society shares responsibility for the welfare and protection of young children, we acknowledge a collective obligation to advocate for the best interests of children within early childhood programs and in the larger community and to serve as a voice for young children everywhere.

The ideals and principles in this section are presented to distinguish between those that pertain to the work of the individual early childhood educator and those that more typically are engaged in collectively on behalf of the best interests of children—with the understanding that individual early childhood educators have a shared responsibility for addressing the ideals and principles that are identified as "collective."

Ideal (Individual)

1-4.1—To provide the community with high-quality early childhood care and education programs and services.

Ideals (Collective)

I-4.2—To promote cooperation among professionals and agencies and interdisciplinary collaboration among professions concerned with addressing issues in the health, education, and well-being of young children, their families, and their early childhood educators.

I-4.3—To work through education, research, and advocacy toward an environmentally safe world in which all children receive health care, food, and shelter; are nurtured; and live free from violence in their home and their communities.

I-4.4—To work through education, research, and advocacy toward a society in which all young children have access to high-quality early care and education programs.

I-4.5—To work to ensure that appropriate assessment systems, which include multiple sources of information, are used for purposes that benefit children.

I-4.6—To promote knowledge and understanding of young children and their needs. To work toward greater societal acknowledgment of children's rights and greater social acceptance of responsibility for the well-being of all children.

I-4.7—To support policies and laws that promote the well-being of children and families, and to work to change those that impair their well-being. To participate in developing policies and laws that are needed, and to cooperate with families and other individuals and groups in these efforts.

I-4.8—To further the professional development of the field of early childhood care and education and to strengthen its commitment to realizing its core values as reflected in this Code.

Principles (Individual)

P-4.1—We shall communicate openly and truthfully about the nature and extent of services that we provide.

P-4.2—We shall apply for, accept, and work in positions for which we are personally well-suited and professionally qualified. We shall not offer services that we do not have the competence, qualifications, or resources to provide.

P-4.3—We shall carefully check references and shall not hire or recommend for employment any person whose competence, qualifications, or character makes him or her unsuited for the position.

P-4.4—We shall be objective and accurate in reporting the knowledge upon which we base our program practices.

P-4.5—We shall be knowledgeable about the appropriate use of assessment strategies and instruments and interpret results accurately to families.

P-4.6—We shall be familiar with laws and regulations that serve to protect the children in our programs and be vigilant in ensuring that these laws and regulations are followed.

P-4.7—When we become aware of a practice or situation that endangers the health, safety, or well-being of children, we have an ethical responsibility to protect children or inform parents and/or others who can.

P-4.8—We shall not participate in practices that are in violation of laws and regulations that protect the children in our programs.

P-4.9—When we have evidence that an early childhood program is violating laws or regulations protecting children, we shall report the violation to appropriate authorities who can be expected to remedy the situation.

P-4.10—When a program violates or requires its employees to violate this Code, it is permissible, after fair assessment of the evidence, to disclose the identity of that program.

Principles (Collective)

P-4.11—When policies are enacted for purposes that do not benefit children, we have a collective responsibility to work to change these policies.

P-4.12—When we have evidence that an agency that provides services intended to ensure children's well-being is failing to meet its obligations, we acknowledge a collective ethical responsibility to report the problem to appropriate authorities or to the public. We shall be vigilant in our follow-up until the situation is resolved.

P-4.13—When a child protection agency fails to provide adequate protection for abused or neglected children, we acknowledge a collective ethical responsibility to work toward the improvement of these services.

Glossary of Terms Related to Ethics

Code of Ethics. Defines the core values of the field and provides guidance for what professionals should do when they encounter conflicting obligations or responsibilities in their work.

Values. Qualities or principles that individuals believe to be desirable or worthwhile and that they prize for themselves, for others, and for the world in which they live.

Core Values. Commitments held by a profession that are consciously and knowingly embraced by its practitioners because they make a contribution to society. There is a difference between personal values and the core values of a profession.

Morality. Peoples' views of what is good, right, and proper; their beliefs about their obligations; and their ideas about how they should behave.

Ethics. The study of right and wrong, or duty and obligation, that involves critical reflection on morality and the ability to make choices between values and the examination of the moral dimensions of relationships.

Professional Ethics. The moral commitments of a profession that involve moral reflection that extends and enhances the personal morality practitioners bring to their work, that concern actions of right and wrong in the workplace, and that help individuals resolve moral dilemmas they encounter in their work.

Ethical Responsibilities. Behaviors that one must or must not engage in. Ethical responsibilities are clear-cut and are spelled out in the Code of Ethical Conduct (for example, early childhood educators should never share confidential information about a child or family with a person who has no legitimate need for knowing).

Ethical Dilemma. A moral conflict that involves determining appropriate conduct when an individual faces conflicting professional values and responsibilities.

Sources for glossary terms and definitions

Feeney, S., & N. Freeman. 2005. *Ethics and the early childhood educator: Using the NAEYC code.* Washington, DC: NAEYC.

Kidder, R.M. 1995. *How good people make tough choices: Resolving the dilemmas of ethical living.* New York: Fireside.

Kipnis, K. 1987. How to discuss professional ethics. *Young Children* 42 (4): 26–30.

The National Association for the Education of Young Children (NAEYC) is a nonprofit corporation, tax exempt under Section 501(c)(3) of the Internal Revenue Code, dedicated to acting on behalf of the needs and interests of young children. The NAEYC Code of Ethical Conduct (Code) has been developed in furtherance of NAEYC's nonprofit and tax exempt purposes. The information contained in the Code is intended to provide early childhood educators with guidelines for working with children from birth through age 8.

An individual's or program's use, reference to, or review of the Code does not guarantee compliance with NAEYC Early Childhood Program Standards and Accreditation Performance Criteria and program accreditation procedures. It is recommended that the Code be used as guidance in connection with implementation of the NAEYC Program Standards, but such use is not a substitute for diligent review and application of the NAEYC Program Standards.

NAEYC has taken reasonable measures to develop the Code in a fair, reasonable, open, unbiased, and objective manner, based on currently available data. However, further research or developments may change the current state of knowledge. Neither NAEYC nor its officers, directors, members, employees, or agents will be liable for any loss, damage, or claim with respect to any liabilities, including direct, special, indirect, or consequential damages incurred in connection with the Code or reliance on the information presented.

NAEYC Code of Ethical Conduct 2005 Revisions Workgroup

Mary Ambery, Ruth Ann Ball, James Clay, Julie Olsen Edwards, Harriet Egertson, Anthony Fair, Stephanie Feeney, Jana Fleming, Nancy Freeman, Marla Israel, Allison McKinnon, Evelyn Wright Moore, Eva Moravcik, Christina Lopez Morgan, Sarah Mulligan, Nila Rinehart, Betty Holston Smith, and Peter Pizzolongo, *NAEYC Staff*

Statement of Commitment*

As an individual who works with young children, I commit myself to furthering the values of early childhood education as they are reflected in the ideals and principles of the NAEYC Code of Ethical Conduct. To the best of my ability I will

- Never harm children.
- Ensure that programs for young children are based on current knowledge and research of child development and early childhood education.
- Respect and support families in their task of nurturing children.
- Respect colleagues in early childhood care and education and support them in maintaining the NAEYC Code of Ethical Conduct.
- Serve as an advocate for children, their families, and their teachers in community and society.
- Stay informed of and maintain high standards of professional conduct.
- Engage in an ongoing process of self-reflection, realizing that personal characteristics, biases, and beliefs have an impact on children and families.
- Be open to new ideas and be willing to learn from the suggestions of others.
- Continue to learn, grow, and contribute as a professional.
- Honor the ideals and principles of the NAEYC Code of Ethical Conduct.

---

* This Statement of Commitment is not part of the Code but is a personal acknowledgment of the individual's willingness to embrace the distinctive values and moral obligations of the field of early childhood care and education. It is recognition of the moral obligations that lead to an individual becoming part of the profession.

Glossary

Glossary

administrator. An early childhood professional who may hold a wide variety of titles and positions: Center Director in a small, single-site program; Site Supervisor within a large, multiple-site program; or a Program Coordinator for a network of centers. Regardless of the particular size of characteristics of a program, the same issues and concerns must be addressed at all programs.

assistive technology device. Any item, piece of equipment, or product system, whether acquired commercially off the shelf, modified, or customized, that is used to increase, maintain, or improve functional capabilities of a child with a disability (Mistrett 2004).

cognitive flexibility. The ability to switch perspectives or the focus of attention and adjust to changed demands or priorities (Diamond et al. 2007).

dual language learners. Young children who are learning two or more languages at the same time, as well as those learning a second language while continuing to develop their first (or home) language.

ecological perspective. The view or belief that interactions with others and the environment influence development.

electronic media. Media that rely on technology to broadcast or store information. Examples include television, radio, DVDs, computers, the Internet, telephones, gaming consoles, and hand-held devices.

executive function skills. Core executive function skills are inhibition (e.g., self-control—resisting temptations and resisting acting impulsively) and interference control (e.g., selective attention and cognitive inhibition), working memory, and cognitive flexibility (including creatively thinking "outside the box," seeing anything from different perspectives, and quickly and adapting to changed circumstances) (Diamond 2013).

home language. The primary language used by the child's family in the home environment. Some children may have more than one home language (e.g., when one parent speaks Chinese and the other speaks English).

IDEA. The Individuals with Disabilities Education Act (IDEA) is a law ensuring services to children with disabilities throughout the nation. It governs how states and public agencies provide early intervention, special education, and related services to more than 6.5 million eligible infants, toddlers, children, and youths with disabilities.

inhibitory control. The ability to resist the temptation to go on "automatic" and to do what is needed to achieve goals (Gallinsky 2013).

interactive media. Forms of electronic media with content designed to facilitate active and creative use by young children and to encourage social engagement with other children and adults (NAEYC and FRC 2012). Forms of interactive media include software programs, applications, broadcast media, the Internet, e-books, and some children's television programming.

multiple means of engagement. Allowing children alternative ways to communicate or demonstrate what they know or what they are feeling, such as through gestures, sign language, or pictures.

multiple means of expression. Providing choices in the environment that facilitate learning by building on children's interests, experiences, knowledge, and skills—for example, providing a chair for a child who is interested in the sensory table, but uses a therapeutic walker.

multiple means of representation. Information presented in a variety of ways so the learning needs of all children are met. For example, it is important to speak clearly to children with auditory disabilities in an area with little or no background noise while also presenting information visually (such as with objects and pictures).

pedagogical philosophy. Philosophy of teaching.

pragmatics. The rules of language used in social contexts (e.g., one would talk differently to the president than to one's mother). Pragmatics includes gathering information, requesting, and communicating (California Department of Education 2010, 99).

prefrontal cortex. Primary functions of the prefrontal cortex include executive function skills (including planning, working memory), cognitive skills, logic/reasoning, and self-control/inhibition of behavior.

preschool or preschool program. Any early childhood setting where three- to five-year-old children receive education and care. Children can experience preschool in a variety of settings, including child care centers (center-based child care and family child care), state-funded prekindergarten programs, federally funded preschool programs (such as Head Start), and private preschool programs.

reflective practice. Thoughtful consideration of thoughts, feelings, actions, and experiences when applying knowledge to practice. This is done to learn from experience and systematic exploration of other approaches or behaviors. May be most effective when supported by peer collaboration or professionals' coaching.

reflective supervision. Refers to several related ideas and approaches designed to help professionals consider, in the presence of another person, their thoughts, feelings, actions, and reactions as they work to support the healthy development of young children and their families.

scaffolding. A process by which adults or capable peers provide a supportive structure to help children learn and play. Scaffolding is helpful when children are faced with a challenge that they can solve with a simple hint, question, or prompt.

screen technologies. Electronic devices with which users view content through a screen. This category may include televisions, computers, smartphones, and tablets.

specialized service providers. Professionals who work primarily with children and families who have special needs or who need services beyond what is typically provided by an early childhood educator. These providers are often early childhood special educators, but they might also include occupational therapists, physical therapists, and specialists in low-incidence disabilities.

teacher. An adult with education and care responsibilities in an early childhood setting. Teachers include adults who interact directly with young children in preschool programs.

universal design for learning (UDL). An educational framework, based on research in the learning sciences, that guides the development of flexible learning environments and that can accommodate individual learning differences (Center for Applied Special Technology 2008).

working memory. Holding information in mind while mentally working with it or updating it (Gallinsky 2013).

References

California Department of Education. 2010. *California Preschool Curriculum Framework, Volume 1*. Sacramento: California Department of Education.

Center for Applied Special Technology 2008. http://www.cast.org/udl/ (accessed July 31, 2014).

Diamond, A. 2013. "Executive Functions." *Annual Review of Psychology* 64:135–68.

Diamond, A., S. Barnett, J. Thomas, and S. Munro. 2007. "Preschool Program Improves Cognitive Control." *Science* 318:1387–88.

Gallinsky, E. 2013. Executive function skills predict children's success in life and in school. http://www. huffingtonpost.com/ellen-galinsky/ executive-function-skills_1_b_1613422. html (accessed July 30, 2014).

Mistrett, S. 2004. "Assistive Technology Helps Young Children with Disabilities Participate in Daily Activities." *Technology in Action* 1 (4): 1–7.

National Association for the Education of Young Children (NAEYC) and the Fred Rogers Center for Early Learning and Children's Media at Saint Vincent College (FRC). 2012. *Technology and Interactive Media as Tools in Early Childhood Programs Serving Children from Birth through Age 8*. A Joint Position Statement. Washington, DC: National Association for the Education of Young Children; Latrobe, PA: Fred Rogers Center for Early Learning and Children's Media at Saint Vincent College.